RAYMOND ASQUITH: LIFE AND LETTERS

This elegant and beguiling collection of letters, edited by Raymond Asquith's grandson, reflects the desires and expectations of an entire generation of Englishmen before the First World War, as well as laying bare the elusive character of Asquith himself. There are touching and revealing letters to friends as diverse as Winston Churchill and Lady Diana Cooper, love letters to his wife, Katherine, as well as witty and engagingly frank anecdotes about most of the major social figures and politicians of the day, from the Archbishop of Canterbury to Lady Violet Bonham-Carter. But the most moving letters are those written from the Front, shortly before his tragic death at the Somme in 1916.

'Witty, informed, acid and deliciously frank about his famous contemporaries'
The Times

'His descriptions of the conditions in the trenches and his comments on the general organisation are bitingly witty and shrewd' *Evening Standard*

The selection 'depicts more elegantly and eloquently than a dozen lesser volumes the lives, standards, hopes and tragic ends of almost an entire generation . . . a superb book' *Sunday Express*

'It sometimes seems that the First World War generated too much in the way of analyses, biographies, criticism and memoirs, but this book says more than most, and says it with more elegance, passion and power' *Economist*

RAYMOND ASQUITH
LIFE AND LETTERS

JOHN JOLLIFFE

CENTURY
LONDON MELBOURNE AUCKLAND JOHANNESBURG

3 1 4 7 2

9 2 0

First published in 1980 by William Collins Sons & Co Ltd

This edition first published in 1987 by Century,
an imprint of Century Hutchinson Ltd,
Brookmount House, 62–65 Chandos Place, London WC2N 4NW

Century Hutchinson Publishing Group (Australia) Pty Ltd,
PO Box 496, 16–22 Church Street, Hawthorn, Melbourne, Victoria 3122

Century Hutchinson Group (NZ) Ltd,
PO Box 40-086, 32–34 View Road, Glenfield, Auckland 10

Century Hutchinson Group (SA) Pty Ltd,
PO Box 337, Bergvlei 2012, South Africa

ISBN 0 7126 1491 5

Printed in Great Britain by
Richard Clay Limited, Bungay, Suffolk

Reading of good authors is like walking in the sun, which will leave a tincture upon us, though unawares of it.

Brian Duppa, tutor to King Charles II,
later Bishop of Winchester,
letter to Sir Justinian Isham.

I have not the slightest feeling of humility towards the public – or to anything in existence – but the eternal Being, the Principle of Beauty, – and the Memory of great Men.

John Keats,
letter to J. H. Reynolds, 9 April, 1818

FOR MY MOTHER
AND HELEN AND JULIAN
THE CHILDREN OF RAYMOND ASQUITH

Contents

Acknowledgements

This book could not have been undertaken without the encouragement of Raymond Asquith's only son, Lord Oxford. To him and to his sister, Lady Helen Asquith, I am grateful for much patient help and advice, as well as abundant hospitality. My next debt is to Lady Diana Cooper, the only survivor of those who knew the subject of the book intimately, and also to Sir Alan Lascelles for further first-hand information and wise counsel.

I would like to thank C & T Publications Ltd. and Mr Winston Churchill, MP for permission to quote from two unpublished letters from Sir Winston Churchill.

I am grateful to Lord Tweedsmuir and to Messrs Hodder & Stoughton for permission to quote from the autobiography of his father, *Memory Hold the Door*; and to the Douglas Library, Queen's University, Kingston, Ontario, for supplying copies of letters to John Buchan.

I would also like to thank the following people who have helped me in my search for letters, and in other ways: the Marquis of Anglesey; Dr Michael Brock; Mrs Giles FitzHerbert; Mr E. C. Hodgkin; Mr T. N. Hughes-Onslow; Mr John Keegan; Lady Lucas; Mr William Montgomery; Sir Rupert Hart-Davis; Professor Hugh Thomas; Mr J. S. G. Simmons and Mr Quinn, the Librarians of All Souls College and Balliol College, Oxford; and finally Miss Mary Vincent for her expert typing, and for skilfully mastering a manuscript which contained many pitfalls.

Other letters from Raymond Asquith no doubt exist which I have been unable to trace. If any reader can let me know of any, care of my publisher, I will be most grateful.

The Asquiths

HERBERT HENRY ASQUITH, b. 1852 ■ ■ ■ ■ ■ ■
Prime Minister 1908-16, created Earl of Oxford & Asquith 1925,
d. 1928, m. 1st, 1877, Helen Melland, (who d. 1891)

RAYMOND, b. 1878, k. in action 1916, m. Katharine, (who d. 1976) d. of Sir John Horner	HERBERT, b. 1881, barrister, poet, m. Lady Cynthia Charteris, d. of 11th Earl of Wemyss, d. 1947	ARTHUR, b. 1883, Brigadier, Royal Naval Division, severely wounded, m. Hon. Betty Manners, d. of 3rd Lord Manners, d. 1939

HELEN, b. 1908	PERDITA, b. 1910, m. Hon. William Jolliffe, later 4th Lord Hylton	JULIAN, 2nd Earl of Oxford, b. 1916 m. Anne Palairet

The Tennants
(mentioned in this book)

SIR CHARLES TENNANT, 1st Bt.
b. 1823, m. 1st, 1849, Emma Winsloe, d. 1906

EDWARD, 1st Ld. Glenconner ('Eddie') b. 1859 m. Pamela Wyndham	FRANCIS, ('Frank') m. Annie Redmayne	HAROLD JOHN, ('Jack') Parl.-Under-Sec. for War, 1912-16	PAULINE EMMA, m. Thomas Gordon-Duff, of Drummuir

m. 2nd, Margot, (who d. 1945)
daughter of Sir Charles Tennant

CYRIL,
b. 1890, Judge,
Lord of Appeal
in Ordinary,
m. Anne, d. of
Sir A. Pollock,
d. 1954

VIOLET, b. 1887,
created Baroness
Asquith of Yarnbury,
m. Sir Maurice
Bonham-Carter,
d. 1969

ANTHONY,
film director,
b. 1902,
d. 1968

ELIZABETH,
m. Prince Antoine Bibesco
(Rumanian diplomat and
friend of Marcel Proust),
b. 1897, d. 1945

CHARLOTTE,
m. 4th Lord
Ribblesdale

LUCY,
m. Thomas
Graham Smith
of Easton
Grey

LAURA,
m. Hon. Alfred
Lyttelton,
d. 1886

MARGARET,
('Margot')
m. 1894
H.H. Asquith,
d. 1945

Introduction: Childhood and School 1878-1897

Raymond Asquith was born on 6 November 1878, the eldest child of the future Prime Minister. He was killed in the Battle of the Somme on 15 September 1916. Innumerable books of memoirs and accounts of the war single him out as the most brilliant and remarkable of all those who lost their lives in it, but the following example may speak for them all. Winston Churchill, in a letter dated 4 December 1916, wrote to Raymond's widow as follows:

> I really could not bring myself to write to you before. The uselessness of anything I could say pressed so upon me that I thought I would wait till later on. But you will have to understand how profoundly and keenly I sympathise with you in your unspeakable sorrow, and how truly I grieve myself for the loss of my brilliant hero-friend.
>
> I always had an intense admiration for Raymond, and also a warm affection for him; and both were old established ties . . . I remember so vividly the last time I saw him – at Montreuil in early May. We sat or strolled for two hours on the old ramparts in bright sunshine, and talked about the war, about the coming offensive, about his son, about all sorts of things. I like to dwell on these war-time memories. These gallant charming figures that flash and gleam amid the carnage – always so superior to it, masters of their souls, disdainful of death and suffering – are an inspiration and an example to all. And he was one of the very best. He did everything easily – I never remember anyone who seemed so independent of worldly or physical things: and yet he enjoyed everything and had an appreciation of life and letters and men and women, and manners and customs refined and subtle to the last degree. Oh how unbearable it must be for you to have lost him! How vain must these and all other words be to ease your grief.
>
> Still you will be brave, you will try like him to smile at fate, and meet it on equal terms. You will remember how many friends you have, and think of the days to come when your little boy will revive his image and carry into the forefront of his country's service the name that all will honour.

There were many other tributes, yet up till the present he has remained an elusive figure, for all the vague superlatives that have been heaped on him.

After a meteoric career at Oxford, he had worked at the Bar for ten years before the war began, and had been married for seven of them. He had been adopted to succeed a sitting member of parliament in a safe seat, and was on the threshold of a political career of his own. The fulfilment and expression of his gifts that would have given him public fame was just about to begin. But, as it was, his talents and powers were fated to bear fruit only privately, within a restricted circle. Fortunately, many letters that he wrote to his wife and friends have survived, and it is principally from these that the following portrait is composed.

It is largely a self-portrait: not on canvas, where the subject can deliberately choose effects of colour and shape in order to produce, often rapidly, the desired effect; but in words, poured out spontaneously over a period of twenty-two years to a variety of recipients. It therefore seems to be free from any except the most obvious and intentional kind of distortion or exaggeration. The precision of meaning and increasing brilliance of style never give an impression of any loss of integrity, or of any lapse into empty rhetoric or false striving after effects.

The materials for the picture come largely from the central figure himself, and the danger, common in biography, of forcing the subject into a pre-conceived pattern, or even a strait-jacket, does not in this case arise. After his schooldays, I have not done much more than to select from Raymond's numerous letters, poems and essays what seems likely to be of most interest, and to bring him most clearly alive to the reader; though I have tried to explain anything about his family, friends, activities and general background which might otherwise 'hinder the reader's understanding and full enjoyment of these remarkable documents of a remarkable life', to borrow a phrase from Robert Gittings's admirable edition of the Letters of Keats.

The context, above all, is important, and may be unfamiliar enough to some readers to need making clear. The years in which Raymond lived will sometimes seem as remote from the present as the Middle Ages, and I am not concerned to comment on the various ways in which life then was more or less desirable or admirable – and for whom – than it is now. The context of the lives of the people who appear in these pages was what it was: from Beatrice Webb and Bernard Shaw to the Duke of Rutland, whatever they thought other people should be doing, they took their own circumstances for granted, and showed no wish to change them.

It was, in particular, an age in which the written word was paramount, and had no competition from the spoken word on the air, let alone from a series of vanishing images on the screen. It was an age of correspondence, and not of last minute telephone calls. By the standards of today all post was, to put it mildly, first class. Letters were still the natural means of all but the most urgent communication, not only for schoolboys to their parents, but for everyone else as well. Raymond's have been classed by a good judge of English literature with those of Keats, Horace Walpole and Charles Lamb. They do something to explain the legendary place he held in his generation, and the fact that all who knew him, even if younger or far older, seem to have regarded him as beyond compare.

Raymond was the eldest child of Herbert Henry Asquith's first marriage, to Helen Melland. The details of his father's life are too well known (or too easily discovered) to need much repeating. When his eldest son was born he was twenty-six; it was five years before he began to achieve prominence at the Bar with his work on the Affirmation Bill and later on the Parnell Commission, which brought his name before Gladstone and (of more immediate value to him) to the attention of the Attorney-General; and it was eight years before he took the bold step of entering the House of Commons. When this happened, his household devised a white banner with the words WELCOME MP inscribed in vermilion; and the seven-year-old Raymond climbed a catalpa tree in front of the house and hung it from a bough, before a row of Union Jacks fluttering from the bedroom windows, to await the hero's return.

At this time the Asquiths lived in Keats Grove, Hampstead, then called John Street, opposite the house where, only seventy years before, Keats had intermittently lived and worked. After establishing himself at the Bar, and entering the House of Commons, Raymond's father rented for several summer holidays in succession the house at Allen Bank, Grasmere, once occupied by William and Dorothy Wordsworth. Raymond's later love, and talent, for poetry must have owed something to these early associations. His forebears were natives of Morley, in the West Riding of Yorkshire, and the family naturally looked northwards for its holidays. After he grew up, both before and after his marriage, Raymond usually spent part of his summer holidays in great content among the Lake Hills.

The family quickly increased: Herbert (originally known as Bertie, but later as Beb) was three years younger than Raymond; Arthur, or Oc, was born in 1883, Violet in 1887, and finally Cyril (known as Cys) in 1890. It was only his nearest two brothers who shared Raymond's early years at all intimately (though no letters between them have survived). But Cyril, in his joint life of his father, gives an illuminating description of the relations that developed between the Asquiths: 'Notwithstanding their cool and casual contacts, the family as a whole were united by a powerful freemasonry, and its members would on occasion furtively fight each other's battles; but a horror of emotional nudism led them to clothe their mutual appreciation with a semblance of judicial indifference, and to deny it all ordinary expression.'

The usual kind of stories – or perhaps rather better than the usual – were preserved about Raymond's precocious powers of thought and expression. At the age of seven, he was able to describe a python's discarded skin at the zoo as 'an outworn fetter broken and cast off by its soul'. And about the same time, when Beb was regarded as a singularly beautiful child, with marvellous curls, Raymond grew tired of having these constantly praised, and 'secretly lopped off one of the best'. When accused, he at first denied but finally admitted what he had done, giving as his excuse 'I cut it off for the robins to line their nests with.'

Before going on to a preparatory school at Lambrook, near Bracknell, Raymond attended a day school in Hampstead High Street run by Miss Janet Case, who was later also responsible for teaching Greek to Virginia Woolf. When he was eight his father was benignly amused to come home one summer evening and find him making a sacrifice to Zeus (complete with a libation of claret) on a small altar that he and Bertie had built under an apple-tree in the garden. His mother's letters to him at Lambrook are of a conventional kind, interspersed with scraps of grown-up news: 'Mr Gladstone made one of his finest speeches in the House yesterday and Father made a short one about a bill in favour of allowing Roman Catholics to be Lord Chancellor and Lord Lieutenant of Ireland. The bill was really Father's idea, but Mr Gladstone took it up. It was defeated by 30 votes.' 'My dearest old Ray, your shower of post-cards and letters was most welcome – I always miss you when you first go, especially now that the House has begun to sit and I have solitary evenings from 8.15 onwards.' And from Monte Carlo, on the way back from Florence in April 1891: 'We bought a bottle of green and white chartreuse [sic] which the monks make and today we have successfully smuggled it across the frontier in Father's ulster pocket.'

That summer the family was struck by a sudden, overwhelming tragedy. Raymond's father had successfully taken silk the year before and now, forsaking the Lakes, had rented a summer holiday house on the Island of Arran. On September 10th, having contracted typhoid, Raymond's mother died. The only surviving evidence of the effect of this on him is to be found in two of his letters: one to Harold Baker, (4 October, 1899), in the same circumstances, (see page 61); the other in 1908, a few months after his marriage, to his mother-in-law Frances Horner, on the death from scarlet fever of her sixteen-year-old son Mark: 'I am afraid that sympathy is not one of my things', he wrote, 'but no doubt it is easier for one person to show his feelings to another when the cause of grief is common to both, as you know it is here. This is the only thing since my own mother died which has made me cry, and still does when particular memories are evoked.'

Raymond has sometimes been accused of callousness and inhumanity. His Oxford friend John Buchan, whose feelings for him amounted almost to veneration, admitted that 'there were times when he was almost inhuman. He would destroy some piece of homely sentiment with a jest, and he had no respect for the sacred places of dull men. There was always a touch of scorn in him for obvious emotion, obvious creeds . . . That was a defect of his great qualities. He kept himself for his friends and refused to bother about the world.' These things cannot be proved, but it may well be that on his mother's death he formed a self-protective mask from behind which he gave vent to merciless and aloof observations, as his powers of expression were developed and perfected. Yet later in his life – even before his marriage which had a softening and humanising effect on him – there are many examples of warmth and tender-heartedness, and his way of affectionately teasing his friends, Conrad Russell and Aubrey Herbert for example, was obviously an important part of his great charm. As Buchan went on to say: 'To such as were admitted to his friendship he would deny nothing. I have never known a friend more considerate, and tender, and painstaking, and unfalteringly loyal. It was the relation of all others in life for which he had been born with a peculiar genius.'

Mr Asquith's reaction to the death of his wife – no doubt a complex one – is harder to analyse. His career was at a crucial stage, and he quickly hired a housekeeper to look after his children, in Hampstead during the school terms and at a rented house in Surrey, near Redhill, in the holidays. He himself moved into a flat in Mount Street from which he conducted his increasingly prominent work at the Bar and in the House of Commons. It was also within a few minutes' walk of Grosvenor Square, the London home of Sir Charles Tennant and his daughter Margot. His biographers have not found much to say about his first wife, beyond quoting a typical, and typically arbitrary, shaft of Margot's later on: 'She was a most unsuitable wife for Henry: she lived in Hampstead and had no clothes.' But two letters have survived from him to Lady Horner, at that time a new but already close friend. They throw a good deal more light on the relationship between Raymond's parents in his childhood, and since they provide the only detailed knowledge we have of his mother, they are quoted here at length, even if the picture is incomplete.

11 September 1892. It is a year today since my wife died and I am going to talk to you about her and myself. You never knew or saw her. She was an angel from Heaven, and God took her back from this miry world with unstained feet and an unspotted heart . . . Hers was one of those personalities which it is almost impossible to depict. The strong colours of the palette seem to be too heavy and garish; it is difficult to paint a figure in the soft grey tints which would best befit her, and yet she was not neutral or negative. Her mind was clear and strong, but it was not cut in facets and did not flash lights, and no one would have called her clever or 'intellectual'. What gave her her rare quality was her character, which everyone who knew her intimately (Haldane for instance) agrees was the most selfless and unworldly that they have ever encountered. She was warm, impulsive, quick-tempered and generous almost to a fault, but in all the years of our married life I never knew an occasion when to do the right thing seemed to cost her an effort. She cared little for society, shrank from every kind of publicity and self-advertisement, hardly knew what ambition meant. She was more wrapped up in her children than any woman I have ever known. To me she was always loyal, sympathetic, devoted; not without pride in such successes as I had; but not the least anxious for me to 'get on'; never sanguine or confident, and as a rule inclined to the darker and less hopeful view of things. I used sometimes to reproach her with her 'pessimism'. What has happened to me lately [i.e. his appointment as Home Secretary] would have given her little real pleasure; indeed, I doubt whether, if she had been here, I should have taken such a step. She was the gentlest and truest of companions, a restraining rather than a

stimulating influence, and knowing myself as I do, I have often wondered that we walked so evenly together. I was only eighteen when I fell in love with her, and we married when we were little more than boy and girl. In the cant phrase, our marriage was 'a great success'; from first to last it was never troubled by any kind of sorrow or discussion; and when the sun went down it was in an unclouded sky.

On 17 October he wrote again, no doubt answering a reply to his first letter:

It is difficult to project oneself backwards. I was young and callow, and self-confident, and ambitious, and probably rather repellent. Women played very little part in my life, I was content with my early love and never looked outside. So we settled down in a little suburban villa, and our children were born, and every day I went by the train to the Temple . . . Gradually – not at all quickly – I got on bit by bit, and in '86, in defiance of all my judicious friends, I stood for Parliament and got into the House. Helen looked on and did not really wish it; but she was an angel and never murmured, although she felt that this was the beginning of the end of our quiet, unruffled companionship. I made my maiden speech (which was rather a success) and the world began to open out, and great and charming people smiled on us.

He met Margot Tennant for the first time only a few months before his wife died. She was soon a close enough friend to take Raymond to a hearing of the Baccarat Case, and realising how tedious the proceedings must have been for a boy of twelve, she tried to amuse him by dropping her handkerchief from the gallery down on to the head of a weary lawyer in the court below. Margot's lack of tact and often of any shred of consideration for other people's feelings later became a byword, but another side to her nature appears in a letter that she wrote to Raymond when she became engaged to his father: 'I only want to say one thing. You must not think that I could *imagine* even a possibility of filling your mother's (and my friend's) place. I only ask you to let me be your companion – and if needs be your help-mate. There is room for everyone in life if they have the power to love. I shall count upon your help in making my way with Violet and your brothers . . . I should like you to let me gradually and without effort take my place among you, and if I cannot – as indeed I *would* not – take your mother's place in any way – you must at least allow me to share with you her beautiful memory.'

Raymond answered as follows: 'I am sure we shall all like you very much and you will get on very well with us, and I will do my best to help you, though I don't think you will need much help with the others, especially Violet and Cis.' Two other letters from Margot show the affection and sympathy that at this time plainly existed between them, in spite of her many foibles. When Raymond won his scholarship at Balliol, she wrote: '. . . Dear dear Raymond, I cannot but feel how proud your mother had she lived wd. have been and how inadequately I can refill her place either in sympathy or joy but you must believe in my pride and affection and gratitude in having you as a step-son and friend. God bless you and give you a worthy future.' Four years later, when she bore a son who lived only a few days, she wrote: 'Your letter was a joy – It seems to me there is no one quite like you, you always touch every situation with tenderness and truth – to know as much as you do is uncommon I believe, but to understand as much is rarer still I'm sure . . .'

Raymond's father evidently kept few personal letters, but from this date on Raymond's letters home from Winchester and Oxford were carefully pre-served, and most of them are dated. The subjects are the usual ones, but the style is already often very different from that of the ordinary schoolboy's letter. The extracts that follow give a vivid impression of his school days. Work, games, epidemics and plans are naturally the staple subjects covered – and of course food, as in a request for grouse or partridges from Scotland, '. . . ready-cooked, as the commissariat is in a bad way just at present, and we are reduced to horse-radish sauce and sardine oil, which are not the most satisfactory things for playing football on.'

There is no hint of reserve, or of the least sense of awe, and indeed Ray-mond's attitude to his father sometimes seems surprisingly off-hand. One let-ter, written somewhat haphazardly on two partly blank double pages of writing-paper, ends with the words 'Perhaps you will not be able to find your way about this letter: it has got mixed somehow. But make an effort.' Nor was he embarrassed about asking for money: 'The stupid man at the school shop tells me that he did not send in to you my whole account at Xmas, thinking I suppose that the whole amount would horrify you. He now applies to me for the balance of some 25/- . . . Being out of funds I have referred him to you.'

Not surprisingly, work comes first. In January 1895 he writes: 'There is almost more to do than at any other time of the year. We have all our Prize compositions this half. The Greek Iambics . . . are a piece from *Atalanta in Calydon*. We only have a week to do it in, without any remission from ordinary work. As there are 100 lines or so to write, there is rather a press of time.' But there are occasional gaps in what was to become a steely self-confidence: 'I must say I don't feel particularly hopeful about Balliol: I hear there are a par-ticularly strong lot of Paulines up: they are fatal people, turn out reams of machine-made verses at the shortest possible notice, and generally know everything. I believe that they get [*sic*] quite a good education. In the very probable contingency of my not getting in, you say I am to get a New Coll. scholarship . . . The worst of New College is that one has to do prepared books, which I have not been doing much this half: that means that I shall only have a fortnight to get it up: still I think I can manage it.' Another letter, to Margot this time, complains of the Winchester mission, in a poor parish in Ports-mouth: 'These people come puling and whining around for money, and when they get it they spend it on incense and candles, or stoles and altar-cloths. On ordinary subjects Father Dolling is an intelligent and above all a practical man, but once get him on to the subject of vestments, etc. and he is a ranting maniac.'

He was also an enthusiastic games player. Most important was Winchester football, a fast and furious game particularly in its six-a-side form, and requiring a dedicated training regime. Raymond ended by being second captain of the school team. Endless ailments intervened, including impetigo and ophthalmia, both luridly described, as well as the inevitable influenza: 'Half College are down with it . . . to work is out of the question; to play is next to impossible. The ground is too bad for football . . . the skating is not good and I have no skates: which is perhaps lucky. About half a dozen fellows have been making a rope of towels and descending by it from a bathroom window about 30 feet into the Warden's garden . . . to a place called Winnall Mere where they had the ice to themselves from 1-4 a.m. This they did three times, but the third time the Warden's gardener having observed footprints in the snow hailed them as they came back, with the result that they will be pretty severely dropped on, I imagine. I was asked to form one of the party and should certainly have done so had I had any skates.'

The winter of 1894-5 was exceptionally hard, but three months later he wrote that 'the general aspect of the place on one of these summery evenings is indescribably lovely . . . Those unfortunates who play cricket all day can form no conception of the bliss of lying in some of the most lovely woods in England . . . We set off about 1.45 [on bicycles] and return by 7.45. By covering an average of 15 m.p.h. we have plenty of time for tea in some nice little village pub. and a good deal of sylvan scenery, in addition to riding 40 miles or so, which enables us to get plenty of exercise – more indeed than we should by playing cricket.'

Even before his sixteenth birthday his appetite for poetry had begun to develop: 'I have read Swinburne's *Dolores* for the sixth time today', he wrote to his father, 'and think it incomparably the finest thing I have ever seen in any language.' His love of old buildings had also taken root, along with the vigorous scepticism that was never to leave him: 'On Sunday evening we substituted Cathedral for Chapel, and it was the most enjoyable part of the day, absolutely cool and delightful: the Norman architecture seemed to radiate coolness: it is simply ambrosial – except for the fact that the Bear[1] preached his Trinity sermon, which consists of a mass of contradictions ingeniously put forward to prove that the object of life is to be a clergyman, and that the object of being a clergyman is to have a black beard and to be Headmaster of Winchester College.'

Finally, political questions are occasionally asked: 'I have undertaken to champion Rosebery at a debate next week. Can you suggest any reason why he should be leader apart from the fact that he seems to be a witty and gentlemanly fellow?' His father's answer, dated 3 October 1896, is of some interest: 'I am disposed to think, tho' perhaps it doesn't do to say so out loud – that R's qualities for leadership are mainly negative and comparative: i.e. there is no one else to whom there are not stronger objections. After disappearing from the stage at Edinburgh in a blaze of fireworks, he ought not to have come for-

---

[1] Rev W. A. Fearon, Headmaster of Winchester, 1894-1901.

ward again so soon to add a postscript to his valedictory harangue – still less to write letters of dubious smartness to *The Times*. His great chance now is to persuade people that his is a force in reserve, and this is not the way to do it.'

Of Raymond's school friendships, the most important and enduring was with Harold Baker, nearly two years his senior, with whom he corresponded at considerable length. The first of these letters date from Raymond's schooldays, when Baker had preceded him to Balliol. The following extracts give a further idea of how unlike the ordinary schoolboy's letters they are:

To H. T. Baker   The Glen,
                                                 Innerleithen, N.B.
                                                 13 January 1897

. . . I must confess however that when I wrote to you I felt stupid and stodgy and unintelligible to an almost unprecedented degree. I did mean all I said and much more besides; and if I refrained from saying more – and still refrain – it is only owing to that spirit of caution which I think we both approved at Winton last half; that grim contrast between fine words and small results which is the very depth of humiliation to a man of any self-respect.

Still as you want me to be definite, I will say as simply as I can that there is no one I have ever known that I would so soon have as a friend as yourself; if anyone is dissatisfied with our bond it will be you and not I; were you nothing more than a mere intellectual phenomenon I should be content to admire you all the days of my life. But you are very much more. If you knew how I hated being definite you would think this a high tribute; but these terrible downright statements always sound so crude! Still I am afraid all genuine emotions are clumsy – at any rate in the mouth of an Englishman; which may account for Heine's dictum, that a blaspheming Frenchman is a more pleasing sight to the Almighty than an Englishman on his knees! . . . Self-control is certainly the true art of life; or to call it by an uglier but safer name Utilitarianism; which is, I imagine what the higher 'Epicureanism' comes to mean, isn't it? J. S. Mill is my idol just now; such a wonderful mind, and yet such a vast deal of humanity, as I have just learnt from his autobiography. But even self-control is capable of degenerating from a virtue to a mania . . .

I return to town on Saturday night, and am very much at your service thence onwards . . . In the meantime try to imagine that I am neither cold nor phantasmal.

To H. T. Baker   Winton [*ie* Winchester].
                                                 5 February 1897

. . . As I think you know, Punch, Andy, Simpkin, Moon and myself were in the habit of holding séances on 11th landing last half, not unattended by a certain nameless drug. On more than one occasion Zimmern came up to hear us read Sophocles, envied our intellectual, and condescended to tolerate our sensual joys. These meetings have been continued this half, the only absentees being Zimmern and Sophocles. About a week ago the former came to me with glum Lutheranism depicted on his greasy features, and told me that he had at length arrived at the conclusion that smoking in a College prefect was a gross breach of morality and as such could not be countenanced by a type of the Divine (as exemplified by himself) – in short, he proposed to call down thunder from heaven – or in default of that from VIth. I argued of course; I pointed out his inconsistent position, and the glorious constancy with which we hugged the only vice which has no evil effect in Society; but it is vain to reason with a German Jew; the Teutonic element of paternal bureaucracy in combination with the Hebrew ideal of Righteousness, brushes aside logic, temperance, and commonsense . . .

To H. T. Baker   The College,
                                                                          Winchester.
                                                                28 February 1897

. . . How is it I wonder that this sacking business has made such a noise? The Bear summoned all school and house prefects to a mass meeting in School on Friday morning: where he harangued us for twenty minutes in a tearful voice on the disadvantages of unconventional forms of vice. He spoke in hushed accents of the abominable crime and exhorted us with passionate fervour to prefer every known form of prostitution and bestiality to the sin of Sodom. He told us in confidence that the Headmasters, in league with the Government, were proposing to increase the legal penalty from two to fourteen years; whereat a perceptible shudder ran through the audience – of whom some eighty five p.c. – by the lowest estimate – were legally liable to incarceration on that charge. The bolder spirits muttered that the law was not altered yet, and registered a mental vow to make the best of the lucid interspace. We were then dismissed with compliments and condolences . . .

To H. T. Baker   Winton.
                                                                Sunday 14 March 1897

Very many thanks for your delightful letter. This week has been one of gloom and misery – only partially enlightened by lectures on the Japanese Alps and other bizarre attractions of the sort. What with the incessant rain, salt fish, Lent hymns, Latin essay and a thousand other seasonable inflictions, life has been hardly worth living: I feel more like some meagre mediaeval ascetic, than a rational full-blooded nineteenth century sinner.

Had I not invented such a perfect device for stopping up my ears, as enables me to read the Anthology throughout the Chapel services in comparative peace and quietness, I verily believe this day would have been my last. Every night since the beginning of Lent Andy and I – just to remind ourselves we are still pagans – go into chapel about 11 p.m. (via Baptistery) and toss for pennies on the altar. Last night Dick[1] being away, Punch, Andy and self climbed over the gate into Crimea and so through the glass door into Cloisters, where the moon effects were sublime: the night was almost perfect, and the beauty of Chantry amazing. Punch who always carries in his bosom a large bust of Apollo Belvedere insisted on placing it on the altar and celebrating a heathen service in its honour.

Apart from these little escapades there is nothing to record outside the stale and fatuous round of daily devotions and blasphemies. Do come down and make life livable – When is it that you are due? . . . was removed by his Mater Dolorosa about a week ago being some £250 in debt. The last thing I saw of him was a frantic creature offering to leave all his trunks and in fact his whole retinue with Andrews, the bicycle man, for the loan of £5. I imagine his family keep him under lock and key now . . .

To H. T. Baker   20 Cavendish Square.
                                                                                    31 July 1897

. . . I found my governor reading a small volume of poems by Alfred Douglas which has just appeared: of course I took it away immediately; I don't think the poor man can have known what was inside – Some of them are quite funny: this for instance in the light of Oscar Wilde's imprisonment.

> Alas I have lost my God
> My beautiful God Apollo
> Wherever his footsteps trod
> My feet were wont to follow.

There is just a reminiscence of "Mary had a little lamb" in the last couplet which adds a certain piquancy of contrast . . .

To H. T. Baker   13 The Links,
                                                                              St Andrews, N.B.
                                                                                  August 1897

My dear Zeus
      A thunderbolt [has just landed] in what is technically called a bunker, three or four seconds after I had jumped out of it: I assure you I have never yet

---

[1] R. Rendall, Raymond's housemaster; later headmaster, 1911-24.

been so near to solving the problem of a future life. As it was I was merely scattered with sand and clods of earth: but the bunker was disfigured for life: it made rather a mess of the telegraph wires too – I consider it a unique and not unpleasing experience, and have been trying to moralize it ever since. Do you think I ought to regard the narrowness of my escape as a divine warning? or as an indication of the special favour of providence? Both the interpretations are plausible: and I have known men who would dedicate their lives to God on the strength of either. Natural vanity inclines me slightly to the latter.

. . . Margot gave me two first editions of Browning's *Men and Women*: I have struggled manfully with them, but cannot feel in sympathy with the man: it is true some of his love pieces are pretty, but they don't touch a responsive note in me: I think perhaps they are too feminine – which to me always means domestic: most love poetry applies equally well to either sex, but there is something distinctively and exclusively female about Browning. Metrically he gives the impression of a man always hard up for a rhyme, but determined to have one at any cost. I am disappointed too in the substance: I had been led to expect mines of deep and helpful philosophy: but find nothing but a few tame moral platitudes, strangely at variance with the effervescent sensuality of many of the poems, elaborately padded, and in some cases impenetrably obscured in masses of crude and crabbed verbiage. The man is inarticulate: his efforts to be what Rendall calls 'terse and vigorous' render him almost unintelligible: when he does hit upon a happy phrase it seems something in the nature of a fluke – But no doubt I have misunderstood him: I didn't go over with a lexicon and a commentary. I wish you could give me a few hints about him: I believe you have the secret . . .

To H. T. Baker   Hyndford House,
North Berwick, N.B.
Sunday 24 September 1897

. . . My only amusing visit was in Perthshire with the Haldanes – Richard Haldane is the greatest philosopher and the greatest politician now alive, though he comes little before the public, being ill to look at and modest by nature. He has written excellent books on Adam Smith and Schopenhauer, and is now engaged on a crushing refutation of A.J.B.'s *Foundations of Belief*, which should be worth reading. He also does all the brainwork of the Liberal Party, and though not in the cabinet thinks for those who are. In the domestic circle he is the most amusing creature I know: he is a great humorist and a thorough-going Epicurean with the finest cellar and the best table in Scotland . . . I can't tell you how sick I am of this interminable round of smart but vacant conviviality, but I have three more visits to get through before I revel in solitude and Aeschylus at Grasmere: the only purple patch is a weekend with Rosebery at Dalmeny . . .

His other principal school friendship was with Geoffrey Smith, two or three years his junior. It was evidently an extremely close friendship, and highly idealised. They do not appear to have met in after life, and Geoffrey Smith was killed in France a few months before Raymond, but his charming letters of this period have survived. They are full of both gaiety and humility, as well as of love of poetry and of ambitious attempts to write it. He sounds from these letters a very engaging character, and though Raymond's letters to him have disappeared, it is worth quoting one of Smith's, since it reveals the spiritual as well as the intellectual level of their friendship:

Butharlyp How, Grasmere. 5 Sept. 1898.

I like your poetry very much; I do often try to look behind the scenes, but it is dark and uncanny work. However, I have some very definite ideas, which I will try to give, but if you find it getting heavy, please shut up and throw it into the fire. I think that there must exist a lot of realities quite beyond the boundary of our power of thought; our ideals and gods and figments of imagination lie in the borderland of this region of realities, and the only way we can make explorations into it is by letting our imagination go in accordance with the rules of beauty and spiritual perspective.

Now religion, by which I mean all superstition and supernatural ideas by which men try to account for things, is in the borderland, but people ruin everything by letting their imaginations roam the wrong way, i.e. back into the realms of *thought*; or rather they do not imagine according to the rules of beauty, which are the only guide to truth. 'Beauty is truth, truth Beauty etc.'; you know the hackney'd lines; this is a pretty conceit if you take it merely into your brain, but when it gets into your passions and imagination it becomes a huge creed. Then it is that one has penetrated into the borders of the borderland and got a glimpse of the blue hazy hills beyond, but all you can see is that the country is much vaster than anything we can know of with our wretched little mass of nerves we are pleased to call a brain. But that it is really there, and that by following Beauty we get near it, I maintain and will do so, whatever Philosophers may say about the association of ideas or any such damned finicking nonsense.

Whether the soul is immortal or not, I have no opinion; very likely, I think; at any rate when I see anybody with a beautiful soul I say with Browning

> Butterflies may dread extinction,
> You'll not die, it cannot be.

Your soul, my dear Raymond, would be such an adornment to my ideal land which I have been trying to explain. But man is a hopeless puzzle; I am much more doubtful as to what he is doing here, than about the existence of my distant hills where Beauty reigns supreme. I am quite sure of *them*; it is the physical world that is the difficulty with all its commercial travellers and poets.

. . . what is important is that a spiritual world of some sort does exist in very truth and that the way to get near it is by following lines of beauty in everything . . .

Raymond wrote to his father while taking the Balliol scholarship: 'There are a very large number of diseased and hideous people up for it. My vis-à-vis is an intellectual looking man with a black beard and flaxen undergrowth over the rest of his face: I am hemmed in on either side by ulcerous and livid Paulines . . . I am crowded with invitations and engagements of every sort, and enjoy myself a good deal . . . As far as I can learn I stay up till Wednesday, but the authorities are strangely secretive. My health is excellent, so I have no excuse for not doing well.'

His father's letter of congratulation in due course was also characteristic: 'I am delighted that you have taken the first place, and I must confess that I would not have been quite satisfied had you taken any other.'

A year after Raymond's death, his widow discussed with her sister-in-law the pros and cons of publishing letters for private circulation among their friends. Cynthia Asquith wrote in her diary for 16 August 1917: 'She says Raymond's to her and Bluetooth [Harold Baker] are so marvellously good that she feels that they will have to be published some day. But, of course, they couldn't possibly be published for a very considerable time without a great deal of bowdlerising. She is, on the whole, in favour of collecting them and leaving them until after her death.'

This is exactly what has happened.

[II]

Oxford 1897-1902

Raymond went up to Balliol in October 1897. The college was feeling the full effects of the great plans conceived for it by Benjamin Jowett, who had been Master until his death two years earlier – Raymond's father having been one of his favourite and most exemplary pupils. Determined that his college should not be one of those described by Bagehot as 'hotels without bells', Jowett had sought to attract to Balliol an elite of ability, to teach it to work hard, and thus to create the best training-ground in the country for rulers and administrators: politicians, educators, members of the home and imperial civil services. In spite of considerable resistance from conservative forces, in whose view Oxford existed partly for its own sake and partly for their convenience, and not at all for the enlightenment or improvement of the outside world, Jowett had achieved many of his meritocratic aspirations, largely by succeeding in making clever and able people want to work. He was naturally persuasive, and he instilled into many undergraduates what he called 'the sense of power' – real or imaginary – 'which comes from steady working'.

The worldly aspect of Jowett's scheme of things often seemed overdone to Raymond's circle. However successful they were they reserved a special scorn for the stuffy and timidly conventional, whom they called 'Heygates', (after an Eton housemaster) and for prematurely middle-aged attitudes of mind, over-concerned with laying the foundations of a career. Apart from the odd Russell or Herbert, the Balliol undergraduates came mainly from the professional classes (with an always strong contingent from Scotland). To many of them at this time the idea of going into business, or seeking mainly to make money, was still beyond the pale. No way of earning a living which did not also provide a supply of spiritual sustenance was immediately acceptable. A first-hand account of this circle is to be found in *Memory Hold the Door*, the autobiography of John Buchan. Buchan was at Brasenose, a place so little touched by the spirit of Jowett that only a few years earlier one of the Fellows (Turner by name) had ended a letter to the parents of an undergraduate who had died with the following words: 'it may be of some consolation to you to know that the young man would in any case have had to go down at the end of the present term owing to his failure to pass Responsions,' (an examination at

29

the end of the first term). Balliol was much more to Buchan's taste, so much so that he afterwards came to regard himself as a sort of honorary Balliol man. As characteristic of this circle, Buchan mentions 'the scrupulous avoidance of parade', and 'careless good breeding and agreeable worldliness', while admitting that some of its members were 'men of the world too young', who 'prized humour and balance too highly'. Though 'affectionate and rather too gentle with each other', they 'wore a swashbuckling manner to the outer world' and were always 'looking for preposterous adventures and planning crazy feats', and always 'ready for a brush with constituted authority'. It happened that this physical exuberance coincided in many cases with remarkable intellectual power. 'In the world of action we were ripe for any adventure, in the things of the mind we were critical, decorous, chary of enthusiasm.' Oxford was still in most ways unaffected by the events of the outside world. Raymond and his friends had a strong appetite for the beauties of nature and literature, and long after their day undergraduates could ride out on summer evenings, down the dusty roads to Wytham or Nuneham, and listen to the nightingales; but the atmosphere seems more full-blooded and attractive than the sometimes anaemic Cambridge world of the same date, as depicted by the budding leaders of Bloomsbury.

Raymond's scholarly and critical gifts soon became a byword. After examining him in his first term, Robinson Ellis, the Professor of Latin, always took his hat off to him when they met in the street; and on one occasion, when Raymond's father dined at Trinity, Ellis on being introduced to him inquired with interest 'Are you related to *the* Mr Asquith?' Apart from his other qualities, Raymond had already moved in comparatively exalted circles, which to some degree also set him apart from his contemporaries, but it is clear from his letters that, far from attaching undue importance or regard to them, his attitude was consistently one of objective coolness and detachment. As Buchan says, Raymond had also inherited important qualities from his father – 'loyalty, hatred of intrigue, contempt for advertisement, and unruffled courage'. He did not court popularity, and since he had no appetite for shallow acquaintances he often seems to have inspired awe rather than affection, not least because he so often scorned obvious emotions and creeds. To all but a few intimate friends he gave out more light than warmth, as is confirmed by a letter to him from one of the closest of them, Aubrey Herbert: 'You shine but you do not burn. You can be Aurora Borealis but never tinder.' What is above all clear is that the things of the mind that appealed to him did so for their own sake, and never as stepping-stones to fellowships or firsts. His rejection of the second-rate seems to have been balanced and usually inoffensive, his only excessive prejudice being against religion and the clergy, resulting no doubt at least in part from a surfeit of second-rate school sermons.

His letters contain occasional references to Jews, sometimes in his usual faintly mocking spirit, though far more genially than when he is referring to the Scotch, French, Dutch, Swiss, Egyptians, Americans, Canadians, Welsh, or finally Germans. It should not – but just conceivably may – be necessary to mention that he is not speaking of the victims of any kind of persecution. His Jews were not the refugees from Russia or Poland, struggling for existence in Whitechapel or Kilburn; they were a handful of Lawsons, Sassoons and Rothschilds, triumphant in their intelligent prosperity, Liberal as well as liberal, masters of the more imaginative kinds of luxurious connoisseurship and hospitality, in some ways trying to be more English than the English, and therefore both endearing and occasionally comic in the style of the *Bourgeois Gentilhomme*, like self-made men of every intervening age, down to the Tennants and the Asquiths themselves. At any rate, by reason of their wits and their accepted position, they were people who found no difficulty in fending for themselves.

Nor are the two or three references to 'niggers' offensive in their context. Raymond proposed a West African as Secretary of the Oxford Union, and he was elected. At that time in England there was nothing either patronising or derogatory in the term, and Raymond's light-hearted description of the episode indicates nothing but support and affection for an exotic figure.

As well as Buchan's, another description of Raymond at this time has survived, by E. S. P. Haynes, afterwards a successful solicitor and author. He admits that Raymond was 'shy and fastidious, and behind his irony it was often difficult to know what he really felt. But as he was sometimes thought cold and cynical I would like to record that his kindness and friendliness to me never varied . . . had I been in serious trouble there was no friend to whom I would have gone with less hesitation for help.' This corroborates Buchan's point that 'to such as were admitted to his friendship he would deny nothing. I have never known a friend more considerate, and tender, and painstaking, and unfalteringly loyal.' Haynes's (very brief) account was written after Raymond was killed, for the benefit of his children. It also refers to his 'luminous bronze hair, physical grace, uniquely infectious laugh; grey eyes, hard in repose but remarkably lively and expressive in talk . . . In early days he would not (I think) have spoken respectfully of martyrs or martyrdom. Yet when a really living issue came it seems as if no shyness or fastidiousness had inhibited his decision.'

These first-hand impressions of others may help to form an outline of Raymond's nature and his context, but a rounded portrait of him as an undergraduate will only appear from the extracts of his own letters. Apart from a few to his father and Margot giving news of his life at Oxford itself, and a few more to other friends, the most substantial series is to Harold Baker, nearly all of them (for obvious reasons) written in the vacations. Raymond's life between terms was never static. The family's London base was a house in Cavendish Square. His father was earning a large income at the Bar, which he could not afford to give up. He was thus prevented from accepting the party leadership in the House of Commons in the winter of 1898, when the Liberals were in opposition (see page 52). Margot also had £5,000 a year of her own, but she probably spent all of it and more, partly on hunting in Leicestershire, and partly on other expensive tastes. Every summer they would take a large house in Scotland for several months, combining family holidays with the entertainment of political colleagues and supporters – most of Scotland being still an important Liberal stronghold. To begin with, these houses were at St Andrews or North Berwick, in or near Asquith's constituency of East Fife. As the family continued to grow both in size and age, its requirements increased correspondingly, and even larger houses were taken, further afield. Dalquharran, a splendid Adam castle in Ayrshire; Slains, a theoretically romantic place[1] on the coast of Aberdeenshire, reputedly Bram Stoker's model for Dracula's Castle; and later still, Glen of Rothes and Hopeman Lodge, both in Morayshire.

Nor did the family remain in London in the Easter parliamentary recess. Fresh air and exercise were considered indispensable, and some readers may be surprised by the enormous number of hours that Raymond spent, usually with delight, on golf courses and grouse moors, in the intervals of savouring his 'beautiful Elzevir Livy', or Wilkes's copy of Catullus. The Asquiths several times took a house or moved into a hotel in April at Littlestone on the Kent coast, where once again golf and sea air were available. Christmas was usually spent with one of Margot's sisters, Mrs Graham Smith, at Easton Grey, near Malmesbury in Wiltshire. And in all the vacations there was a steady flow of invitations either from Raymond's own friends, like Aubrey Herbert at Pixton, or from family friends or colleagues, Lord Rosebery at Dalmeny, the great scientist Lord Rayleigh at Terling, the Grenfells at Taplow and Panshanger, the Horners at Mells, the Poynders at Hartham, near Easton Grey, and innumerable relations and friends of Margot's in Scotland. These were mostly Liberal circles, but it must be remembered that before the bitter hostility ignited by Lloyd George's Budget in 1910, and the subsequent Parliament Bill, social relations between the leading lights of the two parties were strong and close. The Asquiths were on the friendliest terms with A. J. Balfour, and Raymond's father and Margot were actually staying with the Salisburys at Hatfield when the Liberal government was with some difficulty being formed by Campbell-Bannerman in December 1905. Winston Churchill was appointed President of the Board of Trade, and selected as best man at his wedding Lord Hugh Cecil, a High Tory who two years later was to be the leader of a violent and noisy anti-Liberal group in the House of Commons known as the 'Hughligans'.

This peripatetic way of life seems to have suited Raymond, in spite of his early indifference to casual acquaintances. In any case, there was a strong undercurrent of family solidarity among the Asquiths, particularly strong perhaps because it was flexible, and did not make oppressive or artificial demands on the young.

[1] See page 107

To Margot Asquith   Balliol College.
                                                         October 1897

. . . You ask me to tell you of the life up here, but Methuselah with the pen of Swift could hardly do justice to such a subject – much less my humble self in an odd 10 minutes. Suffice it to say that those parts of the day which are not taken up with eating, are spent, by the athletic, in drinking, by the more intellectual in smoking or playing poker. A rather typical thing happened the other day: a man came into my rooms and asked me to join a new debating Society which he assured me contained all the best men in the 'Varsity. I told him that I belonged to so many already that as it was I had to make a speech almost every night of the week: he replied that I need have no fears on that account, it being one of the rules of his society that only one speech should be made at each meeting, (the length being limited to 7 min.) after which the society adjourned to play pool. He was much surprised when I still refused to join.

On the whole it is a life of familiarity without intimacy: which under the circumstances is perhaps as well: this smoking-room intercourse brings out men's superficial qualities only, which are usually the best part of their natures – in fact nearly always up here, as one realises when the *real* man comes out under the influence of liquor. The College is for the most part composed of niggers and Scotchmen: and the prevailing dialect is a compound of Gaelic and Hindustani, which is not easily acquired by the average Londoner . . .

To H. T. Baker   The Glen,
                                                         Innerleithen, N.B.
                                                         28 December 1897

. . . I have also read the first volume of Tennyson's life; very badly written and aranged to my mind; acres of pointless and trivial anecdote and poor Hallam slurred over in the most shameful way; the unpublished poems are in the main execrable; the most remarkable things are his letters at the age of 12. The 'Apostles' must have been an amazing Society in those days too – a cut above the Order of Merit I should think but they are terribly religious and scientific.

I have not begun anything for the Russell as yet; I waver between Socialism and Disestablishment; are either possible? The one would draw Bob Ensor, the other Garbett; the latter on the whole attracts me more, but I have not the necessary authorities here; Socialism is such a palpable fraud, a direct negation of history, equity, expediency, commonsense . . .

My host here [Margot's father, Sir Charles Tennant] – tho' a professed liberal – is the largest employer of labour in this country and possessed by an almost maniacal hatred of trades unions and all their works; debates over the dinner table are, sometimes, dangerously heated – the house being full of radicals . . .

To H. T. Baker   The Glen,
                                                     Innerleithen, N.B.
                                                     31 December 1897
                                                           12.45 a.m.

. . . It is a strange and mixed household I can assure you: statesmen, financiers, admirals from Cathay, Generals from Spain, Etonians, Wykehamists, women – They quarrel about Trades Unions – the financiers and politicians being at daggers drawn – Their only bond of sympathy is gluttony – in some cases genuine, in some assumed to meet the exigencies of fashionable society: apparently it is good form to discuss the entree with scientific fervour, to apply the higher criticism to the turtle soup, and to complain of the temperature of one's claret – if too hot, to break the glass, if too cold to fondle and cuddle it in one's hands and bosom till it acquires the desired heat. These things are a continual source of amusement to me . . .

To H. T. Baker   Hyndford House,
                                                     North Berwick, N.B.
                                                         9 January 1898

This coast is inimitable – one of God's masterpieces – and I have just gazed upon a sunset the like of which mortal never saw: it was as a flock of golden birds disappearing into Hell fire, incomparably, indescribably lovely . . .

I have really been doing quite a lot of reading for me – a little of Heine's Reisebilder – which is exquisite so far as I can understand it (mem. I must learn German) two plays of Plautus – VILE – the only interest an emendation in the *Trinummus* of 'mitum aut ne' into 'catamitum' by a Norwegian scholar called A. Bugge – which possibly accounts for the perverse ingenuity of his suggestion! I have nearly finished Petronius – who to my mind is somewhat overrated (though occasionally unsurpassably brilliant): he is a striking example of the universal rule that writers who are condemned by prudes are always overpraised by the impartial as a proof of their broadmindedness . . .

To H. T. Baker   Hyndford House,
                                                     North Berwick, N.B.

. . . In reading the life of A. T. [Alfred Tennyson] I find to my delight confirmation of a theory of mine I expounded to you last term – to wit that poetry expressing sorrow and despair in sublime and beautiful terms is not usually inspired by real misery: T says in one of his letters with reference to "Tears idle tears" that it was written under the influence of no genuine emotion – inspired by Tintern Abbey rather than by anything human or specific:

which is exactly what I should have imagined. If I were endowed with the gift of rhyme I could have written as good and better in Chamber Court many and many a time under the influence of the buttresses and the stars! What a futile and fortuitous thing is the gift of poesy! I swear I have as much poetic instinct in me as Tennyson, and so have hundreds of others, and they know it: but the art of rhyming is denied them, and the world never hears their thoughts. – There will be as much music in a single heart-beat as in all Homer, but for want of vocalisation no-one listens to it but the owner of the heart – which rather tends to prove poor Oscar's remark that the art of life is the graceful expression of emotions . . .

My dear father has just given me a beautiful Elzevir Livy, in which I revel: your mouth would water if you could see it. I picked up the other day rather a beautiful edition of Suetonius with an 18th cent. translation at the side . . .

To Margot Asquith[1]   Tuesday
[probably February 1898]

Thank you for your charming letter. I would certainly consult you if I got into any difficulty, for I think you know more of the world and take a saner view of it than almost anyone else. At the same time I don't think you need be over-anxious about me just at present. It is very gratifying to find oneself set down as a Byronic profligate: the thing is uncommon nowadays; but I should be interested to know who your hoary old scandal-monger got his information from. On your definition of the 'fast' life, I should think it was comparatively rare at Oxford – for many reasons; perhaps the 2 most obvious are lack of time and lack of opportunity: I can at any rate reassure you about 'women and dice', neither of which are fashionable vices among the saner sort of undergraduate: it is true there are a few fantastic spirits at Christ Church who keep roulette boards and have signed photographs of Mabel Love on their mantelpieces, but they are bores for the most part. As to wine, the place swims in it; it is a social accident of 'Varsity life, but I don't think anyone is much the worse for it, and some people are considerably improved. On the whole I think people are very moderate, and there are only a small number who drink to the injury of their health; for a man with a good stomach and a sense of proportion there is very little to fear.

I think I can see how your friend got his ideas about me: you see, I am a scholar, and the conventional standards of conduct for scholars and commoners are very different – especially at Balliol, which is more or less a forcing ground for scholarship: there is a clique here composed of 3 of the younger dons – bloodless prigs all of them – who want us to live like Turkish women in a harem – brooding over books and entirely segregated from the rest of the

[1] Presumably in answer to one expressing some kind of ill-founded anxiety.

world with its taint of convivial frivolity. They were quite scandalised when I began speaking at the Union: public appearances of any sort they consider immodest. Most of the scholars here submit to these unwritten restrictions – a good deal because they can't help it: they are not only intensely stupid but very dirty, ugly, illiterate and unsociable. Arnold Ward is almost the only exception. Nearly all my friends in Balliol are athletes: they are usually much the best fellows, as well as being far more interesting to talk to and live with . . . a naturally clever mind which has had no training is always a much pleasanter thing to meet than the sterile overloaded machine which serves most of these scholars for an intelligence. The result of all this is that I live a bright amusing healthy life which by comparison with the average scholar's existence might well be described as 'fast', if not flagrantly lawless. The Dons were furious at first, and actually had the insolence on one occasion to tell me that I ought to associate more with my fellow scholars; but having found that I always beat the stupid creatures in their own line, they are very friendly to me now.

This *apologia pro vita mea* has run on rather long but I was anxious to let you know that I still keep a few of the commandments.

Your abandoned but affectionate Raymond.

To H. H. Asquith   Balliol, 13 Feb. 1898

. . . We are getting up a party to go down and canvas at Swindon on the polling day. Some of our rowing bloods are very keen – great big ferocious 15-stone men – many of them Tories, but they all expressed themselves willing to fight if not to speak in the interest of Fitzmaurice. We are taking one of our black men, who is to pose as an Afridi chief in exile, and declaim on the iniquities of the Frontier policy. Amongst others Herbert (rows 7 in the 'Varsity boat) is coming down: he is the son of Auberon the anarchist, and a most delightful creature.

                                                        18 February

On Wednesday Balliol and Trinity made a combined attack on John's with snowballs, getting over Trinity wall and driving them from their garden back through their three quads: we were just about to hunt them into St. Giles's when the proceedings were stopped by the appearance of their President, who was rather angry. A good deal of damage was done to windows etc. and as I was the only man recognised I have been deputed by the Dean to collect contributions from the Balliol raiders to defray it. Raper [President of Trinity] is paying the Trinity bill himself, as he approves of the demolition of John's.

undated February 1898, Balliol

This damnable climate has got its claws into me already: cold, cough, headache, insomnia, every evil under heaven has attacked me, and not from want of exercise either: I have been boxing, fencing, playing tennis, racquets and football every day this term: but these things don't seem to have any effect except to make me sleepy in the day and tired but wakeful at Night.

30 March

. . . I had quite a stormy interview with the College authorities at that grim ceremony called handshaking[1] . . . They accused me of living on my capital – so far as the classics were concerned – though they were kind enough to add that I made more of it than most other people. I ought however to show more disposition to add to it: they relied on me to uphold their reputation against New College: couldn't I do 8 hours work a day instead of 4? and if I couldn't, shouldn't I? why not study German grammars? and as to my leisure hours, was it quite right for me to associate with the nicest people in College? Arnold Ward might be an amusing fellow, but he had never won a Craven: Herbert had nice manners and a pretty wit, but wasn't he in the 'Varsity boat? Surely it would be more profitable too if I discussed Plautus with red-haired Jews and green Paulines, instead of frittering away life in the company of leisured exquisites and elegant debauchees? And this nonsense about the Union: why waste time in practising demagogic arts upon an audience of fools? Balliol was not created for this: rather to chastise the growing insolence of New Coll.: and surely it was the function of her scholars to enable her to do so. And much more of the same kind – folly, with an adumbration of truth in the background: to all of which I replied with as much urbanity as reason admitted. So we parted on the best of terms.

To H. T. Baker   Grand Hotel,
Littlestone-on-Sea,
Kent.
11 April 1898

. . . I read, too, at intervals: have finished H. Richmond, and Mallock, – the latter much to my relief: like most of his books it is a compost of obvious fallacy and equally obvious truths: Where he departs from the platitude he is nearly always wrong; where he disguises it, he is quite inimitable: he does battle with

---

[1] An end of term interview with the Master and college tutors.

phantoms and fights against the air as no man ever did before: at this species of σκιαμαχία [fighting with shadows] you must go far to find his match: give him a lie which he can plausibly put into the mouth of a socialist, and he will play round it with lambent epigrams, riddle it with rapier thrusts of wit, trounce it with the happiest analogies, until one almost believes he is telling one something new. As a matter of fact the book establishes nothing further than that there are more fools in the world than wise men – a very sane conclusion, as even we *democrats* must admit. I am heartily glad to get it off my hands . . .

I have also been trying to grind out verses for the Horace Club with very limited success. Having plenty of pretty thoughts in my mind about Winchester, I imagined I should have little difficulty in writing them down. But the Alcaic stanza is a terrible machine for winnowing out the chaff from the grain, and making no use of either: one might as well whisper sentiment into a coffee-mill and expect it to come out blank verse: one pours in a molten mass of burning thoughts, diaphanous emotions, delicate imaginings, and it emerges at the other end sawdust. For the future the Alcaic stanza shall stand like a grim sentinel in the sacred sanctuary of my mind, challenging false sentiment, demanding an inexorable shibboleth, and stoutly refusing admission to any thought which cannot accommodate itself to the exigencies of the 3rd line. I think it would be a very useful rule for me.

I was much delighted with your letter. As to Mill, what you say is quite true; he never took the measure of humanity, a fault of his education I suppose. When he descends to God and other abstract fallacies he is excellent. But however detached and desiccated he may be, I think there is no doubt that the philosopher does good work if he merely lays down general principles and leaves their application and modification to suit the requirements of particular cases to the student of things as they are.

To H. T. Baker   20 Cavendish Square. W.
                                      20 April 1898

. . . There is quite a jolly little girl staying here now – one Pamela Plowden: it is her first season and Margot is bringing her out, as she has few relations and those she has are apparently inadequate or unsuitable in some way – very pretty and young and too clever to be offensively ingenuous: but I shan't marry her. The more I see and live, the more convinced I become that London Society is the only school for women: it is the feminine Eton, and much more than Eton. They acquire common sense and good manners, which are the essentials of a tolerable woman, without losing any of the so-called feminine virtues, – which to my mind only become virtues by the addition of the two qualities above mentioned. But of course London is the best for everything and everybody and in every way: I wouldn't live anywhere else for millions of pounds: it is a true saying of Sidney Smith's that there is more talent, taste and beauty – not to mention wealth – comprised within the parallelogram formed by Oxford St, Regent St, Piccadilly and Park Lane, than in any smiliar area the world over! A γνώμγ [opinion] which I heartily endorse, though living just outside the great τέμενος [sacred enclosure] . . .

To H. H. Asquith   Balliol,
24 April 1898

There is a debate here next Thursday about Cuba;[1] curiously enough the majority up here are Iberophils: people talk with great indignation of the hypocrisy and aggression of America: one certainly sees the Anglo-Saxon ethos in their policy, and nothing I suppose disgusts the average Englishman so much as to see his own methods adopted by another nation. It is very salutary for us – this holding up of the mirror.

9 May 1898

I went to Cambridge on Saturday . . . to represent the Russell Club as a guest of the Cambridge Liberal Club: the dinner was execrable, and Harcourt's speech – with a few exceptions which recurred at intervals of ¾ of an hour – cheap, dull, and interminable. Paul delivered a number of religious platitudes about Gladstone and his heavenly father: no one quite knew whether to cheer or to say the responses: it was most embarrassing.

May 1898, but undated

The debate here last Thursday wh. was to have been of a humorous description was postponed in consequence of Gladstone's death: in private business funeral orations were delivered by F. E. Smith and Simon (both of whom you met at Arnold Ward's dinner). F. E. made a thoroughly bad artificial speech which took in most of the audience: Simon was more sincere and a great deal better.

29 May

As to F. E. Smith – as far as I can gather, most prominent people up here seem to think that the Union *should* have a special memorial of some kind, tho' there is much divergence of opinion as to the form it should take; a bust is most favoured, and with the money collected, wh. will I suppose be about £500 or

---

[1] Cuba had recently become independent from Spain, helped by the support of the US, which rapidly turned to domination.

so, they ought to be able to get a good one; but it is a risky experiment, and so far as I can see there is nowhere to put it even if it were a success. I myself am strongly in favour of having a special memorial; speaking was certainly the most valuable accomplishment which Gladstone acquired here, and the only one in which he attained any degree of excellence; he was a bad scholar and a bad divine; in fact I suppose most of the faults of his intelligence were due to Oxford . . . I enclose my tailor's bill for the year, which I hold to be moderate; also a bill for my furniture, of long standing, wh. is certainly excessive.

To Arnold Ward   20 Cavendish Square

This is just a line to thank you for the Turgenev . . . It is a wonderful book and quite comes up to your description; the death-bed scene is exquisitely done; and throughout there seems to me to be far more grip on reality than one ever gets in Tolstoi; there is a closer contact with the core of things and less elaborate dalliance with the rind: in fact a much truer realism. Besides there is a much finer sense of humour, which is the real touchstone.

Let me exhort you to go to Pelléas and Melisande; I was in Mrs. Pat [Campbell]'s box for the first performance this afternoon: it is really quite beautiful; she herself is perfect, as is F[orbes] Robertson. I have hardly ever enjoyed a play so much: it sweeps one away into the world of Burne-Jones or Malory; caviare to the general no doubt, and even some of the elect hold it to be diseased and unhealthy; but as a pure fantasy it is exquisite. Mrs. P. C. wanted to have it played behind a gauze curtain and I think perhaps she was right: the idea was abandoned and music substituted, which experts and hypocrites tell me has the same effect.

To H. T. Baker   Hall Barn,
                                                      Beaconsfield,
                                                         Bucks.
                                                      4 July 1898
                                                      1.15 a.m.

. . . Well, well: then of course there is Bimbash [Stewart]: he was at Khartoum with Gordon, and is only 35: but his hair is grey and his mind rather obscene: he is too beautiful for words: a head like Julius Caesar and talks well: I have made great friends with him: he confirms all my prejudices about the General. But how beautiful he is and how well he rides and how brave! I admire bravery in men as much as I hate it in women: I mean real bravery – recklessness if you like – the fine bouquet of a great animal nature, no shilly-shallying with conscience: no side glance at the gallery: no toadying to God: no debate, no hesitancy, no division of the stout heart: just the natural, spontaneous, undiluted, unthinking impulse to DO.

And what lovely women there are too! Anne Dundas who is married, and Pamela Plowden who isn't! and how badly I played bridge: but I won. What are one's real sensations on seeing a beautiful woman? It would be a salutary and valuable exercise in analysis to write these things down: I swore I would before going to bed: but I'm damned if I can. There is little doubt that concupiscence – though at the root of it all – is certainly never on the surface. On the contrary one says How lovely! and one thinks How pure! (and so they are – many of them). I can never conceive a woman as real – unless she be constructed in the spatulate mode – But the really lovely woman – the woman like porcelain and yet compact of flesh and blood, a picture and something more than a picture, redolent of the sweetness of all time, and yet divinely youthful with the primal charm of Eve and the fresh piquancy of London and this great century of ours, with wavy delicate hair, and eyes like the horizon seas, with a nose from Austin Dobson and a complexion from Maeterlinck, with a voice like a reed and like a dove, a figure like some old Greek vase, and an aureole of grace and mystery that never were touched in Greece, hinted at in Chaucer and Burne-Jones, imitated by provincials, parodied by Italians, exaggerated by French, sighed after by all creation – was there ever such a thing seen but now? . . . And then there is the glory of the woods and the sun: the trees here are inimitable and the sun over the links in the park is better than anything but Otterbourne: the house itself is a dream: belonged to Charles II and was given by him to Waller the writer of verses, and the atmosphere of the time hangs about it – full of black oak and poetry. And then there is the strength and the glory of man: the ichor in his veins – the desire to hit and to run and to jump, the outline of a face, the contour of an arm, the two yards of splendid stature . . .

To H. T. Baker

The Pleasaunce,
Overstrand,
Cromer.
2 August 1898

. . . The fact is I am sulky: I have been brought down here under false pretences. I expected to find a handsome athletic comfortable amusing weekend party of the ordinary kind: nothing of the sort: the house is reeking with the gross and human odours which ever cling about the skirts of philanthropy: one sits down to dinner with a rabble of small shopkeepers from Balham and Battersea: when I want to play tennis or bowls or croquet they are playing already: when I want to lie in the smoking room with a pipe and a novel it is already being subjected to the critical gaze of a retail tobacconist: when I want to look at the sea or the sky, some grocer or ironmonger has anticipated me and ruined the foreground irretrievably. One of them actually talked to me yesterday, – prated about salmon fishing and croquet like a member of the Spectator staff. They actually want me to play cricket with them tomorrow! I told my host I thought it was going rather too far: and he poor man agreed with me: he suffers terribly from his wife, who is full of philanthropy and temperance and all that sort of nonsense, and while she is entertaining the good templars and prison matrons and heaven knows what horrors down in Buckinghamshire, he has been deputed to arrange a cricket match between the serfs on the Overstrand estate and the tenants of his Battersea shops: also to entertain the visiting team for three days on the strictest democratic principles at his own table and in his own beds: and here they are eating and drinking and talking their curious dialect, and exhaling a poisonous atmosphere of retail religion through one of the most beautiful houses in Norfolkshire. I call it monstrous! I sympathise keenly with the cultured butler wrinkling his brow and holding his breath with scorn as he pours the best champagne . . . And my host, hating them like death, but moving among them like a radiant god, the epitome of everything that is beautiful, luxurious, and refined, and treating them all with a cordiality that does infinite credit to his forbearance . . . I go from here to St Andrews on Wednesday, where I am told we have a house, which used to be a school, and bears the unique name of St Salvator's: it has an advantage of being near the links and holding forty people – which is always something: whether we all sleep in dormitories I don't know.

I had an amusing night the day I left you: dined at the House with Arthur B., George Curzon, Cranborne and other young Tory sparks: my governor came in half way through after making a phossy-jaw speech and talked about the whole thing in a delightful cynical vein, confirming my view of the modern statesman . . .

To H. T. Baker
St Salvator's,
St Andrews, N.B.
14 August 1898

I suppose by this time the Chateau [Azay-le-Rideau] has received you in its embraces, and you are luxuriating in silver bedsteads and boar hunts and all the other attractions by which the penury of Gallic aristocracy seeks to pander to the budding diplomat. You must write and tell me of your successes by flood and field, with the javelin of Esau and the cunning eloquence of Jacob . . .

We had a hot debate at dinner tonight about Gladstone and Goethe: Alfred Lyttelton and certain other rash spirits – mainly women – having the effrontery to uphold Mr G as the equal if not the superior of Goethe: my governor however with my assistance successfully and eloquently demolished their position, not as you may imagine a very hard thing to do. The ladies decried Goethe for having no heart: and therein ensued another discussion as the exact meaning and importance of that absurd expression: most of them displayed amazing ignorance and prejudice about both points . . . Society – especially the female part – is at its very worst on questions of this sort, on the border line between ethics and religion.

Have you ever been on a "merry-go-round"? A fair has just taken up its position on the shore about 100 yards from our house, and we all go out after dinner and ride on the thing. I assure you it is the most delirious pleasure: the horses move up and down and from side to side, as well as round and round, with every variety of nauseating motion – The scene quite reminds one of the Walpurgis nacht: the throng of half-naked lascivious women, and drunk men like monkeys whirling wildly through space, under the great yellow splashes of gas, and the ἠχή θεσπεσίη [wondrous noise] of automatic bands, and shooting galleries and little dirty boys eating ices and fried fish and every sort of horror. And my grave and statesmanlike father (member for the county and a man much respected in these parts) hurtling to and fro on a painted oscillating horse with a lofty smile of liberal satisfaction in the pleasures of the people, a true apostle of democracy if ever there was one . . .

To Conrad Russell[1]
St Saivator's,
St Andrews
August 1898 (but undated)

I hope you are not going to Turkey in a ship with Italian sailors: they always kill people with boathooks, and are full of fleas. As to the 'Recluse of Yildiz

[1] Conrad Russell, a half-French nephew of the 9th Duke of Bedford, was a highly original Balliol contemporary, later Private Secretary to Joseph Chamberlain at the Colonial Office, and afterwards, even more surprisingly, a stock-jobber and finally a farmer. This letter gives a good example of the mock high rhetorical style then in fashion at the Oxford Union, so often disastrously emulated since. It also gives an opportunity to quote the reply, in a different idiosyncratic vein; dated 8 September 1898, from the Pera Palace Hotel, Constantinople:

'. . . I see you say your knowledge is derived from the daily papers. What an authority to quote. You will be a bad lawyer . . . You seem to be very ignorant of modern history when you say Abdul rules over the Balkan Peninsula. Have you never heard of the Treaty of Berlin . . . in which a great man took part? Again you say "I think I have an examn." A very affected way to allude to Hon. Mods. in which you hope to get a first but are on tenterhooks lest you should get a 2nd.

After this slight criticism of your letter I will pass to other matters. Yesterday there was a race meeting in Asia Minor. Thousands of all nations came to see it. It was very amusing and the sky was rent with plaudits. For the only time since East and West joined in the shout of "Long live Charles August King of the Romans" at Charlemagne's coronation did they unite again and Turk, Seljuk, Chineese, Jew, Basque, Gipsy, Russian, French, Levantine, Armenian, Mongol, Hittite, Celt, Bushman and Parsee called in their various languages "The Russells win!" as my brother passed the post closely followed by me – the rest nowhere. It was really extraordinarily funny to see the Turks moved from their usual lethargy applauding and huzzaing.

Tomorrow I am going to see the Sultan, which I can think will be interesting . . . Ashmead Bartlett is in this hotel and 5 spies who watch him and my mother and me too. When we talk they sit near and write down what we say for the Sultan to read.'

Kiosk' [i.e. the Sultan], as our journalists sportively denominate that great and wise monarch who rules over the Balkan peninsula with an iron hand – albeit well clothed in the velvet glove of civilisation and enlightenment – combining in his person the oriental splendours of Darius and Semiramis with the gentler and more humane virtues of our blessed Father Leo XIII and the Kaiser Wilhelm, blending together in a web as lovely as it is indissoluble the best traditions of the early caliphate, the scholastic refinement of the Eastern Emperors, and those noble ideals of clemency and altruism, which are more particularly associated with the religion of the West – as to him, I say, your warnings are quite superfluous. From myself . . . the tortures of the inquisition could not wring one syllable of blasphemy, one single sentence of disparagement anent that great and good man. By the way I heard rather a good story from our Berlin ambassador about him the other day: he and P. Currie [the British Ambassador] were looking out of the windows of Yildiz one day and chanced to see an oriental funeral go by – a procession of hired mourners, as is the custom in those parts, uttering the most doleful shrieks and groans and pouring dust and dung upon their heads: the Sultan, crossing his hands upon his breast, and rolling the glorious orbs of his eyes in a heavenward direction, turned to Sir Philip, and remarked in a voice trembling with emotion 'I hate this: tears should always come from the heart'. Which is an interesting comment on his Armenian policy.

What do you think of our new Viceroy? Or hasn't that piece of news percolated to those old Whig circles, who don't read the newspapers? I call it a shame to send a man like G. Curzon out there [to India]: it is scandalous the way we lavish the flower of our race on this dull provincial empire of ours: of course he ought to be kept in London: so ought his wife . . . Did you see the account of an interview with [his American father-in-law] Mr. L. Z. Leiter on the subject? Apparently he sent a wire to his daughter to the following effect: 'Warm congratulations: please wire at once attitude of American girl on finding herself promoted to be Vice-Queen of India.' Isn't it rather good?

Margot was intensely keen for me to take her out to India with G.C. in November, where we could have lived in vice-regal splendour thro' the winter, returning in April. I wish I could have gone, but I believe I have an absurd examination in March . . .

I was told rather a good repartee of J. K. Stephen's (the cleverest man of our century) – Oscar Browning was talking about immortality in his greasy complacent way and happened to round off a more than usually unctuous period with the quotation 'Heaven lies about us in our infancy': 'That's no reason why we should lie about Heaven in our old age' said J. K. S. quick as a knife. It looks rather cheap and heavy written down, but must have been good at the time.

Lord Rayleigh arrived today – the man who invented Argon: he is like a fish with red whiskers, and always carries about with him a little phial containing new and undiscovered elements (wh. he is keeping to himself just now): he smells them from time to time, and occasionally eats one, but he won't tell us about them.

To H. T. Baker   St Salvator's,
St Andrews, N.B.
21 August 1898
11.45 p.m.

As usual I am in a gross unspeculative frame of mind – as who would not be after the rude assault of a Scottish Sabbath. Men like baboons scream the name of Jesus 30 yards from the window where I am writing; the sounds of hysterical declamation mingled with the meagre flutings of a choir of thin-voiced anaemic maenads floats in and beats perpetually on my unwilling ear. I went to Church this morning, that being an essential factor in our political methods, and one not yet eliminated by the Corrupt Practices Act . . . As an antidote I read the Vth bk. of Lucretius this afternoon: it was new to me, and much of it is inimitably fine, I think. Old Haldane is staying here amongst others, and coming upon me as I read, took up the English and declaimed 30 lines or so of the corresponding Latin with the greatest accuracy and vigour. I was delighted, for he is a man of no classical attainment. I had a long and interesting talk with him afterwards on the subject of scholarship in general: he has a profound contempt for the English Aristotelians, Platonists, and more particularly for Jowett, and a corresponding admiration of the Germans, amongst whom he was bred. He also told me that he had had MacTaggart to stay with him for three days and thought him much over-rated. He says "he has lived in a cave and is apt to mistake shadows for substance"; but he considers him intellectually remarkable and attractive in character. He and my father are now engaged in a distracting political discussion . . . Latterly they have been more gossipy, and I gather that the Liberal party is in far greater straits than the wildest conservatives dare to dream. There is every chance apparently of John Morley sending in his resignation at any moment. He sees that he has no political future, and is anxious to slink out as honourably as may be on the pretext of writing a life of Gladstone for which he has been offered £6,000 – a bait which they say appeals to him. Harcourt of course they dismiss with a smile: and they seem to think Rosebery will be very chary of coming back yet awhile; he would have to drive a restive and divided team, and a second failure would be fatal to him for ever. J. Morley has just sent my Gov. a sample chapter of his new book (now I believe completed) on Home Rule: it dealt with the Parnell Commission, and tho' as well done as might be, will I think fall very flat upon the world: he rakes about among the ashes of dead things with perfect knowledge and dexterity, but it would take a heaven-born genius to stir a spark from them. The whole controversy is dead and buried, and keen progressives like my father and Haldane talk of it with languid aversion and ill-concealed contempt for the "great" statesman who devised it. My Gov. says that in the last 10 years of his life Gladstone wrecked the liberal party, and broke an instrument which would have gone far towards consummating the counsels of perfection. He also takes the lowest view of his motives and thinks that we should have heard nothing of Home Rule, if his foreign policy – more especially in Egypt – had not been such an egregious failure. And he knew Gladstone as well as most people.

To H. T. Baker   St Salvator's,
St Andrews, N.B.
21 September 1898

I long to see *The Egoist* staged: I don't think I told you I had a drive with Meredith: he is in great distress about it: the man who is "adapting" it has put it into some language which he says is not English, and the poor old boy feels that it will be a travesty unless he undertakes the labour himself.

My hair is brown: there is no getting out of it: it wasn't once, but times are changed: for one thing I've just had it cut – villainously too: I wish one could pass from yellow to grey by some chromatic euthanasia: the intermediate stages are so full of anxiety! The only two general maxims in which I have much belief are *"Carpe diem"* and "never have your hair cut outside Bond St." On these hang all the law and the prophets.

Your description of George Wyndham carries conviction: I see he has contradicted the rumour of his appointment [As Under Secretary of State for War]: I sincerely hope he may not get it: his is quite the wrong sort of intellect for politics – worse than Smyth's I should think. My father still holds by St John Brodrick, who is ugly, rude, deaf and industrious, to my mind quite the best man for the place.

Yes, the 'son' who was beaten was myself: but in case you should imagine that there was any disgrace in the defeat, let me tell you that I was playing with my father against Herbert (who is a very good average player): and my father is quite execrable, a really severe handicap to any partner: so we did well to get within three holes of him – I nearly wrote to the papers about this: I hate being misrepresented: and besides my victories which are many and glorious never receive adequate recognition in the press – Norman the Sub-Editor of the D.[aily] C.[hronicle] dined here tonight: a clever, versatile, well-informed man with a thoroughly journalistic mind, but oily, cunning and untrustworthy to the last degree. He tried after dinner to pump my father about Home Rule, but was evaded in the most masterly way. I must say he told us many interesting things about China and Japan and in a more interesting way than most people with knowledge. They also discussed Local Veto, my gov. again very guarded. (He afterwards told me that when the question of who was to introduce the bill was mooted at one of the early cabinets in '93, old Harcourt declared in a loud voice, that in his opinion the man who proposed that bill would deal the death-blow of the Temperance Cause in England! Really politics is an inimitable farce – and so well sustained too! Still Charley's Aunt went on for three years.)

I have just read some verses which J. K. Stephen sent to Margot – a parody of Myers.[1] One stanza is particularly happy (quite extempore I believe) especially if you remember the original, ending "Show one another what the Lord can do."

> "Lo! when a man obscene and superstitious
> Lo! when a woman brainless and absurd,
> Strive to idealise the meretricious,
> Love one another as the beast or bird!"

The third line a masterpiece, and the repetition of Lo! much in the style of the master. I believe it is unpublished, but you may have seen it before.

What a stupid letter this is! more "outward" I fear than usual: it can hardly fail to bore you: quite a waste of time in fact: but the faculty of independent thought is lost to me for the time being . . .

To H. T. Baker
St Salvator's,
St Andrews, N.B.
22 September 1898
1 a.m.

. . . We were talking the other night of what we would do if we were all very rich. Margot said that she would keep £40,000 per annum for personal expenses, and spend the rest in charity; we all admired such heroic generosity, and I, as in duty bound, impugned the principle; whereon she explained that she didn't mean soup-tickets, but a far more rational scheme: she proposed to endow annually a dozen or so poor but promising young men from each of the Universities with £400 a year, to tide them over early crises, and save many fine talents which would otherwise be wrecked on the rocks of impecuniosity, or driven into the unworthy haven of a premature curacy. The award to be made not by competition, but a discriminating selection conducted thro' competent agents. Of course there are many difficulties in the way; firstly the agents, secondly perhaps the promising young men – esp. if they had to be poor. But I am in favour of some scheme of the sort – tho' I should be inclined to make personal beauty and charm and unfitness for the coarser form of self-sustenation my criterion. Lipton *et hoc genus omne*; should be spoken to about

1 F. W. H. Myers. Author of *St. Paul*.

it – so much more satisfactory and reasonable than the most ideal cookshop, don't you think?

To H. T. Baker
St Salvator's,
St Andrews, N.B.
27 September 1898

. . . As usual I had a most amusing time with old Haldane in Perthshire; he will be a very great man, if not prematurely cut off – like so many of our English sovereigns – by a surfeit of lampreys, or some other unpalatable delicacy; his appetite is quite prodigious – especially for a Hegelian – and seems to increase every time I see him.

Unfortunately – owing to the presence of certain local lairds – the conversation turned largely upon the sectarian idiosyncracies of Messrs Black, White, Green & Brown (all Scotch ministers are named after colours of the rainbow) – that being the only form of shop which has any attraction for this incredible nation. These theological bickerings were relieved by two somewhat laughable incidents; the butler's wife unexpectedly gave birth to a fine boy – the 3rd within the year; this made dinner very late, vastly to my indignation . . . Then some wag at the village church put cayenne pepper in the sacramental wine and the unfortunate communicants were seized with the most soul-subduing fits of sneezing on approaching the chalice, and after drinking were beset by intestinal tortures which broke through the stoic mask and manifested themselves in facial contortions of the most indecent nature . . .

You say history is not a-making at Azay; it is though in the rest of that foul country don't you think? Do you hear anything credible of this Dreyfus business? The thing has lasted so long that even I have been constrained – by sheer force of infection – to form opinions upon the facts and fictions which our Journals ram down our throats. One is inclined a priori to conceive as many people guilty as possible. Henri is a confessed criminal; so is Esterhazy and apparently Sandherr. I think on the whole Dreyfus must be too: no doubt Cavaignac's speech in the Chamber was based upon documents which are now admitted to be forgeries, but since that discovery he still holds to his opinion and as everyone who knows him considers him an honourable man devoid of petty vanities; and as he is certainly remarkably able and intelligent, I think his opinion goes for a great deal. There is also a curious unanimity of all who have seen the evidence, and the further facts that D. is known to have lived, without interference, in German territory, and that when entrusted with the details of a bogus scheme of concentration upon the S.E. frontier, he immediately gave it away to the Italians, if one may judge by the modifications which they made in the disposition of certain fortresses round Nice; and again the consensus against revision of the three *legal* members – the representatives of the Cour de Cassation – on this last commission. These things taken in conjunction with letters to his wife, recently published, incline one to believe in his guilt. The question of motive is the only one which presents real difficulty, seeing that the man was rich; and that seems to me to be plausibly solved by the explanation of Du Paty de Clam – viz. that D. gave away comparatively unimportant secrets in the hope of receiving more valuable ones in exchange, which would of course be of vast use, in furthering the promotion of an ambitious officer . . .

To H. T. Baker   Dalmeny Park,
                                                                      Edinburgh.
                                                              1 October 1898

. . . I arrived here yesterday night from Gosford: it is a comfortable but inartistic house, (Rosebery has execrable taste in these matters) – a regular stucco-castle full of Reckitts blue carpets with silver stars, and other enormities of like nature: the bedroom where I write looks out upon the most suburban sea you can imagine – full of old boots and foam. But there are many fine pictures, especially of Napoleon, Pitt, and Fox – a particularly good one of Napoleon by David. The old house, an 11th century building down by the sea in a very lovely situation, was blown up by R's grandfather: his wife ran away – a curiously inadequate reason one would think. Rosebery has filled it with every sort of curiosity and relic – literary and pictorial: more particularly of the Jacobite period – including the Prayerbook (with notes and corrections in James' autograph) which brought about the Revolution. There is a large house party of dullish people: among them the old Duchess of Cleveland (R's mother) a painted relic of the first Empire in a marvellous state of preservation: face like a well bred parrot, and not a single grey hair on her head: also his sister Lady Leconfield, severe, but sensible, and one Maud Wyndham, sister of your friend of New College, a pleasant, rather pretty girl: also a vast and miscellaneous assortment of military sparks, blasé almost to the point of decomposition: I asked one of them what regiment he belonged to: he replied in a plaintive drawl that he really didn't recollect, but he believed they had buff facings. There is also a Colonial Premier whose name I never gathered but last night I had a most trying experience with him: R. himself always sleeps at the old house, which he has renovated, and he had already retired with most of the others: I was left tête-à-tête in the smoking room with this awful Australian: after talking for many hours about tinned meats and other colonial subjects, I suggested we should go to bed: accordingly we set off – the premier rather wild in his gait: we reached the door of the Duchess's room and my friend opened it and bade me goodnight: I pointed out as respectfully as I could that she was not a suitable victim, and that there were many younger ladies in the house if he was so disposed: he however indignantly disclaimed any libidinous intention, and subsequently confessed that he thought it was his own room, and if it wasn't he hadn't any idea which was: I suggested we should ring someone up and find

49

out, but he merely curled himself up at the foot of the stairs and declared his intention of sleeping there: he assured me that he had often done it before: which I am inclined to believe: a man with a bad head for topography shouldn't mix his wines: but he turned up smiling at breakfast this morning. Rosebery's secretary Waterfield, (a cousin of the great Reginald) must have been very handsome when he first assumed the post as a New College undergraduate eight years ago: he inclines one to believe the worst of his illustrious master . . . Rosebery himself is quite admirable – my ideal of what a man of 50 should be – clever, cynical, sensual, and wonderfully witty and ready: he improves with keeping. I had a delightful walk and talk with him this afternoon, about Jowett, the Union, and Oxford in general. I have studied him somewhat closely this time, and I must say I am not surprised that he is abhorred of the non-conformist conscience. He is a spoilt child, and gives one that impression more than anyone else I know. He is frankly cynical about politics, and completely disillusioned about everything else in the world. He has rooms full of the most priceless bibliological treasures, but he has forgotten where to find things and almost what they are, and doesn't care twopence now about the whole collection which he has taken infinite pains to amass. He has promised to leave me in his will Wilkes's Catullus (he edited Catullus and produced a beautiful edition on vellum: R. has his original copy with MS corrections) and a MS book of J. S. Mill, containing most of Utilitarianism, and many interesting magazine articles . . . I shall be much interested to hear your conclusions about Liberalism – a subject in which I take a philosophical but altogether disproportionate interest . . . I may say at once that I have no views at all at present: my opinions are only developed by opposition: I could rub philosophy off a nutmeg-grater, but cannot spin it out of my own bowels: the latter I think is really the sign of a large intelligence. The 'clever schoolboy' view has much to recommend it – amongst other things the fact of an incidental philanthropy. It is satisfactory to find a creed which is at once gratifying to one's own ambitions and favourable (for the moment at any rate) to the general happiness of mankind: Liberalism is one of the few trades which combine both qualifications . . .

To H. T. Baker
The Lodge,
North Berwick, N.B.
4 October 1898

. . . I can't imagine by what flights of presumptuous and praeter-Icarian sophistry you dare to assert that your letters have a preponderance over mine in quality – though not in bulk: why only two of them have any claim to be called letters at all: the 98 others were mere Papal Bulls and might just as well have been heavy reproofs addressed by that absurd Martin V to Henry VIII . . . the unfortunate Oscar said many truer things and in better form: those that you quote bear the same dully artificial relation to life as Addison's essays, with even a tinge perhaps of something yet more remote and abhorrent – the stucco flavour of French classical poetry – that suggestion of Aristotle misread, misunderstood, misapplied, and cheaply modernised which hangs about anything French that I have read. The fact is we have only begun to touch the core of things in the last 50 years; there is much in the Positivist trichotomy: echoes from the philosophic era fall flat upon ears attuned to science, and the song of things as they are. What a damnable fool, for instance Rousseau . . . must have been: you find the type in almost every age – the Stoics at Rome e.g. – but dear Greece was rid of it: there is something as repulsive in the *a priori* method of thought as there is in the theological – a blighting taint of blatant patent inefficiency. As to Rochefoucauld, I think he must have been a charming man in spite of his Gallicism: I once read an excellent essay of John Morley's on Aphorisms, in which many of his dicta were quoted: I remember copying some of them out – better than those you sent me, but have forgotten them now. Someone said – Huxley I think – that he was the only 'Gentleman writer' that the professionals had ever to be afraid of . . .

To H. T. Baker   The Lodge, North Berwick.
                                                         6 October 1898

. . . If religion wasn't so damned silly, and my father – who is far the greatest philosopher I know – so successful and convincing a disciple of the Real, I verily believe I should totter into the arms of Leo XIII. Here I am – not 20 yet – a mere boy of putrid fibres, diseased nerves and obsolete brain-tissue, and yet I am perfectly certain that, if I took a little trouble, the accidental tutelage of fate would make me a governor of this Empire's destinies. And it is just the same with you – except that you will probably take the trouble and I shan't. It is all very well for wiseacres to prate about the arrogance of youth and to vent their octogenarian satires upon the clever undergraduate who thinks he has the world at his feet – but the fact is he HAS. There's no denying it. We, WE, my friend, are the people who will abolish the Peers and poke fun at the Tzar of all the Russias – if we think it worth while: there is no one else: where are the men of our generation, and what are they? People of meagre intelligence, and no great assurance – civil servants, grocers, minor poets, all of them! But with the brains that you have, and the tub-orator's instinct that has been transmitted to me – anything may be done, especially as we both have enough money to buy dress clothes – which most men haven't now-a-days. It is merely a question of method. We lack motive: if that were there, I would stake my head on our both being cabinet ministers in 20 years from now. The great difficulty of life is not doing things – as the Gentiles vainly imagine – but wanting to do them. These reflections, I fear, may seem a little tumid and arrogant, but I have just come away from a company of twittering bores . . .

Arthur Balfour – the redeeming oasis in this desert of pachyderms, the kind, lovely physician in a vast Cretin-asylum, Christ among the Sadducees, went back yesterday – presumably to manage the Dowager-Empress of China: they should marry her to Charlie Beresford, with Lady C. as first concubine; that is far the best solution of this stupid tangle. A. B. is far the most fascinating man in person and manner that ever lived: I simply love him. The Saxe-Weimars – whoever they are – are staying at the Hotel here: I lunched with them yesterday, and beat the Prince at Picquet: They are singularly stupid and uninteresting even for their class . . .

To John Buchan   20 Cavendish Square, undated
                                                    but between 15 and 20 December

. . . The Whips lunched here today, and offered my father the leadership in the Commons: he defers it to C. Bannerman, being a poor man and unable to give up his practice at the Bar. I have read a pawky letter of C.B.'s, from which I gather he will take it. Rosebery is hated. He has played Fabius[1] too long.

To H. T. Baker   Easton Grey.
                                                                Xmas Day 1898

I have never found myself under quite similar conditions – My host is a typical English squire, who hunts, owns the village, and has a church at the bottom of his drive. If he were not mad he would be intolerable: but he wears no socks and refuses to shoe his horses, though he expects his guests to ride them. This morning we all went to church: my thoughts have been running on mangers ever since. The congregation was small but the occasion a pathetic one: the Vicar has gradually been coming to the conclusion that he has mistaken his vocation, and this was the last occasion on which he was entitled to conduct a service before becoming head keeper to the Duke of Beaufort at Badminton, some miles off. I was much affected: and indeed towards the end of the sermon there was not a dry eye in the church – (N.B. all this is quite true: the fellow dined here last night – another old English custom – and I had a long talk with him in his cups) . . . I had an interesting dinner in town before coming away: A. Milner was there, a most charming man, with a cameo-like mind, clear-cut and as quick as lightning: also Lady de Grey, who has the reputation of being the handsomest woman of our age, as she is certainly the largest, vast and rather passée. She reminds one more of Faustina[2] than anyone else. She is run-

---

[1] Quintus Fabius Maximus 'Cunctator'. Model of delaying tactics.

[2] Wife of Emperor Marcus Aurelius. 'Ancient authority groundlessly interpreted her lively temperament as a sign of faithless and disloyal character.' – Oxford Classical Dictionary.

ning the opera next year, and wants £65,000, so Margot got a millionaire called Cassel to meet her: by the end of the dinner she had got £35,000 out of him, and probably had the rest before she went to bed – or after. Surely the time is ripe for a Juvenal! . . .

To H. H. Asquith   Balliol.
                                                 10 February 1899

We have had snow and frost here all this week, and skating the last two days: I went down yesterday to the frozen fields at Iffley and played hockey on the ice for Balliol v. Trinity: the first exercise I have had this term; we played for four consecutive hours and just beat them: it was great fun.

                                                     21 May 1899

I have been very seedy the last three or four days: my blood has gone wrong somehow, and both my legs have been attacked by a sort of boil or blain, which is painful and depressing.

To H. T. Baker   20 Cavendish Square
                                                     24 May 1899

. . . I am in bed, as you see by the script – not that there is anything odd about that, seeing that it is within a few minutes of midnight; the tedious part of it is that Barlow – who is the best doctor in London – tells me I must stay there for a week; of course it isn't true and of course I shan't do it, but it is a boring thing to say even for a good doctor. I went to bed as soon as I got here yesterday, and am already beginning to feel the *tedia lectuli calentis*[1] and to say my Amen to the conclusion of that same poem *Non est vivere, sed valere, vita.*[2] They put great bandages, poultices, fomentations and other foul appliances on my thighs so tight that I cannot think, so hot that I do not feel, so large that I never sleep. They tell me that I am run down, whatever that means, and that my blood is impoverished – consequently I am compelled to make myself drunk on port, and distend my liver like a goose with all the most succulent delicacies which can be procured. This sounds pleasant but it isn't . . .

---

[1] The boredom of a bed of fever.   [2] Life is not merely being alive, but being well.

To H. T. Baker   20 Cavendish Square.
                                                      28 May 1899

. . . I got up after lunch yesterday and took carriage exercise in the Park, clad in my bright blue coat and Anna straw, the only clothes I have with me – this created a considerable sensation amongst the territorials. Barlow was furious when I told him, and swore that I was not to move from bed again till Thursday at earliest. I suspect he is right as I have just had a relapse in my disease, and one more of these loathsome eruptions shows signs of appearing . . .

To H. T. Baker   20 Cavendish Square.
                                                      31 May 1899
                                                      1.30 a.m.

. . . The thought of the Hertford[1] makes me sick: 6 hours a day in the schools will crumple me up in my present hypertrophied condition – Barlow forbids me to drink champagne, but my father insists on my drinking it, and the veins in my head are like the Missouri in spate – especially as I have been much excited today by visitors after dinner – amongst others the sister of Cecil Rhodes, a vast woman with a pear-shaped stomach: my father asked her what opinion her brother had of Chamberlain, and she replied that he thought him a funny little man: which is probably true. I have also had a letter from George Curzon[2] to-day asking for Greek Epigrams of all things, complaining that no-one out there takes any interest in things other than official, and saying that he works 14 hours a day and that his spine is giving way . . .

To H. T. Baker   20 Cavendish Square, W.
                                                      2 June 1899

Thanks for yours. You won't see any ink yet awhile: I am on a sofa now and out of my bedroom but not allowed to sit at a writing table. I expect I shall handle a pen for the first time in the schools on Monday: I only hope I shan't have forgotten how to use it. My case gets more dismal every day. Barlow was here today and professed himself dissatisfied with my progress: he says he has discovered glands or some nonsense in my thigh which have gone wrong, and I might have to lie up here for another week at least. I told him it was preposterous; he then quoted Dickens – some rubbish about "Little Pip" or a name of the kind at which I was very naturally incensed, and ordered the footman to turn him out of the room. I detest the man: he has no dash. He is coming again on Sunday morning to see whether he can possibly give me leave to

[1] The most important Latin prize scholarship at Oxford   [2] Appointed Viceroy of India the year before.

go back in the afternoon, as he arrogantly says. Of course I shall go whatever he says. I am so hot and bored that I don't know what to do. I wonder whether the Wyndham girl who said Balliol men were prigs was one I sat next to once at Dalmeny: I thought her excessively stupid, but she can hardly have thought me a prig as I made a point of talking dirt to her all through dinner. I don't know her father, but Ly Leconfield seems to me a dull frigid woman, tho' she is said to be alright.

Arthur Balfour and Haldane are dining here tonight: I expect they will come up in a few minutes and comfort me.

To H. T. Baker   St Salvator's,
                                                                  St Andrews, N.B.
                                                                  10 August 1899

. . . This place is divine: in the six days I have been here I have put on 5 lbs. of weight. This is true. The spring has come into my legs, and my face is brown and shiny like the Bear's: We have had the two best sorts of weather: when I came there was mist & drizzle over the sea: I put on a homespun coat and thought of Drake; the rain fell softly on my face and I smiled for joy and bathed my body in hot water. Today the sky has been light blue with a strong sun and keen salt breeze, which makes one feel like an immortal Ostrogoth. I encountered Leslie Balfour, an ex-amateur champion, on the links, and receiving ten strokes, beat him. He is a gentleman but a Heygate of the first water. When I got home on Wednesday I found Margot & my father going out to dine alone at Willis' Rooms . . . So I postponed my journey and accompanied them: we were absolutely the only people in the place – which shows how sharply defined is the limit of the season. The dinner was excellent and we talked of interesting things. It appears that Joe Chamberlain went to C. Bannerman 2 days before the Transvaal debate and deliberately tried to nobble him – to make him promise to let our side in for a war-policy and speak in favour of it himself, – one of the most astounding proposals ever made by a responsible minister. C. B. however was unable to cope with the situation single-handed, and called on my father, who of course told him to have nothing to do with it, and to write a civil letter of rebuke to Joe: the letter, when written, turned out to be so inadequate that my father had to score most of it out and re-write it! and now all the papers are saying what a brilliant success C. B. has been as a leader! . . . Another interesting and distressing thing is that Milner is probably going to marry Mrs Dick Chamberlain, Joe's sister-in-law: she is perhaps the most intolerable woman now alive – well-born, but one of nature's vulgarians: and they are almost as trying as nature's gentlemen. She would really be considered below par in the bar at Basingstoke. Margot is furious, as Milner once made a feeble attempt to marry her. She says that Milner (like me) has an intense admiration for vitality – being little endowed with it himself: and apparently he is unable to distinguish between the real thing and a sort of silly French nervousness which many people mistake for it. It will be a great pity and will considerably impair Milner's efficiency as a statesman: he has already had one row with her for giving away some diplomatic secret with which he had entrusted her, to Rhodes, with whom she is hand and glove: having committed adultery with Dr Jameson while the late Richard was still alive, I suppose she feels that she still owes a sort of allegiance to the Jingo faction.

Another scandal which is causing some amusement just now is the reported engagement of Ly R. Churchill to Mrs Cornwallis-West's son, a young blade in the Guards about your age; my father who was down at Cowes says that his mother was rushing about frantically offering a handsome reward to any man who would elope with Ly Randolph! . . .

To H. T. Baker   St Salvator's,
                                                           St Andrews, N.B.
                                                           15 August 1899

. . . Edward Lawson is here and insists on playing golf: he is a most ridiculous figure on the links sweltering under the sun with his coat off and a moutainous stomach as round as the moon: his servant Nelson, who goes round with him and pulls him out of the bunkers, was at one time the best tenor in Europe: he has also been the champion middle-weight boxer and professional swimmer in Berlin: he now looks after the Turkish baths at Hall Barn and shaves the guests with the most exquisite grace and skill. The little man is also attended by Bimbash Stewart V.C. – probably the bravest man now alive and certainly the wickedest: if he had stayed in the Egyptian army he would have been Sirdar instead of Kitchener – a peer with a fat income and an Oxford degree instead of a wandering adventurer eking out a precarious livelihood by trading on the good nature of gullible plutocrats and cheating his fellow men whenever the occasion offers. He acts as a sort of spear-bearer to the little Jew, very much like the condottieri in earlier times: he knocks down people who get in the way and has his debts paid: he is handsome and witty . . . It is very convenient having Lawson here, as he always has telegrams and one hears how many runs Hayward has made and who is killed at Rennes, before most people. How damnable the French are! one hardly knows who to hate most! there is a self-consciousness about them that makes me quite ill; you never catch them napping: they never forget that there is a situation and that they must act up to it. Demange comes to see Labin 2 hours after he has been shot in the back: "I may collapse" says L "but Dreyfus is saved." How could a man with any largeness in his soul say a thing like that? I wish the little Cretin had been killed, but there seems to be no hope of that: it will probably turn out that he had a prayer book under his vest between the shoulder-blades.

As to Chamberlain – no one maintains that he is an artist except in the sphere of oratory; as a statesman he is quite in the 2nd class – an engineer, not an architect – full of small ingenuity and cleverness, but quite unable to take a synoptic view of things; he has never really emerged from the traditions of Birmingham and the tin tacks that made him; the policy of putting in a screw here and paring off an edge there is all very well for a municipal politician, but it is too patchy for the wider world. Show him a mad dog and he will find a way to muzzle it: confront him with the general problem of canine insanity and he flounders like a woman. I too do not think John Buchan a natural politician; I like him and he has good brains; all I said to him was that there are places in Liberal cabinets of the future gaping to receive the intelligent partisan of 30, whereas on the other side there is no prospect for anyone until the Cecil family is all safely berthed. There are only 2 parties now-a-days, and they are non-political – the party of wisdom and the party of folly: all men of wits are so nearly agreed about what is good and what is possible as to be unwilling to quarrel about the residual difference, except for the sake of keeping up appearances. The mob has to be entertained with the spectacle of a combat of some sort, but it is very like the lion and the bull at Roubaix, neither side wants to fight and one is always toothless. A change in politics is only one of nomenclature, not of principle. If by calling myself A I can make more fame and money than by calling myself B, by all means let me do so . . .

To H. T. Baker
St Salvator's,
St Andrews, N.B.
25 August 1899

You tell me to write and I do so; but really there is nothing to tell. Life goes on here much as usual, and I am still much pleased with it, tho' over tired both in body and mind. Little Lawson is still with us: he was drunk last night and told me a coarse story about Dizzy, who when asked his opinion of a speech which Gladstone delivered in '76 on landing in Ireland, described it as "rhetorical priapism". I screamed with laughter, but can see no particular aptness in the phrase: perhaps you can elucidate it. It is one of the most trying things about life, this necessity of laughing uproariously when vinous old men say things that are dirty but not funny; else one is written down as a prig. However, I always take it as a compliment when people reach that state with me. In this particular case I had my revenge by winning £8 off him at Bridge; when intoxicated he falls an easy victim. Sir Edgar Vincent was here for a few days – a fine figure of a man, a good oar at Eton, with magnificent spirits: how and why he has come to be what he is, or where his money sprang from no one seems to know. Alfred Lyttelton and his wife arrived in time for dinner to-night, and Herbert Gladstone comes tomorrow. My brother declares that he has Viking blood in his veins and has acquired a fishing boat with several gigantic sails, in which he takes me to sea. He steers himself and has a man to help with the sails. I feel that it is very dangerous, especially as I cannot swim 10 yards. I was induced to bathe the other day, and found I had almost entirely lost the little knowledge of that art which I once had. Still it is very pleasant in the boat: one gets out of sight of land with nothing but grey sea and air all round, and there is quite an Homeric feeling about it. My father opened a bazaar here today and made a very witty speech which was received in profound silence by an assemblage of stolid and weather-beaten Dorcades, eaten up with good works and drab with charity . . .

To H. T. Baker
St Salvator's,
St Andrews, N.B.
2 September 1899

. . . What are your views about Cicero's letters? I finished them about a week ago and they seem to me to reverse all the judgments commonly based upon them with regard to the author's personal character; the man emerges not only denuded of all pretensions to political instinct or noble large individual nature, but exposed by his own hand as a vain egotistical, pusillanimous limited creature – a man with all the worst intellectual vices of the 18th Century – cajoled by the hollow bombast of Degenerate Platonists, self-deceived by narrow frigid constitutional catch-words, self-centred, hypocritical, undignified, and essentially unlovable. Have you read Paul's article on him in this month's *19th Century?* taking up of course the opposite side – indignantly denying the only real title to interest which his character possesses – his attachment to Tiro, which he stigmatizes as an 'infamous libel'. At the same time I think the letters increase one's admiration for his literary power, which seems to me consummate: the other great Romans of his time Brutus, Lepidus, Antony, Sulpicius, – barely wrote grammar – let alone style; Caelius is the only one who compares with him in power of epigrams or picturesqueness of expression. I know you despise the verbosity of his speeches, but if you want perfect Latin, almost as pliant and beautiful as Greek, I don't think you can better the Brutus and Orator, which seem to me almost as clever as Tacitus' dialogue, – and as a tour-de-force – the impression of $\epsilon\hat{\iota}\delta os$ [shape] upon a dour and untractable $\H{\upsilon}\lambda\eta$ [material] – unsurpassable . . .

To H. T. Baker
St Salvator's,
St Andrews, N.B.
10 September 1899

. . . My father had a letter from A. Milner this morning, containing two items of interest: (a) the famous despatch of May 4 was badly garbled by Joe, who omitted in the report of it which appeared in the press, bluebook etc, many passages which would have explained what some people consider its excessive vehemence. This is quite in keeping with the rest of Joe's conduct. (b) He thinks the Boers are quite likely to fight: but says they intend to protract matters for a few weeks until the grass has grown on the Veldt, so that they will be able to fodder their horses. I think you are right in assigning Cicero's popularity to the Xtian sympathy with weakness in any form: the assumption that he would have been a christian if he had not died a century too soon forms the basis of many appreciations of him by the school of Early Victorian divines in whose hands the scholarship of the country has reposed for a considerable term of years. At the same time his letters give me a keener impression of selfish vanity even than of weakness: also I can't entirely admit your theory of 'real attitudes': you have only to look at some of his letters to Caesar and all to Antony and compare their style with the references he makes to the recipients in synchronous letters to Atticus, and you cannot for a moment deny that he was given to formal and insincere adulation . . .

To H. T. Baker   St Salvator's,
St Andrews, N.B.
21 September 1899

. . . We have had 2 lineal descendants of the Scottish Kings staying here the last 3 days: Stuarts of Traquair: They are papists and so have to go away before Friday; to look at they are like large bald canaries, and they are very much offended if you speak to them, or if you don't. But I mustn't speak of these things. What am I to say? There really isn't much: I tried to write some Greek Hexameters the other day, but found them quite exquisitely difficult, so am reading the Odyssey instead, which is much more amusing and restful. I have also read through a synopsis of the *Republic*, which is certainly a much saner piece of work than I thought at first sight. Taken in conjunction with my Bosanquet the bulk of it seems to be true, the only important mistakes being the exaggerated theory of communism and the arguments for immortality.

I think I advised you in my last letter to read Ibsen; you really should. Start with *The Wild Duck*: most people think it the least sane and intelligible of all his plays: I like it better than any other: the last 2 acts are about the best thing in the way of satirical comedy that I have ever read: the motif of the play is the "Livslögnen" as he calls it, or "Life-illusion" – the element of optimistic conceit in human nature – the one thing that prevents most people from committing suicide as soon as they arrive at years of discretion – in different men it takes different forms: one believes that he has it in him to be a great poet or artist, another that he is a Napoleon in embryo only biding the period which the Fates enjoin – be it 9 months or 9 years – to burst from the womb of obscurity and subdue an astonished world; a third that his wife is chaste: none of these things are true, but the creature's belief in them keeps him alive: when they are proved to be false then comes the crash: it is to some such awakening as this that most of Ibsen's Tragedies lead up. The life-illusion runs thro' them all: his characters run in 2 moulds: one is the type of self-deceived man, who lives by the Livslögnen, the other the man who conquers fate by sheer vital force – Livsgläd the joy-of-life; as a matter of fact these latter are mainly women. Bron [Herbert] is an excellent example of the latter type, and Rendall might do for the former. What I like about Ibsen is the extraordinary width of his prospect, his fine power of generalisation; he can draw individual characters as clearly and cleanly as anyone, but the scope of his satire is tremendous: for him comedy does not consist in bringing on a man who never buttons his waistcoat or always sits down on his hat, but in the exposition of some broad grim principle which covers all humanity. I think he is really fit to be classed with the great universal geniuses . . .

To H. T. Baker   St Salvator's,
St Andrews, N.B.
27 September 1899

. . . Today is the great day at St Andrews, the medal day: the medal was won by Freddy Tait – probably the finest golfer now alive. I have just come back from the Club dinner, where I went as the guest of Arthur Balfour: it was one of the most indecent orgies which I have ever attended and reminded one of a spritely edition of the Caledonian picnic. My father, who had to respond for the visitors made an exceedingly witty speech: it is a curious thing about him, that whenever he has to do anything, he does it a good deal better than any one else – even if it is making a jocular speech to 300 gin-soaked Kerns from the Kingdom of Fife. Arthur Balfour came here on Monday: every time I see him his charm grows upon me: I believe he has one of the cleanest and clearest brains in Europe, as well as the most fascinating manner. He is bored and blasé about politics, but terribly in earnest about golf and bridge; I make about £3 a night off him at the latter game and £1 a day at the former . . .

On Sunday I encountered one of the few geniuses I have ever met – in the person of the Rev. Jacob Primmer (the very name is an epigram). At 4.30 p.m. I saw a man drive up to the patch of grass in front of our house in a lorry: he unyoked the horse, fixed a red flag in the wheel of his cart, placed a table & 2 gladstone bags upon the tail-board, put up an umbrella (for it was raining and hailing in torrents) and began to speak against Ritualism: in ten minutes he had an audience of 500 people, which went on increasing till seven o'clock, when he dismounted and dined: he held his audience for 2½ hours against God & weather and prejudice, and without a note of any kind: it was a marvellous performance. I will tell you 2 of the stories he told, which struck me: (1) a man and his friend were going up Snowdon: one of them was carrying a large brown paper parcel purporting to contain sandwiches: they arrived at the summit tired and hungry about 2.30 p.m.: they sat down and prepared for lunch: on opening the parcel it was found that instead of sandwiches it contained 3 nightshirts – the moral being of course that the Ritualists offer millinery instead of spiritual food:

(2) 2 young ladies, being caught in a thunderstorm took refuge in the house of a high-church dame: the latter was terrified by electric phenomena, closed the windows and pulled down all the blinds: the young ladies also were frightened: their hostess then declared that their only hope was that she should sprinkle them with holy water: she went and fetched a bottle of liquid, with which she liberally aspersed their dresses: the storm at once abated: the sun shone out: the blinds were drawn: and it was discovered that the bottle with which she had sprinkled them was an ink-bottle! . . .

To H. T. Baker   Hyndford House,
                                                        North Berwick, N.B.
                                                        4 October 1899

I am much grieved at your news. Your letter only reached me to-day or I would have written before – though what use it is to write I hardly know. The formulae of consolation – vary and amplify them how you will – remain barren and profitless to the last – especially in cases like the present, where I can neither prove to you that your mother will live again, nor deny that her death is and must be a serious loss to you: between men of intelligence there is no room for the glossing platitudes of Christianity or the frigid paradoxes of Stoicism: the mystical rhetoric of Paul, the intellectual contentions of Seneca are alike out of place. The only comfort I can offer you with any sincerity is the hackneyed plea that time blunts the edge of our affliction more quickly perhaps than we are disposed to think: it sounds silly enough: but I have found it in my own experience to be true. My mother died when I was 12 – too young to be very callous: she was and is still the only person for whom I have ever felt what a Xian would not be ashamed to call love: and it seemed to me at the time that life, if she were not part of it, would not be worth living: and yet in a month or 2 things began to be very much as they were. This may seem to you irrelevant; but in those days I don't think anyone would have called me hard-hearted: it is my belief that Nature herself provides consolation for the severance of a natural tie – such as the loss of those to whom we are bound by the accident of birth – which she cannot supply when the broken bond is between one of intellectual sympathy forged of our own free choice. You may think I am merely playing with words; but that is not so: I believe there is truth in what I have written, and I believe that you will find in a little while that what has gone out of your life is not so much as you now imagine – a few associations broken, a few habits changed, a few memories added. My attempts at sympathy may seem to you clumsy and brutal: perhaps they are: I was never clever either at inflicting or receiving the thing: for my own part I have always preferred to eat my sorrows in silence; but here are words of a sort: take them for what they are worth, and if it is any satisfaction to you to know that I am exceedingly sorry for you, be assured that it is so; but I firmly believe that you will find the blow lighter than it seems on paper: once the squalid accompaniments of Xian death and burial are over, the mere fact of separation becomes increasingly more tolerable.

To H. H. Asquith   Balliol.
                                                 12 November 1899

Yesterday the coxswainless fours were rowed, which we were expected to win, as we had three blues in the boat . . . we were just beaten . . . there seems to be sort of fatality about Balliol rowing: we are always expected to win and are very formidable on paper, but in fact we never seem to come off. The only other thing which people talk about much is the All Souls Election: it really is rather odd: this is the 2nd year running in wh. they have given their fellowships to the 2 stupidest men in the 'Varsity: the one for law went to Phil Baker of this college, a very nice fellow with charming manners, but the brain of a schoolboy – and a Harrovian at that; he hadn't even done well in the schools, having taken 2 seconds in Greats and Law: the history fellowship was awarded to a New Coll. man called Malcolm, an Etonian, whose father was a fellow before him: he may have been up to form, as he took a good first in Greats and his reputation for work was so great that he was commonly known as the 'Louser'. But most people are very indignant at John Buchan being passed over: he is certainly a much more brilliant man than either of the others and would have found the money more useful: Vernon of this college, who was 3rd in the exam, is to my mind the best man of all, and I think he was very hardly treated. The prestige of All Souls is being rapidly lowered by this type of award.

                                                        Balliol.
                                                 19 November 1899

There is a great row going on now in College: on Wednesday our Rugby team played King's Cambridge, who came over for the match: after wh. they had a big dinner at 5 p.m. and both teams were desperately drunk by ½ past 6: they made hay of the quad, wh. irritated our dons, brawled in the streets, wh. drew down the Proctors on them, and are also being prosecuted by the S.W.R. for wrecking a train and assaulting porters at the station: 3 men have been sent down and the rest gated; but it is thought that favouritism was shown in the selection of victims, and the dons are more unpopular than they have ever been.

Imperial Hotel, Malvern.
3 December 1899

I came down here with Baker to try to shake Oxford fogs out of our systems in view of a week in the Schools . . . The Ireland begins on Thursday and goes on till the following Tuesday: I have made hardly any preparation for it till the last few days, and do not anticipate doing very well in the Exam – I am getting sick of filling my head and loading my memory with vast quantities of useless information: at the present moment I could probably go on repeating printed matter of one sort or another longer than any man in England, but I shall have forgotten every word of it by the end of term – at least I sincerely hope so. This place is certainly quite exhilarating . . . Beb and Oc came to visit me on Thursday . . . they both ate, drank and smoked without a minute's intermission from 10 a.m. when they arrived till 6 p.m. when they left.

Balliol.
21 January 1900

This place is almost unimaginably beastly – rain and fog that one can hardly breathe . . . The whole atmosphere is rather gloomy: Sir John Conroy, the nicest of the dons, is seriously ill with influenza and lungs; John Farmer, the rascally musician, has been seized with an apoplexy and is lying at death's door; the Dean,[1] who has just read in the English papers of the landslip at Amalfi (where he spent the whole vac) is prostrated at the thought of his narrow escape, and finally a certain Abbott – declared to be a brother of Evelyn – committed suicide yesterday by drowning himself in the river. So there is a good deal of tragedy in the air.

31 January 1900

Thanks for your wire: my suggestion [about joining a volunteer force to go out to the South African war] was only provisional, and further inquiries prove on the whole that the objections *are* overwhelming. In the first place, the main functions of the Balliol advance guard – before enlistment – appear to be selecting horses and testing butter; I do not feel myself to be a competent critic of either, and cannot imagine why Hillard[2] thinks that such faculties are peculiarly fostered by a Balliol education. Secondly, when enlisted one would have not only to ride one's horse but to tend it in sickness, to groom it in health, and even to shoe it in emergency: and thirdly the engagement would last for at least 2 years and possibly 5, instead of 2 terms, as I had fondly imagined – All these details were suppressed by the plausible Hilliard.

[1] A. Strachan-Davidson, from 1908-16 Master of Balliol.
[2] Probably E. Hilliard, who became a Fellow of Balliol and Senior Bursar in 1905.

4 March 1900

I was yesterday elected President of the Union – somewhat against my expectation – by a majority of about 40. The man who opposed me, one Cecil,[1] is a sad fool, but has the courage to say what most other fools think, and is therefore a dangerous antagonist at a place like the Union. The times are not friendly to a liberal candidature and I made pretty sure he would have got in. The candidate I nominated for secretary was also successful: He is a West African Nigger, called Nelson for some reason, black as pitch and a staunch patriot; I think his voice and teeth pulled him through: the former is a most magnificent organ, like the sound of heavy guns at sea.

[Raymond's parody of Kipling's jingoistic and highly successful poem *Soldiers of the Queen*, was composed about this time.]

> The sun like a Bishop's bottom
>   Rosy and round and hot
> Looked down upon us who shot 'em
>   And down on the devils we shot.
> And the stink of the damned dead niggers
>   Went up to the Lord high God
> But we stuck to our starboard triggers
>   Though we yawned like dying cod.
>
> Now cod dies hard, and you know it
>   For I've written a book about cod:
> And God dies hard, for Jowett
>   Has written a book about God.
> Yes cod is hard and God is hard
>   But the hardest thing I've seen
> Tough and bluff and bloody rough
>   Is a soldier of the Queen.

To Conrad Russell   Amisfield, Haddington.

It is damnable about the result [of a univiersity prize]. I must say I thought Bluetooth would get the thing, as he did well in the most important papers. But as you say there is no fighting these Jews: they ought to institute some form of 'Varsity competition for which the prize would be a slice of York ham – quite as valuable and infinitely more succulent than the parsley crown for which the flower of Greece competed at Nemea: then perhaps we poor Gentiles should

---

[1] Algernon Cecil became President of the Union the following year, and later a Fellow of the Royal Historical Society; wrote lives of Metternich and St. Thomas More.

have a chance . . . This house is very large, cold and curious: my bedroom where I am writing is about the size of St Paul's, but rather higher. The dining-room is as big as Heligoland, and has a little table in the middle about the size and shape of a sphinx. There is nothing to do except play bridge, as there are several feet of snow on the ground. The stupider members of the party try and shoot duck, which everyone knows is a perfectly hopeless undertaking. Personally, when I want exercise I play battledore and shuttlecock in the dining-room with my hostess . . . it is quite full of naked statues, a motley crew comprising Bacchus, Charles Dickens, Hadrian and the 3rd Earl of Wemyss.

To H. T. Baker

Thurlmere,
Littlestone,
Kent.
17 April 1900

I sit down to answer your letter without an idea in my head – heaven knows if one will appear before I lay down my pen . . . Here I sit at a bay window at one in the morning, looking over a sea streaked by the most divine moon that has ever shone: it is curious that this place which is as ugly as Gibbon's Carthage by day is more lovely than Paradise at night: that is the greatness of night: it is like the Grand Style in literature: only the big things are left – the sea and the moon and the stars – all the little peddling things built with hands are either obscured or transmuted by this lunar alchemy. It is wonderful how the night takes one back at once to Homer and Simonides: the greatest gain of a classical education is that it enables one to think of the night classically and not romantically: a classical appreciation of night is one of the highest aesthetic pleasures – the crisp outline of the moon, the stars like golden bosses on a shield, and the cyanide blue of the background. – Everything is lovely in itself, there is a perfect precision about the heavenly bodies regarded thus which one never realises so completely elsewhere: one thinks of Danae, of Marlowe's "evening air clad in the beauty of a thousand stars" . . . People talk about links with the past: night is a link with a far nobler and far more distant past than any toothless hag who danced at the Waterloo ball: night is not a faded prostitute who remembers the embraces of Charles Fox, but a splendid glittering emblem of eternal youth, conscious of Achilles and Patroclus, Sappho and Phaon, Zeus and Danae – It is the best clue to reality that we have: the unchanging depths of blue, the delightful definiteness of the stars give one a keener sense of what is real and permanent than the conception of triangularity: but it is only by reading the end of Iliad viii and a few passages in Simonides that one is enabled to put away the fleshpots of sentiment, to rid oneself of the corrupting associations of German castles and square pink willing Gretchens, to detach nature from humanity, or at least not to interpret the cosmic order through the morbid medium of mediaeval fancies. Only the man who has read Simonides can look at the moon and see the moon and nothing else: in his vision there is no base alloy of human sentiment – or if there is any it is that nobler sort of dross which forms in his mind impossible dreams of a Charmidean perfection, which is not a thing but a radiance in which things are seen. – But what nonsense all this is – especially when I remember that I am in one of the squalidest lodging houses in England – so typical a lodging house that it might almost have been built by Dickens himself: it is quite unlike anything in real life: there are venetian blinds and drafts and sometimes even boiled cabbage, but never sin: the gas is bad, and there is a notice saying that you may only have 6 inches of water in your bath – Luckily most of our food comes from London, but the residuum of local products is most unpalatable . . . Alfred Lyttelton and St John Brodrick are here with their wives and other paraphernalia: also Herbert Gladstone and others – mainly golfers – whom I don't suppose you would know. Poor St John is ragged unmercifully about the incompetence of the government, their folly in publishing Roberts' dispatches etc.: he often goes purple in the face with anger. I have just had a letter from Rosebery saying that he cannot come to the Union – "he is too old and stiff to take part in sham fights": as my father remarked – a sham fight is just the thing that ought to suit him, seeing his extraordinary disinclination for real ones . . .

To H. T. Baker   Littlestone.
                                                                23 April 1900

. . . I am sorry for John Buchan's misadventure: I expect he felt it keenly: he must be an odd fellow though if he travels about with riding breeches a fortnight after the fox-hunting is over on the off chance of a meet with harriers. I imagine Devonshire must be pleasant to live in just now, if your sun is anything like ours. – Here we have had cicada weather for the last week, a blue waveless sea with Romney Marsh in the background as dry and hard as leather: the air is full of larks, which love a poor soil, and the ground teems with snakes, harmless and otherwise, which give one a keener impression of heat than almost anything else. The first days of summer are as pleasant in their way as the first of spring: both in other respects and because of the inordinate amount of beer which they enable one to consume . . . I read today the chapter in my socialistic book about Lassalle: he too was a wonderful creature, by far the most attractive of the insaner democrats, and worthy to take his place in the triumvirate of great Jews with Dizzy and Heine – On the whole he is the nearest modern parallel to Alcibiades: by virtue of birth, wealth and intellect he moved in the highest circle of German society: he was an acute reasoner and at the same time a violent and obscene controversialist: a brilliant orator, a passionate lover of many women, the undisputed leader of many men – perhaps half the Prussian nation including a king and a bishop: he was a great reformer but yet devoted to histrionic effects, having just that tinge of insincerity which saves great reformers from being great bores and differentiates Alcibiades from Cobden: he lived like a man, worked like a horse, and finally died in a duel by the hand of a rival lover in the 39th year of his age, having done almost as much to mould the destinies of modern Germany as Bismarck himself.

I am also reading (and have now nearly finished) Tolstoy's latest work, called *Resurrection*: my people are mad with enthusiasm about it. It certainly is a wonderful piece of work if you can detach the content from the form, and sink a natural disgust at the mannerisms of the realistic method in admiration for the immense dramatic genius which the core of the book exhibits: but it is in no sense a work of art – full of irrelevant facts and characters inserted to support the thesis of land nationalisation and abolition of all forms of punishment: being didactic the satire is clumsy like that of Roman Stoics and the arguments necessarily rotten. I leave here tomorrow.

To H. H. Asquith   Balliol.
13 May

I went to see Cis yesterday . . . He showed me around the place and gave me an account of the Summer Fields[1] curriculum, with which he seemed completely satisfied: he is certainly a brilliant talker and poured out a succession of precise and gem-like phrases for the best part of an hour during which I was with him, recurring at stated intervals to the fact that he was 1st in Latin and French in the Upper 2nd. The only person who seems to cause him any disquiet is one 'Paget mus' who opens his letters occasionally: but [Mark] Horner has threatened him with vengeance. There are three other people in his dormitory: one of them talks Russian and the other tells Irish ghost stories; so the talk is probably good of an evening.

27 May 1900 (Eights week)

We had a crowded and successful debate at the Union, wh. gave occasion for some fairly good fooling on the ridiculous motion that members of Somerville and Ly. Margaret Hall shd. be eligible for election to the Society. Tomorrow Tree[2] is coming to deliver his address, and the day after that I have to go over to Cambridge to speak to their Union – one of the most boring things one has to do, though I shall be glad to see some of my friends there. I was proxime [second] for the Gaisford [Greek Verse Prize], which doesn't do me much good . . . but as most of mine was written in a cab driving to Aberlady I couldn't expect anything else – especially as I noticed with horror when I was handing in my composition that the first hexameter was ½ a foot too short.

---

[1] Well known preparatory school in North Oxford, to which Cis had just gone.

[2] Sir Herbert Beerbohm Tree, leading Edwardian impresario, elder brother of Max Beerbohm.

3 June 1900

Tree came on Monday and delivered a lecture on the staging of Shakespeare at the Union which was really very good, though the best parts had obviously been written by 'Max'. I gave him a dinner before the address, at which Max, Courtney of the Telegraph, and a man called Joe Knight – a literary critic of sorts – also attended. Tree gave a large supper afterwards which was rather amusing. He is quite nice, but almost half-witted in conversation I thought. He is a most extraordinary compost – with the face and mind of an English Squire and the mysterious intriguing pseudo-impressive manner of a provincial actor. Knight was introduced to me as 'the most learned man in London'; but when a discussion arose at supper about Sidney Lee's theory of the sonnets it appeared that both Knight and Courtney (who had started the conversation) were not only entirely ignorant of what Lee's theory was, but did not even know the initials of the person to whom the sonnets were dedicated: after some argument Knight suggested that it was Mr. H. F. – and everyone was quite satisfied, marvelling at his erudition. I don't think I ever heard so much nonsense talked, but I quite enjoyed it being in fits of laughter the whole time. Max was quite pleasant and intelligent.

On Tuesday I went over to Cambridge to speak at their Union. It is a detestable place to speak in, and the Cambridge orators are as repulsive a crew as I have ever seen: not one of them speaks English – I don't mean the idiom, but the dialect: they all have the manner and accent of Welsh missionaries. Their secretary is a pure-bred Boer called Van Zijl but even he had a strong Glasgow accent. I dined and breakfasted with them, both gloomy meals. I sat next to Oscar Browning who is their treasurer: he had just entertained the King of Sweden and was quite unbearable. There were two nice men, Bowles (the son of T. Bowles) their outgoing president, a person of flimsy intelligence but immense and attractive vitality, and Hylton Young, their new president . . .

To Reginald Farrer
The Cottage,
Sparsholt,
Winchester.
13 July 1900

To one bent upon recruiting a shattered nervous system in one of the most sequestered and genuinely uncomfortable spots in this country it came as a distinct shock to receive by the same post 2 letters demanding papers – I happened to open first the one that was not yours – from the Sec. of the Russell Club, & as politics is to be the wretched business of my life I couldn't well refuse his request for a destructive criticism of the Socialist position, – than which nothing is more in need of destroying – But 2 is too much – I wish I

could write for the Fodder. I like the Society & yearn for intellectual communion with its members, but dinner takes so long at Oxford that there simply
isn't time – For years I have had it in my heart to run delicately amok upon
Kipling, but it is not a thing one can do *currente calamo* [off the cuff], if it is to
be well done, & it is – Time! time! time! there isn't any you know! that's the
difficulty – So please hold me excused – If ever I write a paper in my sleep you
shall have it.

To H. T. Baker   Mells Park,
                                                                Frome.
                                                            15 July 1900

. . . After you left I tided over the interim with Punch more happily than I had
dared to hope – Tuesday evening was so exquisite – full moon and pellucid
air – that we decided to ride into Winton about 10 p.m. and walk up Hills: at
my suggestion we were to call at Rendall's for Andy: luckily we met him coming home from dinner at General Magrath's outside College: he took us into
Rendall's house – R being away looking over Election papers – changed, and
then we went out into Hills: once there it was so lovely that I suggested a walk
back to Sparsholt – our bikes having been left in College – Andy consented and
we all three walked along the railway, across Viaduct, up by Oliver's Battery
and so back by a circuitous route across the uplands to Sparsholt, where we
arrived about 2.15 having started from College at 11, and covered some 9
miles. It was really most enjoyable – quite like old times – Andy insisted on
taking off everything but his trousers and walked naked in the full orb of the
moon – we tramped lustily across the ploughs, "fetching a compass" as Luke
says whenever we got to a field of standing corn, which we often did, as it looked
like short grass in the deceptive light; the nightjars rattled and the young partridges started up fussily in our path, and the moon made everything delicious.
When we got home we ate a tongue and drank four bottles of wine, being very
thirsty – Punch retired at three fifteen but Andy and I sat up till five talking
vaguely but with animation like Socrates after the Symposium about subjects
which could have had no very real interest for either of us – mainly the effect of
premature death upon historical estimates of character . . . We breakfasted
blithely at 10.30, walked into Winton, bathed and lunched with Rendall, who
expressed himself completely satisfied with our escapade . . .
    On Saturday I came here by the route which you sketched for me –
Everything went well and I arrived exactly at the right time owing to the place
being five miles from the station – It is a typically comfortable English country
house in an Elizabethan Park full of magnificent trees. The house itself is
crowded with priceless pictures, which I don't appreciate – my hostess, a clever
and charming woman, having been one of Burne-Jones' earliest models.
There is no-one here of consuming interest except Haldane who has been in

magnificent form – especially when he described to us how the High Church party had come to him to ask him to argue before the Archbishop the case for incense, asperges and the reservation of the sacrament: it is one of the most magnificent situations ever imagined and he described it in language worthy of Gibbon. There is also a very nice little Tory M.P. called Stirling Maxwell, and Bron's filthy cousin Wallop, – a lank and indifferent creature with a ginger moustache, who, I confess is something of an enigma to me. He is supposed to take no interest in anything but the intrigues of fashionable women, but he talked to me with apparent knowledge and enthusiasm about Lord Burghclere's translation of the Georgics, and apart from that never once opened his mouth to anyone except to say that his cousin married Shaw-Lefevre, when Haldane made a disparaging remark about Shaw-Lefevre's sister. The only other person of any interest is one Mrs Gaskell, who is pleasant and passably clever, with whom I had a good talk about Meredith. But beyond doubt the really best thing about my visit – the thing that almost compensated for a five mile walk round the Park which my host took me this evening to explain the various qualities and characteristics of his unique collection of pines, in which he is a specialist – was the bathing. In front of the house is a terrace, beneath which after a steep fall of 100 feet runs a stream which has been dammed into a considerable lake about ¼ mile in length by 200 yds in breadth, covered with waterlilies and fringed with bulrushes, where they bathe: it is very beautiful; but not so beautiful as the two daughters of the house aged 17 and 18 [in fact 15 and 17] – the elder of whom – tho she does not happen to appeal very strongly to me – is about as perfect a specimen of female beauty as I have ever seen. – About ½ past 4 – just before tea Haldane suggested a bathe: no-one but himself and this lovely girl seemed keen about it: however we all went down to the lake as spectators and were amply rewarded. Haldane is an imperfect but courageous performer in the water and to see his immense but stately figure clad in a very scanty bathing dress and recklessly precipitating from dizzy altitudes into this green and flowery pond was really exquisite: the quiet slowness and dignity with which he put himself in the most ridiculous situations proved to me more conclusively than anything else could have done the real bigness of the man – to see this vast white mass with the brain of Socrates and the shape of Nero executing his absurd antics from a thin plank which bent double under his weight and sporting fantastically in the water with a divinely beautiful girl no whit abashed recalled the sunniest days of the Roman decline. Finally he came out and after lurking coyly in the bushes for a few minutes reappeared clad in nothing but a bath-towel and a panama hat and joined us at tea on the lawn where he was soon explaining the theory and history of Buddhism – its superiority to Christianity and its weaknesses as a practical religion – to a host of local spinsters who had flocked in for food and gossip. It was magnificent. At 11-30 p.m. he left in a carriage for Bath 15 miles off having to be in the courts at 10 tomorrow and in the train all tomorrow night and the night after – on his way up and down to Edinburgh where he is pleading on Tuesday. He is a marvellous man, and never loses flesh through it all. I go up to town tomorrow and to Wanborough on Tuesday. Hey nonny nonny! I like this life.

Raymond
P.S. This letter looks longer than it is.

To H. T. Baker   Hotel Mont Rose,
Zermatt,
Suisse.
9 August 1900

I travelled from Paris to Lausanne in a sleeping car with a man who I am quite certain was Oscar Wilde; luckily or unluckily there were two other people in the same compartment, so neither he nor I had any means of testing our convictions.

I consider your description of this country most unfair; it is true that a good deal of it reminds one of the drop-scene of a theatre or pictures on the back of chocolate boxes, but that is no more the fault of Switzerland than it is the fault of Shakespeare that some of his best lines are hackneyed by quotation and vulgarised by the unintelligent admiration of cads. Also there is much that is quite of a different stamp; I don't know whether you have ever been in this place, but it is really very fine – right under the foot of the Matterhorn which in shape and site is I should think the most magnificent peak in the world; the Weisshorn and Rothorn are also just above us, both fine mountains, especially the latter, and on the Italian side of the valley the Breithorn, Monte Rosa, Täschhorn and Dom, all over 14,000 feet. It is impossible to deny them the highest degree of beauty; in vividness of form and definition of outline they are far above anything I have ever seen. It is probably just because of this that one does not appreciate them as much as one should. It is the Gothic strain in one's nature which cannot be put aside – the foolish Northern sentimentalism which feeds itself on half-lights and blurred masses, loves mystery and vapour, suspects clarity and sharpness of outline. It is a feeling I should be sorry to be rid of and will always make me prefer Scotland to this, but one must remember that it is the germ of things like "the Soul's Awakening". So far I have only made two expeditions – one up the Goeker glacier – feeble and dull business – relieved by an excellent cup which Trant brewed in a large india-rubber basin which he always carries; the other up a mountain called the Gabelhorn, about 12,000 feet. One starts at 4 a.m. which is intolerable, and reaches the top about 10 o/c. I was prodigiously bored, except for the last hour, in which there is some rather exciting rock-work crowned by a good view, one might just as well be on a treadmill – plodding on and on, seeing nothing but one's own toes and the next man's heels, and feeling nothing but intense heat and thirst. It is more like pedalling up Otterbourne Hill for 12 hours with a sirocco blowing in one's face, than anything else I know. The only thing I want to ascend is the Matterhorn, which means more excitement and less hard work, but the great Whymper who is staying here declares that it is more dangerous now than it has ever been before owing to falling stones; one man was killed by them last week – under the circumstances it is hardly worth it . . .

SUNDAY

Since I wrote the rest of this dreary and interminable chronicle I have been through an awful experience – the ascent of Dom, a mountain about 15,000 feet high which claims to be the biggest in Switzerland on the ground that Mont Blanc is half in France and Monte Rosa half in Italy. I confess it passes my understanding how people manage to go mad about mountaineering. It is altogether the most painful and tedious sport one can imagine. Myself and two brothers started on Friday after lunch and got back here at 10 p.m. yesterday night. Friday night we spent at a hut about half way up the mountain. The hut has no furniture except a stove at which one can make cocoa and a sort of large manger full of straw in which we and our guides and a solitary German and his guide who arrived shortly after us, slept. We got up there at 6, went to bed at 8, rose again at 3 a.m. only to find that it was too cold to start, there having been a heavy fall of snow in the night. Our guides advised us to turn back, which we refused to do; we waited until the sun was up and started at about 7 a.m. We walked for miles over a glacier, then up some rather difficult rocks which broke off when one touched them, and finally up interminable and almost perpendicular ice slopes, always knee deep in powdery snow, often up to the waist, sometimes entirely submerged, roped the whole way. I was sick three times during the ascent; owing to our late start the heat was terrific. I had three flannel shirts on, 2 pairs of stockings, and my thickest homespun coat and knickerbockers. My brothers being stronger and in finer condition fared better, but we all had to be revived by frequent doses of cognac; the last 300 yards before the summit was rather more interesting – up what they call an *arête* – i.e. a narrow edge of snow – literally a razor edge which one had to stamp down and cut into steps before one could stand on – with a precipice of several thousand feet on one side into Switzerland and on the other into Italy. If we had not been so tired that one would just as soon be killed as not, I suppose one would have been frightened; as it was one plodded on with mechanical precision looking neither to right nor left. We finally reached the top about 3.20 p.m. The odd thing about these gigantic mountains is that there is never room for more than one person on the top; it is literally a vanishing point; our front guide sat on the actual peak; we fixed our ice axes in the slope immediately under him and lay with our heads over the edge clinging like flies, in this odd position half in Italy, half in Switzerland, my younger brother and myself at once went to sleep from sheer fatigue and had to be woken up with brandy by the guides. The view is supposed to be one of the best in Europe – the whole of

72

Switzerland and most of Italy on a clear day; we however could see absolutely nothing except great banks of white clouds apparently miles beneath us and shutting us in on every side: one really experienced the physical sensation of being in Heaven – the Heaven of Italian art – and expected to see Pater Seraphicus stepping across the air, wagging his grey beard, at any moment. As we were rapidly being surrounded by a thick mist we began the descent almost at once, running and sliding most of the way. We reached our hut about 6.30 where we had a long drink, and the base of the mountain two hours later, and reached Zermatt on horses at 10 p.m. The alternation between fearful heat going up – nothing is so hot as sun reflected from snow – and intense cold on the top – had made our faces brick red and shiny. I am still almost unrecognisable. I shall never commit such a folly again. The guides are fine fellows though; one of ours was 67! as tough and tireless as a goat; the other was a young fellow, one of the most powerful I have ever seen, with a face like the carpenter in Alice. As well as being boring to a degree mountaineering is damnably expensive – e.g.

2 guides at 70 frs.	– 140 frs.
1 porter (to carry firewood,	– 40 frs.
provisions, etc.,	
to hut)	– 50 frs.
1 doz. champagne	– 90 frs.
Horses (from base to Zermatt)	– 30 frs.
	350 frs. = £14

That is a lot to give for two of the most miserable days of one's life!

The indoor Swiss are an abominable race – a nation of waiters and governesses, but the outdoor section – guides and peasant girls – are rather nice. Forgive this barren record of events, but imagination and intelligence are crushed here.

To H. T. Baker   Grand Hotel,
                                                          Engelberg.
                                                      20 August 1900

. . . I have done practically no work this vac – which is terrible, and frightens me a good deal, as I have had no opportunities, but begin to fear my capacity for it is irretrievably lost. I am perpetually cast into a deep melancholy by the reflection of my nothingness – that I have done nothing worth doing, and know nothing worth knowing, feel nothing worth feeling, and am nothing worth being! and this is in my 22nd year – it is a startlingly barren record and may well give one pause – all of which I say not to invite contradiction but because it happens to occur to me being an egoist.

I want to write a paper for the Russell on Socialism sometime soon, but don't know how to begin. It is such a slippery phantom that one never knows how to grapple with it – worse than Proteus himself, for he at least had the grace to admit his capture when it came, but this new monster drops and disowns each limb as soon as the opponent grasps it. There is nothing in all the jargon of the creed that you can nail to the counter but what some ingenious apostle murmurs a juggling spell of explanation over it, and straightway coin and counter melt into air and you are left beating a vapour like a new Ixion – beating it very cleverly they all tell you, but it isn't Socialism. You prove that wages are drawn from capital, that nationalisation of land is iniquitous and impracticable, that any form of collectivism removes the spur of ambition, and 20 other things that you have always understood Socialism to mean: but it turns out that it is none of these things but merely an ideal system of ethics, a crystallization of the spirit of benevolence, a handy formula for reminding you that you owe a duty to your neighbour – something lofty and innocuous, manifestly acceptable to all kindhearted and clearheaded men, nothing red or revolutionary.

What is one to say? where is one to begin? there is no Pope in Socialism: is there any *quicunque vult*? and if so how does one obtain access to it? If you see or hear of a book which contains the dogma of this sect in some bleak, intelligible and yet authorised form, with all the glosses up to date I wish you would send it to me. It is not worth writing a paper and then being told at the end by Ensor – "Oh yes – that's what Marx and Henry George thought, but it's all exploded now" – It is useless to discharge the vials of one's invective into a leaky tub.

What a diffuse and tedious letter: but you will have to put up with it. – This life rots the intelligence . . .

To H. T. Baker   Hotel du Parc,
                                                      Lugano.
                                                  1 September 1900

. . . Your letter was forwarded from Engelberg to Brunnen where I spent 5 days . . . I found an uncle of mine there – my father's brother, now a housemaster at Clifton – the penalty one pays for a bizarre shape and a second in Mods. – He is a curiously clever man but has the misfortune to be less than five foot high owing to a fall in early youth. His fate always fills me with pity and interest, though it seems to content him. A cubit added to his stature would have landed him in the cabinet: for he has a wonderful gift of words and hates the clergy: as it is his genius, which is still considerable, is tainted with the squalor native to a second-rate public school: it is wonderful how the tinge of provinciality mars the finest wits, and dulls the brightest blade: it is better to be a labourer in the big world than a king in Liverpool.

We came here in search of weather on Thursday and found little else – the town is unsavoury, the lake suburban, the interests nil. The Hotel on the score of having once been a monastery excuses a thousand discomforts which no monk would have tolerated for an instant . . .

It is bold of you to embark on modern history: even if you master it it can hardly be a permanent possession and is likely to fade from your mind as rapidly as a second-rate novel: but I suppose echoes will remain with you – and perhaps other residua sufficient for the usages of polite society . . .

To H. T. Baker
Sandycroft,
Littlestone on Sea.
25 September 1900

. . . This house has only been built a few weeks: my brother and I are here alone – almost its first inhabitants: it is most comfortable, with plenty of good serious books, a perfect billiard-table, a harmonium . . . also the beds have the most handsome blue coverlets which almost prevent sleep by their beauty. We live a simple pastoral life, playing golf and drinking gallons of Bavarian beer . . . Herbert Gladstone, our nominal host, is borne away by this damned election. Are you going to take any part in your father's campaign? I suppose you will as you say you are at Portsmouth . . . But what a joke it all is! one almost shares Smyth's[1] high contempt for politics at these seasons when the pomp and dignity of statesmanship is thrown aside, when our great men kick away their pedestals, put by their resonant moralities, and devote themselves to the serious business of collecting votes. What an opinion they must have of their high-souled, clear-headed, independent, self-governing countrymen! Really the speeches and manifestoes of the government grandees read like nothing so much as one of Rendall's reports of a debate in Mob. Lib.: "Mr Balfour argued that the government had done more to promote the interests of the Empire both at home and abroad than any other government could have dreamt of accomplishing in so short a time – The Liberals had no programme except muzzling dogs and restoring the Transvaal to the Boers."

"Mr Chamberlain pointed out that all the Liberals – except Mr Perks and Sir Edward Grey – were traitors – he was going to say damned traitors. Were they not soldiers of the Queen? (loud cheers: a voice "Yes") the electors might vote as they liked, but if they didn't vote for him they would wish they had when our gallant fellows came back from the Cape and insisted on his election at the point of the bayonet. Were there not 220,000 of them? Birmingham had always been in the van of progress: let it remain there."

"Mr Brodrick said that the war had been entirely caused by the foolish – he might say the criminal vacillation of Sir Henry Campbell Bannerman – He (Sir

---

[1] School and Oxford contemporary.

H.C.B.) had always sat on the fence. Capt Lambton was a bloody fool."

"Lord Salisbury recommended the electors to vote for Unionist candidates: otherwise (he argues) the Liberals might get a majority."

It is hard to believe that this sort of thing will really go down: you often tell me that I overrate the average intelligence: if it does I shall at length believe you. In any case the mere fact that such things are said is proof that England is not yet fit for Self government: political philosophy is fudge. Here we are back again in the worst days of the Roman Republic: instead of a gladiatorial show our ambitious aedile gives us a Boer War: as it cannot be compressed into the narrow limits of some modern coliseum we view it at 2nd hand thro' an Alhambra cinematograph: instead of a coin largess there are doles to the church and the landlord: as to our *equites* we allow them the mines of Africa and slave labour to work them with – a profitable substitute for tax-farming in Asia: finally there are the victorious legions of Lord Roberts outside our gates to cajole or menace the electors: and so our modern Pompeys are carried into office . . .

To H. T. Baker   Hyndford House,
                                              North Berwick, N.B.
                                                   1 October 1900

. . . My father's polling day is on Friday: he seems confident of an increased majority. It is a great thing that you should have felt the intoxication of a mob oratory: if you can strengthen your larynx and dilute the content of your sentence I see no reason why you should not be Prime Minister soon enough to job me into a soft berth for middle age . . . Of course people like you and I are at a great disadvantage in these banausic competitions: the people who succeed are those who have had a normal education and environment . . . But look at our bloody selves! twice the intellectual finesse of Simon and Steel together, money and status enough to land anyone anywhere in these democratic days, but not the normal antecedents which are so essential. I think of those locust-eaten years in College! a lustrum of Periclean Athens is a poor preparation for public life in 20th century England. The scholarly refinements and emotional indulgence of those years blunt the edge of coarser ambitions which should be one's polestar in this premature middle age that has come upon us: unless one can get away from the sense of having seen and felt the best of things there is a poverty of motive which must tell against one in the future. But perhaps you have left these childish things behind already, as I hope to do one day . . .

I have made some excursions into the better class of socialistic literature during the past day or two. It is a harder bogey to upset than one thinks – a creed which has suffered like Christianity from its disciples: the two great mistakes which they have made are (1) to represent the ideal as one to be attained by force in a few days – and (2) to attempt to justify it by a theory of natural rights, instead of by arguments from history and expediency.

Properly stated the argument may be made very strong and I am not yet sure that it is not unanswerable. One thing becomes increasingly clear to me and that is the necessity of experts in politics. We must pay men and pay them well to do our business of state. Money alone will not secure the right men: I agree with you that the legislator must have some knowledge of ethics and the ends of human conduct, and a corresponding knowledge of metaphysic at least sufficient to rid him of the grosser forms of anthropomorphic superstition. But that is not enough: he must have a real knowledge of political economy and political history, and people who depend for their livelihood on briefs or making engines can hardly reach this or even the semblance of it without charlatanry . . .

To H. T. Baker   Easton Grey,
                                                                        Malmesbury.
                                                                        18 December 1900

Many thanks for yours. I was a good deal pleased about the Ireland[1] – not that it flatters me into the belief that I am a good scholar (which I know myself not to be) but because it is the first flicker of success that I have had for nearly two years: it shows that my star has not completely waned: and I am coming more and more to belief in the potency of fortune: which is my one point of resemblance with Julius. If you were really pleased about it, it is a great tribute to you: personally I could hardly help being galled at seeing an admitted inferior attain something which I had not attained. But I think I am a more competitive person than you. You can at least be assured of my 'magnanimity': except in the one point you mention I am still prepared to submit to your judgement in things classical.

I had a very nice letter from Gilbert Murray, in which oddly enough he especially congratulated me on my taste and general papers . . . though at the same time he seems to have been annoyed at the fact that all the other people on the list except myself declared with one voice that Petronius was the 'lost author' whom they most desired: in my answer to him I took occasion to point out that it was not because I did not admire Petronius that I had not mentioned him, but because he was not a lost author . . .

To Reginald Farrer   Easton Grey,
                                                                        Malmesbury.
                                                                        22 December 1900

Many thanks for your letter . . . I was a good deal pleased at my success, and even more surprised: I always feel like an amateur among professionals in this matter of scholarship.

[1] The Ireland Scholarship is one of the highest competition awards in the Greats school, then even more highly prized than it is today.

The greatest tribute I have up to now received is a paragraph contained in the current issue of the '*Xian World*' (wh. the editor was good enough to send me this morning), stating that my name had long been well known in "Congregational circles" (whatever they may be) and would henceforth be regarded with even deeper respect.

I am staying here for a little mild hunting: my host is a lunatic; but the butler seems a gentlemanly fellow, and the place is charming, so I think I shall stick on as long as I can stand being within 4 miles of the birthplace of Thomas Hobbes – It is something of a strain on a person like myself of a rather idealistic temperament . . .

To H. H. Asquith   Balliol.
6 June, 1901 (immediately after Final Schools).

My examination closed yesterday, and the apolaustic life is now in full swing. The papers were dull but easy enough throughout – except the Greek History which was impossible, involving a minute knowledge of the text of Herodotus which few of us had looked at. However in the course of the 6 days I managed to scribble a good deal of nonsense off my mind and I hope out of it for ever; the thing is a cathartic if nothing more.

To H. T. Baker   Anningsley Park,
Chertsey,
Surrey.
23 June 1901

. . . I am really exceedingly puzzled: my people want me to go to India with Bron and shoot tigers and ride on white elephants with Lady Curzon, which ought to be a sufficiently attractive programme: but I find myself so academic both in the intellectual and animal sides of my nature that I would far rather spend another year in Oxford which I have always determined and to some extent contrived to loathe. This wretched interminable business of eating drinking smoking playing talking and associating with other people really isn't worth it . . .

To H. T. Baker   Clovelly Court,
Bideford.
1 August 1901

I am so sorry when I think of you at Brighton and myself here that I cannot help writing to you, though in a few hours from now – damnably few – I shall be lifting my aching bones from a couch which has hardly had time to take the impress of my body and preparing for the great adventure of the day. For it is the custom of the house to plunge *en échelon* into the Atlantic Ocean as near the centre of it as may be at precisely 5 minutes before 8 every morning. We are rowed out in purple bathing dresses by bronzed descendants of Armada heroes until there is no land in sight but the Island of Lundy and then at a given signal we leap into the blue and bottomless swell and are borne hither and thither like helpless jelly fish in the racing tide. Having sustained ourselves in the waves so long as our strength holds out we crawl again into the boats and are ferried back to a great lugger anchored off the harbour mouth where we find our clothes elegantly disposed by careful valets; we cover our bodies; light cigarettes and are taken back to land where we find a herd of black thoroughbred Dartmoor ponies; each man and each woman selects a mount and we clamber up a sheer precipice where the occasional ash give a perilous foothold and so over a rolling park back to the house where we are welcomed by a smoking mess of lobsters and great dishes of honey and Devonshire cream. It is a curious life, and being a poor swimmer I find it a little tiring – But the place is so beautiful as to repay any fatigues imposed on one by a barbarous tradition. It really is so marvellously beautiful that description is impotent. If you can imagine the softer glories of an Italian Lake crowned by a clean Greek sky and the strong northern air which has fed our Drakes and Hawkins', our Jervises, Collingwoods and Rodneys for countless generations – crimson cliffs thickly mantled with oaks and rhododendrons sliding into a caerulean sea – you have some faint idea of the place. Add to this a square white house standing 400 feet above the sea in a park dappled with fallow-deer, surrounded by smooth lawns and dewy terraces glistening with sun-dials of Parian marble, great trees and luscious shrubs and red garden walls glowing with peaches and nectarines, and shade so cunningly arranged that you can be cool at mid-day and hot in the setting sun and you will admit that Brighton cannot equal it. The cook is good, the wines are good, the servants are good; at ¼ past 7 every morning a handsome rascal in red plush breeches lays by one's bedside a plate of raspberries and a glass of milk with 6 drops of brandy in it to fortify one for the sea, and large flagons of icy cup are alluringly disposed throughout the day in the mossy shadows of ancient beeches. In the morning one reads at length on cushions in the bright air and in the afternoon we shoot deer and rabbits in the bracken or pull in mackerel from the decks of red sailed boats . . .

It is a house where I find it difficult to avoid being thought a prig; if one takes out a good book to read on the terrace, one has to take a bad one along with it – something of Doyle's or Kipling's – which may be hastily substituted when under observation. By dint of steadily abusing G. Meredith as obscure and precious and occasionally attending matins with my hostess in a little white church in the park, I have done much to condone the offence of my intellectual achievement and promise. Nothing is held more priggish than infidelity. But there is one woman here – Lady Manners – with a really beautiful soul; and her little daughter too has a stange fascination for me . . . The White girl[1] troubled me little; but her sister pleased me much. She is quite young – 17 I suppose – and not out yet; not technically beautiful but to my eye much more so than the other – a low broad brow, a delightful nervous voice, and that lively and significant eye which one usually misses in women. She is really very clever both by instinct and knowledge, and while I was there detected two serious Homeric errors in Paul's Essay on the classical element in Tennyson; at these being pointed out he was furious and desired to recall the edition. Curiously enough she is the bosom friend of Lady M. Sackville of whom we were talking – the *altera ego*, the *fida Achates* – and bubbling with enthusiasm about her – they are linked – among other bonds – by a common admiration of Swinburne, *pessimi ominis* as I thought and did not scruple to say. She is also something of a poet herself and showed me a translation she had made of a German poem beginning '*Mein Ruh ist hin*' – which I did not much like – though it was almost shamelessly passionate – partly I think because I have heard the original sung by cads. I really became rather friendly with her for the time, finding in her many of the qualities I admire in boys – especially a combination of purity and vivacity which I am coming to fear is rarer in them than in girls.

Lady Ribblesdale[1] (who also was at Mells) has lent me a house near her in Yorkshire called Sawley, which she promises to furnish with two men servants and a French cook. It was lent her by the Cowpers[2] who refused to lend it to Bron, and she lends it to me in order that I may invite Bron there and he may marry her daughter. She is deliciously honest about her scheme, but I doubt if I can find time to forward it – though Bron – so far as I can make out – is of her way of thinking. But I don't want him to marry yet.

I have just had a wire from Hancock to say that I have a first in Greats. This stirs no emotion in me.

To H. T. Baker
Clovelly Court,
Bideford.
5 August 1901

You tell me to write again soon so I do; and I really have many things to say if only they would come to me in words – they don't but I am sure they are in me. I feel stronger and better in some ways than ever before, but unable to analyse my progress. I think it is mainly due to Lady Manners . . . she really has such a lovely character that it is like a breath of new air to be with her. Her sister who is my hostess is almost equally good in the accepted sense of the word, but her goodness has congealed into certain set forms – Lady Manners is I believe a devout Xian but her goodness is so fluid that one feels she has a medium of communication with all people who worship an ideal in any form.

---

[1] Cecily Horner. Her sister, Katharine, was in fact not quite sixteen.
[1] A sister of Margot.   [2] Bron Herbert was the nephew and heir of Lady Cowper.

She has the sympathetic attraction which only belongs to the great geniuses in morals; so much so that I feel I would not mind explaining to her about Lionel and kindred subjects; and that is the biggest tribute one can pay to a woman or perhaps to a man. Her eldest daughter who is only 14 is very charming and I believe I could marry her if I wished; and as she is the heiress to this delectable place there is a great temptation to do so. But she has slender brains for a life-long companion – at any rate for an optimistic creature like myself who looks forward to 3 or 4 decades of married existence . . .

To H. T. Baker
St Salvator's,
St Andrews,
Fife.
12 August 1901

. . . Hers [Lady Manners'] is the moving working heat-giving goodness: the grosser and pettier obstacles hardly exist for it: the virtues which even the best of men seem to acquire by right of conquest belong to it from the beginning: it is free to shine and warm and project itself sunnily into all the relations of life, with no effort or ostentation but all the charm and bloom of unimpeded energy. If this gives you the idea of a woman who distributes coals and blankets to the poor, it is not the one I want to give you. You commonly ridicule my enthusiasm about people but you must at least give me credit for sensibilities which are jarred by raw displays of the cardinal virtues: and when I can live with a woman for 10 days, drive all over the county by her side with no other companion but a dull pony, and even play singles at croquet with her in the precious hour before dinner, and yet be very sorry to leave her at the end – you must see that it is unfair to make her out a faded philanthropist fanning the embers of a few waning lusts . . .

To H. T. Baker
St Salvator's,
St Andrews,
Fife.
19 August 1901

Your note came to me as a surprise this morning; the post is to blame for my apparent idleness not I. The fact is I wrote you quite a long and – to the best of my recollection – interesting letter as long ago as last Monday night. Cave tells me he distinctly remembers stamping and posting it on Tuesday morning, so it should have reached you by Wednesday at latest. It is most mysterious; I have known the Duke of Norfolk[1] pervert telegrams but he has never yet ventured

[1] Postmaster General, 1895-1900.

upon actual confiscation. I suppose it is the fault of that absurd Declaration Bill – give the Papists an inch and they take an ell, together with anything else they can lay their hands on. It is a pity this should have happened as it interrupts the amoebean process of our correspondence . . . What I mean is that I can write a debating letter but not set the ball rolling – unless the bright incidents of my life present an inclined plane fitted to that purpose; but they don't here in this placid uneventful existence, and I gather that your conditions are much the same, so I don't see where the *primum mobile* is to come from; our letters will be like a switch-back car that has just failed to surmount the slope and falls back, and so to and fro till it dwindles into absolute rest . . .

To H. T. Baker
St Salvator's,
St Andrews,
Fife.
25 August 1901

It is just as I feared! There is nothing in your letter for dialectic to impugn or transform, and consequently there will be nothing in this which you can set to a like service. Still as you seem to put a value on mere ink and paper here is some for you to look at: it may give you a few moments pleasurable anticipation before you break the envelope – though these no doubt will be more than balanced by hours of depression following on the emptiness within. It is all very well for you to taunt me with living a healthy life in pleasant company, but nothing follows from that but health and pleasure, neither of which can be put in a letter and sent to Brighton. I can't retail to you other people's conversations: I can't discuss such questions as Free Will and the Taxation of Ground values: you object to them: and you also object to my giving you a list of guests – What is left? As a matter of fact there are two people here who interest us both in some degree, – Cubby [Medd] and Lionel [Smith]. Lionel, who is living with his family at Bambro, I over-persuaded by a series of impassioned telegrams, though his mother was much against his coming, as she thinks Margot fast and distrusts the stability of the Forth Bridge . . .

To Reginald Farrer
Marshal's Wick,
St Albans.
9 September 1901

Many thanks for your letter. It is wise of you to go to Japan – we all drift there sooner or later. It is better to go of one's own free will than to wait & be driven in the autumn of life like a bloody partridge – (It is my theory that a poorish joke is often well helped out by some coarse fragment of the people's speech – Dickens held it too: but never got further than substituting v for w – & in his most improper moments vice versa. The success of these temperate solecisms sometimes causes me to reflect upon the ease with which a novelist could achieve immortality by putting the word 'fuck' into the mouth of one (or all) of his characters – I shan't do it yet; but I keep it up my sleeve, when other things fail: so please don't anticipate me). All this is in parenthesis because I put in brackets purposely to signify as much. As to Japan, which is the main point, I really think it is exceedingly sensible of you to go there – and as Aubrey [Herbert] is apparently only intending to stay there for a year or so I think it is very sensible of him too. I shall very likely go there myself if I fail at All Souls: & quite certainly if I succeed . . . Have you read any books lately? I read the other day Paul's new book on Mat. Arnold: it is very bad – contains one good story, as usual, and a misquotation from the Odyssey & another from the Georgics: so it is quite what they call scholarly.

I suppose we shall not meet again for some time – unless I go to Japan or the island of St Kitts, or some other place where one is likely to find Balliol men – I ought therefore to give you some solemn word of warning and advice: but I can think of nothing – except to recommend you to marry a Jap – In England one can't marry without making a *mésalliance*. Give my love to Aubrey.

To H. T. Baker   Balliol College,
                                                                          Oxford.
                                                              27 September 1901

Your letter is welcome. I came here on Wednesday night and have got through four of my papers.[1] There are eleven in all – ending next Wednesday morning. It is rather too much. So far we have had Greek Unseen and Latin Prose, both easy: an Essay on "Specialism in Science", "Literature and Education", and a philosophy paper, which showed me I was wise not to read Hegel more thoroughly than I did. I'm afraid I shan't get the thing as I hear there is a man called Tod of John's who is the best philosopher ever seen in Oxford: I think however that I can beat Arnold of Magdalen who is also competing . . . The only exercise I get is at tennis after 5 with the marker when it is almost dark and very dangerous, and sometimes a walk in the Parks. It sounds an un-pleasant life, but honestly I rather enjoy it. The charm with which Oxford is accredited it really seems to me to possess, and never more palpably than now. My amazement at the moon rising over the trees in the Parks yesterday even-ing caused me to be locked in there; but luckily it is almost as lovely here in the Quad, where one is locked in at ten in any case. There is also a spaciousness and tranquility about the Broad just after the lights have been lit – due partly to its emptiness – which lays quite a spell on one's imagination. Probably also the six hours *per diem* of strenuous if rather hysterical brain-exercise contributes to one's general sense of well-being . . .

[1] The examination was for a fellowship at Merton College, which was not awarded to Raymond.

To H. H. Asquith
The Pleasaunce,
Overstrand,
Cromer.
8 October

I have been thinking over the possible alternatives since this Merton fiasco. They seem to be three:
1) To settle down at once in London and begin reading in someone's chambers, or whatever one does in early stages of the law.
2) To go up to Oxford for next term on the chance of something turning up in the way of fellowships outside the ordinary run of things.
3) To go up for another year and read another school. . . . It is no use being at Oxford unless one is part of the machine; I don't care about standing in the market-place until someone chooses to throw me a penny: especially as no one is really likely to do so . . . my best plan is to go up and read Law pretty hard for a year, taking the school if I thought I was far enough advanced to do myself credit in it, if not having a shot at the despised All Souls next year. There is certainly very much more chance of an impartial verdict in the law department than in History: and it is always worth competing so long as one knows it is one's own fault if one fails . . .

The whole thing would have been very much simpler and more satisfactory if I hadn't made such a stupid mess of Merton . . . I can never remember being more disgusted about anything; as I was quite fit and well during the examination, and that is all one ought to require in these competitions. You might let me know what you think about my scheme by return: if it is to be carried out I must lose no time in securing rooms and getting into my stride.

To H. T. Baker
The Pleasaunce,
Overstrand,
Cromer.
10 October 1901

. . . I hear vague rumours of a mystic plum offered by St John's: if they do announce a competition I shall steel myself to enter for it though it will probably be intended as nothing more than a solatium for the brilliant but seemingly unacceptable Tod. I have today received the apologies of the Warden of Merton. He writes in a most friendly spirit, representing himself as my champion and lamenting the system of majority voting by which he would have me believe that his amiable intention was frustrated; some at any rate of the examiners considered my claims to be very strong, he tells me: and therefore I should not despair, but look forward to successes even more important than that which I have achieved in narrowly missing a Merton fellowship. My spiritual anguish – with which I thought you showed a deficient sympathy the

other night – is much assuaged by these admissions and still more by the
envelope of material conveniences with which I am here enclosed . . .

To H. T. Baker

Balliol College,
Oxford.
17 November 1901

. . . I hope however that you noticed Rosebery's handsome reference to me at
Edinbro': in form it might certainly have been more felicitous: his "two
generations of Hertford Scholars" was a little wide seeing that there has not
been one in the family as yet. I am afraid he will never take enough trouble
about his facts. I am getting on badly with my law. The fine burst by which I
completely mastered contracts has died away and I am stranded impotently on
the shoals of jurisprudence – the most irritating quasi-science that ever was
begotten by bad philosophers upon an intractable material. It seems to me to
matter so very little what system of classification you adopt provided you stick
to it: but one has to wade through pages of foggy writing on such subjects as
whether the State can be regarded as a Person in whom rights inhere: the
answer makes all the difference in the world to jurists but none at all to anyone
else: however the answer, if it is to have any value as truth, cannot be given by
jurists: it is outside their learning and belongs to philosophy. All they should
do is to say I think that the State is (or is not) such a person and base my system
accordingly. As it is they are in the position of a man who being employed to
index a work of reference insists on interfering with its contents. The study is
very debauching to one's intelligence, especially if relentlessly pursued: it keeps
one on the lower levels without any chance of a rise: one might just as well be
on a stool in Threadneedle St for all the spiritual sustenance one can get out of
it . . .

To John Buchan

20 Cavendish Square.
19 December 1901

Very many thanks for your letter. I ought to have answered it long ago, but I
am so stupid nowadays and so industrious that I didn't. I think you are probably lucky – as you say – to be out of this poor old country . . . But I expect you
are having a dullish time too: there can't be much work to do for a civilian in a
beseiged town like Johannesburg . . . I imagine you spend most of the day in a
cellar thinking what would happen if De Wet turned up. The great event here
of course has been Rosebery's speech last Tuesday. The old funk is coming back
at last: he was forced into it rather cleverly by the Lib. Imp. press wh. made
such a fuss about the speech for months before-hand that anything less sensational than an announcement of his return to politics would have been such

an anti-climax as would have made him ridiculous in the eyes of Europe. I didn't even hear the speech: I wish I had: my father says it was the best he ever made in his life – delivered in a railway shed full of snow and Derbyshire miners and as long as the Manchester Ship canal: most of them can't have heard a word. The whole thing was wonderfully stage managed by Perks. who provided a special train to take the platform people back to London in wh. was served a dinner wh. must have cost £10 a head. The meeting seems to have been violently jingo, and murmured loudly at the very mild criticism wh. R. passed on Milner. He wants us to explain to the Boers that we are going to make things very comfortable for them if they give in and spend millions on restocking their farms etc. But there seems to me to be a 2fold difficulty about offering them terms: firstly, they know well enough that whenever and however the settlement comes about we are bound in our own interests to spend a lot of money in re-establishing them *in statu quo ante* and getting the civil machinery to work at the earliest possible date: consequently they have no particular inducement to surrender. Secondly, they will never accept terms which do not bind us to bring back those fellows in Ceylon and elsewhere: and how the devil we are to do that I don't quite see. The permanent deportation of the majority of the Dutch population seems almost a necessity. Still, it will be interesting to see what effect the speech will have on the poor old Liberal party . . . But we shall see some some fun I make little doubt.

As R. says, if there is no alternative govt. to the present one we may as well put up the shutters and dig our cabbages. 18th century methods worked well enough while we had a talented aristocracy, but we can't afford nowadays to limit our choice of ministers to a few stuffy families with ugly faces bad manners and a belief in the Nicene Creed. The day of the clever cad is at hand: the future is with Perks. I always felt it would come to this if we once let ourselves in for an Empire. If only Englishmen had known their Aeschylus a little better they wouldn't have bustled about the world appropriating things in the way they have. A gentleman may make a large fortune but only a cad can look after it. Anyone who knew what Cleon did at Athens or Pallas at Rome might have foreseen that: and I suppose a lot of people did, but not till it was too late. It would have been so much pleasanter to live in a small community who knew Greek and played games and washed themselves.

. . . honestly I haven't the ambition of a louse and I don't see why I should pretend to it. There are a few things and people at Oxford that I intend to keep close to as long as I decently can, and I don't care a damn about the rest. If one fell in love with a woman or believed in the Newcastle programme or had no dress clothes it might be different. But the world as I see it just now is a little barren of motives . . . But I suppose I may have what they call a spiritual awakening any day: and then I shall shout and lie and make money with the best of them . . . The law is a lean casuistical business: it fills me with disgust.

To H. T. Baker

Balliol College,
Oxford.
28 February 1902

I am so dazed with the logic chopping of international lawyers that I do not know if I shall carry through my project of writing you a letter; if I do parts of it are pretty sure to be in bad German – a language one picks up quickly from reading foot notes by Vattel, Hügner, Geffckens and others. Sentences such as *"man kann Lord Granville nur dankbar sein dass er dass gute Recht der Neutralen so entschieden gegen Französische Willkür vertheidigt hat"*[1] roll very easily off my pen. Thank God I am not yet infected with the villainous French of Wellington's communications with Massena! Internat. law is a much more arbitrary system that I thought at first sight: it has been built up on no other principle than the temporary interests of temporarily dominant states, and consequently there is a vast mass of conflicting precedents which jurists select and compound with a caprice limited only by ignorance or national prejudice – one can't help being struck though – looking at the thing from an impartial and common-sense point of view – by the fact that England has been almost always right – apart from the accident that she has usually been able to enforce her views – and America almost always wrong . . .

To John Buchan

Balliol,
2 March 1902

. . . You seem to have taken S. Africa into the hollow of your hand: it must be a pleasant sensation doing work which produces an ostensible result: it is one which those who read the Digest in Oxford rarely feel, I can assure you. Whether anyone else in England feels it I should be puzzled to say: it is certain that no one has a right to. The political situation almost sends one to sleep by its tediousness: the blank futility of our public men on both sides is a thing one never hoped to see outside the neo-celtic school of poetry: if they made W. B. Yeats 1st Lord of the Admiralty instead of Selborne the picture would be complete: the general effect is that of a flock of sheep playing blind man's buff in the distance on a foggy day. Now Arthur Balfour has got influenza anyone but CB could turn the government out in a week: they were beaten in a division the other day – but that was because Gerald Balfour who was leading them is even stupider than CB. Rosebery continues to prance on the moonbeam of efficiency, and makes speeches at every street corner: but he might as well call it the Absolute at once for all the meaning it has to him or anyone else: no one has the least idea what he wants to effect, and beyond a mild bias in favour of good

---

[1] It is thanks to Lord Granville that the rights of neutrals have been so effectively protected against arbitrary encroachments on them by the French.

government and himself as premier, nothing can be gleaned from his speeches – unless it be a determination to exasperate the Irish at any price. Meantime Lulu Harcourt who is a wicked but not unpractical person has taken the precaution of securing the entire organisation of the party for the pro-Boers: he has acted throughout on the old Macedonian maxim and the honoraria have been on the most lavish scale: it has been a great time for secretaries of local liberal associations, who have now an additional motive for desiring the end of a war wh. necessitates an income tax of 1s. 2d. in the £ – as well as violating every principle of justice and humanity. By way of a counterblast Rosebery has now started a thing called the Liberal League wh. appears at present to consist of 3 persons, himself my father and Grey, backed by a squad of titled ladies, who believe that the snobbery of the lower classes is greater than their greed: I trust that this may be so: they say there is a good spot in everyone if one knows where to find it.

The only important accession to the new party is Bron.

To H. T. Baker   Altachiara, Portofino

. . . I like this place immensely – tho' we have only seen the worst of it as yet – rain and wind the whole time, but when the sun comes as it must soon it will be perfect. It is a large white villa built 20 years ago by Aubrey's father, high up on the rocks above the sea at the very end of the Genoese promontory. The Mediterranean is as blue as a sapphire tho' the sky is grey. We look straight down on it 200 feet below from the terrace. The garden is full of delicious things – orange trees with the fruit still on them and peaches in bloom which are quite lovely. In a few days there will be wistaria. The hills behind are covered with silver olives, and the village below is deliciously splashed with green and red and white. When the hot nights come and the full moons it will be a paradise of sensuous delight. The rooms are exceedingly cool and comfortable, tho' there are a few scorpions in the rears; and the food quite excellent. My bedroom, where I am writing, has "Horatius" written over the door and I am waited on by a handsome youth called Vergilio. We work fairly steadily and in the afternoon climb on the rocks which I enjoy. Aubrey missed his footing today and fell off into the sea luckily, whence he was recovered by a retainer who follows us in a boat.

To Mrs A. L. Smith   Portofino,
                                                       28 March 1902

Thank you for your letter. There was no need to apologise for writing it; anything which concerns Lionel has the greatest interest for me. Lionel's case seems to me to be a fairly easy one to diagnose, but hard to remedy. When one hears of a clever man not doing himself justice it usually means one of two things: either that he is not clever; or that he is not interested in exerting himself – lack of brains or lack of stimulus. Lionel has very good brains (though he has other qualities which are much more remarkable than his intelligence) – but he does not seem to me to be interested in getting the most out of them. The very best brains in the world take one a very little way if one has not the will to use them; the worst will take one almost the whole way, if one has. A man of fair abilities – at Oxford or outside – can get practically anything if he wants it enough: St. John Brodrick is a case in point. If one is to do one's work easily and well one must have some strong motive power behind one: and this may be either interest in the subject for its own sake, or some more selfish impulse – ambition or vanity.

Lionel, as you know, has probably less of these two latter qualities than any man alive: he has not even the ordinary combative self-assertive instinct which is almost a physical impulse in most men's compositions, and which one would certainly expect to find in a person who plays games so much and so well as he does – the instinct to push other people out of the way and show yourself the better man if you are – and perhaps even if you are not. It is a pleasant quality to contemplate, this wonderful diffidence – and contributes to his peculiar charm, but is a bad one to possess in the vulgar and competitive world . . . Of course what a man does in the schools can never make any difference to the estimate which his friends form of him, but I suppose Lionel, like the rest of us, will have to earn his bread and butter and it does seem rather a pity that he shouldn't get the ordinary fruits which would drop into his mouth if he would only open it. It is not that he is lazy: The *amount* of work he does is amply sufficient if only he would put a little 'devil' into it: it is the spirit in which he does it which produces the 'lifeless' quality you speak of. One reason for this is that he has no definite objective: most men of his age – whether from inclination or necessity – have a settled profession in view, and even if they do not take much interest in the academic work for its own sake, they yet pursue it with some fervour in preparation for a larger struggle outside. But I have sometimes talked to Lionel about his profession and he has not only no ideas about it but apparently no wishes: all he will say is that he ought to make some money for the sake of his sisters and would jump at any job which offered him a prospect of doing so.

He is not a man of what they call strong intellectual interests (you won't be offended at my saying this? for I doubt if even you can value him more highly than I do) – he is still inclined to take the boyish view of work as an irksome interlude between one game and another: this is partly because he is such a true athlete, partly, again, owing to his constitutional diffidence. Philosophy, as taught at Oxford, is a little dull if one stops short at the limit marked out by the schools – that is, on the brink of the really vital and interesting questions: the stuff one is taught seems mere pedantry and jargon until one can bring it into connexion with these bigger issues, but once one does so it comes to have a real bearing on one's life and can hardly fail to interest the most apathetic student. But here again L is pulled up by distrust of his own powers and prefers by nature to rest in authority and habit rather than to launch out on individual speculations for which he thinks his equipment inadequate. Most of us, no doubt, err on the other side, but I am inclined to think it is a more fortunate error – certainly a more profitable one from the immediate standpoint of the examinee. The best thing I can think of is for you to get Mr. J. A. Smith to give him some private and informal instruction by way of discussions and so forth rather off the lines of the schools. 'J.A.' is very lucid and very candid and very keen, which one does not feel about many of our Oxford philosophers: he is also rather shy of forcing his opinions on his pupils, but if you could somehow persuade him to talk to Lionel in an unofficial and untechnical way about the larger topics of metaphysics and morals which must be of interest to all human beings, I am sure it would be a good thing, and I believe it is almost the only thing which could give Lionel a real living impulse in his work and overcome his reluctance to speculate on subjects as to which everyone of his intelligence is entitled – if not bound – to form an independent opinion.

I have often wished that I could give him some of my own superfluous vanity and selfishness: an inoculation with some of the commoner vices would make him far more capable off playing his part in the world – a few small ambitions, a little low cunning, a little of the cheap intellectual agility of the mercenary examinee would send him dancing through the schools on three hours' work a day. But it is too late now to try and degrade his character, and the other alternative – that of rousing a real interest in his subject – is the only one that is likely to be effective. I hope it may be so, but whatever he does in the schools, he is such a wonderful and priceless person that you can always afford to laugh at an examiner who makes a mistake. I wish he were here with us; this place is delicious – glorious sun and sea: I am sure it would be good for him.

To Margot Asquith

Altachiara,
Porto Fino,
Liguria,
Italy.
6 April 1902

Many thanks for your letter. I am sorry your weather is so beastly: ours is much the same at present but has been – & I hope will be – magnificent. The sea is always deep blue whatever colour the sky may be; & when the sun shines the whole place is a paradise of sensuous delight, – heavy scents & brilliant flowers: the peach & cherry blossom are quite wonderful, & look particularly well agst. a background of silver olives amongst which they are usually planted. The coast here is not at all unlike Clovelly – magnificent grey rocks covered with stone-pines down to the water's edge: & the house is in much the same sort of position, only more immediately above the sea. There is not a very great deal to do – which is perhaps as well since we are all supposed to be working: but the rock climbing is dangerous and interesting & the bathing good – I went up the biggest mountain near here the other day & got a magnificent view – the maritime alps running right down to the sea with snow, & the Apennines which are an extraordinarily beautiful range I think – so clean-limbed & tight-skinned & well-modelled: they remind one of an athlete's body or a well-made face with the shadows cleverly arranged in it. The natives are most courteous & picturesque: our boatman Alfredo is the handsomest man of his type I have ever seen – small & sinewy with perfect little aquiline features – The neighbours are pleasant too – especially one Brown, who is British Consul at Genoa but lives here in a delightful old castle on the promontory opposite us: it was built in Crusading times & has walls 15 ft. thick: he bought it 40 yrs. ago for £50! He is very good company, & hospitable – especially to German Princesses, who throng the castle: – one particularly odious one (of Thurn & Taxis) with whom we sometimes have to play ping-pong: it is almost worth it to see her eat her tea afterwards – such ingenuous gluttony is most refreshing in an adult. His other guests are 2 or 3 rather beautiful Irish girls and an unusually stupid Austrian called Count Sechindorf who is said to have been married to the Empress Frederick. Such is the ménage of 'the good Mr Brown': but there is also 'the naughty Mr Brown' who was turned out of the Guards some years ago for an offence agst. the moral code & now lives – as we like to believe in sin – in a large painted villa immediately opposite the good Mr Brown: but we are not allowed to know him.

Our own party consists of 9. Aubrey Herbert our host is an excellent person – full of spirits, good imagination & good brains though thoroughly unmethodical: he has rather a tiresome pose of pretending to be mad, as very sane people sometimes do, but he is getting rid of it by degrees, & his good qualities are so many that one easily forgives his carefully planned absurdities & eccentricities which smell of the lamp. Another nice fellow is John Kennaway, son of an old West Country squire with an enormous beard whom you may know: he has been in the House since the middle of last century . . .

To H. T. Baker

Altachiara,
Porto Fino,
Liguria,
Italy.
21 April 1902

. . . I have thought quite seriously of giving up schools and Oxford and civilization of all kinds and becoming a wild and brutal colonist. What is the good of it all? The marvellous education I have had. The great books I have read, the agonies of intellectual acquisition, the trophies of intellectual conquest. The wonderful and beautiful people I have known. Here I am at the end of it as stupid, as incapable, as uninterested, and as promising as ever. This is cheaply and theatrically written; but if you examine yourself you will probably see that it is true of you also . . . You are a mere conduit pipe, a sewer of time, a hollow thing fixed in one place through which runs a stream now sweet now foul but running always and leaving no deposit or at best one which is heavy, melancholy, and malodorous. You never grow; you learn and forget; extend and relapse; feel and are as though you had never felt; fight and win – or lose – and are as though you had never fought. There is no accretion, no progress . . . What is the good of knowing about the Interdicts? Or the works of Verrius Flaccus? Or seeing that Sappho was a genius? Or revering the stars? Or thinking that one would do noble things if there was an opportunity or an audience? Or worshipping a person whose happiness one cannot affect? Of course all these things are good in their way, and from time to time one feels them to be so – but sitting down in a calm moment one also feels that they are fragments and ragged ends, pearls without a string, or pieces of nothing at all. The ignorant armies which clash by night are better off; they at least clash; but here one sits with handsome clothes, good food, friends, books, brains and muscles – and nothing happening to one for ever and ever. It is not surprising that clever people are driven into poses of foppishness or brutality . . .

The Bar, Courtship and Marriage 1902-1914

'The world as I see it just now is a little barren of motives. The law is a lean casuistical business: it fills me with disgust.' (19 December 1901.) 'Politics is now nothing more than a wordy wrangle . . . Consequently the soul turns inward and consoles itself with literature and law.' (2 March 1902) 'A mill is no use without grist . . . moreover there is the eternal lack of motive.' (21 December 1902.)

Naturally, one must allow for the changes of mood to which brilliant men with exalted standards are particularly prone. But these thoughts, expressed in letters to John Buchan in South Africa in the year in which Raymond won a fellowship at All Souls' to crown his firsts in Mods, Greats and Law, indicate beyond doubt that his successes on paper failed to give him inner contentment or even satisfaction. Early in 1903 he made an expedition to Egypt, largely in order to arrange for his Balliol friend Phil Kershaw a position on the staff of the Chief Secretary Lord Cromer, having first sounded Margot on the advisability of such a direct approach. Egypt stirred his curiosity, but not, as will be seen, his enthusiasm.

Back in England in April, he began working seriously at the Bar, in chambers in Inner Temple, spending week-ends either at All Souls' or at the country houses of friends. Fortunately for him, a distinct motive, of increasing power, appeared in his life during the next year, as a result of further visits to Mells, where he first met Katharine Horner in the summer of 1901. He was invited on a summer holiday with the Horner and Manners families in the mountains of Carinthia, fifty miles south of Salzburg. By July 1904 he was writing Katharine passionate letters: ('You know how I would like to give you the whole world if it were mine, and the sun and the moon and all the stars . . .'); complaining bitterly when they were not satisfactorily answered, retracting his fury on the receipt of even 'a lonely sheet of abuse' or muted self-defence; and asking her to forget all his 'silliness and extravagance and peevishness'. Besides further visits to Mells, he went to Venice with the Horners in September of that year, and to Ireland with them in the summer of 1905.

Most unfortunately, none of Katharine's letters to him has survived, and it

93

can only be supposed that she destroyed them after he was killed. It is obvious that she returned his love from an early stage, but she was probably held back by a natural shyness and by an element of elusive remoteness, as well as by genuine humility and diffidence in the face of the intellectual heights at which his love for her was pitched. Apart from a natural mutual attraction, one of the links that attached them from the start was a deep love of poetry, largely self-generated on her side, and the fruit of education and environment on his. When they finally married in the summer of 1907, she was not quite twenty-two. Not surprisingly for the time, Katharine's mother had wanted her to see a little more of the world, and a few more potential husbands, before making up her mind, and it was not for two years that her strong disinclination to do either of these things was rewarded. (The conventions of the day even made it difficult for them to see much of each other except at crowded social functions or rather formal week-end parties: hence the tone of some of the courtship letters.) There was also another worldly objection, that whatever Raymond's earnings at the Bar might eventually be, he had at that time no money of his own, and by the standards of the day was therefore not in a position to support a wife. In those days, and in those circles, this obstacle could be worn away only – if at all – by the passage of time and the obdurate determination of the couple concerned. Raymond's father and Margot, though neither had capital, had large incomes which they spent freely, and in the event they both gave him an allowance. However wayward and wild Margot's observations might sometimes be, her comment on their engagement was that 'Raymond and Katharine are the most perfect combination of in-loveness and friendship marrying at the right age, with the right knowledge of each other, that I have ever known.' Apart from his letters, an interesting essay of Raymond's has survived, long but unfinished, and referred to on page 131. The subject is Sentimentalism, and its disastrous consequences. Though too long to include in full, it throws valuable light on his general critical approach to the world, and is therefore worth summarising.

Between the ages of six and eight he had been deeply affected by a song that his nurse sang, and he could 'therefore understand how the most vivid effects can be produced upon an uncultivated taste by the most cheap and obvious means'. This, he goes on, does not apply in the case of pictures, tunes, stories and poems. At the shallow end of speculation, random ecstasies and frothy aspirations (usually of women) are often co-ordinated in a 'fantastic, inconsecutive, vague, superficial and pretentious' pattern which is the finest flower of sentimentalism. Those who are capable of feeling at all strongly cannot avoid it without the 'critical apparatus of culture', and an insistence on 'a reasonable degree of definition in any object that excites the emotions'. It is only by 'precision of outline' that true works of art and genuine passions can be verified.

The degrees of illusion vary. Byron, a striking creature, is thrilling 'in the sense that some fleshy actor, overblown with wine and gallantry, would be thrilling in a spinster's parlour in the provinces, where an eye which has long rested on antimacassars is gratified by the spectacle of a bull or a bottle, and the starved heart responds', only too glad 'to idealise the second-rate'. Though it did not prevent his writing 'fine lines and fine stanzas', Byron could never get it out of his head 'that the universe was a mere adjunct to his own personality, a scenic background to the drama of his own emotions'. Then there is the case of 'those who are moved by objects of true value to crises of false exaltation and trivial exuberance', in contrast to Wordsworth – the hero of the essay in so far as it has one – who was justified in his confidence that 'he could express his feelings, about a sunset for example, in a worthy form'.

Snobbery is to be deprecated; but Bohemianism is equally perilous; and when we turn to the ecstacies of Rousseau 'they give us no confidence, but leave us cold, empty and suspicious'. His great intelligence was 'distorted, obscured and at times almost deranged by the impetuous and disturbing incoherence of his emotions. . . . His reason was not only sound, but profound and acute. When it worked, it worked well – but under certain circumstances it was simply in abeyance.' Wordsworth's intelligence, on the other hand, was at ordinary times a very ordinary instrument; 'but it was illuminated and advanced by his emotions to the point of genius'. Sentimentalism covered both 'the man whose natural passions are so weak that he is impelled to supplement them by studied and ingenious fictions, and the man whose natural passions are so strong that his reason reels before their onset'. And the victim of it, since he 'amuses his imagination with fantastical pictures of the world and of his fellow men . . . is framed for contemplation rather than for action', where his foibles will inevitably let him down. The essay ends abruptly at this point, and it is difficult to see why, after having plainly taken a good deal of trouble with it, Raymond did not pull the threads together and complete it. But even as it stands, it is the most powerful (and readable) indictment of false perspectives, false sentiment and therefore of false values that one could wish for.

Raymond's love letters are among his best and most brilliant. However eloquent, they are never rhetorical, and their intensity comes most obviously from the heart. But as they are inevitably repetitive, and in some cases temporarily reproachful as well as lyrical, they are not quoted in full. For the period that followed, immediately after their marriage, it is not surprising that only a very few letters have survived, since Raymond and Katharine were together except when he was away on legal work on the western circuit, or she paid visits of more than a few days to her old home. Their first child was born in October 1908, and was called Helen after Raymond's mother.

Eighteen months later, Raymond embarked on his first long-drawn-out case, concerning an arbitration on the Newfoundland Fisheries at the International Court at The Hague. This took him to Holland from June to September of 1910, during which time a second daughter, eventually named Perdita, was born. He wrote home almost every day, and these letters, even when describing such unpromising material as a fisheries arbitration, are typical fruits of his vitality and imagination as well as his powers of expression. Not surprisingly, he went on making progress at the Bar, where besides these qualities his competitive spirit, mentioned earlier, was no doubt another source of his success, however unambitious he may have been in the conventional worldly sense. Once he had surmounted the initial dreariness of working at the Bar, he admitted to Buchan that 'it somehow seems a more independent and individual career than any other'. By 1914 he had been made a Junior Counsel to the Inland Revenue, and in the previous year he had been adopted as prospective Liberal candidate for Derby, where the sitting member, Sir Thomas Roe, was to retire at the next election.

Politics had by now long ceased to consist of the often contrived differences of opinion between Liberals and Tories diagnosed by Raymond when Balfour was Prime Minister. Lloyd George's budget of 1909, the ensuing Parliament Bill and the threat to swamp the House of Lords (with the King's agreement) with enough new creations to give the Liberals a majority there; the passionate divergences on Ireland, and on the merits of Free Trade and Tariff Reform; all these had bitterly divided the world of politics and had filled it with more personal animosity than had been felt for twenty-five years.

After his adoption in January 1913 Raymond made a number of hard-hitting speeches at Derby – eight in 1913, and another seven in 1914. At the first of them he mocked and taunted the Tories in characteristic vein by recollecting 'during one autumn night at the house of a friend, Mr Winston Churchill coming in with a bruise on his cheek as big as a man's fist, inflicted by some enthusiastic sportsman who, at the termination of a debate in the House of Commons, had thrown a book at him by way of a final and conclusive argument in favour of free speech . . . Of all the mean and dubious expedients the Tory party employ in the desperate hope of discrediting the Liberal Government none is more contemptible or less effective than those recurrent outbursts, that have neither the dignity of nature nor the charm of art; neither the freshness of spontaneous passion, nor the finish of good acting.' He went on to say that the Tories had 'got rid of Mr Balfour because he was too subtle for them . . . too fond of evasions and subterfuges. They [had] substituted Mr Bonar Law because they wanted what they called a plain, blunt man, who would hit hard, and ride straight.' But he had now been 'twisted completely out of shape by the alternate pressures of the different wings of the Tory party. This man who was so blunt had been sharpened until he was nothing but edge . . . instead of cutting the throats of foes he merely cut the fingers of friends. . . . This blunt, plain, straight man was now resorting to all the old evasions and tortuosities they knew so well under the Balfour regime.' But he was not the man for the job. 'If they wanted a man to play the bull in a china shop, a mad bull, but an honest one, Mr Bonar Law could do it very well. He roared, lashed his tail, and beat about among the crockery in a most exhilarating way. But to take the bull from the china shop, where it was doing such good work, and to invite it to walk along a tight-rope across Niagara – that was asking too much, more than bovine nature could accomplish . . . as when he was asked by the Prime Minister whether or not he intended to repeal the Insurance Act, and he replied "Certainly" and had to write to *The Times* next day to say he meant "Certainly not". . . .' On another occasion he described Bonar Law privately as 'the victim of his own rhetoric: his words are like a team of performing fleas which take the bit between their teeth and run away with the showman.' His speeches contain more in the same vein on the other main political topics of the day, Home Rule, Welsh Disestablishment, the Food Tax policy, and the problem of low wages, particularly for agricultural workers.

However showy Raymond's own use of words might sometimes be, he always remained in control of them with the greatest assurance. In 1902 his few months in active politics lay far ahead in the future. The extracts which follow indicate that in the intervening years it was in his correspondence, as well as his legal work, that he continued to develop the clarity of his mind and the sparkling precision of his language.

To Reginald Farrer

Marshal's Wick,
St Albans.
20 July 1902

Many thanks for your letter. The Law School is fitter for galley-slaves than gentlemen: but I suppose it might be argued that it is better to be a good galley-slave than a bad one, so I will accept your congratulations.

Have you had your absurd viva yet? It will bore you to tears when you do. I cried like a child when I saw at close quarters the sort of people who had presumed to estimate my knowledge of Law. I sat there long enough to insult the senior examiner & then flung out of the room in a passion of sobs.

You have heard no doubt of Aubrey's mad folly? going to Japan at 10 days notice as an honorary attaché! can you imagine anything more feverishly absurd? To put oneself 12000 miles away from anybody fit to speak to, in a country where the men have no faces & the women have no feet, & the houses are made of paper, & the books begin at the end & end in the middle, & the scenery is imported every year from the Savoy theatre & retained on the hire system until Gilbert & Sullivan want it again in London! The proctors ought to forbid him to go: but they always do their duty at the wrong moment – like everyone else who does it at all . . . You have an election going on in your country have you not? why don't you stand? one must do something you know. We are going through a domestic crisis: our cook was discovered 2 days ago to be cheating us out of £80 a month: he tried to bolt but we brought him back & he makes the soup with a private detective standing over him to see that he doesn't put strychnine in it – or if he does that he is hanged for it after-wards.

To H. T. Baker

Marshal's Wick,
St Albans.
17 August 1902

. . . I went yesterday to the Naval Review on Selborne's yacht the *Enchantress* – a vessel 35 years of age and quite unseaworthy; it does not answer to the helm and cannot either leave or approach a pier without the aid of a tug. I was only persuaded to go by the representations which were made that Botha, Delarey, De Wet, and Kitchener would be on board; but the Boers proved as elusive as ever and took the train to London as soon as they arrived. Consequently I spent a very dull day – I got up at 7 in the morning and stood on deck talking to fools till evening. I had some conversation with Goschen, who looks like an old clothesman, but it is not uninteresting. Selborne told me all there is to know about the ships (which is that all but six of them are quite obsolete and useless), and the Bishop of Winchester gave me minute descriptions of the interior of Osborne and the Royal Yacht, together with a categorical denial of certain things which he said he is said to have said to our Late Queen. Buckle was there too – a grinning yokel, 6ft. 3ins. high and as much again in girth; he ate six quails and drank a bottle and a half of champagne for lunch. On the whole I was bored and tried almost to despair. How you can think the Navy interesting passes my understanding. Thank God I didn't stay for the illuminations which were all extinguished by a thunderstorm . . . But I am so acrimonious and out of sorts just now that I see nothing good in anything. I can never remember being so completely discontented; I suppose it is the climate which is detestable here. W. James has an excellent chapter on the Sick Soul in his last book on 'Varieties of Religion' [i.e. *Varieties of Religious Experience*] in which I find some self portraiture. It seems to me a very good book – brilliantly written at any rate – from what I have seen of it; you should read it. I have gone through with *Barchester Towers* which without ever boring me yet leaves a lasting impression of feebleness; if your scene and incidents are on such a very small scale they must be very much better done to be worth doing at all . . .

To H. T. Baker

Marshal's Wick,
St Albans.
28 August 1902

Lady Helen Vincent is here: her beauty in the evening is very remarkable, and, I suspect, moderately assailable: her sister at any rate allowed Hugo Elcho (who is one of the ugliest men in the Empire, though by no means the least witty) to beget the present Duke of Leinster upon her body: but against that one must set off the fact that her other sister, Lady Ulrica Duncombe, jilted the Bishop of London as soon as he mentioned the fact that he looked forward to copulation as one of the incidental delights of their married life . . .

To H. T. Baker

Marshal's Wick,
St Albans.
9 September 1902

. . . I am much pleased that you find quality in one whom I have always admired – and should probably now admire, if I were fortunate to enjoy the opportunity, fully as much as you do. I congratulate you sincerely on having taken a step (which I hope you will this time not retrace) in the right direction: a normal attitude towards women is clearly the only key to the encroaching problem of middle age; and if your new-born appreciation does nothing else it must at least make you tolerant of my very temperate admiration of some women whom I meet in London and elsewhere which you have hitherto put down to a mixture of snobbery and caprice – especially when you reflect that they are commonly not only as beautiful as Barbara but also well enough instructed in your trinity of topics – poetry, politics, religion, to make conversation a possibility and criticism a duty. But whatever may be the intrinsic worth of women or their value as sources of pleasure there can be no doubt of their paramount influence in affairs great and small: we live under the most absolute gynaecocracy which the world has ever seen . . . and whether your ambition bends towards politics, society, or mere selfish comfort it is a fact which you must take into account among the first . . . Old Sir Charles [Margot's father] is staying with us – one of the most extraordinary men I have ever seen – 78 years old, a very fine billiard player, as good a man at the short strokes of golf (which do not require much strength) as any professional, and a very decent shot though he shot poor Eddy [his son] the other day in the bone of the eye, and another man in the balls – the only apology he vouchsafed to him was "Oh, Rosebery shot me in just the same place 30 years ago!" He is as vain as a peacock and sucks down the grossest flattery which his family administer to him in choking doses. His wife is here too, covered with emeralds and big with child! Another odd couple who are here are Lady Ottoline Morrell (née Bentinck) and her husband, whom I wish you could see if only to appreciate the incredible felicity of Lady Poynder's remark that he looks the sort of man who ought to be chained to a rock. He is Titanic in stature, classical in feature, philanthropic in disposition – the very picture of a sucking Prometheus.

To John Buchan

Marshal's Wick,
24 September 1902

. . . A civil servant who does his duty in South Africa is sawing away the branch he sits on: and whether he does it or not the branch is bound to fall in a year or two, and 'where will the baby be then, poor thing'. It is different for you who have done difficult work under a charming and appreciative chief: but when Milner goes there will be no one to appreciate and nothing to be appreciated – no work in fact which could not be done as well by the Master of Balliol and much better by Hancock[1] . . .

Have you entirely given up the idea of coming back to the Law? I can't help wishing that you would return: it somehow seems a more independent and individual career than any other: but of course in your case there is the large advance you have made in an administrative line to be taken into consideration: it seems a pity to throw all that overboard, and I daresay at this time of day it is really better for you to stick to it.

To H. T. Baker   Prince of Wales Lake Hotel,
                                                                           Grasmere.
                                                                       3 October 1902

. . . I have visited Wordsworth's Cottage, seat and grave, but have not yet had courage to open his poems though I have them with me in a handsome volume. I wonder if you find the same as I do about Pollock's *Torts* – I mean that fragments of it abide with me whether I will or no, like the smell of onions? I constantly find myself repeating "*Damnum* (said Hankford J.) may be *absque iniuria*", and "What if cattle belonging to a foreign ambassador are distrained damage feasants?" Do you know the answer to this montrous hypothesis? It only occurs in a footnote, so perhaps you may not. But I am in rather a morbid state just now – I have dreamed the last three nights of the Duke of Sutherland, which only happens when I am in poorish health. I see in *The Times* today that he has become a member of the Lib. League and so perhaps Mrs F. Thomas put it into my head from afar. Nothing like the influence of a good woman is there? . . . You may think this a little incoherent and fantastical; perhaps so! We are none of us quite sane, and the sudden blossoming of my spirit today in this wintry season may have made me unusually light-headed. What you say about Margot's petrifying influence is very true. There is no incitement to a person socially indolent to interrupt a stream of pleasant utterance by any active contribution; at least so I find; but I stand in an official relation to her and I can never bring myself to take any steps about a person to whom I stand in an offical relation; if she were a stranger it would be different. The least taint of status paralyses me – I could make myself a new character and a new intellect if I could start in a world of people who had no preconceptions about my present ones. I often think it would be pleasant and interesting to do so.

. . . I love this country with a passionate appreciation. It pleases me to stand alone on mountains in wind and sunlight and name to myself the peaks and lakes which I know. Today I almost persuaded myself that I was immortal, as the ranges unrolled themselves before me.

---

[1] Famous head porter at Balliol.

To H. T. Baker

Easton Grey,
Malmesbury.
28 December 1902

. . . I find the speculative department of my mind a little rusty; and in general I am filled with a kind of intellectual despair which always comes upon me whenever I am not reading at a definite area of matter for a definite purpose – the feeling of being behind hand with one's foundations – a blank ignorance of history and economy, a futile grounding in philosophy, a few fading memories of classical literature. One consoles oneself with the reflexion that one has a 'trained mind', a gymnastic intelligence with all the apparatus of method ready to be put in action at any moment; but a mill is no use without grist, and unless when one can learn or remember something the wheels bombinate aimlessly in a vacuum. Moreover there is the eternal lack of motive. Nothing can save me now but a moral crisis of some kind. I look forward to it with nervous anticipation and trust that it will take a transient and unobtrusive form . . .

To John Buchan

Overstrand, Cromer.
11 January 1903

I hardly know what news to tell you about England. We Liberals go on winning bye-elections which Rosebery and CB both claim as scalps: whereas they really seem to be due to Kipling's infamous verses about our German alliance . . . The farce of a division between the parties grows more evident every day: no two people seem to disagree about anything – except Rosebery and Bannerman: and neither of them have anything you can call an opinion except about one another: and of course the unlucky thing for us is that they are both right . . .

My people want me to go to Egypt in a few days and take 2 months or so there: they think Oxford is bad for me: but neither Bron, Conrad nor Bluetooth can come with me, and I don't at all fancy going alone, so I shall probably loiter on in England – more and more enervated by the motiveless comfort in which I live.

To H. T. Baker

The Pleasaunce,
Overstrand,
Cromer.
13 January 1903

. . . I have just come in from an intellectual tea-party given by the Sidney Webbs to myself and the two Bernard Shaws. Mr Webb and Mrs Shaw seem to count for very little in general society, though as Aristophanic complements I believe them to be highly prized. Webb is like a pawn-broker in appearance and has climbed to his present pinnacle from the dust of a second-hand bookshop I am told and can well believe – not that I dislike him – he seems to me to have stuff in him, and is certainly most enviable in his wife – a woman of great beauty (though forty-four) and charm: she has a most lustrous eye, most graceful figure, and any quantity of intelligence. She never says silly things about the lower classes as most Socialists do, and generally speaking gives one the impression of not being a Christian. She told me she had everything she desired – work, exercise and love – a very sensible trinity: though I fear I showed her involuntarily that love with Sidney was not quite my notion of the emotional ideal – still I am told they are very much in love with each other: also I could not help puzzling myself a little when my eye strayed over him as to what sort of exercise he was precisely adapted for: it can't be said that he is shaped for any sportive tricks. I think the life of these people would have pleased Plato – indeed it pleased me in the transitory encounter of the tea-table: to impinge on it at dinner-time would probably be disconcerting I felt – so strongly that I persuaded her to dine here tomorrow night. Bernard Shaw is very like his *Saturday Review* articles: he talks too much and keeps on saying that the earth is flat: but if one has plenty of time he is really quite amusing and full of gesture and vivacity . . .

To H. T. Baker   S.S. "China".
                                                     3 March 1903

In 2 or 3 hours we arrive at Port Said . . . It was very rough in the Bay and almost every one was sick except Phil & me: I think I must be an unusually good sailor as I never felt a qualm. Phil was a little shaky but staved off a crisis by flying to the rum cask. One feels very fit on the sea I must say. I have never eaten or slept so much in my life, which is saying a good deal. Phil has behaved very well – except for making love to Molly Bell, and throwing a fork at the Bishop Elect of Nagpur, a civil whining man rather like Steel – who would talk about Faith at the breakfast table . . . Gibraltar was very jolly: we were there on Shrove Tuesday when there was a fiesta – which means that lovely women squirt dirty water at one out of their windows & Moors walk about swindling in a stately way. The only people who look thoroughly vicious, miserable and absurd are the English soldiers. The Spanish are delightful and so is the white Spanish claret – but the soup which is made of sea-water with beetles and hair-pins in it is poor . . . There is plenty of time to read, much of which I foolishly filled by ploughing through *The Heart of Midlothian* – which altogether passes the due limit of prolixity. Scott's characters may be as well drawn as Meredith's but – like Dickens' – they are neither attractive nor familiar – they fit into no scheme of the world either as one knows it or as one would wish it to be . . .

To H. T. Baker   Cataract Hotel,
                                                         Assouan.
                                                    22 March 1903

You are not a good correspondent – in fact no one is. The only letters I have
had from England since I left are a bill for clay pigeons and an invitation to join
the Middlesex Mounted Infantry . . . We dined alone with the Cromers one
night in Cairo and had a very pleasant time: he is exceedingly sensible and full
of interests and she is very beautiful though not of great intelligence . . . Then
we had a week in the desert with young Honks[1] and Charles Rothschild[2] who
had a great camp for natural historical purposes. We had 22 camels, 30 black
men of various nations, and one Cingalese boy of 15 brought by Rothschild
from Colombo on account of his skill in taxidermy. He was rather a bonny boy,
not unlike a gross edition of that hackneyed picture of the young John
Baptist . . . Then we came on up here by train – about 600 miles south of
Cairo, which takes 24 hours on these railways. It is a very pleasant spot and I
could well endure being exiled here for a week or so – as Juvenal was by Domi-
tian. The Nile – which is an absurd river always and usually a very ugly
one – is here quite picturesque, broken by islands of which the chief is Elephantine behind which the most exquisite sunsets take place every night passing
from the palest green through every shade of yellow to the deepest purple with
such unnatural rapidity and precision that one almost suspects the hand of
Beerbohm Tree. The remains on Elephantine are late and shabby: but those on
Philae which we visited to-day – though only Ptolemaic in date – are very
beautiful and must have been still better before a great part of them were
submerged by the new barrage – an imposing affair but not more so than the
Tower Bridge. The fact is Egypt is an infernally ugly country: its monuments
have nothing to commend them but their age and a few thousand years more
or less do not fix in the imagination an object which is not already attached
there by some thread of classical association – a casual lie of Herodotus is not
enough for the purpose. The tiny pyramid of Mycerinus is interesting from M.
Arnold's excellent poem – but who cares a fig for Cheops or Chephren. Still I
have enjoyed this expedition quite as much as I expected and have no wish or
reason to complain. Phil's vitality and power of holding drink make him a good
companion: he was known by our native henchman as Ibn-el-gusasi or "Son of
the bottle" – but it is easy for the most temperate of topers to win fame among
this wineless people and in this admirably dry climate. The average temp. at
noon in the shade here is about 100 – but one does not feel it as oppressive and
can even play lawn tennis in it with the prospect of an exquisite cock-tail ahead.
It is certainly a most healthy place . . .

---

[1] Francis Henley, later 6th Lord Henley, Balliol contemporary.
[2] Distinguished naturalist, father of 3rd Lord Rothschild.

To John Buchan   Ghezirah Palace Hotel, Cairo.
                                            28 March 1903

I have been in Egypt just a month – which is too long a visit for a tourist and too short for a statesman. I know no more about the politics of the country than I learned from reading Milner at home, and no more about its antiquities than I gathered from Baedeker – though I think infinitely less of them. Still it is a good thing to have been in a country where any form of self-government is so clearly out of the question as it is here: you have only to walk the streets to see that these people are slaves by nature, a nation of beggars, sluggards and cheats . . .

There is no facet of our insularity which will do us more harm than our sentimental passion for representative institutions in season and out of season.: the only representative bodies here are quite farcically incapable and laughably impotent: if public attention could be judiciously directed to these phenomena it would do more than 50 Lib. Leagues to wipe out the trail which Christ and Gladstone have left on the political philosophy of Englishmen. Still, these reflexions only add point to those criticisms of Milner which declare that his Egyptian career has unfitted him for dealing with the Boers – who are I imagine a very different breed to these mongrels here. The monuments of this country are disappointing: they have age and size but mostly no beauty . . .

The natives offer one all kinds of shooting from lions and boars to rabbits and cats, but it usually ends in a few quails. . . . We rode from our camp 3 days on camels to the Pyramids of Ghizeh – a most dreary and exasperating business. For mere vileness nothing equals camels: 30 miles in a day of 7 hours is thought good going, and after it one is as tired as 4 times the distance on a horse could make one. One has no means of controlling their paces or of accommodating one's seat to them: they groan and spit and rear and bite and if one tries to pull them off water they lie down and roll on one. I wish they were all dead. We went up the biggest Pyramid and also inside it – the latter most unpleasant: one is pulled up and pushed down passages of glassy sliperiness so low that one's back bumps the roof as one crouches and so hot that it is impossible to breathe and so dark that one can see nothing but the bats which flap in one's face, by 3 black men who stink horribly and catch hold of one's ankles at the critical parts . . .

We dined with the Cromers who were very pleasant and did what they could for Phil: he has practically been promised the next vacancy . . . but will have to go back to England for the present. We leave by the Orient boat tomorrow – and I shall not be sorry to leave this city in the streets of which one cannot walk without being pursued by a mob of scoundrels who importune one in every possible way – some begging one to shoot animals that don't exist, others attempting to sell one antiquities on which the paint is hardly dry, and others again to show one sights that are ludicrously familiar to those who have enjoyed a public school education . . .

To H. T. Baker
All Souls College,
Oxford.
12 May 1903

. . . By not coming [to Mells] till Sat. I shall avoid being taken to Wells Cathedral. Let me advise you when you do go to insist on sitting with Katharine on the back seat of the dog-cart. Cicely will drive on the outward journey. Coming back I recommend you to insist on driving yourself. Cicely is too humane: she spares the whip and makes one an hour late for dinner, which is intolerable. I have been moving in the great world lately – at Cav. Sq. on Friday where I played bridge with the Duchess of Devonshire – a dowdy old German pol[1] – & then Sat. – Mon. with the Leo. Rothschilds at Leighton – a temple of luxury which Keats and Spenser rolled into one would lack words to describe. The Pleasaunce is a mere doss-house beside it. The claret and roses are among the best I have seen: one plays golf and bridge for 6d points with deaf men who talk racing shop: but there are practically no women which saves trouble: and the baths are as big as billiard tables . . .

To H. T. Baker
Anchor Hotel,
Porlock Weir.
3 January 1904

I send you a parody (for Maurice's *Spectator*) of Warren's poetry which consists [as] you know in applying tags from *In Memoriam* to dead Peers or Princes he has known at Magdalen.

On a Viscount who died on
the Morrow of a Bump Supper

Dear Viscount, in whose ancient blood
the blueness of the bird of March
And vermeil of the tufted larch
are fused to one Magenta flood;

Dear Viscount – ah! to me how dear
Who even in thy frolic mood
Discerned (or sometimes thought I could)
The pure proud purpose of a Peer!

So on that last sad night of all
Erect among the reeling rout
You beat your tangled music out
Lofty, aloof, viscontial;

[1]Edwardian slang for a loose woman.

105

You struck a footpath with a can
And with the can you struck the bath;
There on the yellow gravel path
As gentleman to gentleman.

We met, we stood, we faced, we talked
While those of baser birth withdrew:
I told you of an Earl I knew,
You said you thought the wine was corked;

And so we parted: on my lips
A light farewell, but in my soul
The image of a perfect whole –
A Viscount to the finger tips.

An image! yes: but *thou* art gone;
For Nature red in tooth and claw
Subsumes under an equal law
Viscount and Iguanodon.

Yet we who know the larger Love
Which separates the sheep and goats
And segregates scolecobrotes,
Believing where we cannot prove,

Deem that in His mysterious way
God puts the Peers upon His right
And hides the poor in needless night,
For thou, my Lord, art more than they.

(Herbert Maudlin).

To H. T. Baker   Carinthia.
                                                    July/August 1903

I notice you haven't written to me, but I said I would write to you and I will. I
live in a Post Office, and if one lives in a Post Office one is almost bound to
write letters . . . the rest of the party live in a public house about 50 yards
away; there is a marsh between us spanned by a single plank by which in dry
weather a man of good balance can cross dry shod, but you will never manage
it. The baths luckily are in the Post Office . . . I went hunting one day with
Hoppy [Lord Manners]. We slept at a hut in the hills and had each missed a
chamois before 6 a.m. I have just come back from a 4 days mountaineering
expedition – Edward and Katharine [Horner] and Betty [Manners] and
I – We slept two nights at an Alpine hut and one in a most expensive hotel at a
fashionable watering place called Gastein where we enjoyed the company of the

King of Roumania. We walked about ten hours a day, sometimes over snow peaks, sometimes through sweltering valleys. I enjoyed it as much as anything I have ever done, and I daresay you would have done too in spite of the height of the hills and the hardness of the fare.

To Mrs Horner
Slains Castle,
Aberdeenshire.
12 August 1903

Your letter is one of the most charming I have ever had . . .

I must thank you again for the courage and kindly initiative which you have shown toward me: these are qualities which men imitate at Oxford in their cups: but they are rare and the more admirable among water-drinkers of strong intelligence. It is sad to think how many people there are who persist in waiting like violets to be picked: and very fortunate that there are also a few like you who have the charity and skill to turn over the stones under which they hide their silly heads. I suppose that the harvest of desirable men and women is really larger than one suspects, but there is no doubt that the labourers are surprisingly rare. I think it so wonderful of you to trouble yourself about making new friends: the tendency of most people is to stop when they have scraped together a pittance and live on their capital – but of course it is a wasting capital: I am always rather sad when I remember how many friends I have outgrown – people who appealed strongly to some transitory phase in one, and ceased to please when the phase ended: but probably you have been wiser in your original choices, and more constant in your own moods.

I'm glad you find London a change for the worse: it was certainly trying you rather high to put you suddenly between St John [Brodrick] and Buckle: St John always reminds me of the Trojan Horse, and Buckle ought to be eating turnips on a stile in the home counties . . .

I will not tell you much about Slains: the topic is a painful one: there are no grouse and hardly any trout: but it is only 2 miles from a 2nd rate golf course: there are big stables and a collection of pictures of William IV which must be almost complete; but no bathrooms – I rather resent roughing it in a castle – especially when there is a good modern hotel within sight of the windows. It is large, dark, cold, damp and empty – full of the noise of waves and seagulls, bleak but not wild, and uncomfortable without being in the least romantic . . .

To Mrs Horner
Slains Castle, Aberdeen.
7 September 1903

. . . We live a placid life here in very inclement weather – bridge, golf, and fishing. I brought Evan [Charteris] and Miss Barrymore back from Dunrobin, where Winston pursued her with relentless vigour and the most honourable intentions – repeatedly laying his heart and career at her feet: but she would have none of it. She certainly has great beauty, and charm and sense – though Harry thinks her plain. But they are all gone now and succeeded by Colonel Collins, an intelligent soldier of gentlemanly deportment, though somewhat emasculated by contact with the respectable part of our royal family: also Arnold Ward whom you know, and my father's brother who is only as high as Queen Victoria though much cleverer: Pamela Tennant arrives this evening: it will be interesting to see how she and Margot get on: the allegory she wrote in which Margot figures as a princess in a glass house, herself as a beetle beloved by God, and my father as a muscovy duck, has made things a little strained. We have a scandal here to amuse us: Major Hay, a brother of Lord Erroll's, and ex-grenadier, who for some years took refuge from his creditors in the Burmese police, has now come back like a homing pigeon to live at the Kilmarnock Arms in the village, together with a certain Mr and Mrs Hopwood, whom he insisted on bringing with him when we asked him to dinner: Collins vouched for the respectability of Mrs H. whose appearance is mature but meretricious: since then however, she and Hay have been surprised in compromising circumstances in an arbour in the kitchen garden, usually employed by our Fraülein to sleep off a surfeit of raspberries. It was most unlucky for them but has added a great zest to our life: we constantly entertain the trio and gloat over the jealous agonies of Hopwood, a gloomy looking cad who hunts in Cheshire, and is the uncle of Edward Grey's wife . . .

To Lady Manners   10 October 1903

. . . We had a storm yesterday and went out to watch the waves: I ventured too far out on to a rock and was knocked flat on my face against a granite floor by one of the biggest rollers ever seen on this coast: I never felt such a blow: luckily I fell in a crevice and wasn't washed away: but I was stunned for a few seconds, and when I got up my face and knee were streaming with blood. Margot is always splendid on these occasions: she took me back to the house and covered me with ice and raw beef: but in spite of all I am a most revolting sight today and shall be for a week or more – lame in one leg, blind in one eye, and with a nose like Cyrano . . . I'm glad you can't see me: you would never speak to me again. I thought my nose was broken at first, but the bone seems to be alright, though it is swollen and purple like a bloated Emperor, or a big plum . . .

To Mrs Horner   20 Cavendish Square, W.
                                          3 November 1903

. . . I was up till 4 this morning watching Stepney and Cantuar – both drunk – trying to cheat one another at poker; it was a very even match: for tho' Stepney was far more cunning, Cantuar was far less drunk. Such is All Souls Day.

To Katharine Horner   Pixton Park,
                                                    Dulverton.
                                              24 December 1903

I am resolved to give you a Xmas present, so I am sending a book which I happened to bring with me here . . . A great deal of it is very boring and not to be read, but some parts – especially the first half of the poem on Conversation are neat and pointed, and make rather a refreshing contrast to the modern dust-throwing School; you will complain that it is not at all dim or unemphatic, and so little wistful that there is hardly so much as a snipe mentioned from cover to cover: but poor Cowper had a precision of expression which is rare in religious maniacs and rather admirable when one remembers that most of his life was spent in the company of 3 hares and an unattractive woman of 57 . . .

P.S. I enclose a card just received from a friend in the Colonial Office to compensate you for the dullness of Cowper – interesting if you collect autographs: it is the first authentic instance of this handwriting since Tekel Upharsin and shows traces of old age.

[Copy of Post Card.]

Never mind Protection it is ready for all who want it.

                                                      GOD.

To Aubrey Herbert   20 Cavendish Square, W.
                                            6 March 1904

I was very glad to get your letter from Athens – especially because of the assurance in it that you are not going to Japan. If you had gone it is quite certain that you would have been shot: no one I like ever goes to a war without being either killed or wounded; and for you even Peace is quite dangerous enough. In this war I am on the side of the Russians – the only man in England who is I believe: but I can't help feeling that they are made of the same stuff as we, and the Japs aren't; the Russians write books which we like to read, they make music which we like to hear, they paint pictures which we like to see, they live in country houses and play bridge & own serfs: even their religion shares many of the errors of our own: they are more like the English than any other foreign nation: but the Japs have done nothing for thousands of years but write the wrong way round & paint unrecognisable pictures of red mullet on bits of scented paper: they have even abolished their feudalism which was the only attractive thing they had: they are small and yellow & imitative – which is the worst of all the vices to my mind: and just because they wear frock coats and yearn for the factory system our shallow pressmen imagine that they are like the English.

Your letter shows a sad lack of enthusiasm about Athens: you could never have written that jolly poem of Ernest Myers.

"Bear me back across the ages to the years that are no more,
"Give me one sweet month of springtime on the old Saronic shore;
"Not as one who marvels mournful seeing with a sad desire
"Shattered temples, crumbling columns, ashes of a holy fire;
"But a man with men Hellenic doing that which there was done,
"There among the sons of Athens, not a stranger but a son."

But I'm afraid you will never be a Phil-Hellene, Aubrey: if only you had been taught Greek how you would have loved it: it was just what you needed too to make you a great poet, to steady the oscillations of your vagrant fancy & limit the licence of your intemperate vocabulary. However it is better to be too full than too empty, better to die of an apoplexy than of inanition: you have the wine of life & others have the headache . . .

To Aubrey Herbert   Ascott,
                                                                                                                          Wing,
                                                                                                          Leighton Buzzard.
                                                                                                              1 May 1904

. . . your letter was very nice and consoled me in my depression. I think I am too fussy about my health: it is really better than it used to be but seems worse because I try it by higher standards – constantly find myself in situations which make a larger demand on one's vitality & quickness of thought than any which one used to meet. It is the change which comes from living with women & making them the criterion of one's social efficacy instead of men – I suppose it bears in upon every one a sense of his own inadequacy at first: but probably one's nerves & muscles train one into the requisite state of responsiveness with practice. There are several differences which make life with women a more difficult & anxious task than life with men: it is partly that their minds work quicker than ours and on different lines, and there is the effort of accommodating oneself to their methods & their pace which causes a kind of intellectual stitch; and partly the sexual impetus which makes one want to please a woman more than one normally wants to please a man so that one's desire outruns one's ability (which is an unfamiliar situation for most of us): and partly also that the opportunities of pleasing are fewer merely owing to the conditions of social life: & therefore the effort is less diffused & more intense in the slender moments into which it has usually to be condensed: there is no common life at clubs or colleges in which men & women can get so used to one another as to behave quite naturally & so daring as to be dull at the times which destiny appoints for dullness even in the most brilliant of us, and so tolerant as to endure in others these intervals of lethargy with faith & hope & to give credit for activities which are in abeyance, for intelligence which temporarily does not sparkle, for emotion which temporarily does not glow. Men see enough of one another to take a good deal on trust; just as we have all seen enough of the world to believe that a chair goes on existing in the empty room which we have left – perhaps as the good Berkeley thought because God is always looking at it with the corner of his eye even if no one else is: but women see men so little and at such long intervals that their faith in the existence of the non-apparent is necessarily a weak one: the wit that flares and goes out, the passion that breathes & is still may well be accidents incapable of repetition; what guarantee have they that God or anyone else is secretly tending the fires & will blow upon them once more in his own good time? we have doubts about a ship which signals us once & not again, or a meteor which is luminous only in leap year: the ship may be a phantom & the star an opaque body; the signal may be an illusion & the light a freak: they are not things to argue from or build upon. The more transient & occasional are the moments of contact the more emphatic and intense one must make them: the fewer the data of the induction the more damning is the weight of a single negative instance; in the hectic communion of the dinner table, in the scanty and precarious solitudes of a house-party one must express the pith of a month's speculation, the heat of a month's emotion; & if it so happens that one's brain is torpid or one's sensibility for the moment blunt, the fleeting crisis has come & gone & left one discomforted and discredited like a runner whose ear has missed the pistol, with one opportunity irrevocably gone & a heavy mortgage upon the next in the shape of arrears of ill-fame which must be paid in full before one can start level in the subsequent stage of this coxcomb's progress. And it is this effort always to sparkle & always to glow which brings home to one the latent inadequacy of one's vital and mental furniture. Poor Aubrey! I have written you a great dull essay – on a subject too which you can hardly be expected to understand with your perpetual surplusage of physical & spiritual energies. But you will forgive it because it is better than writing about politics or law or commerce or war which are all sufficiently dealt with in the press: & in a way it is personal without being egoistic exactly & therefore a good topic for a letter. It is 2 on Sunday morning so I must stop – a respect one owes to Christian prejudice when staying in the house of a Jew as I am – Leo Rothschild, the greatest master of luxury in our age – perfumed baths, & asparagus in your bedroom, & the Prime Minister to play golf and bridge with.

To Lady Manners   1 July 1904

I knew I should be miserable as soon as I left Avon; and my misery squeezes a Collins out of me as quickly as a confession is wrung out of a coward on the rack. It seems almost impossible now I look back on it that you can have been so good and I so bad – that for all these days I can have taken Katharine away from you without a qualm and you can have borne it without a murmur! But now at any rate you have got her and I haven't, and I see how inconceivably selfish I have been: she has eyes that would draw a limpet off a rock and deaden the conscience of an archangel: and that must be my only plea, though I know well enough it is a bad one, and cannot excuse conduct which was an outrage against you and a sin against her, for it prevented her from giving and you from receiving the joy and comfort to which you must at all times have a stronger claim than I, and at this time more than ever.

You will think all this mere cant and rant: and in a sense it is: because the awful thought comes to me even while I write that I could not trust myself not to do it all over again just as badly as before: all the same it sometimes happens that one sincerely regrets a sin which one obstinately repeats: and the sober truth is, Con, that by being so good as you are you make it terribly easy for others to be as bad as I am. You put yourself and your sorrow[1] so much out of sight and show such a whole hearted interest in the fortunes of others that it tempts us all to go on our way in happiness and half forgetfulness of your constant pain and the marvellous effort by which you efface the appearance of it. You were encouraging me all the time to be happy at your expense, to drink up the springs of your consolation and warm myself at the fire which is lit for you – and now when I see what I have done all I can offer you in compensation is a kind of death-bed repentance which is to give me my sin and the pardon for it by a single sneaking manoeuvre.

But you have Katharine to yourself now and I know how sweet and dear you will find her now that there is no me to tar her against her will with the brush of my own selfishness. Frances told me in the train that you were so miserable last night, and when I remember what a happy talk I was having on the terrace with Katharine, I blush with shame: but you will at least not let her suffer in your opinion for a fault of imagination that was altogether mine. And some day later on perhaps you will let me come down again to Avon when you are alone and I can give you anything that is worth having in myself without taking away from you, as I have done so cruelly this time, what is so infinitely more worth having in another. Forgive me, Con, if you can for all my abominable wickedness and remember my temptations.

---

[1] At the death of her eldest daughter.

To Lady Manners
Terling Place,
Witham,
Essex.
2 July 1904

. . . If I ever become a religious person it will be in quite a different way and for different reasons: it will be because of an imperative claim which I can't help making on the universe that the facts shall correspond to my will: that a desire for something intrinsically good should be for ever unsatisfied seems to me unbearable – and may one day I suppose seem unbelievable.

It consoles me to be able to sit down and write to you: it is the first pleasant thing I have done in this great ugly uncomfortable laboratory, full of radium and adenoids and Lytteltons . . . [J.B.S.] Haldane has repeated to me verbatim a conversation which I had with him 3 weeks ago as to the effect of carbon monoxide on white mice, and I haven't spoken to Katharine even languidly, on any topic at all . . .

To K. H.
20 Cavendish Square, W.
23 July 1904

. . . I would rather find a letter from you than a scroll of Sappho among the Pyramids. I hoped for a moment that it might be the Philippine, but then I remembered the dingy little books I ordered for you. It is most dear of you to thank me for them so sweetly – I only wish I had something to offer you that was worth your taking. You know how I would like to give you the whole world if it were mine, and the sun and moon and all the stars: And two buckram books seem a poor symbol of the present I make you every day in my soul. But I'm glad you like the essay on Rossetti and look forward to discussing it with you when the dim day of our next meeting comes round, if ever God lets it. The others I fear may very likely bore you. I can recommend the first half of the one on Virgil – and the Marcus Aurelius is well done in spite of the intolerable tedium of the theme: and perhaps you will like Mazzini because I think he is one of your odd heroes – like Kropotkin: but you must on no account read the one on Greek oracles which is full of unimportant things – But Myers always has a certain distinction of style and a wonderful sensitiveness to that mysterious margin of twilight feelings which Wordsworth and Virgil understood in their different degrees. But I am rambling about things which do not matter.

Yes, the ball was a wretched business and leaves me still humpy and angry. . . . you must be almost ashamed to be loved by such a feckless unhandy kind of oaf – my only excuse is that I have never much wanted before to have lonely talk with a woman and so I have no tricks. I ought to have fallen in love with someone like Margot who would find a solitary and peaceful nook in the

Black Hole of Calcutta . . . Still, it is a comfort to me as I told you at the time that you were in such a great mood of beauty and I can call up in lonely moments the lovely shape of your head which I deliberately fixed by study in my imagination where it still lasts . . .

To K. H.

Dalquharran Castle,
Dailly, N.B.
8 August 1904

O, Katharine, Katharine how can you be so hard and wicked and unkind to me? You are completely wicked all through in your head and in your heart from your magical hair down to the silver buckle on your contemptuous instep. There is not one jot of goodness in you anywhere and not one tittle of badness left out. Think of your sins while there is time and repent: think of your irreverence, think of your pride, and above all think of your cruelty – your black unappeasable and in-any-one-else-unforgivable cruelty and then your hypocrisy too – that is almost the worst of all: your vile pretence of sympathy with slugs and your gentleness with wounded beetles – and then your ruthless wanton cruelty to me who – in God's sight at least – am more than many beetles. It is monstrous that your eyes should be full of tenderness and imagination and that your lips should have the exquisite curve of sensibility and that your brow should be low and white and wonderfully moulded into a radiant promise of simplicity and sweetness – and then that it should all be an empty and deceitful symbolism and nothing behind it but the loving kindness of a tigress and the warmth of newts and adders! Oh why why won't you write to me? You faithfully promised me you would, but perjury is a slender addition to the list of your abominations.

. . . [send me] Just one paragraph of scolding, with leave perhaps at the end of it to write to you again in 10 days and tell you of my bag on the 12th and why Rufus Isaacs didn't have a bigger majority at Reading, and what I think of the friendship of Diderot and D'Alembert – you might have done that much your pride and prejudice notwithstanding you really might: but you didn't think it worth while: or did Con persuade you that it was wrong? or – most likely of all – have you been too much taken up with encouraging the advances of this damned fat indolent Count your mother tells me of? . . .

To K. H.

9 August 1904

At last the letter which I longed for has come and I was most delighted to get it – so delighted that though I wrote you a rather fantastic letter less than 24 hours ago I can't help sitting down to write you another now which I hope may be more to your taste, less fanciful and unbalanced, more sober, sensible and full of information.

You will like to know no doubt about our house and the way we live. The castle is plainly but tastefully built of a pleasing whitish stone with crenellated turrets and slits in them to fire arrows through: it stands on a slight eminence above the river Girvan which flows into the Atlantic Ocean about 5 miles off at the town from which it takes or to which it gives its name . . . The rooms are large and well shaped but poorly furnished and infamously decorated – though the library contains some fine Raeburns and a Kneller of the usual type. There are 5 reception rooms, 24 bedrooms, kitchen, 4 bathrooms, offices etc. But there are no beds in the bedrooms, no water in the bathrooms, no fire in the kitchens, no officers in the offices, and no one to receive or be received in the reception rooms. Margot has put up a green tent of great architectural beauty (it can be had for £11.10 from the military stores in Savile Row) in the gardens, and there she sleeps at night, while the rest of us rough it in the Castle.

There are two fine hunters in the stables which we ride when the weather is suitable, and we enjoy sporting rights over a considerable acreage of the adjacent country. Our groom is stone deaf and our keeper's son has recently become insane which adds to the interest and excitement of a life in itself sufficiently thrilling. We speak sometimes to the groom through a megaphone or communicate with him by means of the motor horn; and at dusk 3 or 4 guns go out to try and get a shot at the keeper's son about flighting time. There are salmon, sea trout and brown trout in the river and Beb yesterday caught one of 5 lbs: we shot a few duck there this morning but were disappointed in finding only 7 of the 70 snipe which the keeper had promised us: you will be anxious to learn what are the prospects from the moors, and I must confess that the news we have is somewhat conflicting – some authorities predicting a record year while others hold that it will be no more than average.

. . . There is a golf course about 4 miles beyond Girvan which is easily accessible by motor: the fastest time we have done so far is 21½ minutes but it takes somewhat longer owing to the unfavourable nature of the gradients. The course is said by many to be the best in Ayrshire but when you remember that the county also contains Prestwick and Troon you may be forgiven for doubting this: in my own opinion – which I give you for what it is worth – it suffers from 2 cardinal defects: in the first place it has no short hole – no hole I mean which *you* could reach with your cleek from the tee: and secondly, it is extremely uneven – by which I mean that the hard holes are too hard and the easy holes too easy. But we have really no right to complain and I would rather play on it than at Perugia or Upper Tooting. We play bridge at night – often till 2 in the morning: and during those parts of the day – somewhat exiguous parts I fear – which are not devoted to sport I do a little desultory reading.

The library is a fine one, containing as it does several back numbers of the *Edinbro' Review* and a complete edition of Sir Walter – always a favourite with me as I think you know: he has not the wit of Dickens, nor the ease of Thackeray, nor the high purpose of George Eliot, nor the minute delicacy of Miss Austen, but when all is said and done there is a broad humanity about him, a naturalness, a geniality, an insight into humble character and a command of humble idiom which puts to shame your modern scribbler such as Meredith – who always seems to me I confess to be a kind of unhealthy mixture between a snob and a contortionist thinly veiling adulation of the upper classes by the disingenuous obscurity of his style. He lacks certainly the true epic note which I find in Scott: in reading him I always have the feeling that I am dealing with an English gentleman, don't you? though of course he was really Scotch. But I should like some day to have a good long talk with you about books. I feel sure we should agree. We are both rather old fashioned aren't we? But I have left barely a page for politics which I know you dote on.

To K. H.   17 August 1904

. . . The lonely sheet of abuse which you have sent me for a letter this morning deepens my growing gloom: it is the letter of a bully: if I were a woman I should turn: but I am only a coward so I don't. On the contrary I do exactly as you bid me – and that, without the solace of thinking that you care a straw whether I do or not. I retract everything disagreeable I have ever said to you and I repeat and multiply and intensify everything agreeable – if I have ever said anything agreeable. As to your growing old and ugly – that was a mere rhetorical flourish: you could no more do it than a square could grow into a circle or an egg into an oak tree. And as to your being cruel and proud and faithless and hard – I take all that back too – back enough that is for me to be allowed to see you and hear from you again – but with mental reservations and in the same sense as an ambitious and enlightened priest repeats the creeds for the sake of a Bishopric . . .

To K. H.   Enoch Station Hotel,
Glasgow.
24 September 1904

. . . How I wished when we reached Boulogne that you and I were going to cross the channel in a gondola with no bother about turning round at the Rialto and just a single *avanti* to last us over 30 miles of water. But even the channel is absurdly narrow: couldn't we some day go to Tasmania in a gondola? Last night in my train bed I dreamed again and again that we were still on the Grand Canal and I stretched out my hand to you, but could never find yours though I knew all the time you were there, and each time I woke up with a feeling that I was going to have a very bad headache all the rest of my life. Perhaps you were lying in your bed at Ravenna and deciding that you would make yourself more remote . . .

To Mrs Horner
Dalquharran Castle,
Dailly, N.B.
28 September 1904

I passed through Glasgow on my way here and couldn't help noticing how different it was from Venice, and even now I am snugly back in my castle, small differences keep on striking me . . .

. . . What a pity there is no Epistle of Paul to the Venetians! It would have been a great opportunity for him: you remember his very stiff Collins to the Corinthians: it was his metier to stay with people and enjoy himself very much and then write to say how very wicked their way of life was. I feel sure I could have kept several of the commandments at Corinth, but Venice would enervate a Lyttelton . . .

But all this is nonsense, and I do want to thank you, dear Frances, more than I can possibly express for the heavenly time you have given me this last 4 weeks. It has been a dream of delight from beginning to end and you have made it go as smoothly – and alas as quickly – as a dream . . .

30 September 1904

Dear Miss Horner
Once more you are not being very kind to me, and my last spiky letter had such a success by your own confession that I am sorely tempted to write another on the same lines: but alas I have lost the power even to yield to temptation when it goes against your wishes: you have so often in the last month made me retract things which I knew were true and repeat the contrary of them that I have lost all shame and dare not even tell the truth or act it for fear of being made to unsay it or undo it the next instant. And after all why should I be ashamed of that? Galileo recanted under the compulsion of pains far slighter than your displeasure a truth of which he was far surer than I am of anything in the world . . .

It looked so fat and it felt so fat – that deceptive envelope of yours -- and I believe even you would have been touched if you had been able to see the delighted anticipation with which I stowed it away in my pocket to read and rejoice in at leisure, and the almost tearful gloom of the denouement when the whited sepulchre was opened and disclosed nothing but a ravening wolf. (Forgive me for using so inelegant a mixture of Biblical tags but it reminds me of all the new things you told me about the Bible, and of all kinds of delightful talks we had in delightful places about Saints and Basilisks and other things which never existed or will) . . .

To K. H.   7 October 1904

. . . Fortunately or not I get back a little of my reason when I leave you. I too have had a letter from Con, in which she says of you and me "temperaments not circumstances will be the bar to your ultimate happiness – and that is harder to overcome". What do you say to it? it seems rather hard to be diagnosed at a glance and definitely ruled out of life as an incurable, doesn't it? If she is right perhaps it would be worth while one of us making an alteration, shall we draw lots to see which is to change the spots? . . .

To K. H.   Breamore, Salisbury.
                                                         October 1904

. . . The shooting is good here, but the company so bad that more than 3 days of it would make me insane: perhaps less than 3 days will: so will you promise to be very sweet to me for the few hours at Mells before they come to shut me up? The downs were so divine today with the yew trees and berries of all possible colours, that I could hardly bear to look at the partridges instead: and indeed you nearly had an "autumn letter" from me – all about tints and splashes – only just not: it was touch and go for a little . . .

When I got to Salisbury yesterday and found no train I was in 2 minds whether to walk on to Mells. I believe I could have got there by midnight – perhaps in time to find your window still yellow. And then you might have come down and let me in as you did once at Clovelly . . .

To K. H.   Panshanger,
                                                         Hertford.
                                                     12 November 1904

. . . I think what makes me really write to you now is the feeling of emptiness that I had after Friday night. I expected too much I suppose. It is a mistake ever to expect much of London. But some days when I have been with you I come away happy and satisfied, even though very little has been said; last night I had a feeling of gloom and futility – of barren and disconnected talk, like the crackling of thorns under a pot and the sense of a thin dream-conference in which you were real while I was a shadow – of wheels revolving without advancing, purposeless motion in a vacuum without grip or progress – And yet you were very real indeed – more beautiful than ever, but more than ever inexorably yourself – remote elusive and unattainable. But of course I am making heroics out of nothing. What real communication is possible in the middle of family silences only tempered by Herbert Jekyll's snores? Still, that doesn't make the emptiness any less empty – nor does it exhaust the whole grievance against fate which is always in the back of my mind, though it may account for a single evening's failure. For I do honestly believe, though it's probably foolish to say it, that if we were in a desert island I could make you love me, and that makes me resent all the more obstructive facts and conventions of our little bit of the world which are none the less real for being totally artificial . . .

To K. H.
Penrhos,
Holyhead.
20 November 1904

. . . Blanche Stanley asked me many questions about you at dinner – I said you were in my opinion good looking, intelligent and shy. Was that right? I had the same feeling I have when Lady Sassoon says to me "Don't you think Plato an interesting philosopher?" She – B. Stanley – said to me what everyone who speaks of you says – as I told you the other night – that all girls – like all men – long to know you well because you are so beautiful, but are puzzled how to do it because you are so uncommon and remote. But if you dislike me dwelling so much on your elusiveness I will remember not to do it . . .

I will stop now because it is 2 on Sunday morning and I am tired and shooting loosens the brain from the skull and makes it roll about when one moves one's head . . .

To K. H.
20 Cavendish Square, W.
21 November 1904

. . . It is only the humility of those who would be mad if they weren't humble that has an insipid and ungracious nature: but yours has a very different flavour – because it is the splendid irrational excellence – a thing for which there is no reason or origin except the dim presentiment which is at the back of all tragedies and all religions that the race is not to the swift nor the battle to the strong, that brightness drops from the air and that the world is full of strange accidents, and unconquerable perversities.

I know very well the feeling that makes one say a thing out in order to push it away from one. I think it is partly a kind of sacrifice to fortune – an anticipatory propitiation of the malignity of God – the same reason that makes a man throw his ring into the sea. That sounds as if it were mere caution and timidity: but it is a much more complicated and mystical thing than that, and the same person who quails before the uncertainty of fate will go swaggering into a den of lions with pure arrogance: because both things come from despising the law of probabilities, which we all do in our best moments and should always if only we could shake off the original taint of mathematics, which came into Adam after the fall. But though I love your unreasonable fears I hate to think that they should give you any real concern: and unless you were ill, I don't think they would. I am not tired of you yet, Katharine, and I believe I shall not be for a little while still – perhaps till we are both so old that we are tired of everything. Indeed my fear takes a different direction – that I shall not have time to get tired of you – time and opportunity – before I die. Everything else I shall at least have a chance of exhausting, but not you . . .

To K. H.

1 Paper Buildings,
Temple,
London, E.C.
26 November 1904

. . . I don't think I shall have time to come to see you this evening as I am very busy constructing a defence for a lady called Katharine, who is accused of fraud. But I have thought of another plan. This is it. I was going to Taplow tomorrow, but I have found out that the King is going, and as it gives me a sick feeling to be in a house with even minor royalties I am writing to Mrs Grenfell to say that she must let me off. Of course if she says it makes her number uneven I shall have to go. But I fancy it will be all right. That being so, my Sunday is free and I propose to take the sea-air somewhere on the South coast. What is the station for Rottingdean? and is there a tolerable inn there? and if there is what is it called? and am I likely to be able to get a room there? and if I did would there be any chance of my being able to meet you somewhere on the downs and go for a walk? or would you be too closely looked after by that funny little woman? or would Baker be there at the inn? or would he walk over from Brighton?

Will you let me know by return the answer to these questions? and particularly about the station and the inn: because I should be inclined to risk some of the others.

Is there any chance of my seeing you at Lady H. Bentinck's dinner tonight or at the Fitzwilliams' ball? . . .

To K. H.

All Souls College,
Oxford.
3 December 1904
Very late

. . . It is certain that one gets a faith and illumination from love which puts peremptorily aside the reasoned observation of colder brains. Only today I lunched with a clever man whom I hate, who says and sincerely thinks the most horrible things about women, and admits no exceptions in his doctrines: but I found that his words fluttered round the room like dead leaves and never made an entry into my brain at all – though he was plausible enough and circumstantial and full of instances and inductions – but all the time I was thinking of the light in your eyes, and the grace of your figure as we sat in the drawing room on Thursday, and his theories seemed such dim and thin illusions that I could not even consider them or reply at all . . .

At the play I thought of you all the time because as you know the Shrew is called Katherine, and some of the lines startled or shocked or delighted me by the odd contexts in which they put your name. There is one bit that Lady Brownlow would have liked – where the Shrew says very haughtily "They call me Katherine who speak of me" and Petruchio answers "No: Kate: plain Kate!" But it made me quite angry when she was beaten and bullied and starved by her great fat brutal husband, so that once or twice I nearly interfered – "What man would dare to woo *curst* Katherine" says one of the men.

Do you think your father will make a rule that you mustn't marry anyone till Cicely is married? Most of the play is at Padua, and I thought I recognised in the painted scene the place where we bought fruit that day when the Arena was shut up and I was so poor-spirited about climbing the wall, and you so perverse about sitting on the railway lines when the train was coming. Do you remember? How far off it is! and how spoilt I was in those days! It seems unbelievable to me now that there ever should have been a time when I could sit on a sunny balcony with you all the morning and by a shady moat with you all the afternoon, and then ride back with you through a starry valley at night, or lounge in a gondola with no Jekyll to interrupt our talk by snores and no anxious hostess to re-arrange her guests at absurdly short intervals of time.

O Katharine when I look back at what I have written I feel that you must think the last part vapid and rambling, and the first part common or pompous – just as I showed you my bad poem last time we were long apart, so now I show you the bad silly parts of myself. I won't ask you to forgive it – only to remember that one doesn't give oneself away except to a person to whom one would give everything else in the world as well . . .

To K. H.

Hatfield House,
Hatfield,
Herts.
6 December 1904

Thank you for your beloved letter. It comforts me for a mass of small afflictions. By an odd accident it was opened by Dick Cavendish, as the butler brought it to him among his own letters, but he tells me he only read the first two words, and he is such a good fellow that I would as soon he read my letters as anyone . . .

This is, to my mind, about the nicest house in England, it is full of very nice people and I don't want to leave it a bit and the only thing which could make me want to leave it is seeing you, and that's exactly what I shan't do . . .

To K. H.   Tring Park,
                                                                            Tring.
                                                                 14 January 1905

. . . I have been reminded of you – if I needed a reminder – by 2 separate things today – first by Botticelli's madonna with the red eyelids which I went to see after lunch in the National Gallery – it is beautiful but I'm not sure that it is the redness of the eyelids that makes it so – and her eyes are quite secular compared with yours; poor Botticelli was aiming at you when he made those big spaces in all his women between the eyebrow and the eye but he never quite succeeded, and it has taken God 400 years working steadily with many failures and corrections on a painter's hints to produce at last in flesh the divine type which Botticelli conceived but could never quite express . . .

To K. H.   1 Paper Buildings,
                                                                           Temple,
                                                                     London, E.C.
                                                                 20 January 1905

. . . I like you to complain when it implies that you care for me or my letters. Damn me as much as you like if only you like me as much as you damn me. And your explanation of my not having written – that perhaps I had met someone else – is even feebler. I had met someone else: I am always meeting someone else: that is just the trouble: if only I were always meeting you! that would be a really good reason for not writing – because then I could be speaking instead. It is an insufferable inconvenience not always living in the same house with you, and one I find it increasingly hard to endure. And to think that Bowlby is actually doing it now! walking with you on the cow hill or still more likely reading the Bible to you in an attic! O Katharine dear, it is not to be borne. And he even jumps gates better than I do. It is the thing he does best in fact. They made him a master at Eton because of it . . .

To Lady Manners   20 Cavendish Square, W.
                                                                 29 January 1905

. . . But I suppose John [her son] has gone back to school by now, and you will soon be coming up to town again. It wasn't his house [at Eton], was it, that was burnt out the other day? I was dining with the Sassoons that night and a telegram arrived from the little Philip to say that he wasn't hurt, but that there had been a smell in his room and he had poured a bucket full of eau de cologne over the floor and made it alright again.

I'm glad you like *The Grey World* – I haven't begun it yet – and indeed have read very little but law books lately – only two old novels which I was assured were full of genius and impropriety – *Madame Bovary* by Flaubert and *Moll Flanders* by Defoe – but I can find very little of either in them, and was much bored by both . . .

To Lady Manners   30 January 1905

. . . I think I wrote to you from Killerton which I hated, but since then I have had a very pleasant holiday. Two days at Pixton, where Aubrey went shooting in silk stockings on a white pony – and then at Hartham for Xmas and a week after. You've probably heard all about that party from lots of people – I enjoyed it very much in spite of Winston making a political speech which lasted without intermission for 8 days. He was the autocrat – not only of the breakfast table – but of the lunch, tea, dinner, bridge and billiard tables: and Jack considers it bad form for anyone to interrupt him. Then I was snowed up for 3 days at Asquith House[1], and after that I had 4 days at Belvoir and 2 balls, in which Marjorie [Manners] just saved me from dying of weariness. I think she is a little frightened there by her precarious position in the household, which makes her more human and attractive than she is in more commanding situations – she interests me a good deal – she is so puzzling, illusory, impalpable, whimsical and dissatisfied – a mixture between a monkey and a moonbeam – I doubt if anyone will ever be much in love with her, but she is a capital companion . . .

I've just come back from Mile End where I heard the poll declared – H. Lawson in by 76. It has been a most comic election, neither of the candidates could make up their minds whether they would get more votes by boldly confessing that they were Jews, or by still more boldly professing that they were Christians. But the event has proved a victory for the Church . . .

To K. H.   20 March 1905

. . . You were to have sat between John Fortescue and BRON at dinner, which would have made you all right I know, and Bron was so handsome and delightful. He came home with me and has been here talking till now – almost 2 in the morning. He told me that his life was perfectly happy, and only 3 things worried him at all – his sister being a theosophist, and the prospect of

---

[1] Margot's hunting box at Melton Mowbray.

certainly having a title and probably having a wife! So I feel rather easier in my mind about those violets – though heaven knows if *you* wanted him to have a wife his objections would vanish quickly enough! . . .

To K. H.   8 April 1905

. . . Shall I tell you what I have done since I saw you? It is very boring, but perhaps I'd better so that you can have no excuse for not telling me every step you've taken, and every word you've spoken or heard or written or read.

All yesterday I was in Court – 5 hours – at the end of which we won our case, in spite of our chief witness having delirium tremens. Then I dined with the Sydney Buxtons – Mrs Buxton whom I like has red hair and pale blue eyes and had put on a green velvet dress with the object of looking like Beata Beatrix but with the result of looking like a rather plain mermaid. (This is blood: I have cut my finger and may very likely bleed to death: it won't stop: I wish you were here to tie it up). Then I took in a nice Germanish woman called Baroness D'Erlanger – rather pretty and clever: but I talked stupidly to her and also to Lady Helen Shaw Stewart who was on my other side – like a good tempered horse: she rested her nice cold nose on the nape of my neck and looked at me out of the side of her head.

I repeated 3 conversations which I remembered having had with other women of the same appearance in 1902 and from stories which Margot told me when I was 15: and while she was still laughing at them as if her heart would break I went to sleep: when I woke up the women had gone away and I found myself sitting next to Herbert Jekyll and talking rather brightly about the Tramways Act 1870. Then we went upstairs and I talked very brilliantly for 70 minutes to Lady Solomon (whose husband is a colonial statesman), first about cynicism and then about the curious fact that in Surrey there are trees but no water and in Lancashire water but no trees: I sign my full name in case you have forgotten it.

Raymond Asquith

and the address is at the top of each sheet.

To K. H.   1 Paper Buildings,
                                                                          Temple,
                                                                    London, E.C.
                                                                    11 April 1905

. . . I have finished *Peter Ibbetson* and was disappointed to the end. It is nice to think of two people enjoying themselves so much as that: but the Duchess got rather dowdy and philanthropic and I don't like her having holes in her gloves: then it is very boring where they make friends with their great-great-grandmother and I nearly died of fatigue when they actually got back to the

Mammoth: you might as well make love in the South Kensington Museum: it shows they were getting tired of one another: and then all that nonsense about metaphysics at the end – as silly as Hegel but not so well expressed. I'm afraid we must differ about this book as we do about Hector, unless you can over-persuade me (by fair means) when we meet – But there is one place where he says "It seems that I was fated to fall down and prostrate myself before very tall slender women with dark hair and lily skins and light angelic eyes – Fortunately for me it is not a common type". I agree with that – though perhaps it is an insult to call your eyes light or angelic – I don't think I know what to call them except holy. I am pleased with that word.

I have tried in vain to dream as they did: but with the most horrible results: last night I dreamed first about the law of mortgages and then that a woman called Mrs Algy Grosvenor said to someone in my hearing that I was so repulsively ugly that she couldn't think how anyone could endure to be in the same room with me.

I have just come across rather a nice thing in an old law book – a case of Charles II's time about whether a husband must pay for things which his wife orders – the judge said "Again, if such cruelty shall be sanctioned and wives shall not be allowed necessaries, England will lose the happy reputation in all foreign kingdoms which her inhabitants have achieved by their respect for their sex, the most excelling in beauty, which, as in this climate it far transcends that of the women in all other lands, so has this Kingdom surpassed all other countries in its tenderness and consideration for their welfare."

. . . I had a nice evening with Maurice [Baring] who remained in excellent form till nearly 4 in the morning and we didn't get to bed till later than that because Maurice said there was one cab in London with three wheels and we must find it to go home in. But we never did.

. . . and last night I dined with 20 rather drunken young men and afterwards went – heavens knows why – to a ball where I had supper with the beautiful Miss Hozier[1] – She is beautiful – She must be. Otherwise how could I have spent 40 minutes talking to her? For she is certainly nothing else.

Tonight is my play-party . . . I believe I shall faint in the middle from sheer sadness – O how I wish it were just you and I sitting down on those hard chairs in the dining room at Mells to a simple meal of lettuces and cheese and a new moon and no rule about going to bed at eleven. I need such a lot of you just now to bring back happiness and purity out of all this muddiness which makes me hate myself so dreadfully. And instead I am looking through a window grimy with soot and rain at a lot of ugly people moving drearily about an ugly street – and then a vulgar dinner and a vulgar play – and at least one companion whom you think vulgar! Please make a purifying sacrifice for me with bitter herbs and salt and fire, so that I shall not be quite unrecognisably gross and horrible when we meet at Avon . . .

[1] Afterwards Mrs Winston Churchill.

To **K. H.**

Hôtel Windsor,
Dinard.
20 April 1905

The wild folly of leaving England, of ever doing one's duty, of ever living with one's family and of ever doing what they tell me to do and not doing what you tell me to do, is terribly clear to me at this moment. I have been miserable both in mind and body since the first moment I lost sight of your face on the drive at Avon, but never so irretrievably miserable as now.

My father and I motored for 3 days from Dieppe in bitter bitter cold along indescribably straight roads, stretched like pieces of white tape along a counter, through indescribably dull country – with every sort of accident, persecuted by God and man, bursting tires in a hailstorm, running short of petrol in a desert, pulled up and detained for hours by officials because our chauffeur had no birth certificate nor any photograph of his absurd cockney face – and finally we arrived here at 9 tonight cold and tired and hungry to find a snow-swept watering place with bad overcrowded golf links 3 miles away and squalid rooms with oil stoves and match-box walls in an hotel full of Jews, hunting women, hunted men, and all the congested vulgarity of Leicestershire, Park Lane and Bayswater.

Cis has been already turned off the golf links for insulting an aged member of the club, and Violet and Oc (who have come straight from Venice, from lying in Francesco's gondola and eating pink risotto in our smuggler's cabin by the Frari) quite in the abyss of despair. And the most damnable part of all is that the place is a lobster pot: we are in fact cut off from getting out. We thought of going to Jersey but there is no boat till today week: nor owing to the Vacances de Paques is there even a boat to Southampton till Tuesday night 25th. Isn't it *awful?* I am going to try and find out tomorrow if I can't get a boat on Monday from Cherbourg, but even so there are probably no trains to take me there. O Katharine, when shall I ever see you again? and how can I possibly live through it? And then I must tell you a thing which makes me hate the French till the blood spurts out of my fingernails.

We got to St Malo at 5.30 in the motor: it is separated from Dinard by an estuary about a mile wide over which boats run once an hour. We waited till 6.30 when the last boat was to go over, and the little stoat of a man who commanded her decided after some reflection that it was so rough that he couldn't go again! a boat mind you in which you or I would willingly have gone to America – or even Tasmania . . . No wonder they lost the battle of Trafalgar. We had to drive round 50 or 60 miles by land. How I loathe the French.

. . . I believe one of the things that is making me unhappy and ashamed is the terrible unrestraint of the letter I wrote you last night which I fear you may think very laughable: but when the thinking part of my mind is dull (as it always is) and tired (as it was then) and yet the recollecting part is a crowded treasury of very lovely images, the result must always be a little like that. And then comes your dear quiet little letter and makes me hot all over to see how all the love that *should* be put on paper can be put there quite simply and beautifully with no rhetoric or rouge or circus tricks . . .

To K. H.   Dungeon Ghyll New Hotel,
                                                          Langdale,
                                                          Ambleside.
                                                      10 June 1905

. . . How I longed to have you by me when I went out for my walk this evening. It was chilly but very beautiful, and I would have been a good comrade to you and made you put on a cloak – not your white one because to look like a white peacock is not appropriate here, but only where there are yew hedges: I think you should have the one that makes you look like a beautiful married woman. It is light longer here than with you: and first of all the sun made a braid of lemon coloured fire along the crinkled edges of the hills which stand like a steep wall at the head of this valley: and then a cuckoo made noises in the echoing folds of the mountains under a cold northern moon: and at last a kind of sacred stillness came with no sound but a very far off sheep bell. And then I came back and read a book called *Hieroglyphics* by a man called Machen, whom I think I have told you of: he usually writes weird and terrible books which I admire, but I believe you said you didn't: but this one is a literary essay: I think you would agree with it – quite clever but not first-rate – saying that the hall-mark of great literature is what he calls "ecstasy" – a sense of the mystery behind appearances, which he finds both in the *Odyssey* and in *Pickwick* – which sounds silly – but his quotations from *Pickwick* – not the parts customarily regarded as funny, but bits about snowstorms and clouds and winds – and it makes me see what he means and inclines me to agree – especially as he rules out Thackeray, Jane Austen, and George Eliot by his principle. Much of it is mediocre but some quite excellent. I will give you the book. I will give you everything . . .

To K. H.   Prince of Wales Hotel,
                                                           Grasmere.
                                                       13 June 1905

. . . I walked up Helvellyn today – a big but easy mountain and lost my temper with the North West wind which buffeted me and pushed me off the path in quite a sudden human way like a policeman till I nearly cried from impotent rage: and finally it took my green hat roughly from my hand and hurled it down a precipice. I was tired and meant to leave it there: but then I remembered you liked it so I climbed laboriously down and recovered it.

Darling, you are wrong to say I don't think of you on my walks. I think of you the whole time: today I tried in the wind to make a poem about you – contrasting mediaeval you with hard polished modern Paris, but it came so badly that I gave up. I wish I could write a poem about you: you deserve so many and such good ones: but I haven't got a grain of art in me from head to heel and you must be content to love me as a clod if you can love me at all. I meant to write to you about sentiment but I am so terribly tired that I will do it another time or never.

Pamela [Tennant] has asked me to Wiltshire on 16th July: couldn't you insist on going? at present the party consists of Winston and Lady Vera [Herbert]: he will probably strangle her in the first 10 minutes and then there will only be one lady to three men . . .

To K. H.

Sandycroft,
Littlestone-on-Sea.
19 June 1905

Thank you a thousand times for your dear letter from Paris which I found awaiting me here this morning – you are quite quite wrong to say that you can't express things adequately: you say to me most simply and beautifully things precious enough to ransom the world, and so long as you can say them truly I like them better that way than with any quantity of embroidery and verbiage and your clean way of leaving all that out is what I call your reticence and what I love – partly because I am afraid my temptation lies the other way. I can't even write to you about a sunset without making all kinds of tame phrases . . .

I thought a little about sentimentalism when I paused to take breath among the boulders, and it seemed to me that a large department of the vice consists just in this. I mean in giving rash intemperate inadequate inept expression to an emotion which may be genuine enough in its way: it is often a fault of art more than a fault of the heart: pictures like "The Soul's Awakening" (if you are lucky enough to know it) and books like "The Choir Invisible" and letters like Bowlby's come in this class: perhaps it is all obvious: but some people think that it is always the hollowness or triviality of the emotion itself (apart from the form in which it is exhibited) that makes sentimental things absurd. I tried in a rough way to think out the whole subject for myself and some day when I have time I shall write an Essay on it: I should like to make a Platonic dialogue of it but I shall never have enough time for that: there would be 3 characters – Bowlby, the real sentimentalist, myself a kind of doubter (who would of course come out best of the argument) and you, who are not at all a sentimentalist but, on second thoughts, what I now call a 'romantic' for want of a better term: there would be a picture of you as a frontispiece and some very pretty speeches (spoken by me) describing the beauty of your face and nature. No: you are certainly not a sentimentalist, and *Tristan* is not a sentimental book! You are quite right about that. It is like you – romantic. By a romantic I mean a person of most lofty and ardent nature – a person who is gloriously blind to prudential considerations, practical obstacles, low explanations, of high things; so much convinced of the strength and truth of his own emotions and of the overbalancing value of them as to believe that all the weight of the matter and evil must kick the beam against them: feeling so strongly and so deeply the divine spark in passion as to be almost insensible to the physical and wasting basis of it – never deceived about the quality of his emotion which is always pure gold and never dross, but never quite admitting that even the purest gold is a volatile and evanescent element subject to all the mortal processes of attrition and decay which menace baser materials – never I mean sensible to the most daunting of all facts that intensity is no guarantee of permanence – you remember the lines which I have in mind of Polonius to poor Ophelia.

> "For Hamlet and the trifling of his favour
> "Hold it as fashion and a toy in blood,
> "A violet in the primy youth of nature,
> "Forward not permanent, sweet not lasting,
> "The perfume and suppliance of a minute,
> "No more!"

and some verses of Shelley's – you will know where they come from, I don't –

> "When passion's trance is overpast,
> "If tenderness and truth could last
> "And live, while all dark passions keep
> "A mortal slumber long and deep.
> "I should not weep, I should not weep."

I have got it wrong, but it is something like that. This type rushes to picturesque extremes and absolute conclusions: it says "We are in love: let us fly together! We are oppressed: let us be anarchists" and is always putting theoretical syllogisms into practice with courage and unhappiness: either he takes the world for an ideal republic, and sees in it the reflected glamour of his own glowing state and believes that it must accommodate itself to the full stature of his aspirations or he realises the harsh and unmalleable nature of things, refuses to make any compromise with it, and sets up the frail and fiery standard of his dreams in hopeless rebellion against the invincible constitution of the universe. Like your dear Celts they go forth to battle and they always fall. I could write much more and much better about the romantics, but I am falling into the prize essay manner, and also my father and Jack Tennant are talking politics so loud that I cannot follow my thoughts. It is a great bore because I wanted to write you a really long nice letter, and especially to find out more of what you mean when you say you live in a grey world.

You make yourself out to be only "the shadow of an angel with bright hair" but you are much more than that to me. You are everything in the world – as vivid and wonderful as a woman can be.

Write to me again and tell me more clearly what you mean – I must stop now because of the lateness – it is two – and the noise, which is unbearable. I went last night when I was alone in London passing through, to see Tree's play. Viola looked very pretty and charming in her rotten part and I went to see her afterwards and left her with a kind of baffled interest which I always feel in her. I go back to London and work on Monday.

Write to me, write to me, write to me, beloved. With much unsaid, good-night.

RAYMOND

I started out to put this letter in the pillar box so that it should catch the early post: and read it through before sealing it and I see it is so hollow and stilted and absurd (the result of constant interrupting) that I only send it because it may challenge an answer – if only of disgust.

O, Katharine dear, I oughtn't to send it: it is frigid and horrible: but this reason overbears me. Forgive me dearest, and think no more about it. This illiterate postscript is written by moonlight.

R.

To K. H.   20 Cavendish Square, W.
                                                         19 June 1905

Your dear letter which I found when I got here this afternoon gives me no address which is perhaps a hint that you have heard enough of me for the time. Anyway it would be an argument for not writing if I had any natural gift of abstinence – or even temperance. But partly because my last letter was so unforgiveably pompous and empty – I recollect that it contained the word "attrition"! fancy that in a letter to a lovely Chaucer Child like you! a thing barely natural if Sir Thomas Browne were writing to Jane Austen – and partly because I am feeling very low and miserable this evening, I am sending this with obstinate passion to Tours in ignorance if it has a chance of finding you there – or anywhere. I enjoyed my time at Littlestone – brilliant sun and sea with the loudest noise of larks I ever heard – I played golf well and talked a good deal to Arthur Balfour and Lady Elcho who have an extraordinary charm for me – both singularly, and particularly in combination – she is worn and faded but I think one would always jump among lions to redeem her glove . . .

Do send me your Mallarmé prose. I am sure it is very good. And if it wasn't you know that my ignorance and partiality would make me doubly blind to any faults. But I feel in my bones that it is perfect – and in exchange I will give you my essay on Sentimentalism – when it is written – I began to write it on Sunday but the first 10 pages turned out to be all about Oscar Wilde – I suppose because you said you had been reading his essays. It struck me at the time that there was something very whimsical in the apposition of your name with his. But you will not think it as strange as I do. You belong to the choir of young-eyed cherubims. He did not . . .

To K. H.   20 Cavendish Square.
                                                                   4 August 1905

. . . I have never been here in August before and I don't suppose you have either: you can't conceive the dreary drooping deflowered depopulated morning-after-the-ball appearance which it presents – the sickening miasma of stale smoke, dead violets, dusty rooms, melting butter, tinned food, drunken servants, sleepy cabmen, and exhausted members of the White Hungarian Band – Everywhere the ashes and odours of yesterday's debauch . . .

To K. H.   10 August 1905

. . . I was afraid you would fall in love with Stanway – But remember that it is just as worldly to marry for a Tudor house as for a million pounds.

If you decide to spend your life in the Cotswolds I shall buy a cottage in the Quantocks and look at you through a telescope: and some day I shall come when Ego isn't looking and bind you and gag you and put you in a gondola at Bristol and take you to Samoa which is like Avalon – only in the Pacific . . .

Then I had meant to quarrel with you about Racine as well, but perhaps I had better pretend to like him. Couldn't you bring some of his writing to Ireland and show me what is good in it? I think my nerves will have to be much more shaky than they are yet before I shiver at *"La fille de Minos et de Pasiphae"*. But I suspect I am what Maurice [Baring] calls "Tone-deaf to the language". It appears that Mat. Arnold was too; and I wouldn't mind betting that Yeats is. I say nothing of Racine's skill in construction or of his nobility of sentiment which are probably unexceptionable and so far as mere diction goes he has just the same metallic and rhetorical quality which your Yeats objects to in Macaulay and Scott – though of course in a much more exquisite degree. What a pity you haven't read Lucan. He seems to me very like Racine, but withers away if you read him after Virgil.

There: I have done it after all – given you a rough coarse draught of insular philistinism; and you will never forgive me if I don't take it all back, which I do at once . . .

To Mrs Horner
Glen of Rothes,
Rothes, N.B.
27th August 1905

As I am writing this I suppose you will be taking your last look on the mud flats of Mallaranny[1] or perhaps undressing in a hail-storm on the Plage . . . I enjoyed it all tremendously from alpha to omega – except perhaps a few moments in Clive's garden when Katharine was unkind to me and a few other moments on my last night when I was unkind to you, and made you come down dozens of flights of stairs in a dressing gown to rescue your daughter from the dawn.

It *was* my fault, and I *did* keep her up by being rather unreasonable on purpose in my talk. You were divine to be so forgiving. You are the most forgiving person there is. But I still feel ashamed about it. You gave us an ell and we took two. You spent all the days in arranging our pleasures for us and then we turned you into a night porter as well . . .

Baker's jealous depression, Dolly Gladstone's fluent follies, Elizabeth's[2] clamorous egoism, the hideous furniture, the ceaseless rain, the croquet hoops and Wellingtonias on the lawn, the possibility that Lady Sassoon may swoop down in a motor from Tulchan at any minute – all this is more than my weary spirit can support. I can only gutter feebly like a candle.

. . . I suppose those 2 children [Edward and Katharine] are on their driving tour now – I'm not certain that you ought to have let them go. They are sure to lose their way or catch cold or something. It is like sending the Babes in the Wood on to the Stock Exchange. I should feel happier if I were there to look after them, see that Edward spent enough on his dinner and Katharine had her lemon in the evening and got to bed in good time . . .

To K. H.
Glen of Rothes,
Rothes, N.B.
28 August 1905

I have been in a kind of stupor ever since coming here or I believe I should have written before – a sort of half dazed indifference to everything that goes on around occasionally sharpening into impotent irritation when I miss a grouse or have to listen for more than 40 minutes at a stretch to Elizabeth shouting about herself. There is something very stale and tame about family life after that delicious spell we had of freedom and joy. But I have preserved some very vivid pictures of you to feed my memory on in this sad pause and twilight of time. I can still see you quite clearly standing in your short white skirt and wet

---

[1] The Horners took a house at Mallaranny in Mayo, where Raymond stayed with them before joining his family in Scotland.

[2] Raymond's half-sister, then aged eight.

green shoes on the platform as my train steamed out – standing in that divine
equipoise which you laugh at me for insisting on – wrongly, because it isn't
merely having an eye on each side of your nose and a shoulder on each side of
your neck, but a thrilling mystery of proportion – a union of grace and strength
and breeding – which I fear one sees oftener in a horse than in a woman – not a
simple thing that can be enclosed in a magazine metaphor or exhausted by trite
analogies with larches, lilies, leopards and such like, but an inexpressible
essence which I have seized and shall enjoy for ever and ever not by any of the
five common senses but by an extra one which you have developed in me along
with the material you provide for its exercise – a sense which has nothing
whatever to do but apprehend the things in Katharine which aren't in anyone
else, things which God put there in a moment of drunken genius in the year
1885 when there was a great wave of experimentalism in the air and Gladstone
invented Home Rule and everyone was doing rash novel and imaginative
things hoping for the best but not knowing a bit how they would turn out . . .

To K. H.   Glen of Rothes.
                                                31 August 1905

. . . I finished Orestes in the train – It gets rather exciting later on, but the
dénouement where Apollo comes in and says that Orestes must marry
Hermione whose throat he is in the act of cutting is rather comic – I suppose
intentionally when Orestes, Pylades and Electra are all preparing to kill
themselves it is very striking how Pylades says most sentimental things to
Orestes but never a word to Electra whom he is by way of loving and is at any
rate anxious to marry. A modern could write a powerful scene in the converse
sense – where A on the wave of a hopeless passion for B sacrifices himself for
her brother. If I were going to kill myself for the convenience of Edward I think
I would say a word or two to you first. I am also going through the Iliad again.
Do you know what these lines mean? [1]

'Ου νέμεσις Τρῶας καὶ ἐυκνήμιδας 'Αχαιούς
Τοιῆδ' ἀμφὶ γυναικί πολὺν χρόνον ἄλγεα πάσχειν

The old men of Troy say it about Helen when she walks on the walls. I haven't
suffered many woes for my Helen yet, but I will if you make it necessary.

We have no guests here at present but Archie Gordon, Mervyn Herbert, and
others come on Monday. Also Mrs Grenfell. Dolly Gladstone when she was
here kept trying to make me talk about you but I wouldn't. She praised very
much a poem of your youth called the Woodman's daughter and I was obliged
to confess I had never heard of it. Do please send it to me. I know I should love
it. The very name is full of romance. But you never will show me anything of

---

[1] Small wonder that the Trojans and the well-armed Greeks should suffer woes for a long time
for such a woman as this.

what was for a long time almost your whole self. You are like all the rest – you think I am a hard scoffing cynical brute with whom you can risk nothing, unproductive and falling like a malignant hammer on those who have the courage to produce. O Katharine dear, you know quite well that if you wrote the merest nonsense with your lovely hands it would be wine and moonlight to me, and I would fight Dr Johnson with my tongue and Charles Fry with my hands to prove that it was honey of Hymettus and bloom in the top grapes of inspiration and anyone less stupid than those two there would be no need to fight, because they would know that what I said was true . . .

To K. H.
Cortachy Castle,
Kirriemuir, N.B.
19 September 1905

You have not been very kind to me. I nearly sent you a card on Sunday to complain. It would have been like this – Aug. 24 to Sept. 17 = 25 days: 2 letters. Not a very generous allowance. And 3 in 26 leaves the average still rather starved – even if I can count the one I got yesterday; and I hardly can because it gives the idea of having been written more from shame than love – an overdue debt reluctantly extracted, a mechanical smile yielded to the photographer's importunity – and what a feeble attempt at the beginning to carry the war into my country – you didn't write because I should have no time to read! . . .

To K. H.
Glen of Rothes,
Rothes, N.B.
25 September 1905

. . . All the same I believe I would rather have this indolence in you than a sham assiduity. It is so very characteristic of you, and contrasts agreeably with the greed of acquisition and industry in retention which are the ordinary practice of women . . .

I had a very pleasant visit at Cortachy in spite of two balls. Indeed I liked one of them – the one at Glamis. The place is an enormous 10th century dungeon. It was full of torches and wild men in kilts and pretty women pattering on the stone stairs with satin slippers . . . I was glad to find I had enough illusibility left to fancy myself in a distant century. It gives one a certain thrill to sit out in the room where the King was murdered in Macbeth. I confess one had to depend more on the scenery than the company. But Sybil Brodrick is a very nice creature I think, and much improved both in looks and other ways. She had a tremendous success with Aubrey – mainly by virtue of a detached and abstracted expression which she has somehow acquired. I suspect her of being in love with some youth whom St John disapproves – possibly Paul Phipps! She is here now, and so are her parents, who irritate me a good deal in their totally different styles. The rest of our party was not much to boast of: but I am always happy with Aubrey: he and I played chess till six in the morning when we got back from Glamis. Lady Airlie[1] of course is charming and I think the most beautiful woman of her age I ever saw. But her daughter is one of the largest most uncouth and terrific beings you can imagine with a sledge-hammer rudeness which leaves one stunned and bruised. Eventually I had to tell her so. There was also Lady Arran – a Dutch woman with Titian hair, Rubens body, and Greuze intelligence. But she told me I was like a Tiger Lily, so we got on very well together . . .

To K. H.   26 September 1905

. . . I was a brute to badger you into writing when you were feeling ill and wretched; and indeed I am a brute to badger you about it at all, because in my heart, as you know very well, I make no pretence of being on an equality with you and if one's deserts made one happy which they never do, I ought to be more content with a wave of your hand or a scratch of your pen a few times in the year. But we know how religious people call themselves worms of earth and are furious when God doesn't treat them like Emperors, and I suppose it is the same with me. At any rate I long to be perpetually reassured that however little time and thought you may give to me there is no one else to whom you give more; and when I don't hear from you that belief crumbles very easily. But I agree that letters are extremely unsatisfactory: they are a device and a compromise, – a compression into 2 dimensions of what can only properly exist in 3 or perhaps in none, full of tiresome iterations and cloying clichés, with all the faults of a statue which pretends to portray motion. And I think you feel this formal and unreal quality in correspondence even more than I do: because with all your delicious ritual of sentiment and superstition, of thrills and tremors and fancies and sensibilities to influences which do not touch anybody that is not made more than half spirit by its own beauty, you have a far clearer and more candid vision of things than I have and a sincere apprehension of reality which my muddy blood and peddling analysis can never give me. You feel the silliness of shows and the importance of words so strongly that you can hardly amuse yourself with them: but I am afraid I am a kind of middle-class Mountebank with one frothy lobe to my brain full of a charlatan's conceit in building up sentences which are a vulgar embroidery on the truth which I cherish, and one stodgy lobe of a shopkeeper which topples over these gim-crack towers and tells me it was a false economy ever to set them up. And I think there must be a third part of me as well because it can't be with either of those two that I see and worship the pure fine light of your spirit and know myself unworthy to confront it. There is a kind of purity which is not merely

[1] His hostess at Cortachy Castle.

technical if you know what I mean – no accident of blood or chance, no lethargic loyalty to a local code, but an active and pervading perfection which works some ambrosial change in the whole texture of a person's being, body and heart and mind . . .

To K. H.   6 October 1905

It is tiresome of me to write again so soon. I've nothing to say beyond the ordinary old thing. But the posts are so infernally slow here that I know I can't hope to hear from you before Monday and I am too impatient to wait in idleness till then, though heaven knows letter-writing is only one remove from idleness and a very vain and shadowy approximation to what I want. If only there were a kind of Telehapsy by which one could touch people a long way off! The country would make more out of it than ever they will out of telegrams. Fancy if I could suddenly pluck your sleeve for sixpence so that you would turn round and think of me with your eyes, or kiss the hem of your skirt for a shilling – Wouldn't it be delightful for me and embarrassing for you. How you would blush at your tea with the Aunts when you became aware that Norton in Chelsea was quietly stroking your hair, or found Bron's arm stealing firmly round your waist from the middle of the New Forest. On the whole I am glad that telehapsy hasn't been invented yet . . .

We have had every room in the house choked up with bores this last week and stormy weather outside, so life has been going rather heavily. But Olive [Macleod] and her papa left this morning for Dunrobin (have you seen the Duchess's play?) and Victor for the south and other people for other places, where I hope they may get more nearly what they deserve than they did in this charitable home for the incurably tedious. The only consolation is that I won £30 from them all at bridge, so you see the game has its uses as a scourge, if not as a pleasure. In order to get out of their way Beb and I have been finishing off the shooting in spite of savage weather. Yesterday some partridges lured us on to the top of a high moor and then left us blind and bleeding in the fiercest hailstorm I have ever seen. We lay flat on our stomachs screaming for mercy while the north-east wind drove sticks the size and shape of mauser bullets through the backs of our ears. Today we wrapped ourselves in Shetland shawls and went after grouse – bitterly cold with snow on the hills and in the air, but quite lovely.

In a minute I shall be writing about tints, so I will pull up. But there really is a tree here which the Scotch call gheen – a kind of wild cherry – which has leaves like transparent red flames, and the birches are covered with half sovereigns – canopies of sequins on a silver stalk. I am getting fond of this place, as one does when leaving time comes, and now that the hills are brown and empty I look back sentimentally on the hot days when the heather was pink, and the grouse plentiful, as a man may think of the splendid youth of his wife and fortify his loyalty to her grey hairs, but if old women were as beautiful as autumn moors, old men would have little to complain of. And you will be, my beloved, because your eyes are lakes which time cannot ruffle or dry up, and your throat will still be smooth and round and white when the Pleiads are a heap of ashes.

I forgot to say in my last letter that I entirely disapprove of your midnight ramble with Ego, and I think your Mother was perfectly right in objecting to it – Ego is not the kind of boy to walk over ploughed fields at 4 in the morning for mere love of nature, and your story about the others getting lost is shockingly thin.

To Mrs Horner   10 October 1905

. . . I am left in solitude here – Beb and Oc have gone to Avon, Margot to Gosford and my father to make speeches in Fife. I don't know how anyone can be very serious about politics when every year in the middle of October my father says that Liberals must keep their powder dry and Winston says that Arthur Balfour is a woman, and everything goes on exactly as it did before.

No one here but Violet and May Tomlinson. I shoot by myself on the tops of hills, and read Ovid in front of the fire – very agreeable after the congestion of fools we have had here the last 10 days. All the best bedrooms have been filled with the valets of the greatest bores in Britain, and the only big bath always occupied by the chauffeur of my father's wine merchant – just because he plays bridge and voted against the Government on the Irish Supply – the merchant I mean, the chauffeur didn't even do that, and drives damnably . . .

To K. H.   11 October 1905

. . . O why why aren't you here? It is quite early and everyone has gone to bed, and a warm still night with stars and owls. We could walk for hours on the moors with the grouse chuckling round us and hares slipping away from our steps and the Orkneys coming up out of a moonlit sea in the distance. Elizabeth said to Violet the other day 'What face would you like best to live with always', and Violet said 'Katharine's': and E. said 'Of course it's a beautiful dreamy face to meet at the top of a steep hill when you're tired with climbing up it, but it's not an affectionate face to live with always.' I wonder if it's because I've usually been with you in hilly places that I disagree with the last part of that? you must take care not to be too much on the plains. But it doesn't really matter, because I don't think I want an affectionate face to live with always . . .

To K. H.   20 Cavendish Square, W.
                                                26 October 1905

. . . London is horrible – cold and wet and empty: no tall bare limetrees, no quiet October downs, no golden girls – or boys either – who remind me in the very least of you – I have made two attempts to be reminded of you – in some less tantalising way I mean than by vividly unsatisfying memories. I asked Bron to dine with me tonight, because he is fond of you and you of him, and that seemed a kind of link though a very perilous one. But he was away and couldn't. And then I wired for Phil, but he was away too and never turned up, so I had an expensive and voluptuous dinner by myself, very wretched and reflecting all the time what a brute you would think me if you could have seen – (I could live on grape nuts and barley water with you, but when you are not there, there's nothing left but eating and drinking and crying) – And then I remembered about that girl in *The Blue Moon* who was said to be like you, and I went off there when the thing was half over, and she came on and I saw the likeness and then she opened her mouth and sent out a voice of such penetrating vulgarity that I ran sickly from the theatre before I had been there ¼ hour, and came back home to write to you. But I find I can't even do that because I am full of disintegrating regrets – not the clean self-controlled elevating kind which make lovely tears on the paper with clear edges and bright colours and fill one's mind with tender images and inspiring illusions, but the sort which leave one flabby and diffuse without shape or force or dignity or anything else desirable.

You can't think what it is to come back here after those perfect days at Mells to soot and squalor and damnable professional routine. I have spent two whole days deciphering the ill-spelt letters and ill-shaped figures of a fraudulent and illiterate bagman and now I have to tell my client that he has no case and consequently no further need for my services. And there were you in your walled garden wasting God's sunlight and your own sweet beauty on a half-witted old woman who cares for nothing but plasmon and manures.[1] I hate this life of guesses and snatches and half-satisfactions and silly hopes and silly regrets. But I am much too tired to do more than hate it. Even this very minute I am round again on the other tack and almost loving it when I remember how very happy I was at Mells and shall be again unless you put my name in a sealed box . . .

---

[1] This hardly does justice to Miss Gertrude Jekyll, famous gardener and garden designer, whose brother married Frances Horner's sister.

To K. H.

All Souls College,
Oxford.
29 October 1905

. . . if you were here I believe you would steady me and with something to
balance me I feel sure I should make a good swan song because my pulses are
going so fast, and the slowness of them at normal times is what makes me so
dull and stupid. All I really mean is that I have got a bad cold in my head and
the top of my chest . . . I had such a terrible night last night – full of mean-
ingless dreams like tons of hot soft cotton wool with one's soul helpless and suf-
focating in the middle of it; and I daren't go to bed for hours because I know it
will be the same thing over again.

Tonight we have had a long long dinner with 30 or 40 solemn people in our
beautiful hall and wine-drinking afterwards which I thought would never end.
A professor of Economics talked to me about Charles Fox till I screamed, and
the faces of all the men swelled till they became like round hazy mountains
with all the coarseness of size and none of the mystery of distance – and then
we went to the smoking room and I stood up and harangued them all for 40
minutes – telling anecdotes, reciting poetry, even talking politics for fear the
man should begin again about Fox. I could hear my high rapid voice like a
swallow talking and see their slow features moving in appreciative correspondence with my words, only long after the words were spoken – like the
jerky inconsequent mobility of faces in a cinematograph, or when you see a
man hitting a pile in, a long way off, and then at last hear the sound of the
blow. And then I told them that Mrs Humphry Ward had begged me with
tears to become a Papist and I had consented and must go away and write to
her about it: and I suppose that is what I am doing now . . .

To K. H.

Impérial Hotel,
Paris.
21 December 1905

. . . Yesterday was the vilest day I have ever spent – would have been I mean if I
had *chosen* to spend it as I did. From 11 a.m. till 2 I was closeted with H.R.H.
Prince Ibrahim and his man of business, a ruffian called Clitzin, Neapolitan
with Turkish blood, fierce moustaches, fierce eyebrows, bald scalp and yellow
skin creased like a toad's belly, gives himself out as a famous duellist and
briseur de coeurs, and only just got out of Turkey in time not to be hanged for
assassinating the last Sultan but one. He didn't understand much about the
case. Ibrahim did. He is intelligent and speaks both English and French
well – more horrible to look at than you can imagine, a long immensely fat
body, legs shorter than a dachshund, a face broadening rapidly towards the
chin, dull wicked eyes and a mouth like a sensual tench, which droops in the

middle of a sentence and has to be pulled together with a slow effort to finish it.

At 2 we stopped talking business and went to lunch at Durand's – a meal which lasted till six in a small hot room full of smoke, wine and obscenity. When I got out Cassel's agent came to see me and tried to bluff me into giving up the job by lies. Luckily I could prove them lies. Then at 8 I had to go back to Durand's and dine with the Prince, another vast meal. Then we went to a sumptuous box at a music hall where there was an excellent performance – half-naked women on the stage paying us the sweetest attentions, as the Prince is a great patron of the art. Then from midnight till 2 in the morning a great supper party. I got to bed feeling that I never wanted to see food or drink again. A rich oriental is the most poisonous thing there is. This man made me think tenderly about the worst of our English Jews – (But perhaps you will say I always do that) . . .

To K. H.   Grand Continental Hotel,
                                                                Cairo.
                                                      5 January 1906

. . . I am afraid I have no contributions to offer for the New Blank Book. My knowledge of French poetry is confined to Cinna, Phèdre, a few pages of Mallarmé, and a few sonnets of Ronsard and Du Bellay which I read in Belloc's book and liked very much: also a poem called Le Captive by Chénier which comes in *Shirley* which I am reading now. I don't care about the poem but I like the book all the more perhaps because I have been taking a course of Jane Austen which bores, irritates and depresses me beyond words. Everything is so prim and tepid and formal. One can't feel any interest in the respectful feelings which a governess entertains towards a curate, and you don't often get anything more unrestrained and elemental than that in these novels. Her idea of a good character is a person whose "sentiments are just", whose "language is well chosen" and whose "information is correct and varied"; and a bad one is merely a young man who writes to a young woman without being engaged to her. Brontë is like Aeschylus after this – the best parts of Aeschylus after the worst parts of Euripides – a day-spring of passion and poetry and mystery after a bowl of gold-fish in a rectory parlour . . .

To Aubrey Herbert   1 Paper Buildings,
                                                            Temple,
                                                      London E.C.
                                                    20 March 1906

I wrote you a very dull letter to Bagdad and here is another to Damascus. Good letters like good love-making come only from an exuberance of spirits – the overflow of a personality in spate, not from the shorn and parcelled tricklings of an existence like mine. But there is a certain value in the mere transmission of bits of paper. They prick the memory even when they do not tickle the intelligence of the receiver . . . If you knew what the address at the head of this sheet meant it would give a double zest to your pleasures. It means hundreds of dull men sitting in hundreds of dull rooms with hundreds of dull books – men who bear the same relation to real men as a pianola does to a piano, rooms which bear the same relation to real rooms as a bus does to the Parthenon, books which bear the same relation to real books as beetles bear to butterflies. I take one out of the shelf and the binding crumbles in my hand like a mummy, musty odours of decay exhale from the leaves and clouds of noxious and ancient dust choke my eyes. The window panes are covered with the dung of London pigeons, and from the room above I can sometimes hear the clerks spitting onto the pavement. Once a month or so I have something to do; but the rest of the time I stare with sightless eyes & unregarding brain at books which ought to be burned for dullness by the common hangman. It is the best way ever found out of rotting one's brain. I really believe it would save time & trouble to do it by drink instead. But I have given up drink – as an experiment – for about a fortnight now. The only result is that I sometimes feel faint. Never give up drink, my dear Aubrey. Never give up anything. You sink at once to the level of the animals if you do.

I supped last night with Mervyn[1] & Bron. Bron is more black against society & especially women than ever before. He has been living with the Grenfells in the full flow of the social tide these last two months & now he creeps in & out of their house by the back door & is conducted straight to his bedroom by a servant holding a green umbrella before him to prevent his seeing or being seen. I think I am coming round to his view. There are half a dozen women & perhaps a dozen men whose company I enjoy – but not in the way one gets it in London, tempered by a hundred conventions and restrictions & pomposities with bows and grimaces and hurry & clatter & insincerity – women twittering like tired birds and men tinkling like empty glasses.

I won't write anything about politics – except that F. E. Smith has astonished the ignorant by the brilliancy of his maiden speech & Belloc has announced in the House that he never goes to bed without drinking 2 pints of beer. I have an idea for you when you go in: go in as a Labour candidate – don't you see the theatrical capability of that? the young aristocrat with ideals & sympathies which carry him passionately out of his class – a tribune of the people – Gracchus, Rienzi, Tolstoi – anyone you like. It would explain your clothes too. Write to me again & come back soon.

---

[1] Aubrey Herbert's younger brother.

To K. H.   In the train near Lyons.
                                                                5 a.m.
                                                           12 April 1906

. . . I am in a train which is 9 furlongs, 5 chains and one rod pole or perch in length, and there is only one carriage which has no beds in it, and that is mine. I offered £5 to everyone I saw in uniform at the Gare de Lyon, but no one had a bed to sell; so I have been sitting stiffly like Yeats' soul for 8 hours in a straight blue garment, among 5 Frenchmen of the lower middle class with a head-ache and a body-ache and a soul-ache. Frenchmen of the lower middle class put on yellow leather slippers before they go to sleep – I tell you this because it may be that you have never slept with one. Think how you will astonish some cautious anthropologist who has spent 50 years in the study of native customs by the inductive method, when you quietly say to him that Frenchmen of the lower middle class always look to you as if they slept in saffron slippers! It is in these ways that women get their fine reputation for intuition . . .

To K. H.   Grand Hotel,
                                                               Ajaccio.
                                                           14 April 1906

I have just got here, as far as a first glance goes I believe it would only need you to make the place Paradise. We came in a little ship which went very fast, but looked like a canoe and would certainly have sunk if there had been a ripple on the water. It was very hot and we had beds like coffins, dark and dank and nar-row, with sheets like boards, and blankets like damp earth. But about 4 in the morning we arrived, and by 5 we were off the ship with the sun rising in a sapphire sky behind the mountains of this most divine bay. We had baths and coffee and now I am sitting in the most delicious garden snatching a few minutes before the post goes to tell you again very quickly and shortly that I love one of your eyelashes more than all the other women in the world, and the stars and the sea and God and the Mother of God. And as for emeralds and rubies and ivory and roses and attar of roses and a deep pool in a wood and the tops of windy mountains and the inside of a pomegranate, they are things that a man would empty into the dustbin if he had seen the little bow of your lips and knew what was worth keeping. But perhaps really one should be careful and tender with all beautiful things because of your beauty, prizing the community in kind which their quality has with yours, instead of scorning the difference of degree, as Xians are good to all men because Christ was a man, and not bad to them because they are worse than he.

I wonder how this tropical garden would suit you as a setting? less well than a bare spring wood in England: but I think you would like it all the same, as you liked the garden of Violante so much. It is hotter here where I am sitting now than on the hottest midday in an English summer, though it will be an hour yet before fortunate Meg comes to twist your hair into a golden crown for you: and the air is very clear and bright with butterflies – and what is very rare out of England – full of the song of birds. There are big palm trees which look real and not as if they had come from the winter-gardens of a provincial hotel, and orange trees loaded with fruit like lamps, and mimosa and great hedges of white irises with the dew still lying on their petals and some very graceful fragile trees with scarlet flowers like trumpets, which have a look of the most sophisticated voluptuaries and the air is quite drowsy with damp heavy scents which the sun is sucking like incense from the flowers. But it is really so very like the descriptions of such things in books that it would be folly to go on writing about it – unless one could pull oneself together and re-arrange one's impressions into unconventional shapes and torture one's ingenuity for a new vocabulary to describe them. But this kind of beauty makes one sleepily – not brilliantly – drunk; it is enervating and narcotic, and until I get into the hills with my rod you will have to forgive these trite and torpid phrases of journalism.

In this garden one's mind would always be in a siesta, even before breakfast. It is the kind of garden in which you couldn't walk in your little straight white dressing gown as you can most exquisitely at Mells. Here it would be too simple and modest and northern. I like to speculate lazily how you would dress yourself for this garden – I think you would be covered with clinging dragons of green and blue silk with orchids in your hair and big raw emeralds hanging around your neck. But I know you would make some new and amazing effect . . .

O how I long for you to be here! we would spend such heavenly days fishing together in the high mountain streams and walking slowly home at sunset under the slanting shadows . . .

To K. H.   All Souls College,
                                                                      Oxford.
                                                                  6 May 1906

. . . I came here yesterday by a train which started 5 minutes before the 5 o'clock for Frome. I saw my father on the platform and your father too. Why does God visit the sins of the fathers upon the children and squander the happiness which should belong to the children upon the fathers? I nearly cried to think of them jogging comfortably down to Mells without an emotion in their battered bones, and myself, who would have given the world to have been in their places, broken on the wheels of an Oxford express. I could scarcely have had less will in the matter if I had been put into the train by a giant or a governess. The advantage in freedom which a boy is supposed to have over a girl, is not much to boast of.

To K. H.
The Manor House,
Sutton Courtenay,
Abingdon.
13 May 1906

. . . since I last wrote I have barely had a second to myself – work in the day time – other people's – and pleasure in the evening – also other people's. It is a shame that I should have to be writing to you now instead of bathing – It is a perfect day, quite fit for you to walk about on – and the sun is shining brilliantly on masses of yellow flowers and the rooks cawing in the elms. The whole place looks divine. If only you were here my darling! How can God allow you not to be? I almost cry when I remember last year. How very happy we were in our red boat on the grey river. I am sitting on the green seat at the end of the garden: why won't you come gliding on your little high feet down the path between the box hedges with a red rose in your hair and your eyes like dark dew in the early sunlight. Perhaps you have never seen what I often saw when I was a boy in Winchester – the dew on the great stretch of perfect turf very early on a summer morning with a quality in the fresh air of radiance which I could never describe because it seemed to have all the best points of light and shade fused in a miraculous combination, brightness and softness, coolness and haze, a kind of lucent and vivified darkness more like the effluence from some holy symbol than the light of common day – and all this I used to see framed in a large grey Norman arch which opened from the quadrangle upon the playing fields – Your eyes are like this. I love you . . .

To Conrad Russell
Drummuir, Keith.
25 August 1906

I would rather have rain in Banff than sun in Bayreuth. I am heartily sorry for you, Conrad. The gleanings of the Spey are better than the grapes of the Danube. Perhaps you do not know that the political unrest of what are known as the Danubian principalities (not to be confused with Persia) has always been a source of great trouble to the Chancelleries of Europe. I can hardly believe that you will be very happy in such a milieu . . . Bongy [Bonham-Carter] is staying with us at Rothes. He is in one of those intervals between two professions which occur so frequently in his life (and would occur so frequently in yours if your political conscience was rather more robust) and being no longer engaged in a job or to a woman, his genius is in its fullest bloom. He sings Polly Oliver and The Golden Vanity 3 or 4 times every night to an enormous audience and imitates ducks, cocks, etc. without a moment's intermission throughout the day. The chief (and almost only) topic of conversation is a gigantic upas tree (to borrow an expression from Bryce's History of the H. R. Empire) of fraud, concealment, and intrigue, which has sprung up in the damp heats of the silly season and overshadows with its malignant foliage the whole of the Asquith, Grenfell and Horner families, Hugh Godley, Archie Gordon,[1] and a number of other supernumerary characters of lesser interest. It is extremely uninteresting in substance and extremely complex in detail. It suffices therefore (v. p. 174 of H. R. Emp.) to say that it threatens the friendly relations of each group and each member of each group to every other group and every other member of every other group, if not, indeed the continued existence of each and all the persons involved, as simultaneous units in a heterogeneous society. The crops continue much as usual.

To **K. H.**   Glen of Rothes.
19 September 1906

. . . I have sent back your Zola to Buck. Gate, but I fear you would not have got it before you left. Today was marked with a white stone for me because I finished, after infinite weariness, the first volume of *Le Crime & le Chatiment.*[2] The hero has been in bed all the time with a sick headache, except for half an hour when he was cutting off two old women's heads with a hatchet. I wonder why anyone thinks it a good book? Could you find out for me from Eddy Marsh? It is his metier to know that kind of thing . . .

To **K. H.**   23 September 1906

. . . By the way, I have written a poem — I made it today walking alone in the first rate wood. It is meant as an additional stanza to [Meredith's] *Modern Love*, and deals with the Desborough crisis, Ettie being My Lady and Violet Madam — It wants putting into shape but here is the rough draft.

> My Lady tactically takes a bone
>   From Madam's shelf (Meat on it? here and there!)
>   And hungry Madam finding cupboard bare
> Thrusts at her snaky-tongued with eyes of stone —

[1] This refers to an obscure drama, evidently gripping at the time, according to which Lady Desborough had been indulging in an excessive flirtation with Archie Gordon, who was a son of Lord Aberdeen and not much older than her own son Julian. He was also on close terms with Violet Asquith, and may have tried to become engaged to her in 1909, not long before his death in a motor accident. It appears from the poem above that Lady Desborough distracted him from his feelings for Violet, who nevertheless remained her devoted admirer all her life.

[2] Dostoevsky's books did not begin to appear in English until after this time.

"You've made him sad with sin – or very dull,
  "Sir Truth-be-Damned or Mister Meaning-Well,
  "A Kilted Kill-joy, or a showy shell
"Glengarried, glowing, godlike, and —— a gull."

"Nor gull nor liar" sweetly makes reply
  My Lady – "or if liar, then a white one,
  "A ptarmigan, out-Georging Washington,
  "Clear-eyed, whole-souled" – Then Madam angrily;

"He drives with you: he lies for you; he's caught
  "And you go free through flame – a salamander"
  To whom My Lady with a sugared candour
"Why spare the Sporran if you spoil the Sport?"

To K. H.   Tulchan Lodge,
                                                    Advie,
                                          Strathspey, N.B.
                                        26 September 1906

. . . I love you for telling me everything you do and especially for your way of telling it. The little hill towns must be, as you say, beyond imagination, and I suspect that they make a nearly perfect setting for your beauty, my tall lily girl: I can see you like a white angel in the twilight streets of sheer and sinister Volterra. We will certainly go there, my darling, as well as to Cumberland and Venice – Nothing shall stop us. Only, if Eddy, who is remarkably abstemious takes ¾ of the day for meals you will have to allow me at least half. You never told me by the way whether you were drinking Chianti as I ordered you to do. I beg you to do this Katharine dear, the water of Italy is full of death.

You never told me either what was said in your talk with Oc at Avon which you describe as "odd and sad" – I am glad you are fond of him: to be loved by you is a shield and sword against the devil, because you are pure as a tall candle before the Holy Rood, and evening stars of a million forgotten worlds have melted in your eyes . . . I am fond of Oc too, and I rather regret that we have always been on such uncompromisingly unsentimental and even uncommunicative terms. Our family are naturally very undemonstrative but also naturally clannish and I think we should all be prepared to make considerable sacrifices for one another at a crisis . . . You are quite all I have, my darling angel, and all I ever want – So will you be true to me for a little longer, my Katharine? I know that Italy swarms at this season with rich and idle and handsome young Englishmen, and if you meet them the temptation will be strong upon you to complete the moon and cypress landscape with a man, and to them quite irresistible. And then you will tell me with a smile of lovely indulgence that you are going to "love them side by side with me" as you do Yeats. But you know how I rebel against these parallel passions, and you must remember that parallel lovers are not like parallel straight lines: they meet long before infinity; and then there is the hell of a row . . .

I have very little matter of fact to set against your chronicle of Romance – This is a lovely valley commanded by the moon, just as was the Vale of Rothes (I often think now with sick self-reproach of one evening there when you lingered to look at a pink moon and I pressed on because of the midges and the gong – fit types you will say of the things which I run from and to! – oh, if I had those minutes back again). There is excellent grouse driving and the King, who was here last week, seems to have shot so badly that there are plenty of birds left. No one here but Sassoons and Rothschilds, except one gentile called Wynne. Saturday is the Jewish Day of Atonement which they solemnise by a 24 hours fast, so I shall go off then for a week-end with Ettie, thereby missing a musical heiress who is coming to Rothes . . .

To K. H.   28 September 1906

. . . Did I tell you that Olive [Macleod] was going to take a sort of secular veil by becoming one of the Vice-Principals of Newnham at Cambridge? I think it is a wise resolve, don't you? a far more appropriate haven for her than a nunnery would be for you. Frances is profoundly right not to let you become a Papist. A priest meddles with your life infinitely more than a family. It is not the creed of the Catholic Church which I mind, but the administrative system. Still I would almost rather have you a Papist than an actress. I can't understand how, seeing as much as you do of the Campbells and the Trees you can be blind to the unbearable second rateness of the profession and everyone who has anything to do with it – in England at any rate – except Viola, and she avowedly hates, mocks and despises the whole thing.

What you say about Frances perhaps leaving Mells in the middle of October rather frightens me. Do persuade her to stay till the end. The flowers and the trees and the downs and the stars are all at their very best there, and it would be a sin to desert them for the death-in-life of London . . .

To K. H.   Glen of Rothes,
                                                                 Rothes, N.B.
                                                                 10 October 1906

. . . Cicely left a few hours ago, having told me just before your letter arrived the sad news about letting the Manor House[1] – selling Buck. Gate doesn't

---

[1] A threat that did not materialise.

matter nearly so much I think. You can live just as well in Bloomsbury as in Mayfair. London is always London, and one part is no worse than another within reasonable limits. But not to have the Manor House is a good enough reason for the blackest depression and until something irrevocable is done, I shall never believe that it can happen. Even from the standpoint of economy, it seems very doubtful policy. No one can live always in London, your family less than any, and I feel sure that Frances would never try to: but taking places is very much more expensive than keeping them – and from all other points of view your leaving Mells is not to be borne. Of course, you couldn't bear it, because you love it: and I couldn't bear it either because I love you and I love the dear memories of happiness with you which cluster like Pleiads round those pointed gables – the blinking moments when the world went out on summer nights, and the yellow lights in the latticed windows as one came back from an October walk. If all these things go, nearly everything goes and we might almost as well have made the compact of divorce which Frances wanted in the summer. An occasional tea-party in the Bloomsbury parlour, and occasional visit to Crewe Hall – I suppose that is what we have to look forward to. The fire is dying in the grate and kinship with the stars is difficult in Bedford Square. At least you will not be able to accuse me of consolation! I never felt blacker in my life. It began even before your letter came – I don't know why or how. Everyone has gone away except Margot and me and May Tomlinson, and it is the saddest of autumn days with pale sunlight and yellow leaves. I went for a solitary walk in the afternoon and lay on my face in the heather, and everything in the world seemed to have stopped except the chuckling of the grouse all round me, and the ceaseless withering of everything inside and out – I was as nearly sincere as one ever is in wishing to be quietly extinguished. Life seems an impossible thing to deal with – purposely made unhandy – this wretched round of desiring and not desiring, attaining and not attaining, endless and fruitless as the sea – And death is very likely worse – The only thing is that I know this is a mood in me, and I know that your despondence is a mood in you, and moods must pass: they always do – often quite quickly.

It must pass: it absolutely must. I know well that we shall be very happy when we are together again at Mells. We shall, darling Katharine, shan't we? promise me that . . .

To K. H.   11 October 1906

You must forgive me if you can for writing you two such morose despondent shrivelled letters. I can't forgive myself – especially when I remember how I have sometimes scolded you for being moody. If some one attacked you I don't think I should run away; but when you are menaced by melancholy I see the bully just as large as you do and take to my heels in tears. It is abominable, and the very thing which makes women stop loving men. It is a great shame, my darling, when I have always pretended that you could count on me, suddenly to fail you in your need, and however little you may really care for me, it must add to your burden to know that my courage is as capricious as my charm.

A few days since I was full of life and confidence, open to every sensation, eager for every adventure, ready to run through a hundred careers and love a hundred women, responsive to all kinds of strange calls in things, and quarrelling with the niggardly circumference of fate: and then suddenly everything collapsed: I seemed unequal even to the little weights I have to bear, the little efforts I have to make, and quite unworthy to sustain the love of which I had before felt very sure. – And then your letter came showing, I thought, that I was almost as insecure as I deserved to be, and after considering the alternatives of killing myself or falling in love with Cynthia, and finding insuperable objections to both, I was quite at an end of my resources and simply went on enduring with no policy but the dim hope of better times. And now I think the better times are coming, though I cannot have any confidence till I know how much estranged you have been by the limpness and folly of my last letter . . . Will you send me a line to Gosford, Katharine, to tell me that you have forgiven me once more for my unforgiveable trespasses against you?

This is my last night at Rothes. It is very black and the rain is coming down in sheets, but every now and then I can hear the coots calling from the pond and that comforts me because it is the same wild angry cry which used to make you knock upon the wall and give me an excuse for seeing the most lovely vision eyes have ever been blessed with. Or have you forgotten all that, Katharine, and the stars in the pines and your golden dress on the heather?

"These things seem small, and undistinguishable
"Like far off mountains turned into clouds"

Do you remember how we admired those lines together? That is how our happiness here seemed to me two days ago – a fading dream which could never be recaptured. But it is all coming back again on the cry of the coots, and it will be so real and substantial by the time I reach Mells that it will need an effort of dislimning malignity of which I believe you are not capable to prevent my forcing upon your reluctant imagination the joy which I have already almost recreated.

To K. H.   Gosford,
                                                                Longniddry, N.B.
                                                                15 October 1906

Thank you very much for your long letter which I was delighted to get this morning in spite of the sadness of it. I think it was foolish of me to envisage life without Mells, but I couldn't help doing it: that was why I wished I had not written. It is worth making a million efforts and enduring every hardship to keep the Manor House: with that lovely background, life in a slum could be borne; but without it a palace would be oppressive. I do hope and pray you will manage somehow to keep it . . .

To K. H.
Pixton Park,
Dulverton.
18 November 1906

. . . I am slowly ploughing through Swinburne's book about Blake. There is some capital invective in it by Swinburne, but I am quite unable to get pleasure from the parts by Blake. There is not enough inspiration in him to excuse the lack of grammar. I can't understand how a man who is held up as an artist *par excellence* could have endured to turn out such unfinished stuff. But I admit that his view of things (as explained by Swinburne) – his belief in the equality of soul and body, and his contempt for the Christian virtues of chastity and humility – has in it a good deal that attracts. But I wish I could drop this habit of writing down my own damnation in every letter I send you! Last time I spent pages in demonstrating that I was a depressed and depressing wreck, and here I am again emphasizing all the defects in my taste and judgement to which you most object, and underlining literary views which put me almost as far below you in aesthetics as I am in morals.

Angel girl, the more I think of the differences between your spiritual furniture and mine, the harder it seems to explain this strange accident of your loving me – It must be some twin strand in the complicated cobweb of the senses that has unpredictably attached you to me for a miraculous moment, and when you wake up from this unconsidering swoon of childhood and feel the natural breezes of the world in your face, this link of gossamer will be broken and blown about the sky with dead leaves and thistledown and slanting rooks. And when that happens I know how cold and young the world will look – just as it does on some raw day at the close of February when one feels development and discomfort going on in the air, and discomfort without development in one's heart – the sense of being left behind and alone is an old illusion which Nature has shaken off in the budding of a new life in which one has no part . . .

To K. H.
Hartham,
Corsham,
Wilts.
26 December 1906

. . . But what a lovely night now – the moon on the snow – what a night for wolves and chestnuts – O Katharine, if only we were in our mountain shanty! I can see you very clearly kicking the caked snow off your foolish little shoes on the threshold and crouching on a cushion by a log fire, wet and glowing, the pure bright blood in your cheeks and your great eyes shining like silk – And I would get you a brown blanket for your skirt, and pull off your drenched blue stockings and bathe your beautiful feet in a basin of hot water and verveine, and all the air would thrill and quiver with the radiance of your loveliness and the stars would cluster round the lattice to look in upon the divinity of you, just as they stood over the inn at Bethleham and Orion would draw his sword to keep guard over your door and the Great Bear would leave the pole star and circle all night long about the glory of your little head.

Won't it all happen very like that, my angel? How good you were to me at Avon – even on the last day when the flame of your affection began to flicker a little under the trial of seeing me all day and so much of the night. I shall always love Avon because of the wonderful things that have happened to us there. I think of it more than of any other place as the cradle of our love, and it will always have a romance for me which I believe not even Mells can equal. The path by the Linnhay is patrolled by angels out of paradise, it is not a grass track between deserts of heather, but a moonbeam leading to the highest sky, and if I ever see the San Graal (and you have made it very likely that I shall) it will be floating above the mist in that clump of pines . . .

To K. H.   Chatsworth,
                                                                 Chesterfield.
                                                           29 December 1906

. . . How you would loathe this place! It crushes one by its size and is full of smart shrivelled up people. Lady Helen [Vincent] is the only beauty here and Lady Theo Acheson the only girl – quite nice but not very interesting. I have been a long walk with her in the snow this afternoon – sometimes up to our waists: but I never found it necessary to lift her out of a drift. There is some very mild tobogganing and a good deal of bridge, but shooting and skating are prevented by the snow, and there is only *one* bathroom in the house which is kept for the King.

I am going to have a good look at the pictures tomorrow – there are a thousand here, nearly all good and the library which is the best in England . . .

To Lady Horner   All Souls
                                                             12 January 1907

. . . Comfort continued at a high level even after you left – Kitchener couldn't have kept house better than Katharine did – consummate efficiency and no apparent effort – We had Aunt's leg twice in one day, and should have had it again if she had remembered to order it . . .

I have got back to "the dedicated life" again. It *is* Hell though I have a certain amount of work for once. But Cavendish Square is quite un-inhabitable – Margot's nurse is still there, which means that I have to sleep in the bathroom. Also all the servants are new and mad. There is one man who has boots which chirp like crickets all through dinner, and another who hands one brown sugar with the partridges instead of bread crumbs. I had to come here to get away from it, but I have been richly punished by finding only one man in residence – and he has a cork nose and no roof to his mouth and is writing a County History of Northumberland.

To Lady Manners   The College,
                                                                        Winchester.
                                                                  9 February 1907

. . . I can't tell you what a relief it is to have something fixed at last.[1] I had never thought of it as a near possibility and was prepared to continue for a good while longer the exciting but uncertain conditions under which we lived. I hate asking favours of anyone, particularly of my family, but think in this case it is right to accept them when they come unasked: and both Margot and my father seem to think that they can provide us with a competence without unduly pinching themselves. I shall never regret the time of our rather protracted court-ship, because it has been full of glamour and sweetness from beginning to end, and if I were only a man of genius I could have made a hundred volumes of immortal lyrics out of the days that we have spent together at Avon alone. But it did seem a pity to see the irreparable years of our youth slipping by in a re-lation which – however delicious – was yet imperfect and intermittent – like the great pearls of a necklace sliding from their broken thread into the sea. I am very happy about it and so I think is Katharine: but there will always be a strange and uncaptured element in her which rebels a little against any authorised alliance – And I am not sorry for this because I hope it will prevent me ever growing lazy or confident in my love.

I suppose we shall live in a mean and uncomfortable way at first, but I believe she will enjoy the freedom and independence more than she minds the discom-fort, and if only by a miracle she can go on being fond of me, everything will be well. In the meantime we want to be as secret as possible for as long as possible about our arrangements and only to be publicly engaged at the very last decent moment – partly because we both feel the status of an engaged couple to be a ridiculous and farcical one – quite unworthy of a serious episode, partly because we are quite certain to alienate people by unbecoming and irregular demeanour – never exhibiting the correct emotions, never using the correct

---

[1] Katharine's parents had now agreed to her engagement to Raymond.

catchwords, neither talking of "our great happiness" nor pretending that we are "unworthy" of it or of one another, constantly laughing at moments when we ought to cry, and perhaps crying at moments when we ought to laugh (though this is less likely) . . .

To K. H.   20 Cavendish Square, W.
                                                                      16 February 1907

. . . I suppose you are at Rome by now comfortably installed with Con, bathed and perfumed, re-clothed and in every way renewed, and perhaps drinking coffee on a sunny balcony among the scents of freesia and verveine. Happy Katharine! think of me sometimes in this dreary city – only leaving it to go in bad trains to other drearier ones! It is so mild here today (though very grey) that I think there must be real heat and golden sunshine in Italy and in a week you will be among figs and lizards – which are nicer than the pigs and blizzards among which my lines are cast. What a grumpy ungentlemanly dog-in-the-manger sort of letter this is! You might think I were grudging you your pleasures: I'm not: I long for you to have blue skies and golden suns, and come back with brown hands and round cheeks. But I suppose I didn't fully realise before you went away what a perfect blank your going would make in my life, and that is why I have subsided like a pricked balloon into a heap of crumpled pleats.

I walked in the park this afternoon and thought how much better autumn suits London than spring: there is something impotent and mechanical about the faint efforts of a London spring – a lack of élan and spontaneity – more like the second childhood of a dotard than the lusty uprush of youth . . .

To K. H.   22 February 1907

. . . Your account of Rome makes me sick with jealousy – less because Lord Lascelles is there, than because I am not – you would have to be at a very loose end before you fell in love with him. He certainly can't be described as voorish.[1] Indeed I am surprised to hear you so describe Rome – I must have got a totally wrong impression – to me it seemed more like Lancashire than Latium – wet and cold and full of trams and municipal buildings, with a few faked ruins such as the Forum and the Amphitheatre incongruously insinuated by the Local Authority to attract tourists. But of course I never saw the sun there, nor the Campagna nor the crocuses.

Please write me a full account of your fashionable dinner party. I have quite forgotten what they are like; I never dine out – except sometimes with Bron

---

[1] A private expression meaning mysterious and sublime.

and Conrad – dear Bron – he is delightful now and looking extremely handsome. Thank God, my Katharine, you are an emotional freak – your not loving him is almost stronger proof of it even than your loving me . . .

To **K. H.**   All Souls College,
                                                                                                                      Oxford.
                                                                                                                      28 February 1907

I wonder if the night in Rome can be more lovely than it is here in Oxford? I don't think so – because there is a sensuous warmth in the Italian air which is infinitely agreeable and plunges one into ecstasies which our climate cannot normally provide; but for begetting the simpler and more purely devotional moods of adoration there is nothing to equal the incomparable austerity of our northern stars. Some day I will show you the Great Bear wheeling round the spire of St Mary's as you can only see it from the quadrangle of this College; it forms a severe and glorious diadem for the brows of those who fell at Agincourt, whose souls our Founders directed us to pray for. We will come over from Sutton, my Katharine, one glowing night in August and watch the sky there when the air is kinder than now but still with a religious sharpness in it; and we will see if the spire and the stars remind you, as they remind me, of the lovely fragment of Simonides and the lines of Coleridge about Mont Blanc:

> "O struggling with the darkness all night long
> "And visited all night long by troops of stars"

which I have always for some reason rated very high. But in August we shall not hear what I hear as I write – the wild cries of reeling students drunken in the middle distance. And perhaps it is as well; because for you they would always be a pain and a disfigurement of the beauty of night: women are cut off from that corner of experience as men are cut off from another by the fact that they do not bear children: but for me these drunken cries emphasise and complete the passionless serenity of the heavens, as the orgies on Citheron emphasised and completed for Athenians the quiet severity of the Parthenon. I am glad that I learned in the appropriate season the poetry of wine, because if I saw drunkenness now for the first time I believe I should condemn it as bravely as you do . . .

To Lady Horner   Avon Tyrrell,
                                                                                                                      Christchurch.
                                                                                                                      30 July 1907

I think being married is much nicer than not being married, and I feel that we both of us owe a great deal to you for putting the idea into our heads. I remember some years ago suggesting to Bron that it was more agreeable travelling first class than third. It had never occurred to him before but he has often told me since that it has made the whole difference to his life. Of course the parallel is not perfectly exact – But I do feel rather strongly that one of the pleasantest features of our new situation is the fact that we are – for the first time in our lives – out of a crowd . . .

How delightful the wedding was! I confess that I thoroughly enjoyed it – from the moment when I took Bron to hire a pair of grey trousers from a friendly neighbour – to the time when I got that deliciously homey feeling one gets from seeing Lady Lister Kaye at the reception. Passages from Scottie's terse and pointed address still flit through my mind in the watches of the night – I find that they strengthen my character and enlarge my vocabulary – Do you remember when he said "Ask, inquire, request, investigate, scrutinise, interrogate, examine, cross-examine" – each succeeding word making clearer and fuller the meaning and message which were hinted at in the first quiet monosyllable! That is what I call oratory . . .

To Lady Horner   Hotel Grande Bretagne,
                                                                    Florence.
                                                          11 September 1907

. . . We skimmed the cream off the Uffizi this morning, and saw the Duomo, Or San Michele, and San Miniato in the afternoon. It is a rich diet – almost disturbingly rich after the rather meagre masterpieces of Umbria – But I was very much charmed with Siena – though I wish the cathedral could change its stripes, which remind me more of the absurd zebra than of the noble tiger. We are taking Italian art rather seriously and have read three books by Berenson. Do you think he can be right in supposing that the test of a good picture is that it should make you sweat without having to take exercise? It seems to me that there is a great opening for someone to write a book on art who not only knows about pictures, but can also think . . .

To Violet Asquith   20 Cavendish Square.
                                                              7 February 1908

Really, Violet, you ought not to have taken my Liddell & Scott [Greek Dictionary]; not only was it bound in light blue morocco but I have had it for fifteen years; so for God's sake tell me what you have done with it, as my position without it is exceedingly difficult and painful. As to my Ibsens, they turn up one by one in various corners of your room; and I have no serious complaint to make about them. But I do implore you to bring back safe the 3 vols. of Arthur Machen which you have taken.

If you had any conscience it would take more than the company of Eliza to keep your spirits up. But you have none: and it is with difficulty that I sign myself

Your loving brother Raymond

To Violet Asquith (in Switzerland)   49 Bedford Square.
10 March 1908

Certainly nothing sadder than Mark [Horner]'s death could have happened. I was very fond of him indeed. When one knew him well he had the most singular charm, partly due to an exceptional power of interesting himself extremely in things and people outside the ordinary circle of his life. In some ways he had the most remarkable character of any boy of his age I ever knew. Frances has shown the greatest courage all through but she has been terribly distressed of course and really very ill with a bad cold which prevented her from sleeping and almost prevented her breathing, and temperature varying from 103 to 96 . . .

The funeral was at Mells on Saturday and was a most affecting ceremony, as there was genuine grief among all the people there. Lear, the parson, was by way of having a kind of memorial service on the Sunday evening. His sermon was the most ghastly and formal piece of stupidity I have ever heard. I never saw an occasion worse used. The church was crammed with peasants from the outlying villages prepared to sob at the simplest eloquence; but Lear's line was to curse them for not coming to church oftener and remind them that life was short and it was well to lose no time in mending their ways. 'You have had a warning', he said. 'Profit by it.' This way of treating the situation pleased no one very much. And matters were not mended by reading a poem of Longfellow's called *The Reaper*. Poor Edward cried with disgust and indignation and I should dearly have liked to kick Lear round the parish.

To K. A.   Royal Hotel,
Winchester.
26 May 1908

I hope you are well and faithful. I am. Last night there was a riot here and they had to call out the soldiers. I didn't take any part on either side. The reason of the riot was that the corporation had caused an old cannon which is used as a place of assignation by local lovers to be moved from the bottom of a hill to the top . . .

It is quite warm here but not sunny. The limes and the hawthorn are beginning to scatter odours. I am still suffering a little from brain anaemia; it is fortunate that the brain is not much used in my profession. I am also suffering terribly from lack of Fawnia.[1] I must go back to Court now.

To K. A.   27 May 1908

. . . Here the heat and summer smells are delicious. I have just come in from dining with the judges which was rather tiresome: but before dinner I went for a 7 mile walk by myself to a cottage which Bluey and I had near here. Everything tended to make me very sentimental but I had to keep remembering to think of Frank Maguire and Elsie Kenchington – murderer and murderess. Every day I detest my profession more and wish more that I were rich.

How happy we should be on these· hot days in the country – and how wretched we are. There was another riot here last night in spite of the fact that the chief rioter of the night before had been enlisted as a special constable at a salary of 3/6 per night. The Mayor telephoned for the military but the Chief Constable telephoned that they were on no account to come: so the Mayor has complained to the War Office of the commanding officer and to the Home Office of the Chief Constable. Let me know where you are for Sunday: it is possible (tho' unlikely) that I might get away Sat. night . . .

To K. A.   31 May 1908

I couldn't send you a letter yesterday because from 10 in the morning till 11 at night I was in Court with only 3 intervals of ½ hour for food. Our Armenian witness who is very like Lady Sassoon but much cleverer fainted at the conclusion of her evidence and nearly expired in the lobby of the Court. Hawke the defending Counsel, who had only 3 hours sleep the night before made a speech lasting 4 hours during which he was sustained by doses of brandy furtively administered by his junior from a bottle under the bench. By the end of the day the prisoner was the only person in Court who looked fairly fresh and tidy.

He went into the box and gave his evidence with the greatest self-possession and owing to our lack of materials Radcliffe could get no damaging admissions from him in cross-examination. At 7 o'clock the judge began to sum up and at 8 the jury retired to consider their verdict. We waited in Court till 9.30 and then the judge told us to go and get some dinner: so we came down here and hurried through a rather nervous meal expecting every moment to be summoned back to hear the verdict. It was not until each of us had heartily consumed a bottle of champagne that any sign of returning vitality appeared.

As we walked into the great courtyard of King Arthur's Castle (where the trials are held) the scene was very poor. A thick white mist had suddenly

---

[1] His private nickname for Katharine.

climbed up the hill from the river and floated in wreaths about the air: through it glimmered faintly here and there the street lamps like magical censers gently swung by unseen acolytes: there was nothing visible to support them and yet they were held up and even seemed to swim a little in the thick air at the distant end of the courtyard. A company of 100 policemen was drawn up to keep off the people: and as we came out they all began to march with a crackling tread, clearing away the great crowd which had collected to hear the result so that the judge might pass; and then suddenly there was the blare of the judge's trumpets and the judge walked out, a dignified old man, very tall, wrapped in his long scarlet robes, stepped into his state coach and drove off to his lodgings . . .

To K. A.   Slains Castle,
Aberdeenshire.
10 September 1908

. . . I am sending you an extract from the Westminster in which the Rev. Jacob Primmer (one of our greatest protestants) suggests to God a good dodge for making the Popish procession a failure next Sunday. It will be interesting to see whether He is or is not above taking a hint. But how different from your Daddie and the 5th November! . . . [of which he mildly disapproved on humane grounds].

(Cutting from newspaper)

PRAYERS FOR RAIN

AT THE Protestant meeting in the Queen's Hall, Edinburgh, last night, the Rev. Jacob Primmer and several other speakers, denounced the Roman Catholic doctrine of Transubstantiation. Referring to the Eucharistic Congress and the procession connected therewith, Mr Primmer said the Lord could employ means of making it a fiasco by sending down rain.

To Cynthia Charteris   The Kirkhouse,
Innerleithen.
17 September 1908

I am delighted to hear that you and Ego are coming to us on Monday. This is just a line to pin you down and make it more difficult for you to break faith (as the whole of your family have a natural tendency to do).

Bring tennis shoes and racquets, golf clubs, green stockings for confirmation and a small crystal beaker to quaff the waters of St. Ronan's Well . . . You shall be met at any station you choose to name by the clansmen.

To K. A.   Gosford.
                                                                1 October 1908

. . . Prize [i.e. Cynthia Charteris] has been having a flirtation with a nasty little man called Mallock who wrote *The New Republic* and comes here for a few days every year because he and Lord Wemyss are agreed that nothing should be given to the poor and particularly nothing which belongs to Lord Wemyss. I believe Margot made a floater at lunch today by asking him how long he took to write *"The Mighty Atom"* which it appears was really written by Marie Corelli! But Cynthia was a good deal occupied with him and I haven't been able to get a word with her till this evening . . .

To K. A.   Avon Tyrrell,
                                                            Christchurch.
                                                        29 Novemnber 1908

Hugh Cecil becomes daily more entirely given up to all forms of chambering and wantonness. He cares for nothing but eating, drinking, hunting and cards; lies in bed till eleven in the morning reading loose novels, and grumbled loudly this morning when he was driven off to church behind the white horses.

I wish I were a fanatical Christian of high birth. It is the only way to enjoy oneself. But I suppose my turn will come in the next world . . .

To K. A.   49 Bedford Square, W.C.
                                                            10 December 1908

. . . Edward rang me up while I was having my bath in a great state of agitation because in spite of him and Goschen[1] both pleading guilty the Westminster and St James' each had a paragraph about it, and the Westminster with its usual damnable inaccuracy had said that they both pleaded to being drunk and disorderly, whereas E. was only charged with obstructing the police. Frances hadn't seen anything about it so far and he suggested that I should come round and assist him in explaining it to her. But I strongly advised him to say nothing about it and trust to her not seeing it in the papers. I had read both of them without noticing it; and I remember Geoffrey Howard tearing out law reports from all the papers for a week after he was arrested at a pols' dancing club which was raided some years ago with the result that Lady Carlisle[2] who would have turned him out of the house if she had found out does not know about it to this day In this case it may make the dew fall heavier if it is discovered, but the chance seems worth gambling on. It is very bad luck.

[1] Bunt Goschen, an Oxford crony of Edward's.
[2] Instead of his being turned out, Castle Howard was later left to him rather than to his elder brother.

I spent all this morning in intimating to a Major in the Indian Army that his grandfather instead of being the legitimate son of an Irish Peer as he had supposed was the bastard of a butcher in Long Acre. It was very uphill work, as he was every inch a soldier and like all soldiers entertained an obstinate belief that he was also a gentleman – which it took 2½ hours of the most minute argumentation to eradicate. Then in the afternoon I spent 3 hours roaring like a Hyde Park secularist at 2 rather pretty but very deceitful women who had falsely pretended that they had supplied false teeth to a vast multitude of bed ridden spinsters and felt myself inadequately rewarded when they were sentenced to a year's imprisonment . . .

To K. A.

Royal Hotel,
College Green,
Bristol.
26 March 1909

Thank you for your exquisite letter. How monstrous to wrap up the Junior Dean in a petticoat! whose was it? not Fawnia's I hope. But still more monstrous to take away poor Patrick's scholarship. The folly of the young is nothing to the folly of the old . . .

To K. A.

Lympne Castle,
Lympne,
Kent.
24 July 1909

I came here at lunch time and we drove off in a motor afterwards to Littlestone, 10 miles away, and played golf till dinner. The air was sunny and full of larks and I enjoyed myself. After dinner we played bridge, some of us, while the younger and more mercurial spirits danced and sang. And now I have come to bed in a room in the old part of the house which no one has ever slept in yet because it is supposed to be haunted by a monk – the least terrifying of all possible apparitions. But I should be well content to sleep in the room if it were haunted by the Devil himself. The bed is tall and covered with pink silk, the walls are 6 feet thick, the furniture which is not too crowded for beauty or too scanty for convenience, is of the best Jacobean oak, and the ceiling is of an admirable camber. There is a dressing room and a bathroom panelled in oak and equipped with a large bath of the most flawless and creamy porcelain.

The whole house is very beautiful both within and without, and though there would be little more for you to do here than there is for me at Mells, I

can't help thinking that you would like it. It stands on an eminence commanding the channel and Romney Marsh – a wide flat expanse intersected with
canals and embellished with windmills, a prospect with the illimitable planitude
of Koninck irradiated with the soft diffusion of Cuyp's golden light.

I like Annie – she is a strange mixture of Philistine and connoisseur,
laborious taste and undisciplined intelligence, and has the power (which only
the combination gives) of making a house both comfortable and picturesque, a
conversation both inane and tolerable. She would have been a good wife to
Andrea del Sarto, but a poor mistress to the meanest of stockbrokers; the ends
of the world have not come upon her eyelids, but the water is hot, the pillows
soft, and the brandy very old. And the children too are lovely and limited,
sweet and pure and brainless, fitter to be painted by Paul Potter than by
Sargent, benign and bourgeois as angels on the bioscope.

As you may imagine it is all very agreeable and entirely to my taste. As for
me – wherever two or three thousand pounds are gathered together, there I am
in the midst of them. That whimsical devil Ballard[1] seized the occasion to send
me away without any dress clothes – a pretty trick to play upon a young man
who is going to spend a few days in the society of wealthy angels.

I have to get up infernally early on Monday in order to appear in court
against Horatio Bottomley.

To K. A.   49 Bedford Square, W.C.
                                                        13 August 1909

. . . Today I had an interview with the Premier of Newfoundland who is claiming that about ½ Canada is really part of his wretched little island and wishes
me to submit arguments to the Privy Council in support of his fantastic
hypothesis.

He was so much impressed by a previous opinion which I had written for his
government on a matter of Constitutional Law that he begged me to publish it
as a magazine article – an act which would involve my immediate expulsion
from the profession . . .

To Lady Manners   Lympne Castle,
                                                        Lympne,
                                                        Kent.
                                                        14 August 1909

. . . London was quite insufferable: I worked 10 hours a day in a room like the
Sahara in the endeavour to master in a week a controversy which has engaged
the brightest intellects of England and America for exactly 126 years next

---

[1] Raymond's manservant.

October. It is characteristic of this country that when at last the question comes up to be finally settled, we leave the selection of the arguments to be presented at the Hague to the discretion of an inexperienced stripling exercised during the few moments which he can afford to spare from golf during the last fortnight of August. However, I have now done all that can be done for the present with the materials which they have supplied, and have fortunately discovered an intelligent Canadian who has devoted to the subject the greater part of a long and arduous life spent in the purlieus of Pimlico, and he provides me from time to time with volumes of printed argument from which I do my best to excise the poetry. Considering how much prose there is in the poetry of the New World, it is remarkable how much poetry there is in their prose. It seems that anyone of American origin is liable in the middle of the most closely reasoned legal argument to break out into some lyrical ebullition about Liberty being the inalienable privilege of every rational creature, or what not. And it is this kind of joyous outburst, more appropriate to a lark than a lawyer, which I have to try to restrain.

. . . Do you notice how, whenever L. George has made a particularly outrageous speech, he arranges that it shall be immediately followed by a 'bereavement'? and then the newspapers point out that this kind of thing evokes all that is best and noblest in our public life, and the whole affair passes off very pleasantly. After he gave the Cabinet away to the Daily Mail his daughter died, and now after Limehouse his sister . . .

To Conrad Russell   Avon Tyrrell,
                                                   Christchurch.
                                                   23 January 1910

Many thanks for the Watson dossier. I have read the articles with great pleasure: especially the one in which a Veteran Diplomat urges with much force that if Margot had succeeded in her attempts to marry Arthur Balfour or Rosebery, they would constantly have been taunting her with the fact that her grandfather was a 'journey-man weaver', whereas my father, being himself a person of low extraction, would take pride in the fact that her father at any rate was a baronet. Let us meet soon. Could you dine at Bed. Sq. some & which night this week?

To Cynthia Charteris   49 Bedford Square, W.C.
                                                   9 March 1910

I expect that you feel about French rather as I do when I am supplicated to become a member of Parliament – divided between a loathing for drudgery and a liking for éclat. I hope you will decide as I have done. You are too young to be public. A public woman loses caste. A public man gains it. Besides, nothing kills charm like a profession . . . However much you may charm across the footlights you charm infinitely more across the dinner table. To offer your 'hyacinth hair and Naiad grace'[1] to the stalls is like pelting a mad bull with white violets. Don't do it. I sympathise with your wish for pocket money. But remember that I owe you nine shillings. Shall I buy you a tortoise with it?

To K. A.

> Queen's Hotel,
> Birmingham.
> 14 March 1910

I hope that you spent a pleasant day at Taplow. When I left this morning the stage was crowded with all the properties of Spring – sunlit dew, carolling larks, gambolling lambs, etc. Lord Curzon, with whom I breakfasted, was positively the only unvernal object on that scene . . .

To K. A.

> Chateauneuf-sur-Loire.
> 14 May 1910

. . . We lunched at a place called Dreux and got to Chartres at about 3, the glass in the Cathedral is certainly as good as one can want, and the interior gives a fine general impression. I lighted a candle for you before the shrine of the black Virgin. It is a very fine one, much bigger than anyone else's and cost a franc.

We reached Orleans at 6, and would to God we had stayed there. But it was so early that we decided to push on here another twenty miles, and find ourselves now in an inn of a very squalid kind. We ordered a bottle of 84 claret for our dinner but it was like vinegar. A Frenchman had dinner with us, but we were both too frightened to speak to him as I believe etiquette demands, and about the middle of the meal he got up with a loud snort and left the room. The worst of speaking to foreigners is that they answer you back and then you are done because you don't understand a word. Bluey is very bitter about the French; he says that whenever you say anything to them they repeat it again with a different accent. After dinner there was a procession of the local fire brigade with helmets, torches and music all round the town, followed by the inhabitants singing, and by Bluey and me not singing. It is worth noting I think, that torches are far the cheapest way of making an impressive and picturesque effect . . .

[1] A misquotation from *To Helen* by Edgar Allen Poe,
> Thy hyacinth hair, thy classic face,
> Thy Naiad airs have brought me home
> To the glory that was Greece,
> And the grandeur that was Rome.

To K. A.
Gd. Hotel De Paris, Nevers.
15 May 1910 Whitsunday

. . . Our hard night at Chateauneuf passed off better than I dared to hope. I slept a good deal in spite of the sandpaper sheets, and Bluey has so far had no rheumatic symptoms. Still I regard the episode as a blot on my life. Nothing can justify discomfort except being able to brag about it afterwards. If it is really dramatically acute one can tell the story to one's grandchildren, as for instance that one found a pig in one's bed or that the floor was black with bugs; and again if it was part of a recognised achievement – if in consequence of enduring this hardship one had killed an exceptionally large tiger or climbed an exceptionally high mountain – such things become a saga and fill up gaps at dinner. But the bare facts that one motored 20 miles further than one had intended and as a result lay between coarse sheets are irredeemably tiresome and unrecitable, intolerable at the time and useless hereafter. It is simply like having been for one day in penal servitude. It is physically and spiritually degrading. I shall write to Galsworthy and perhaps he will make a play about it . . .

. . . We started early and saw two very interesting churches; the first at a little place called Germigny was Carolingian, restored but very well restored, very massive and simple with round arches – a great pleasure after the riot of points and pinnacles. We went in and sat there for a ¼ hour watching a dozen little girls being rehearsed for their first communion which was to take place later in the day: they were plain and unmelodious and in quite the wrong frame of mind, as they kept turning round and giggling and ogling us, but their white dresses and veils were extremely pretty and there was something very primitive and charming about the whole scene.

The priest had spasms of gout and swore horribly about the singing at the beadle. Then we went on a little further to St Benoit-sur-Loire where there was another very early church – an abbey, built at the beginning of the 11th century with a wonderful porch in 2 storeys of round arches. It reminded me a little of Torcello. We listened to the service for a while. There was a very large congregation, mostly peasant women with brown faces and white caps. The strong sunlight made it very gay and clean and seemed to dry up and burn out the vulgar richness and more pestilent part of Popery as the brandy burns the fat out of a plum pudding.

Then we drove on to Bourges where I found your letter. The Cathedral – hunch backed as usual – is very fine and the glass even better than Chartres; at any rate there is more of it. Between there and Nevers we encountered a dust storm and became encrusted and granulated to a horrible degree. We also burst a tyre, and while it was being mended I found some stinking Horehound; also Orchis maculata, greater Celandine, a handsome kind of purple stock which I think is Cardamine bulbifera and Bluey Hesperis mathomelir, and a tallish white flower which I believe to be Saxifraga granulata, dubitante Bluey. Nevers is an attractive place with shady squares and boulevards and a nice renaissance chateau . . .

Bluey has a telegraph code for motorists with which we amuse ourselves; it consists of ridiculous words like those you see on the backs of encyclopedias, and by means of it you can order any number of bedrooms and any style of furniture. Last time we ordered six cots by mistake. It was a waste Helen not being there . . .

To K. A.   Hotel d'Europe,
Avignon.
17 May 1910

. . . We lunched at a place called Montelimar, the Nougat Mecca. I caused two boxes of this succulent sweetmeat to be despatched to you. They say that it is made better there than anywhere else in the world. But whether it is worth making at all I do not know. At Orange we inspected the triumphal arch and Roman theatre – both quite admirable. Did you know that it was from this place that our William III drew his title? Probably you did. For my part I had always vaguely connected him with the Orange Free State.

We got here about six. The Rhone is very fine here – broad and green and fringed with thick bushes, and the town looked very noble in the grey mist. This hotel is spacious and comfortable. We drank the famous Hermitage wine at dinner which is really equal to its reputation. After dinner an insufferably fat woman played upon a large golden harp, extracting throbbing cadences which interfered a little with the pleasure of my cigar . . .

To K. A.   Avignon.
18 May 1910

. . . We have a very elegant suite upholstered in crimson and gold, and there is a peace and dignity about this place, especially when it rains, which is very grateful. It seems to me exactly the place for a retired Pope to come to and I think it was very clever of them to see that so long ago as 1307. I like the place – But the thing which has struck me most and which I shall always remember with surprise, is that the red Hermitage is very distinctly better than the white. I had come here with the contrary impression, derived from Andrew Lang – But he must after all be a superficial creature, and the world is right not to treat him very seriously.

I think I may say that we ticked off Avignon during the 2 hours of fine weather this afternoon. The Papal Palace is quite perfect, so far as anything empty can be. And I liked the Cathedral very much. The architecture is almost domestic in its well-bred sobriety – and inside it is nearly pitch dark (which is a great asset in a church of this period) – and in stalls in the apse the choir in scarlet robes intone the mass in a solemn and lonely delirium. The space which would be the aisles is taken up entirely by a series of little side chapels, and in these the people who would be the congregation clear their throats and spit: so that in the nave it is very comfortable and there is room for holy feelings. In the largest of the side chapels a very old woman was conducting a service in French: here it was forbidden to spit – But the rule was violated . . .

To K. A.   Nîmes.
19 May 1910

. . . Today we drove to Arles, lunched and saw the sights in an hour; the cloister of mixed styles is much the best thing there I think. Then on to Nîmes, stopping en route at a place called St Gilles where there is a 12th century church with the most gorgeous facade which is the only happy example I have ever seen of architectural statuary. Much finer to my mind than the South portal at Chartres.

At Nîmes again we were very expeditious. The amphitheatre and Maison Carrée are both admirable but a very little time suffices. Then we drove on to the Pont du Gard which is sublime. I walked along the parapet from end to end and found a number of unknown (and so far as our efforts went unknowable) flowers both on the bridge itself and in the dry bed of the river. The only one of a dozen new and lovely varieties which we could identify was a wild jasmine – bright yellow and deliciously scented. Thence we drove quickly home . . .

To K. A.   20 May 1910

. . . Today it has been pouring as usual and we had some thunder. I suppose it is this damned comet. Not even Bluey can wag the tail of a comet. Nevertheless we motored to Les Baux – not very far off, and quite one of the most extraordinary places I have ever seen. We lunched at a little place called St Rémy where there is an inn with an excellent cuisine, and some inconsiderable but exceedingly elegant Roman monuments. Thence we drove up a steep winding road for 5 or 6 miles into the hills – the most unnatural kind of hills with a foreground of impossibly Leonardesque precipices and a middle distance exactly like the background of a Mantegna landscape – little green bushes scattered as from a pepper-dredger over grey stones bare enough to look half painted and altogether unfinished. I suppose that the rock is limestone but it must be singularly soft because instead of blasting it they cut it (where the road goes through) with a knife as clean as you would cut cheese, and where it is exposed to the weather the mere force of the wind is enough to pit it with deep and fantastic pock-marks. When we had wriggled up to a great height we came upon this extraordinary village of Les Baux, holding now about a couple of hundred people, but in the 14th century a populous place and the impregnable seat of the most powerful Seigneurie in the South of France. One of the Counts of the Baux was Emperor of Constantinople about 1380. Many of the houses are simply cut out of the soft rock, with all their furniture – chairs, tables, beds, chimneys, wine-presses and kitchen-dressers, and you look from their windows down hundreds of feet of sheer rock wall. There is a great ruined castle on the summit partly built, partly excavated, and entirely protected by precipitous bastions of natural rock; and then in one of the little streets you will come upon a tiny church with fluted columns and elegant renaissance detail of the 16th century.

Dante is said to have taken the architecture of his Inferno from the scenery of this region. It reminded me a little of that equally renowned work (unknown, I think, to you) *King Solomon's Mines* by Rider Haggard. We drove back through Arles and past a ruinous monastery called Montmajour with a fine cloister and an eighth century subterranean chapel. In the museum at Arles is the golden hair of a daughter of one of the Lords of Les Baux whose skeleton was dug up some years ago. After 500 years it is still a lovely colour though a little lacking in mass. That fearful bore Mistral has written a poem about it. He is the Yeats of Provence. He has exploited Provence as Yeats has exploited Ireland. He has invented a language, a literature, a temperament, a costume, and even a cast of countenance, which have turned Provence into a going concern. The poor wretched overworked peasants spend all their scanty leisure in adulterating their naturally pure French and twisting their unnaturally natural hair into Greek modes. The bookstalls groan beneath the poems of Mistral, the streets and museums are plastered with his portraits, the square obstructed and dominated by his statues. He has a goat's beard, a pot-belly, and a felt hat and looks as if he would have made a good President of Nicaragua . . .

To K. A.   30 May 1910

No letter from you today and only 5 minutes left for me to write to you. We have been delayed this evening by a tea-party; the Premier of Newfoundland came – a pink plump rough-hewn sort of creature, very like men whose function it is to stand outside bathing machines and teach little boys how to swim by ducking them. There also came a man called Young who is going to act as Secretary to the tribunal. He really belongs to Bryce's Staff at Washington, and is married to a daughter of Old Ilbert, whom I remember at Oxford as being rather pretty; but she appears now to go in more for being clever.

It turns out that in addition to 5 English Counsel and two Canadians we are to have the assistance of 3 ex-attorney generals of Newfoundland! Really the thing is becoming rather a farce, when you have a team of eleven. I hope it won't mean that we shall be paid less. The Newfd. premier says that 6 weeks is the minimum time we shall take . . .

To K. A. Hôtel du Vieux Doelen,
The Hague.
31 May 1910

. . . I am glad that you are melting a little towards Visey [Raymond's sister Violet] – she was quite abnormal when you saw her at Archerfield; normally I don't think she is theatrical or insincere – certainly not if handled firmly; though I admit there is a thin crust of nonsense borrowed consciously or unconsciously from Margot; but it is part of her training more than of her nature; and if you put your foot quickly through it the birds begin to sing and everything is all right . . .

To K. A. 1 June 1910

Thank you very much for today's letter which arrived safely this morning though addressed to "The Hague, London" but don't reckon too much on the intelligence of the post office.

I am taking advantage of a temporary lull in the proceedings to begin a letter which I probably shan't be able to finish till later. The tribunal holds its first formal sitting at 4 this afternoon. But nothing will happen then except a little speech by the President in praise of Peace – The real business will not begin till Monday. Meanwhile difficulties have arisen about the conduct of our case, and it looks as if the energies of our General would be exhausted before battle is joined by quelling mutiny in the ranks. The tribunal has decided that there are to be four speeches on each side delivered alternately, England taking the first. It is settled that Finlay opens for England and that Robson closes; the trouble is about the two intermediate speakers, who are to be a Canadian called Ewart and a Newfoundland Attorney General called Sir James Winter: Ewart knows more about the case than anyone else as he has been working on it for three years or more, but he appears to be so much biassed in favour of his own country that he is quite unable to distinguish the good parts of our argument from the bad, and inclined – according to Finlay who dreads, distrusts and detests him – to dwell at inordinate length and with equal emphasis upon every possible point. As for Winter, he has all the appearance of being a mere dummy; he admittedly knows very little about the facts of the case; it is apparent from his face that he is devoid of the divine faculty of reason so frequently useful even to the advocate; and though phonetic peculiarities lend to his discourse a certain element of the picturesque, the poverty of his vocabulary is inadequately veiled by a profuse variety in pronunciation which enables him to give an individual flavour and an unexpected sound to the few rather ordinary words which at short notice he is able to command. However, they are all sons of the Empire, and I suppose we must take them as we find them. But for my part I would sooner have this case argued by a boy scout than by Sir James Winter. Finlay said that he never had a case in which he took less pleasure or had more unpleasant and embarrassing wrangles; Robson has already threatened three or four times to throw up his brief and go home; Peterson and I, who have been temporarily thrown out of work by these domestic quarrels in which we take no part, find useful employment in drawing up a report upon the cheaper varieties of Dutch cigars of which we are making an exhaustive study. However, things seem to have quieted down again for the moment, and tomorrow we shall get to work again with Robson on our argument which is now seriously behindhand owing to these constant interruptions – or rather would be behindhand if there is any chance of its having to be delivered before the middle of July.

Since I began this letter we have attended the first meeting of the tribunal which lasted about half an hour. It was held in a small stuffy room, densely crowded and totally unventilated. The English Counsel pre-occupied all the places of vantage at the head of the table allotted to us, leaving the daughter Nations to fight for the limited accommodation provided at the back of the room; so that there was a perspiring mob of Colonial Attorney Generals and prime ministers seething and weltering below the salt, gnashing upon one another with their rugged jaws and thickening the air with a melée of strange slogans in their native idioms. The President of the tribunal, an Austrian called Lammash, made a speech in rather elaborate pigeon English about the blessings of Peace, and then we all trooped out again. We are to meet again on Monday and sit 4 days a week from 10 to 12 and from 2 to 4. The great feature of life here is the interchange of visting cards on an enormous scale. Great piles of them are brought up to my room every hour with the most outlandish names upon them. I have never had a card in my life, but Lady Robson very kindly writes my name on her card and I discharge my duties vicariously as her son.

I must stop now to catch the post. Give my love to Frances. I adore you always.

To K. A.   9 June 1910

I have the unusual joy of two letters from you this morning, one from Clonboy and one from Bed. Sq. It really is monstrous their not having finished the road yet: they have been at it for a month and a half. We ought to make a row about it – though for my own part I dote on the smell of pitch – the bad part is that you can't touch it without being defiled. As to the heap of circulars and bills, I gave no instructions about them, and so far as bills are concerned, I don't see my way to paying any for months. But as I am going to be away for so long it might be a good thing I think if you would run through the heap with a view of discovering whether it contains (a) a notice from the rating authorities to say that they are going to raise my rateable value (b) a notice from the National Provident Society asking for payment of my insurance premium (c) any invitations to dine, lunch, sup, sleep or what not, with Lady Cunard. Documents falling into any one of these 3 classes will require immediate and firm answers by me, and had better be forwarded. Bills can be disregarded unless accompanied by writs: but should not be destroyed.

Last night the Robsons and I dined with Fitzpatrick, the Canadian C.J. at a Dutch Restaurant called "The Old Devil", on the road between here and Leyden. He drove us out in his motor about 5 or 6 miles and we found a dozen or so of fellow guests, including the American Arbitrator, Gray, (a judge of the Supreme Court in the U.S.) and a bevy of transpontine beauties. We dined in a large airy room, very clean and mostly consisting of windows, all open, so that at last one began to feel cool. The food was simple and good, but very slowly served, and the champagne very sweet. Gray and Fitzpatrick both seem very nice men and I should say, very capable too. I was partnered with Miss Fitzpatrick, a darkish girl, moderately pretty and gifted or cursed with the kind of confused vivacity which Americans seem to be born to: there were no boundary lines between her talking, her laughing, her eating, her drinking: each process seemed to flow into the other after the manner of Hegel's opposites, but without resulting in anything which you could call a higher unity: indeed I found it so difficult to disentangle any meaning from her composite communications that for fear of seeming deaf or a dummy I was driven to imitate her own methods and to take refuge in a boisterous agglomeration of all my functions, whether of thought, speech, feeling, or mere assimilation, in the hope of producing a general impression of cryptic and inarticulate bonhomie. On my other side I had Miss Robson with whom at rare intervals I was able to communicate in the ordinary language of the dinner table. I have never before found myself in company where the only way of maintaining one's self respect was to speak with one's mouth full. Opposite was Gray's daughter, much the prettiest of them all, but rather too tall thin and faded, with a very large mouth, but white teeth, straight nose and dimples. She seemed roguish, but I got no chance of dalliance with her, because after dinner I was nobbled by a girl whose name I never found out, who told me that she always stood up for 20 minutes after meals in order to get thin; so I thought that I was bound by good manners to stand with her. It was a very long 20 minutes. About 11 we all motored back. In the motor the girl who wanted to get thin began re-arranging the button-hole of a young Canadian who was of the party: he told her with a caressing intonation that she was "a sweet little fusser": and so she was . . .

To Edward Horner   15 June 1910

Many thanks for your wire which I have just received – I wish very much that I could dine with you on 5 July but I'm afraid there is not the least chance of my getting away from here till the last week of July at earliest. The arbitration in which I am engaged (between England & United States) began on June 1 and Finlay's opening speech will not be concluded till the end of this week. After that there are seven more speakers to come, 3 British, 4 American, (of whom I am not one.) The proceedings are necessarily rather slow as none of the judges understand English and none of the advocates (except Robson) speak it. The Americans of course speak American; Finlay speaks Scotch; and we also have on our side a Canadian and a Newfoundlander who speak the dialects of their respective dominions: this is perhaps not without its advantages, since the limitations of their vocabulary are to some extent disguised by the peculiarities of their pronunciation, and they continue to give a great variety of sounds – none of them familiar – to the same word. However the proceedings are both lengthy & costly, & calculated therefore to satisfy the nice feelings of honour entertained by the two high-spirited nations concerned. Fortunately this hotel is going to be pulled down at the beginning of August, so I suppose I shall get away then at any rate. You must have finished your schools by now, I imagine, & be serving your sentence of rustication. I hope that you have been as lucky in the examinations as I was; I remember that the weather was so warm that I was able to drink a quart of Moselle Cup in the quad during the luncheon interval on each of the six – or was it seven? – days. Katharine tells me that you are depressed by the simultaneous betrothals of Cynthia & Mary [Vesey to Aubrey Herbert] – It is a double bereavement hard to be borne. The older wines are now all drunk, and I fear that you may be becalmed for a time in the interval between two vintages, until the younger liquors mature. But there is always whisky & soda, varied by light wines from the wood. You would not like Holland. The women are meek & shiny, and tend to be square rather than round.

To Aubrey Herbert on his engagement   Hotel du Vieux Doelen
                                                   16 June 1910

You are consummate. Your luck amounts to genius. To be frank with you, a more glittering prize was never awarded to a more mis-spent life than yours. The prodigal son and the man who got a penny for an hour's work are left panting in the rear. The practice of eating your cake and having it has been reduced by you to an exact science; and by an added touch of almost unnatural dexterity you eat and have every one else's cake as well. For a very long time nothing has pleased me so much (nor you either I dare say) as this news which I had simultaneously from you and from Katharine. Both of you are now firmly secured within the particular little plot of society which also contains Katharine and me – whereas either of you might so easily have strayed into some alien and inaccessible orbit. Mary was capable of marrying an Irishman and living on an island: you might have been entangled either with a dowdy aristocrat or with a flashy cosmopolitan, a Hapsburg or a Levantine; but you have secured breeding without dullness and beauty without vice. This shows that it is possible to rise, as well as to fall, between two stools. It used to be one of your obstinate prepossessions, I remember, that I did not appreciate Mary at her true value; and it may be that when I first knew her I did not fully take her in: I have always thought that she had not Cynthia's unparalleled skill in dressing the shop-window. But no one could accuse me now of lack of appreciation. She is superb, one of the jewels of the universe. Some day or another I suppose I shall fall in love with her, and then in deference to your incurable dramatic instinct we shall shoot one another on the sands at Dieppe. I can see you now making all the arrangements with the greatest possible gusto; and Bron explaining that his position in the Government makes it difficult for him to act as second to either of us. But in the meantime we shall all be very happy together. I well remember the day when it first occurred to me that Mary was one of the most beautiful women in Europe. It was last August when Katharine and I were at Venice. Mary had just come down from the Dolomites and we were to take her out to dinner. I walked with her from our hotel across the Piazza to the Vapore, and it was like walking with an archangel: there was a depth and radiance in her beauty which beat back the twilight as a strong swimmer divides the waves: it was as if the brightest star were reflected in the darkest sapphire; the church of St Mark was enriched as she passed and as I led her through the tables of Florian's I was thrilled with a sort of celestial snobbery, a pure racial pride which Kipling and Nelson and Tariff Reform and all the rest of our imperial assets have never been able to stir in me. However, I must rein in this rhapsody or you will suspect that I am already in love with her. But it is only that I have strong feelings about beauty which are nevertheless impersonal very often. When are you going to be married? Not I hope for a little while, because I am cooped up in this damned flat prosy rectangular land till the end of July or thereabouts, and I want to dance at your wedding . . . Bless you, my dear Aubrey – I wish we were drinking together to this great exploit of yours.

To K. A. 18 June 1910

. . . I am sorry to learn your news about Cynthia, but the operation is a very safe one and will probably have the effect of raising her vital powers and getting rid for ever of the headaches and vapours from which she has been used to suffer. Still it seems rather hard to lose both your appendix and your virginity within a single month – However, it never rains but it pours – For my part I should rather resent the lack of an appendix in my bride: in quite a young girl I think it is more becoming to have an appendix, I should regard its presence as a guarantee that she had been properly brought up, and its absence as a sign that she had been tarnished a little by contact with the world. However, (like Sir Ian Hamilton) I am rather sentimental and old-fashioned about women, and I daresay Beb will be content to take her as he finds her.

I have had a letter from Hugh [Godley] grousing a good deal about the state of the world and particularly about Mary's marriage. It is certainly a bad business for him the way all the best things are being snapped up by more or less dark horses – I wish I might live to see the Duchess of Rutland's face on the simultaneous announcement of engagements between Marjorie and Oc and Diana and Cis respectively. As I don't belong to an Empire-building family, I take a certain pride in belonging to a mother-wrecking one.

To K. A.   22 June 1910

I am so glad that at last your long wait is over, and the baby safely born . . .

I am longing to hear further particulars from Frances, and whether Dr. Easton fulfilled her expectations. I do hope that everything will go well now, and that you will have no tiresome set-back. When you are a little stronger I will run over for a couple of days to see you. Probably I should be able to see more of you if I came, not next Saturday, but the one after. And the baby would be more personable by then too. I hope that you are not too much disappointed at its not being a boy. It is a pity, as variety is certainly more amusing, but there is not much difference between the sexes now-a-days, and what little there is shows a tendency to decrease. Anyhow, I daresay Helen will prefer having another doe to play with; and until they reach the ball-gown period girls are certainly cheaper than boys . . .

To K. A.   23 June 1910

. . . The first of the American speakers who had promised to finish tomorrow, has now announced that he will probably continue through all next week. His accent, which I wrongly took to be that of New England, turns out on the contrary to belong to the Pacific coast, where he was for many years engaged as a porter on the Canadian-Pacific railway. His speech has so far been confined entirely to an analysis of certain doctrines of the Roman Law – It seems to our notions a strange function to assign to a porter; but he manfully proclaims his propositions in the voice of a man accustomed to announce the names of railway stations and his Latinity would drown the noise of buffers . . .

To K. A.   24 June 1910

. . . I hear that Helen regards McKenna as its father, but shall be bitterly disappointed if the child's appearance gives any warrant to such an appalling attribution . . .

To K. A.   26 June 1910

. . . I hear that your conduct towards the new baby is so harsh and unwelcoming as to provoke a reaction among the servants at Bed. Sq., who have now got a strong early-Victorian feeling that the despised and ill-treated child will turn out to be a Cinderella and put Helen quite in the shade.

    . . . The American Shunter is still booming away like a bittern . . .

To K. A.   8 July 1910

Another day of boring booming balderdash from Mr. Warren. His speech is tedious and incoherent beyond description, but it is so carefully prepared and so automatically delivered that he reads out aloud not only the substance of what he wishes to say but also the stage directions. It produces a very comical effect when at the end of some impassioned passage of declaration about the greatness and goodness of the United States the orator adds in exactly the same exalted tone of voice the word 'Period'. It is worse than Selah in the Psalms. One wonders he doesn't sometimes add 'Sensation in Court', 'Cheers' etc. Sometimes he will read from a document, then interpolate a comment, then say 'continue reading' and so proceed with the rest of the document. If ever the Court interrupts him with a question he is completely floored and says that he would prefer to answer it tomorrow, and when tomorrow comes he produces and reads a type-written answer prepared for him I suppose by Root, who appears to be the only man among them with brains above the rabbit level. Any nation ought to be ashamed to be represented by such advocates. Unfortunately I don't suppose very much will depend on advocacy in this case, or we should win hands down.

    Last night I dined with Fitzpatrick and took in to dinner the daughter of another of the Arbitrators Miss Drago. She was divinely lovely, at least so it seemed to my starved gaze . . . She was more like Stella [Mrs Patrick] Campbell than anyone else but with a much better skin, larger and darker eyes and plenty of breeding which Stella lacks I think. Her head has a good shape, perhaps a little too big, and her hands lovely, but her back was not straight enough; and this was really her only fault, except her almost total ignorance of English.

    Her father is or was Minister for Foreign Affairs in the Argentine and

Spanish is her native tongue. She spoke French, as far as I could judge, not very fluently or correctly, and I did my best to reply in the same language, but as you may imagine the conversation was of a very elementary and fragmentary character. I have never reproached myself so bitterly for my folly in not learning to speak French nor you for your cruelty in not teaching me . . .

I have written so much about Miss Drago that the post is going. But you won't make this a grievance because, lovely as she is, she is dust compared with my starry Fawnia, whom I love and worship world without end. ('Period')

To K. A.   10 July 1910

. . . Your news is interesting. I am glad Patrick [Shaw-Stewart] is going into partnership [in Barings Bank] with Revelstoke, as it will withdraw him from competition at the bar—I see no reason why he should not be a very good financier, if he can obliterate his education, which I believe is very quickly done in a Bank . . .

I am dining tonight with Finlay at Scheveningen – I fear Miss Drago will not be there. I knew that you would be rather rusty about her, but I can assure you that she is very cold and demure. You might suggest to Ego to come out and have a look at her – I don't know why you say, as if it were a grievance, that all men are the same. They are not all the same even to the extent of agreeing to admire beautiful women, but if they were I don't know why you should complain of this, since it is entirely to your advantage . . .

To K. A.   12 July 1910

. . . I wish you wouldn't try to put off on me the responsibility of finding a name for your child. I have provided it with a surname which, but for my very handsome act in leading you to the altar at St Margaret's it would certainly never have had, and I really think that you ought to provide it with a Christian name. After all you are a Christian and I am not . . .

To Conrad Russell   17 July 1910

Your 2 sheets of stamps came in the nick of time. Katharine tells me that there is a law under which you are fined £50 if you don't name your child within a month, so I sent the stamps off at once & the whole of both sheets are to be affixed to the child in the presence of a public official. I think you once told me that something of the kind was done to Lord Amberley. I hope it won't mean that my grandchildren will all be buggers or bigamists. But I daresay they would have been anyhow.[1]

[1] (No sign yet. Ed.)

I am exceedingly tired of being at the Hague, but see no chance of getting away till near the middle of August. I haven't your facility for living contentedly in foreign countries. The Zoo here is very bad too. There is practically nothing in it but a Chiff-Chaff (called in Dutch Tjif-Tjaf) – not even zygodactylous you know.

To K. A.   18 July 1910

. . . I have finished Virgil now, and nearly finished *The Ambassadors*: it is more exasperatingly refined and more heavily veiled than almost any of the others: I don't wonder that he thinks it his masterpiece: one has to keep one's wits about one to be sure that one is reading a novel at all and not merely watching someone else in the distance having his nose tickled with a cobweb – not vigorously enough to make him sneeze, unless he were James himself . . .

To K. A.   20 July 1910

. . . A strange thing happened this afternoon: I had gone with Peterson and the 2 mysterious ladies to see the Mesday pictures: as we walked away along the street, I noticed a Dutch boy dancing along the pavement and waving his hat in the air; there was such an undutch vivacity in his gestures that I said to Miss Fox (with whom I was walking) that he must have a gadfly after him: and then suddenly we saw Peterson (who was a few yards ahead with Mrs Fox) begin dancing and waving in exactly the same way: and next moment I became conscious that we were in the middle of a swarm of bees, and I began dancing and waving too; they bustled against one's cheeks like bullets; but the odd thing was that they didn't go near either of the women, who stood still in the middle of them with perfect serenity and watched our antics with amusement. They very soon left off bothering me and after I had run about 20 yards I was quite free of them and unbitten; but poor Peterson they pursued much further; he was stung in 3 or 4 places on the head and face and kept shaking bees out of his pockets and sleeves for quite a long time. When I had got away from them I turned round and watched other passers-by running unwittingly into the swarm, and at once beginning to behave like madmen. It was really very comical; the Dutch look more ridiculous in such a situation than probably any other nation: in about 3 minutes the road was piled with bicycles and trays of beer bottles or butcher's meat—all abandoned by their owners or carriers who had gone dancing and screaming down the street with no idea except to avoid the bees. It was like one of those cinematograph scenes which one sees at the music halls. Why they made such a dead set at Peterson I can't imagine. I believe they have a way of settling on the lips of poets, but Peterson is not in the least like the infant Pindar. Equally mysterious was their complete disregard of the 2 does. Do you think that it shows that they come from Hell? or from Heaven? They may come from either for all I can discover about them. The younger one goes to the School of Economics. Do you think that would have anything to do with it? . . .

To K. A.   21 July 1910

I was delighted to get your letter this morning stating that the baby is now beautiful. I think it shows that you are really getting well again. Is she also very clever? I remember that Helen became quite a little Bernard Shaw at about this age. But do you really still feel ill, my dove? and look green? Were you only painted when I saw you in bed that Sunday? Do, for heaven's sake take your Mother's advice and have a bottle of Burgundy to your dinner. Tell Ballard to get you a catalogue from my wine merchant and ask your papa to choose you a really first class wine from it. I am sure it would do you good—Anyhow you had better have a glass of port wine at 11 a.m., and more after luncheon and dinner. This is precisely the occasion when your previous abstinence might prove really useful—Don't abuse it. The whole point of being normally abstemious is that when you do indulge you may be really stimulated. Habitual soakers, such as I, lose this advantage, and instead of being invigorated are merely faintly muddled by doubling or trebling the dose . . .

To K. A.   23 July 1910

It was very business-like of you to have the baby "registrared" as well as vaccinated. I can't help believing that when I am able to take my mind off international law, I shall be able to come at something better than Mary Juliet [to call her]. However, if she has been vaccinated 3 times, I don't see why she shouldn't be "registrared" 2 times. When that is done we might have her appendix, tonsils and adenoids removed . . .

Couldn't we, by the way, have called the baby Yelling? it struck me as rather a good name when I read it in yesterday's "Times" – It appears that Detmar Blow [a contemporary architect] is the 3rd. son of the late Yelling Blow. (One might as well be called 'Howling Gale' at once). Could you inquire whether it is a girl's name or only a boy's? and do you think that Mary Yelling Asquith or Yelling Mary Asquith sounds better?

This must be the 7th time that Detmar's engagement has been announced. Is it thought that he will stick to this poor girl? I also see with regret that Lady Westmoreland is dead. In her the Flesh has lost a notable pillar: her spacious desires burned like a beacon in the anaemic world, and will assuredly add lustre to whichever of the other worlds they may by now have been transferred. I should not be much surprised if Charon fell into the same error about her as about Dirce.[1]

To K. A.   30 July 1910

Miss Fox, by the way, among her other points of resemblance to you, nourishes the desire to own a Great Dane. I would rather that she had one than you. She has a flexuous nose like Gertrude Bell. Do you know the sort I mean? It waggles at the tip when she speaks – and even when she thinks at all hard. It is a quality which seems to go with a certain type of mind. She and her Mother gave me a serious talking to last night about the injustice and inequalities of the present structure of society – quite a little sermon on the Mount. I found myself defending (as I always do in political discussions) the privileges, usurpations, splendours, luxuries and tyrannies of the upper classes. I dare say there is something in it. But I can't bear the idea of grouse shooting being abolished . . .

To K. A.   2 August 1910

. . . I am very sorry indeed about Edward's third [class degree at Oxford] – I was afraid that Frances would take it to heart, and I confess I don't see any plausible line of consolation. If one is disappointed, one is disappointed, and there is no more to be said about it. – It is like being hungry, no amount of talking will make you less hungry. Food stops hunger, but words don't. It is useless to tell the sufferer that he would be less hungry if he had eaten more at his last meal, or had trained himself for years to do without food. The emptiness is a brute fact which cannot be evaded or denied. In this particular case I don't even know whether Frances would prefer to believe that Edward had the brains to get a first if he had used them conscientiously or that, however much he had worked, he could never have got a first. But, as she seems from your account to feel his lack of industry as a personal grievance, I should think the second view may be the more acceptable to her, and I feel pretty sure that it is the more correct. I don't think women realise what a very stiff and very technical test is 'Greats'. It is nearly impossible for a man who is not a good enough scholar to read Latin and Greek fluently to get a first in Greats: unless, that is, he has something like a genius for metaphysics. Mothers see their sons making a good show in their table talk, distinguishing accurately between Holbein and Titian,

---

[1] The reference is to the lines of W. S. Landor, on a great beauty crossing over to the next world.

> Stand close around, ye Stygian set,
>   With Dirce in one bark conveyed,
> Lest Charon, seeing, may forget
>   That he is old and she a shade.

Keats and Yeats, and so forth, and infer that nothing short of indolence or malice could cause a mess of Greats. This quite ignores the technical side of the thing. No doubt Edward has a general intelligence much above the average, but he has never had the requisite technical training to deal with a test such as Greats. Of course more of one's life is spent (mercifully) at the dinner table than in the schools, and the social and practical virtues are really more useful than the purely academic. But it is futile to dwell upon this, as women in general (and perhaps Frances in particular) are apt to regard all kinds of success – I mean proclaimed and certificated success – as equally to be desired, and all kinds of proclaimed certificated failure as equally to be deplored. If one is by way of looking at the thing from a large point of view, the imperfect relation between the academic and the practical test of ability seems to me a material consideration – But of course no one would pretend that the immediate pangs of disappointment are in the least alleviated by bloodless propositions of this type, however irrefutable. For the moment, indisputably all triumphs are equally sweet, and all failures are equally bitter, and it is precisely this which makes one so exceedingly sorry for poor Frances and so utterly unable to suggest consolation. But it seems to me unfair to Edward to pretend that this unhappy result brands him as being either criminally ungrateful or universally inept. Of course it has been unfortunate for him that owing to his always living with these brilliant young men, and superficially resembling them in habits and catch words and so forth, he has come to have an impossible standard applied to his own more moderate and less disciplined wits. I hope that he is not very much depressed himself about the whole thing. It would be a pity if he became too diffident, but I should have doubted (if you had not assured me) that this was a serious danger. Of course you, my angel, are absurdly and incongruously (though none the less charmingly) diffident. I have never been able to understand how you have managed for so long to nourish your spirit of self-distrust in face of the reiterated acclamations of everyone you meet testifying with passionate unanimity to your incomparable excellence in every possible direction. However, that is your way, and I'm not sure that it does not add a bloom of exotic sweetness and mystery to your peerlessness.

To Lady Horner   3 August 1910

A thousand thanks for your letter. I can't tell you how much in this twilit dungeon one prizes a gleam of light from the real world. I'm afraid you must have been wretchedly disappointed by poor old Edward's third – of course you know (and reject) my view that these academic distributions are all rot, and it would be merely irritating to enforce it. For my own part, I would sooner put my trust in Princes than in examinations. But that doesn't in the least prevent my sympathising intensely in your disappointment. Anything that one wants very much has infinite value, and it is damnable not to get it. I remember when

I failed to get the Hertford after being 2nd the year before, I nearly drowned myself with disgust. But of course it has never made a pin of difference to me since, nor ever will – even at the day of judgment. Still for the moment the pang of defeated expectation is quite unbearable. I think that people who don't know Oxford are apt to forget how very technical the test of 'Greats' is: I mean that unless you can read Latin and Greek almost as easily as English it is nearly impossible to get a first, and very hard to get even a second without an amount of labour which cramps your style for the rest of your life. The idea that general intelligence will carry you home is quite a mistake. Edward has any amount of intelligence – also he is bright and beautiful (which I never was) – Why not be content with that? But I am beginning to dispute about tastes, which is always futile. Shelley's father would rather that little Bysshe had made 100 at Lords instead of writing Adonais. Of course there is a good deal to be said on both sides. Anyhow, Edward has done much better than Cardinal Newman who had to work 14 hours a day for his third. If only he would become a Roman, like Laura,[1] I don't see how he could avoid being Pope some day. I believe you would like that. It is a big position. But I suppose my father would grumble about it.

This loathly worm of an arbitration is wriggling slowly to its end – my responsibilities are over and tomorrow I am going out to live for the remaining week at Scheveningen to repair the ravages of industry and boredom by sucking in a little ozone. It is a kind of Dutch Brighton, but less sunny and more moral – one can run into the Hague every morning for the Arbitration in twenty minutes on a tram. Robson made an excellent speech I am glad to say and now Mr. Elihu Root is winding up the case for the U.S. He is supposed to be the ablest man in America, I only hope that this may not mean that he is the most long-winded. They have a way of accepting that as a test . . .

To K. A.   Nieuwe Litteraire Societeit,
                                                          'S-Gravenhage.
                                                          8 August 1910

Not a streak of news. Indoors Root, outdoors rain: both slow and inexorably everlasting. Root has been speaking now for 3½ days and has not finished his argument on the 1st of the 7 questions. However, he has sworn to get through by Friday evening. But I don't believe he will. Americans simply don't know how to stop: they are like people beginning to learn the use of the bicycle whose only way of stopping is to run gently into something: so far the 3 Americans who have spoken have run gently into the tribunal and collapsed: the Court has stopped them: they could never have stopped themselves. I only hope that the Court will have the pluck to stop Root: it would be a true kind-

---

[1] Margot's niece, Laura Lister, became a Catholic on her marriage to Lord Lovat.

ness to him as well as to us: if he is not stopped he will go on until he dies – Every day the thing becomes more difficult to bear: the repetition of phrases and arguments which a month ago was merely nauseating is now maddening: it is all one can do not to scream: the alternative is to go to sleep, but there is always the danger of waking with a scream.

Please don't call the child Hermione. I don't really mind Mary Juliet: besides if she has been registered so, it doesn't matter what is done at the font: Mary Juliet she will remain . . .

To K. A.   11 August 1910

. . . I dined last night with old Finlay at the smart restaurant at Scheveningen – Suddenly about ½ past 10 as we were all sitting round the table smoking I began to feel very faint and left the room with the object of getting some air; but before I could get outside I actually did faint – fell down on the floor like a dead owl and had to be swept up by waiters: everyone was very nice and humane, and no one dashed cold water in my face or stuffed nasty smells at my nose: so that as soon as I was laid out in the open air I came to and felt perfectly well again in 5 minutes. However, they made me go home to bed and be examined by a Dutch doctor. He said that there was nothing the matter with me (which was indeed sufficiently obvious) and that my heart in particular was an organ of exceptional power. I said to him "Why did I faint?" He said, "Because you are so long". So I suppose when I get home I shall have to be amputated or truncated in some way or another. Robson wanted him to say that I must stay in bed today, but he saw no reason for that. His only advice was that I should not drink or smoke much! How tragically alike are the Dutch and the English doctors! I could almost fancy that I was listening to Sir Thomas Barlow. But of course one pays no more attention to doctors when they say this than one does to the patter of an auctioneer. It is their way of making conversation. I had an excellent night and have done nothing but drink and smoke ever since with the best possible results. The incident has been useful in providing me at last with a little item of news to put in my letter to you – I fear they have been growing very barren and jejune lately.

It is not really surprising that one should faint after being steadily bored for 3 months – there is a limit to what my constitution can stand in the way of boredom, and my only wonder is that I didn't reach it earlier . . .

To K. A.   49 Bedford Square, W.C.
                                                                                  3 April 1911

. . . I have had a pretty wearing day – 6 hours travelling and 6 hours consultations already and it is only 8.30 and I expect at least another six hours work before going to bed. I am snatching a moment to send this scrawl in order that you may not think or even say (as you are apt to do) that I am brutal and callous and indifferent. You know in your heart that I adore you, my vicious angel!

To K. A.   24 April 1911

. . . I worked all day at my chambers, and had a late dinner at a Club. I ordered a teal and they brought me a quail: a stone for an egg would have been a trifling disappointment in comparison. Then I went in late to the Palace and saw the Russians who have sadly fallen off. Mordkin has become a 2nd rate coquette and Pavlova smothers her genius in technique. She does nothing but dither on the tips of her toes and pretend to be the antennae of a butterfly. This deceives nobody. She and Mordkin will not dance together or even look at one another . . .

To K. A.   Queen's Hotel,
                                                                          Birmingham.
                                                                          1 May 1911

. . . We had a tiresome day in Court and made very little headway. The witnesses we called were all cretins – deaf, blind, toothless, dishonest, illiterate and stupid beyond the wildest dreams. The Exeter witnesses were intellectual giants and moral paragons compared to these people.

One had not only to roar at them but to repeat each roar a dozen times before anything passed through their dull ears to their duller brains. It was heartbreaking and throat cracking work. But we got out at four and played a round of golf before dinner in fine weather. Since dinner we have been in consultation for 2 hours and I am just scribbling this to catch the midnight post . . .

To K. A.   Wollaton Rectory,
                                                                        Nottingham.
                                                                        14 May 1911

I suppose that at my time of life I ought to be grateful for a new experience; it is solemn and rather shattering to find myself for the first time sleeping in a rectory. I hope that I shall sleep well because my host has just informed me that breakfast is at half past eight! He said it in a calm even voice without any preparation or periphrasis, as if he were offering me a good cigar or introducing me to a beautiful woman. If one was going shooting in the morning it would be all very well, but considering that one is by way of spending a quiet Saturday to

Monday in the country it seems hardly credible that one human being should have the hardihood to make such an announcement to another.

It seems to me to be something tremendous and devastating: an earthquake or an avalanche would surprise me less and would scarcely discompose me more. Harold Russell,[1] my introducer, who doesn't drink port and usually breakfasts at 8, thinks nothing of it. There is really something wrong with the Russells – a defect in voluptuousness without the complementary quality. They have the vices of the Spartan without their virtues – acidity without efficiency and insensibility without athleticism. My principal consolation is the thought of how much more Edward or Bluey would mind it all than I do.

The walls are plastered with stuffed penguins and the heads of dead squirrels, and there is a vivarium full of yellow-bellied toads which come out and crawl about the floor. I do hope that you won't get too fond of natural history – It is a dirty science.

Sunday morning.

I was quite punctual for breakfast having been wakened by church bells while it was still almost dark. It is only 10 o'clock now, but already the parson and his two daughters have taken part in early communion, family prayers, and Sunday School: and in half an hour we shall all set off to Matins. What a life! The clergy are almost as hard worked it appears as the bar. He is a curious old boy, this parson, a mixture of gentility and clownishness.

There is one pretty daughter and one ugly one. The ugly one is called Marjorie, has a face like a vicious horse and is rather down-trodden by Sheila, the pretty one. Sheila has eyes of an admirable blueness, but her hands and feet are rather too large and from what you tell me I should guess that her stays did not cost enough. She is a little like Denys Finch-Hatton – a handsome face but rather too much of it. But there's no denying her eyes: and she has cleverness too – though exceeding slightly in the direction of sprightliness – and I can imagine her dealing in practical jokes. She sang a good deal last night.

However it is better being here than alone at the Hotel and all the others have gone away somewhere. The place has a nice garden and small park round it and near by is Wollaton Park where the parson's brother-in-law lives – a fine house I believe built by the man who made Longleat: we are going to see it this afternoon . . .

To K. A.   1 Paper Buildings,
                                                  Temple, E.C.
                                                 29 July 1912

. . . I came up alone in the train, lunched at Brooks', ordered you some cigarettes and a lawn-tennis racquet; found Paper Buildings in an empty idle slug-

---

[1] Conrad's eldest brother, engaged in the same case as Raymond.

gish and depressing state, so fell to upon my poem on does, of which I send you a sample herewith. It swelled in the writing and is only a fragment which I am too sick of already to complete. To make it an artistic whole we would both have to add and to omit a great deal. It is a failure, but parts of it are a passable parody . . .

[The final version of this poem, 'In Praise of Young Women', went as follows:]

Attend, my Muse, and, if you can, Approve,
While I proclaim the 'speeding up' of Love;
For Love and Commerce hold a common Creed—
The scale of business varies with the speed:
For Queen of Beauty or for Sausage King
The customer is always on the Wing—
Then praise the nymph who regularly earns
Small profits (if you please) but quick returns.
Our modish Venus is a bustling minx,
But who can spare the time to woo a Sphinx?
When Monna Lisa posed with rustic guile
The stale enigma of her simple smile.
Her leisured lovers raised a pious cheer
While the slow mischief crept from ear to ear.
Poor listless Lombard, you would ne'er engage
The brisker beaux of our mercurial age,
Whose lively mettle can as easy brook
An epic poem as a lingering look.

Our modern maiden smears the twig with lime
For twice as many hearts in half the time.
Long e'er the circle of that staid grimace
Has wheeled your weary dimples into place,
Our little Chloe, (mark the nimble fiend)
Has raised a laugh against her bosom friend,
Melted a Marquis, mollified a Jew,
Kissed every member of the Eton Crew,
Ogled a Bishop, quizzed an aged peer,
Has danced a tango and has dropped a tear.
Fresh from the schoolroom, pink and plump and pert,
Bedizened, bouncing, artful and alert,
No victim she of vapours or of moods –
Though the sky falls, she's ready with the goods –
Will suit each client, tickle every taste
Polite or Gothic, libertine or chaste,

Supply a waspish tongue, a waspish waist,
Astarte's breast or Atalanta's leg,
Love ready-made or glamour off the peg.
Do you prefer 'a thing of dew and air'?
Or is your type Poppaea, or Polaire?
The crystal casket of a maiden's dreams
Or the last fancy in Cosmetic creams?
The dark and tender or the fierce and bright,
Youth's rosy blush or Passion's pearly bite?

You hardly know, perhaps, but Chloe knows,
And pours you out the necessary dose,
Meticulously measuring to scale
The cup of Circe or the Holy Grail.
An actress she at home in every role,
Can flout or flatter, bully or cajole
And on occasion by a stretch of art
Can even speak the language of the heart,
Can lisp and sigh and make confused replies
With baby lips and complicated eyes,
Indifferently apt to weep or wink,
Primly pursue, provocatively shrink,
Brazen or bashful, as the case require,
Coax the faint Baron, curb the bold Esquire,
Deride restraint, but deprecate desire,
Unbridled yet unloving, loose but limp,
Voluptuary, virgin, prude, and pimp.

To Conrad Russell
Mells, 8 August 1911

. . . Perdita I am going to bring up as a Socialist. By the time she is marriage-able all the money will be in the hands of Socialists.

. . . I spent Sunday with Lord Haldane on the Wiltshire downs inspecting Territorials. We saw a corps of 4 thousand boys: they were little orphans, but Haldane got it into his head that they were little Orpens, and made them an address on the hypothesis that they were children of the painter of that name . . .

To Patrick Shaw-Stewart
Mells, 31 August 1911

Many thanks. Before I got your letter I would have betted that the word 'Pray' did not occur in a cheque book. It surprises me more than would the word 'cheque' in a Prayer Book.

To K. A.   Edenglassie,
                                                              Strathdon,
                                                               Scotland.
                                                     18 September 1912

. . . I rather like Runciman though he has a white forehead and looks more irretrievably urban than anything I have ever seen on a grouse moor . . .

To K. A.   Dallas Lodge,
                                                             Forres, N. B.
                                                     24 September 1912

. . . Life here is very pleasant because one is out all day shooting in the sunlight, and in the evening there are hot baths and cold champagne and mild bridge. But the intellectual lethargy and vacuity of the atmosphere are almost beyond belief. Frank occasionally announces that he would like to shoot Lloyd-George, but this is the nearest we ever get to a speculative proposition or a spark of temper: this is our lightning and our thunder – and all other differences are drowned in the mild effulgence of universal comfort and benevolence which undulates in tranquil waves round Annie and her daughters. I daresay it might make Edward want to stand for Parliament. What a good idea that is by the way. Could we not stand against one another and kill 2 birds with one stone? . . .

To Lady Diana Manners   Holker Hall,
                                                          Cark-in-Cartmel
                                                        5 October 1913

. . . Bron's fishing place in Ireland was funny enough – owing to Juliet Duff (Duffy II) who loathes nature (and especially fish) sitting for hours every day in the rain on the bank twiddling her long yellow Bakst fingers while Bron remorselessly flung his line; and coming down to dinner in a chin-strap of pearls which made her face almost unbearably like that of a nice hack. Salmon flies by the way are pretty Bakst, I think you would like them. Here we have Lady Essex and the Archbishop of Canterbury. Poor Cantuar is going to pieces. His eyebrows are bushy enough, but his brain is going. The first night when Dick asked him to say grace at dinner, a look of blank idiocy came over his face and I had to save a rather difficult situation by prompting him audibly. The words "For what" set old memories vibrating and the powerful mind clanked into action.

To Lady Diana Manners   Mells, Xmas Day 1913

. . . I must apologise for sending you Aubrey Beardsley's drawings but I do so want to lead you back from your tainted and artificial ideals to a simpler saner more childlike outlook upon life. Anyhow they will do for Bonar Law's bedroom next time he stays with you.

Here we have to knock along as best we may without the faintest element of corruption – not a hint of decay, not a breath of Bakst: on the contrary, Christmas cards, Morris dances, children's prattle, woolwork, goodwill, and so forth – all that ever was joyous and clear and fresh . . .

To K. A.   Penrhôs,
                                                                      Holyhead.
                                                                  5 June 1914

My luggage didn't after all turn up till after dinner. I bought a night shirt in Birmingham – such a brute – but luckily lost it in the train. Lloyd George was here when I arrived but went off with Edwin by the night train. He had all the women well in hand – Barbara in particular posturing before him in the most audacious way and Visey [Violet] herself rather crumpled up with adoration like a nun . . .

[IV]

War, 1914-1916

In the first week of the war, the usual strange assortment of guests continued to assemble for lunch at 10 Downing Street among them Edward Horner, who made the original suggestion that Raymond should go out to the front as a war correspondent. If his dispatches had been in the same vein as his letters to his friends, the paper would no doubt have flourished. But instead, amid the general confusion and the sheer unfamiliarity of what needed to be done to win the war, he spoke at recruiting meetings, continued with his legal work, and made plans to enlist as a soldier, though it was not till after Christmas that he succeeded in joining the Queen's Westminster Rifles, along with other inexperienced Londoners including the twenty-year-old Harold Macmillan. His characteristic detachment remained unaffected, and his sense of the ridiculous, always keen, found rich scope for expression.

Until he left in January to train in camp on the edge of Richmond Park, his letters to Katharine are naturally few, but a new correspondent appears on the scene who was to inspire some particularly brilliant flights of fancy. Lady Diana Manners was the youngest daughter of the Duke and Duchess of Rutland, and a distant cousin of the Manners family at Avon. Referred to in the letters both as Dotty and Dilly, she had in the previous two years become the rising star and soon the leading light of the circle of friends – mostly Edward's contemporaries and therefore ten years or so younger than Raymond – known to each other as the Coterie. In their youthful exuberance and independence they seem to have looked up to Raymond with a special veneration for his irreverence and his light-heartedly cynical wit; and until Katharine's death over sixty years later, though the lives they led had little in common, Lady Diana remained perhaps her most devoted and sympathetic friend. Raymond had known her elder sister Marjorie (by then Lady Anglesey) since before his marriage, and had stayed with her family at Belvoir since Lady Diana's childhood. She was now twenty-two. Raymond was delighted by her 'flashing mind and dazzling skin', and noted that 'her wit illuminates her complexion like forked lightning playing on a bowl of cream, and her beauty sweetens her wit like honey on the point of a dagger'. Edward, among others, was in love with her, but the group on the whole seem to have managed to conduct their relations with each other without burning their fingers, though at the same time without ever suffering from cold feet. In a way that may seem strange today, they were willing to a considerable extent to accept conventional restraints on their conduct, however impatient they were of the authority by which those restraints were imposed.

Raymond's friends soon began to be killed. The first was John Manners, the elder son of Con, his great friend and confidante from the days of his courtship. Aubrey Herbert was slightly wounded, and taken prisoner, but managed to escape and was actually back in England before the end of September. His method of joining the army had been distinctly informal for a young member of Parliament, or indeed for anyone else. He had simply ordered an Irish Guards uniform from his tailor, discovered the route which one of the battalions was to take to the station on its way to France, and fallen in beside them in the street. After the war he became almost totally blind, and his sight had already begun to fail. Julian and Billy Grenfell were killed in May and July 1915 and later on Charles Lister and Ego Charteris. Bron Lucas was killed very soon after Raymond himself, and Patrick Shaw-Stewart in the next year. Edward Horner was severely wounded in France in May, but after convalescing at home for a few months, he succeeded in going out to a staff position in Egypt. Profoundly bored there, he pulled every string he could lay his hands on in order to rejoin his regiment, and was eventually killed in France in November 1917, a year after the last entries in this book, and only a few weeks after a fire had destroyed Mells Park, the family home that had been let since 1902.

Raymond became increasingly restless under the leisurely routine of training with his regiment, and the doubtful prospect of active service, and transferred in July into the 3rd Battalion of the Grenadiers, already severely depleted. His attitude to the war had hardened into 'an invincible pride and a stiff indifference to the brutal muddle of the universe'. His detachment from the deaths of his friends grew more formidable as time went on; and as for the ever increasing danger to himself from shells and bullets after he went out to France in October, he took 'the same sort of interest in it as an ill-tempered tourist may take in an uncomfortable hotel'. He was in and out of the trenches between 15 November and 30 December, when he came home for ten days' leave. There are various references to the staff positions that were pressed on him from time to time, but his scorn for them only briefly relented at the beginning of 1916. From his return to France in January till April he worked with Intelligence at Montreuil. After the birth of his son Julian on 22 April he had a few days' leave, and then returned to his regiment in the middle of May.

At home, conditions for Katharine became increasingly difficult and worrying. Apart from the general unfamiliar horror of war, the death in action of many devoted friends who had played such a large part in their lives and the constant and immediate danger in which Raymond was living – of which he did not deign to spare her the details – there were nagging everyday problems which showed no signs of going away. Raymond's income from the Bar dried up as soon as he joined the army, though he retained a half share in the fees for a certain number of Inland Revenue cases. But the house in Bedford Square, the background to seven years of exceptionally happy married life, was too large for Katharine and her children. It was soon shut up, and she stayed at first briefly in Downing Street, and later at her parents' house in Lower Berkeley Street (now Fitzhardinge Street) off Manchester Square, with intervals at Mells.

Raymond's wartime letters vividly bring out the strange contrast between life in billets, with birthday dinner parties and visits to other well-found messes, and on the other hand the ceaseless shelling, sniping and mortar bombing in the trenches themselves. The abrupt transitions from one to the other recall the universal indifference to impending danger described in Tolstoy's autobiographical story *The Raid*: 'It was as though it were impossible to imagine that some of these men would not be coming back by the same road – it was as though all of them had already left the world long ago.'

To Conrad Russell   The Manor House,
                                          Mells,
                                          Frome.
                                          August 1914

. . . There is the Hell of a crowd here this weekend – people sleeping not only in one another's beds but in flower-beds & cony-burrows & places where you would hardly dream of putting even the Son of Man.

To Lady Diana Manners   August 1914

. . . Beware of saying in public all or any of the following things:-

(1) God save the Kaiser.
(2) God damn King George.
(3) I hate war because it spoils conversation.
(4) I love war because one gets ravished.

The atmosphere here is appalling. The crisis has brought out all that is best in British womanhood. Katharine still keeps her head. But Cicely Lambton[1] and Frances Horner have sunk all political differences and are facing the enemy as one man. They have cornered all the petrol, sold all Charles Kinski's

---

[1] Cicely Horner had married in 1908 the Hon. George Lambton, the famous trainer. One of his closest friends, Count Charles Kinsky, had been an attaché at the Austrian Embassy and won the Grand National on his own horse, Zoedone. Although aged 60 in 1914, he served with the Austrian cavalry on the Russian front to avoid having to fight against his English and French friends. He died in 1919.

hunters, knocked off two courses at dinner, and turned Perdita's pony-cart into an ambulance. Cicely thinks that everybody ought to give up everything except racing, which (she tells me) has ceased to be a sport and become an industry, and that everyone should enlist at once except George because the whole of Cambridgeshire depends on George continuing his industrial career at Newmarket, and where, (she asks) should we be at a time like this without Cambridgeshire? So far as I can judge it is a matter of hours or at the best days till I begin to do my duty. One asks oneself what it is. Shall I pretend to be a veterinary surgeon? or a St Bernard dog? or what? Anyhow don't be surprised if you hear of me barking about the streets of Brussels with a keg of brandy tied round my neck . . . How I wish you were at the War Office, Dottie, instead of Kitchener. We should all sleep easy in our beds or I for one should make a bee-line for the colours . . .

To Lady Diana Manners   Undated, August 1914

. . . I was chid this week in London by Nancy Cunard[1] for failing in brio and insouciance and forced to plead guilty to a certain lack of blitheness. Of course her ideal of indifference is almost inhumanly high, as she is not only insensible to the standard emotions and inoculated against the germs of love, death, honour and glory, but utterly unaffected by changes of social and spiritual atmosphere palpable enough one would think to asphyxiate a cossack. Certainly in London the fog of war as they call it had got into everybody's lungs, and the air was thick with the feeling that England expects everyone to make a fuss, and that if you did make a fuss – even quite a small fuss, for at a time like this no fuss is too small – you would be personally thanked for it by the Prince of Wales. I saw at once that there were two things to be done (1) to make some small unobtrusive fuss of my own (2) to interfere as much as possible with the people who are making more serious fusses. So giving up my dream of going out as an Army Chaplain on the staff of the Bishop of London, I put my name down for a thing called the London Volunteer Defence Force, organised by Lovat and Desborough, having the following among other advantages (a) it is not yet in existence (b) the War Office may stop it ever coming into existence (c) Patrick belongs to it (d) no member of it can be called on to perform even the simplest act of duty for several months (e) no member of it can possibly be killed till Goodwood[i.e. August] 1915 at earliest. Then I went to a most amusing place called the National Service League Offices, where a vast swarm of well meaning and inefficient patriots are employed for 14 hours a day in first classifying and then rejecting the applications of a still vaster swarm of still more well meaning and inefficient patriots for posts which they are utterly and obviously incapable of filling – deaf mutes who fancy they might be useful as in-

---

[1] Rebellious daughter of the well-known hostess Lady Cunard.

terpreters, baptist ministers who volunteer as *vivandiers* and so forth. I spent a very pleasant afternoon trying to put these people into classes. There were 4 classes but the qualifications for each class were so peculiar that none of the 2000 applicants whom I examined were eligible for any one of the 4. Next week the committee are going to alter the classifications, and it is hoped that someone may scrape into one of the classes. It will be a proud day for England when this happens . . .

To Conrad Russell   18 August 1914

I can't tell you how much I sympathise with your sufferings. People like you are the true heroes of this (or any other) war. To seek the bubble reputation at the cannon's mouth is bloody enough, but to get up at 2 in the morning and stand about for hours in a heap of horse dung, to live on bad food eaten in moderate company – all these things are beyond bearing.

Old E[dward] sends news to the same effect from Winchester where he has joined the N. Somerset Yeomanry: only I suspect his sufferings are worse than yours as he is a new boy & a voluptuary instead of a veteran ascetic.

The fact is that one is bound just now to be either very uncomfortable or rather ridiculous. And I can assure you (if it is any comfort) that one feels something of a rabbit as one walks onto the lawn with a racquet in the company of a few derelict does. There is a feeling in the air that everyone ought to make a fuss of some kind. I went up to London last week & found it seething with futility. I flung myself with gusto into the maelstrom of misdirected effort and ostentatious altruism. I put my name down for an organisation wh. Lovat & Desborough are promoting for drilling middle-aged breadwinners out of school hours. Probably the W.O. will stop it, and quite right too. Then I went to the office of the National Service League, where an enormous staff is employed in rejecting the applications of well-meaning idiots for inappropriate positions – Boy Scouts with fixed bayonets see that one comes to no harm in the lift, and old women fill in innumerable printed forms which old men in other parts of the building tear up. The nett result of my activities was to reject an application by Evan Charteris to be an interpreter and to recommend the immediate deportation of a man who said he had taken part in the Franco-Prussian War.

K. of Chaos, as they call him [Kitchener], seems to be a sad mixture of gloom, ignorance and loquacity: says the war will last 3 years, had never heard of the Special Reserve, and can't be persuaded in the Cabinet to give his mind to anything but Welsh Disestablishment on which he descants at inordinate length. Fortunately he has already been persuaded to give up his original ideas about the new army & to shelter himself behind Jack Tennant.

I'm afraid the Irish trouble will blaze up again next week. How bloody everything is . . .

To K. A.   Brooks's,
                                                    St James's Street.
                                                    20 August 1914

I spent some hours yesterday at an agricultural show at Derby, drank a bottle
of the very worst champagne in a marquee and made a buffy speech in praise of
Beet Sugar. Sir Thomas [Roe] took me round the ground afterwards introducing me to queer people and making wild inquiries about the Exhibits. Such
e.g. as whether honeycombs were made by rabbits. I nearly bought a Belgian
hare myself to commemorate eponymous merit . . .

To K. A.   Travellers' Club,
                                                       Pall Mall, S.W.
                                                     2 September 1914

. . . I dined at Downing St last night. Edward Grey was there – rather gloomy.
They all seem to think Turkey will come in against us before the week is out.
The story of Russians in England is untrue: but Tyrrell (who was at dinner) is
very keen to bring the Japs to France. There is very little news. Bluey tells me
that French complains that he is constantly left unsupported on both flanks
without warning. Also that our ministers at Amsterdam say that 300,000
Germans have left Belgium for the East in the last few days. I fear this may
mean that they are contemptuous of France rather than that they are frightened of Russia. They can't afford to fall between 2 stools.

Norah [Lindsay] and Frances came to Bluey's after lunch – F. just off to see
E. who had asked for 25 cigars! Such a hauling down of the flag of profusion is
a startling departure from idiom and looks as if he were really taking things
seriously. The W.O. is in a panic about the projected recruiting campaign, as
they have no means of dealing with the men they have got already – 30,000
yesterday and ½ million in the last month.

To K. A.   49 Bedford Square, W.C.
                                                     3 September 1914

. . . Last night I dined with Edwin [Montagu]. Bron and [his sister] Nan
were there, Margot, Libby [Elizabeth Asquith], P.M., the McKennas and the
Lulus [Mr and Mrs Lewis Harcourt]. There was bridge at which I won a little
and after they had mostly gone Bron[1] held forth about the strategy of the war
in an interesting, and for all I know accurate way. I have just come back from
one of my sentimental rambles in Hampstead. I confess I am soppy about the
suburbs. There was a rich melancholy radiance over the place this afternoon
which gave a peculiar charm to some of the older streets and houses . . .

---

[1] Bron Lucas was by now in the Cabinet.

To K. A.   10 September 1914

. . . Not much news here. There was no dinner at Downing St last night, Margot being in Scotland, so I dined with the McKennas where Pamela was the only woman: the rest, Birrell, Tyrrell, P.M., Edwin, Wedgwood Benn, and the head of the Criminal Investigation Department whose name I never made out. He seemed a heavy sensible sort of man, very much down on Spy-mania. But they have a theory that one of the British Cable Companies has been tampered with, and is somehow helping the Germans, and that Lord North-cliffe is or may be involved.

I have just been lunching with Bluey. It seems that they are still satisfied with the progress of the battle and have regained confidence in Joffre who has sent three of his generals under arrest to Paris – the one who wrongly announced the fall of Namur, the one who failed to support French at Mons, and another.

They have heard nothing more about John [Manners] or Aubrey and have no notion when or where they were lost. Bluey thinks that the Irish Guards must have been severely handled quite recently owing to bad leadership, as they have a telegram asking for the appointment of a competent commander for them – the man who succeeded to Morris after he was wounded being apparently a bungler . . .

To Conrad Russell   The Manor House,
                                                                Mells,
                                                                Frome.
                                                       13 September 1914

. . . Last week we had a meeting near here to explain to the common people all about the war. The speakers were (1) The Duchess of Somerset (2) myself. Funny enough. But tomorrow I understand the nation splits up again into its component atoms on the rock of Home Rule. I had a meeting at Derby next week with the Duke of Devonshire & other Tory bigwigs which has just been cancelled & I hear of others sharing the same fate. The other five, stirred up no doubt by A. J. B.; are shaking with rage at the notion of putting the Irish Bill on the Statute Book, even though it is to be accompanied by a Suspensory Act postponing its operation till after the end of the war and by various pledges about amendments & the absence of coercion etc. I should guess the public will think our compromise a reasonable one. However it is something gained to stop all these recruiting meetings. One or two are well enough, but it is becoming clearer daily that everyone perfectly understands the situation, that recruits are enlisting far quicker than the W.O. can deal with them, and that there is nothing left for public speakers to do except abuse the Kaiser in stronger & stronger language. I begin to feel more cheerful about things. If we really do win this battle in France I believe the war will be over by Xmas. The gossip in London is (1) that Joffre has sent 3 of his generals in chains to Paris (2) that Admiral Troubridge is to be court-martialled for bungling the Goeben business (3) that George West has been shot as a spy (4) that Lord Northcliffe is mixed up with a British Cable Company which has been bought by the Germans & gives away our secrets. But I daresay you have heard all this, none of which is true – or even likely except (1) . . .

To Aubrey Herbert
                                                    Hopeman Lodge,
                                                    Hopeman,
                                                    Morayshire.
                                                    20 September 1914

I am more than a little pleased that you are safely back again: though from the moment I saw your name in the casualty list I had the strongest possible presentiment that it would all end happily and gave Mary my word of honour to that effect. It was thoroughly characteristic of you to be shot and lost but equally characteristic to be found and healed. I would always put my last shilling on your luck in these little things. I saw your mother the day after you arrived and she gave a most satisfactory account of you. So I hope that you are not being much bothered by your wound in spite of the nasty looking hole it made in your breeches. I went to my father's Edinbro' meeting on Friday & then brought Katharine up here to recover from an influenza she has had. When I return to London next week do let me come and see you. I long to hear an account of fighting from an intelligent amateur so please have your quiver full both of prose and verse. Though as a matter of fact I suppose a battle is far too much like a railway accident to be susceptible of description. Give my best love to Mary. Au revoir.

To Lady Horner   22 September 1914

. . . It was very sweet of you to support so unmurmuringly my vast family through all this time of famine and pestilence, and my conscience pricks me for having repaid you by ungracious alternations of captiousness and inertia. The War certainly plays the devil with one's character. The way it takes me mainly is to fill me with an unbridled passion for contradicting people – specially women. But doubtless this has not escaped your notice . . .

To K. A.
1 Paper Buildings,
Temple, E.C.
9 October 1914

I was glad to find your letter awaiting me. You must have had a horrible journey and I wish very much that you had been more extravagant. I was extravagant but all the same had a horrible journey, got very little sleep, and Bongy's dog was sick in my hat.

I found some work to do here, so am staying till tomorrow, the 3.30 train. I dined last night at Downing St and found them all rather gloomy – P.M., Grey, and Winston, specially the latter who had relied on the French to co-operate with his Naval Brigade in saving Antwerp.[1] When it became clear that the French couldn't or wouldn't do this the Belgian army threw up the sponge and for the last 3 days has been making for Ostend in motor buses. The Naval Brigade (Oc with them, but apparently not Patrick who is Embarkation Officer at Dunkerque) got into Antwerp some days ago and have been fighting in the trenches there, but were to begin their retreat last night in the direction of Ostend. If they reach there safely they are to be brought straight home again to complete their Education. Bluey told me at luncheon yesterday that the whole of our 7th Division was in Antwerp, but Winston at dinner said his men were the only English there – a curious difference of opinion on an important point . . .

To K. A.
19 October 1914

Bongie has just rung me up to ask if I will go up to Fife next Friday to address an annual meeting of delegates from my Father's constituency which is to take place on Saturday afternoon. It is about as repulsive a proposition as one could be faced with, involving 2 costly and uncomfortable night journeys and doing no human soul any earthly good. One can't dole out heroics about Belgium to a few dozen hard-bitten Scotch wire-pullers, nor can one possibly make the party speech to which they are accustomed at this time of year. The P.M. himself is out of London today, but comes back tomorrow and I suppose if he really wants me to go I shall have to, hence the wire which I am sending you about Sutton . . .

To Conrad Russell
Walmer Castle,
Kent.
2 January 1915

What the devil do you mean by saying that I shall be a worse officer than you? You know more about birds but I know more about cards; I have a stronger

---

[1] The Antwerp expedition, conducted mostly with untrained troops, was an irresponsible venture of Churchill's, only saved from disaster by good fortune.

stomach than you and a weaker conscience, and though better educated am decidedly more vulgar.

As to your advice, of course I know that you get shot if you argue with generals – you seem to think I have never heard of the Charge of the Light Brigade – But what do you mean by 'telling lies in reason'? What sort of lies? Who am I to tell them to? and when? Please let me know at once as I have to join my regiment on Monday and should not like to make a bad impression by blurting out the truth about something on my first day . . .

To Edward Horner[1]   April 1915

Your letter asking for a gold pin for your servant does you great credit. May I send you out an emerald ring for his nostril? and some attar of roses for your charger, and a Dégas for your dugout, and a sheet or two of Delius for the gramophone – or would a little something by John Sebastian Bach be more seasonable in Holy Week? and 'some precious tender-hearted scroll of pure Simonides' for use in the latrines? It seems very horrible that you shouldn't have had these things long ago: but you know what our War Office is like – the same old carelessness about equipment etc. as it showed in the Crimean War. And after all, War is War unlike Peace . . . as indeed we all of us have had the opportunity of learning from Landseer's admirable pictures in which the two are so firmly but subtly distinguished. I'm sorry to hear that you are becoming colourless: I can imagine that the conventions of the trenches are rigorous and oppressive but in time I believe you will loosen the yoke and teach your senior officers—prohibited by their traditions from reasoning why – at any rate to ask themselves.

I am in bed – your bed – with my 2nd dose of typhoid inoculation . . . having had a reasonable expectation of crossing the channel this week either as a staff officer or as a platoon commander, though it is hard to say for which position I am the less fitted. However for the moment I have fallen between two stools and shall continue discharging somewhat unsensational functions in the neighbourhood of Clapham Junction.

To Edward Horner[2]   April 1915

(A) *Landseer*: a middle-Victorian painter and friend of animals. Your ignorance about him is a fine testimony to the purity of your artistic education. He did 2 pictures which one used in my childhood to see in most lodging

---

[1] On arriving at the front, Edward had written home asking for a gold tie-pin for his soldier servant.

[2] Edward had evidently written back denying any knowledge of Landseer but asking if temperance was spreading on the home front, following the example set by the King.

houses entitled "War" and "Peace" – War being symbolised by a white horse partially disembowelled, Peace by a white lamb sitting in the mouth of a disused cannon . . . (B) I don't think the drink question is going to be treated in a drastic or disastrous manner. People are saying, just as they did at the time of the House of Lords crisis, TRUST ASQUITH, and I think you can. Haldane has given up drink. But you might have guessed that. If the war lasts much longer I believe he is capable of giving up Hegel. Per contra, Lloyd George, hitherto a life-long teetotaller, now calls loudly for brandy after every meal, and Margot can touch nothing else. When I was at The Wharf last Sunday the P.M. got a telegram from Port Said signed by Oc on behalf of the whole Naval Division in these terms. 'All of us amazed and alarmed at reported spread of temperance. Stand fast.' This appeared to affect the P.M.'s mind much more powerfully than the King's letter in *The Times*. I'm just off to a banquet at Montagu's to celebrate the 647th anniversary of the P.M.'s P.M.-ship.

To K. A.   Brooks's,
                                                            St James's Street.
                                                                 12 May 1915

. . . Here they seem to be expecting an air raid on London, and have established an elaborate system of picketing all the approaches for the purpose of stopping vehicles suspected of signalling to aircraft. My colonel got an order last week to detail 6 officers for "responsible work of a secret and confidential character". He chose me amongst others, and I thought we might at last be going to do something interesting, but on coming up this afternoon with the 5 others to get instructions from the W.O. was disgusted to find that we were merely to be responsible for arresting suspicious vehicles on the North Western approaches to London whenever the W.O. anticipate a raid. It is all night work – 7 p.m.-7 a.m. – and means that one gets no dinner and no sleep. However I hope we may not have to go on duty very often. If we do I shall certainly fade away. The idiocy of taking men from Richmond to picket roads in the north of Middlesex is striking. Probably the men will shoot a lot of innocent people by mistake or in revenge . . .

To K. A.   Camp,
                                                             Richmond Park,
                                                          Roehampton, S.W.
                                                                 13 May 1915

. . . There is no news of any sort except that Haldane has appendicitis – if true an awful warning against the water-waggon. There is no doubt one can't play these tricks with one's constitution. It is better to burn the candle at both ends than to extinguish it at both ends.

Poor sweet, you must be dog dull with nothing to do – Hotel life is so ghastly at the best of times. If you stay till Edward[1] is brought up to Boulogne, give him my love and find out if there is anything I can send him. His wound has already taken its place at Downing Street as the battle ground of competing obscenities and Margot and Montagu have heated and unseemly squabbles as to whether the liver is or is not in the stomach. You had better find out for certain from Arbuthnot Lane. There is no other way of silencing her . . .

To Lady Diana Manners   24 Queen Anne's Gate.
                                                                                            May 1915

I hate, and despise, and condemn you. You are mud, you are the entrails of a toad, you are the stump of bad burnt-out cigars, you are the bits of dirty nonsense that collects in the pockets of a beggar's cast off trousers, you are the excrement of a million bats, the close stuffy smell of a stale goose, the stuff that caterpillars slough off when they become butterflies, the stone that builders reject, the stinking bubbles emitted by sinking Huns, the lowest rung of the infinite ladder which leads up from the bug to the woodlouse. I don't understand how you can be so cruel and white and dastardly and like a poisoned dagger as to go away from a thoroughly suitable party at 20 minutes to 11. Lady Anglesey is neither here nor there. Marchionesses are all very well in their place but their place is Hell. There is no straw like the last straw.

You will get a letter very like this from Alan [Parsons] by the same post but don't read it.

To Lady Diana Manners   Sutton Courtenay.
                                                                                            May 1915

. . . I can't tell you of the staggering beauty of this place today, and wouldn't if I could; it would be as much as my place is worth. All the same such is my incurable romanticism that I often regret never having been with you except in the company of pimps and actors, cocktails and chandeliers. Have you, Dilly, ever given Nature a true turn? as a thing in itself, I mean, not as décor to a personal relation. For my own part, I think well of it in both respects; but then my hair is white, and my brain even more torpid than A. J. B.'s.

---

[1] Edward had been severely wounded in France. Because of the influence of George Moore with General French, arrangements were made for Katharine and her parents, and Diana and her mother, to go out with the famous surgeon Sir Arbuthnot Lane to France and bring Edward back first to the base hospital at Boulogne and later to England. Lady Diana wrote in *The Rainbow Comes and Goes*: 'It was, I suppose, natural that this privilege – worse, favouritism – was considered outrageous by the many. One cannot but sympathise with their deprecation, but which of those many would not have grasped at the same chance?'

Honestly this is not meant as a sermon . . . It is just part of my general curiosity about you, and about all the possible reactions of your nature, to untried stimuli . . .

To K. A.   Camp,
Richmond Park,
Roehampton, S.W.
27 May 1915

. . . Today I had luncheon with Lady Sybil [Grant] at Primrose House. She was kind and friendly and rather unintelligently voluble. She seems to want conscription. It is very odd how many people do now-a-days. The idea they have at the back of their minds seems to be that if their lovers are being killed, it is only fair that their footmen should be killed too. I don't feel that myself.

Among the more dashing young officers in this regiment there is a growing spirit of disaffection. We are wasting time here on duties which make for weariness but not for efficiency. The Colonel is becoming conscious of this I think, and takes one or other of us aside from time to time to communicate mysterious hints that we may be wanted abroad at any moment. But we none of us believe him now. I think he must have bitched all our chances when they asked for a subaltern two months ago and he told them that none of us were ready. Several of the subalterns are scheming to have themselves transferred to some more active unit. It is a great effort getting out of an old rut and into a new one, but unless prospects improve in the near future, I think I shall do something of the kind myself. Edgar [d'Abernon] suggested to me on Sunday that I should transfer to the reserve of the Coldstream Guards. They push one along very quickly I believe, and it is a fine regiment, I suppose about the best . . .

To K. A.   28 May 1915

. . . I'm sorry that Edward's recovery has been slower than they expected, but I heard from Frances yesterday that things were going better. It is simply bloody about Julian.[1] I quite thought that his strength and pugnacity would pull him through.

I don't know why you scold me so much about Derby. It really would have been difficult, if not impossible to get leave again so soon, and in my opinion a most idiotic way of spending it if got. The people there really can't expect to have a soldier boy and a stump orator all at once. I had quite a nice

---

[1] Julian Grenfell died of wounds on May 26.

letter from Thomas[1] about it, not in the least reproachful. He is bent on making Roe resign now or soon, and thinks the coalition a good excuse, as perhaps it is.

My mind becomes hourly more perplexed about my military position and prospects. Today there really seems some reason to think that our 2nd Battn. will go out in a unit – not at once but in a couple of months perhaps – substituting some of us for their own home service officers, of whom they have a fair number. If this is so it is worth staying on here . . .

To Lady Diana Manners   11 June 1915

When you firmly and abruptly left that consecrated sideboard I watched you go as I have seen a convicted murderer watch the judge, who has just sentenced him, moving indifferently away to lunch, in dull and desperate mutiny against an utterly reasonable callousness.

I suppose it is a hard enough job for you, poor child, in the contracted spaces in which we live, to keep 3 or 4 lovers in a tolerably good humour. Last night you seemed to me more than usually absorbed in the pure technique of your jugglery, and less than ever solicitous about the substance. Your only interest in the eggs, I mean, was that they should be all in the air at the same time. Yes, you were less human than I have seen you lately. If possible I would say that you were less beautiful; but I can't. You have nine and fifty ways of solving "the problem" and every single one of them is right . . .

To Lady Diana Manners   18 June 1915

. . . We all dined with Lady Howard [de Walden] last night. . . . I thought her perfectly charming. I don't know why you said I shouldn't. Serenity without torpor, dignity without rigour, mental activity combined with muscular rest, an eye both glowing and candid, but not a trace of morality or sincerity in any offensive sense of the words, and above all a whole-hearted and discriminating passion for Dilly, which shows that her heart, her brain, and every other significant and considerable organ are respectively in their right places. She seemed to me most open-minded and elastic; well ventilated and perfectly garnished for the reception of seven new devils, on the spur of any given moment; eager without being breathless, fresh without being rustic, and genuinely disposed to treat all of us as persons, rather than things . . .

[1] J. H. Thomas, Labour MP for the other division of Derby since 1910.

To Conrad Russell   24 July 1915

Your letter[1] is a powerful indictment, and though I don't agree with it I am glad to see that a year of soldiering has not blunted the edge of your pen. It has turned mine into a ploughshare . . . I am entirely in favour of the Stanley-Montagu match. (1) Because for a woman any marriage is better than perpetual virginity, which after a certain age (not very far distant in Venetia's case) becomes insufferably absurd. (2) Because, as you say yourself, she has had a fair chance of conceiving a romantic passion for someone or other during the last 12 years and has not done so and is probably incapable of doing so. This being so I think she is well advised to make a marriage of convenience. (3) Because, in my opinion, this *is* a marriage of convenience. If a man has private means and private parts (specially if both are large) he is a convenience to a woman. (4) Because it annoys Lord and Lady Sheffield. (5) Because it profoundly shocks the entire Christian community.

Of course I see your point when you say you wouldn't like to go to bed with Edwin. I don't mind admitting that I shouldn't myself. But you must remember that women are not refined, sensitive delicate-minded creatures like you and me: none of them have much physical squeamishness and Venetia far less than most. You say she must have weighed the consequences and so she did, quite carefully: but what frightened her most was not the prospect of the bed being too full but of the board being too empty. She was afraid that her friends might give her up in disgust; but after sounding a few of them – Katharine e.g. and Diana – she concluded that it would be all right and decided to flout the interested disapproval of Mr. H. H. and the idiotic indignation of Miss V. Asquith.

Your character sketch of Edwin is done in much too dark colours. You are obviously prejudiced against him by the fact (if fact it be) that he steals birds' eggs, a vice utterly immaterial in a bride-groom. I agree that he has not a drop of European blood, but then neither has he a drop of American. I don't agree that he is a wet-blanket in Society. He is moody certainly, but is capable of being extremely amusing and (specially during the last year) has succeeded in attracting some very critical and some very beautiful women. He is broadminded, free from cant, open to new impressions, tolerant of new people. I do not think he will be either a dull or a tyrannical husband, and I understand that the terms of alliance permit a wide licence to both parties to indulge such extra-conjugal caprices as either may be lucky enough to conceive . . .

I have been in camp here for three months, not getting much forwarder, so far as I can judge, either in military efficiency or in prospects of foreign service. So I am now exchanging into the Grenadier Guards, which may sound to you a queer thing to do for a middle-aged middle-class chap like me. But a good many men of my kidney are doing the same thing. It seems to be about the only way of getting properly trained and decently treated by the W.O. and certainly

---

[1] Criticizing the engagement of Venetia Stanley to Edwin Montagu.

provides the best (and last) chance one is likely to have of being killed on a
fairly warm day. I fancy the Huns will be stiff before Xmas don't you?

To Lady Diana Manners   13 September 1915

. . . You much misunderstood me, Dilly, if you thought (as indeed you didn't) I
meant that the desultory chatter of half-witted women was less likely to
debauch your mind, than the wild cataract of praise which leaps in glory at you
from the mouths of men. Far from it. Nothing is so deteriorating as that
ceaseless trickle of discoloured drivel which distils itself from the miasma of idle
women's minds, dribbles down their dank and wispy beards, and collects
in stinking pools about the floor of places where they knit. So wouldn't it
perhaps be less dangerous for you in any view of the matter to come back to
London? . . . How I wish you had been at Downing on the Zepp night; we saw
it all so well and so comfortably. The F.O. gun banging away from the actual
window out of which Duff looks down for custom in his bonnet, the P.M.
going on stolidly making absurd declarations at bridge, the Zepp itself at the far
end of the search-light looking like a radiograph of your broken ankle. I took K.
and Moira Osborne[1] down to the city to see the fire. They were very sweet but
just a touch indignant with me for not with my own hands waking up the Dean
of St Paul's and making him unlock his bulbous Church and show us all the
Kingdoms of the earth from the top of it . . .

To Lady Diana Manners   Brooks's.
                                                           21 September 1915

. . . You see even in times of profound peace, we who seek for joy, draw bitter
and perilous breath: pleasure is the biggest game that any man can hunt, and
the shyest – shy as the rhino, wayward as the walrus: the end may come at any
moment, the door be slammed upon the flame, the feather blown to Hell by the
wind. And now when there is a war, you can hardly hear yourself laugh for the
clamour of banging doors and howling hurricanes. I am not thinking so much
of people being killed; so far as my personal crust is concerned it is not broken
by anybody's death in the war, and will not be even by my own. To that extent
I nail my crust to the mast; or support it upon the inverted egg-cup of
invincible pride and a stiff indifference to the brutal muddle of the universe. I
will not catch at God's skirts and pray. I will merely send him to Coventry
(where by the way he will find himself represented in Parliament by Ramsay
Macdonald, so true is it that there is a use for everyone however humble). I am
taking quite a short view and thinking merely of the continuous depletion of all
the sources of life and joy which has been going on under our eyes for months
past . . .

[1] Lady Moira Godolphin-Osborne, married in 1920 Oliver Lyttelton, afterwards Lord Chandos.

To K. A.   Bovingdon Green Camp,
                                                                    Marlow.
                                                          28 September 1915

. . . The weather has broken now and it is pouring in torrents. My prospects of really serious and strangling boredom have never been higher.

The Company is poor, and the bridge low, slow and indescribably bad. We are much outnumbered at mess by the officers of the Welsh Guards but the laugh is on our side. You should see us raise our eyebrows when they address their commanding officer as 'Colonel' or talk about 'mufti'. "Guy and Pauline" has arrived but not the chocolate. It was sweet of you to send them.

I must stop now as I am lured into the endless sewer pipe of a military rubber. One might as well play cat's cradle with Penelope.

To K. A.   Guards Division,
                                                                Base Depot,
                                                                    B.E.F.
                                                          23 October 1915

. . . I have to go now. Thank old E. for his sweet letter which I have just got and will answer anon. He talks of joining the Grenadiers, and if he is going to fight again I believe this would be much the best and pleasantest plan – But I don't see why he should fight any more.

A kidney seems to me a sufficient oblation upon the altar of patriotism. When I have lost one too we might repair together to the Staff of some 1st rate general . . .

To Lady Diana Manners   Rouen.
                                                          24 October 1915

. . . How I wish you were here, and how you would love it, so much more than I do; the dirt and the difficulty of getting the right clothes (which you would always flashingly surmount) and the utter irregularity and unusualness of it all. You would see it all so much more dramatically than I do. People complain that the war is not "realised" in England; but as far as I am concerned it is certainly not realised in France. Saturday evening on the Underground is the impression I get . . .

To K. A.   Grand Hotel de la Poste,
                                                                    Rouen.
                                                          24 October 1915

We have been on our way to the trenches ever since tea time yesterday: it is now luncheon time today and we have got no further than Rouen. We wait 5 hours at every station and travel like cattle, about 10 in a carriage and always at night so one gets very little sleep. We go on again this evening and arrive (I believe) at Bethune sometime tomorrow, and after that no one seems to know what becomes of us.

We got here at 7 a.m. and the men, poor devils, are all shut up with a lot of Indians in a dirty kind of shed in the station until the next train is ready for them. The officers I'm glad to say are allowed a free run of the town and my Captain and I have succeeded in getting a good shave and a hot bath and in a moment or two we hope to be beginning a thoroughly buffy lunch, which will be pleasant enough as we have lived entirely on hard boiled eggs for the last 24 hours, and should not have got even them but for the Y.M.C.A. Canteens the value of which I never fully appreciated before.

We have already quarrelled with most of the staff officers we have had to do with and I can't tell you the loathing and contempt in which they are held by the others. If you heard the way they talk I believe you would think I was right not to become one: though of course one may find in the end that there are more uncomfortable things than general abuse.

I wonder if I shall get my brother officers to face the cathedral. I rather think not. Caneton Rouennais with a good stoup of Burgundy will fill up most of the available time. I always thought that I should be able to do a lot of reading and writing at the war, but so far – in spite of vast tracts of derelict and unoccupied time – I have read nothing except the Continental edition of the *Daily Mail* and written nothing except the most banal and laborious letters. One's brain is even more in abeyance out here than in camp at Richmond or Marlow. One seems to spend one's leisure moments either in making up arrears of sleep or in snatching feverishly at the last roses of summer in the way of hot water and cold wine. I see clearly that you will always write much better letters from England than ever I shall from France . . .

To **K. A.**   3rd Battn. Grenadier Guards,
                                                 Brit. Exped. Force.
                                                 26 October 1915

. . . We met our Battn. coming from the trenches yesterday and marched into billets where we are very comfortable and shall remain if all goes well for about a fortnight, so it is worth while sending things here. There are only 3 officers in my company including Capt. Vaughan who came out on the draft with me and we live and mess together. (An orderly has just come in to say that the post has gone so you won't get this for days).

We have an arrangement for hampers to be sent twice a week from Fortnum and Mason with delicatessen etc. At present we have an assortment of cakes and sweets which Rumpelmayer might envy. We had rather a tiresome journey from Rouen here with a good deal of waiting and marching in heavy rain, but we are comfortably housed now in a French village the name of which I believe I am not allowed to state. But in any case I do not know it. I suppose we are 10 miles or so from the firing line. One hears the guns poundering away all the time. We do a couple of hours drill in the morning and nothing much in the rest of the day, though if we can get some suitable ground I believe we are going to have some bombing practice.

The day after tomorrow we are to be reviewed by an important person (a relative of the Kaiser's). I dined last night with our O.C. (Corry) who has a very good sort of house as H.Q. and gave us 6 courses and a variety of different vintages all good.

There are only 14 officers in the Battn., ½ as many as there should be according to the book and only 3 of them have had more than a fortnight's experience of this war. Our Adjutant is Oliver Lyttelton whom I was glad to see and also seems to do the job very well. John Ponsonby is our Brigadier (the 2nd Guards Brigade). I have not seen him yet, but his quarters are just opposite to ours . . .

To K. A.   27 October 1915

. . . We live an easy life in billets – a little drill in the morning, a walk with Oliver or someone in the afternoon, a bottle of wine at dinner, and a feather bed to sleep on. The most laborious thing one does is reading through and censoring the soldier's letters. They are usually very long and very dull and full of formulae which hardly amount to idiom. The only things I ever scratch out are the expressions "hoping this finds you as it leaves me" and "now I must draw to a close". But God knows my own letters are very little better . . .

You would like this country because there is such a fine show of Rat Tails, just turning colour too. I suppose in another week the beeches at Mells will be at their best. What is the political gossip? Is the P.M. recovered? – how are Lord Derby and Nurse Cavell doing with the recruits?

I constantly think of you my angel, sporting with Brutus[1] and the chils, among the blackberry bushes, and every time I think of you I adore you more. Keep well and lovely.

To Lady Diana Manners   27 October 1915

. . . This war is a pure convention, like debates in the House of Commons, the birthday honours, and all other public (and most private) events. Usually there is a hell of a din here of big guns, today absolute calm. Why? because the King is at the front and they don't want a damned noise when he is there. Why have a damned noise at all, whether he is here or not? Pure convention. In the old

---

[1] A Great Dane.

days when we had no shells everyone wanted a noise but now we all know there are masses of shells, so why let them off? . . .

I think you would love being in billets here; there is a sort of strangeness about it that would appeal to you. Two or three rather muddy officers in the parlour of a French cottage and a few faithful servants, very like soldier servants in books, playing with the women in broken French in the kitchen next door, being sweet to children and making terrible smells with onions: outside big guns booming at a safe distance, dispatch riders, ambulances, etc., rattling over the pavé, in fact all the minor nonsense of war; if only a female spy of consummate beauty with wild hair and pinioned arms could be suddenly brought in by a sergeant major, you would have at once the 3rd act of any moderately bad play not by Galsworthy . . .

To K. A.   29 October 1915

. . . Dottie tells me by the way that old E. has broken out into a silver leprosy. It sounds most becoming and also characteristically extravagant. I wrote to him yesterday advising him not to do any more active service, but if he was bent on losing another kidney to do it in the Grenadiers. I think we do get better looked after than the other regiments, though they give us bloodier jobs in the field. However if they want to keep the division in existence they will have to put us in cotton wool a good deal this winter.

It would be a much pleasanter life, if one had one's friends in the regiment; though I must say I have been lucky in my company and like both my captain and my ensign.

Today we have been digging trenches or rather watching the men dig which was rather boring, and last night we had a concert which was worse. Needham[1] is very efficient and a great standby. He showed me a letter he had written to you yesterday.

Yesterday we had an awful fiasco. The whole division was to have been reviewed by the King at a place about 6 miles from here but after marching almost to the appointed spot in drenching rain we were told that the review had been put off on account of the weather and so we marched back again. I found out afterwards that the real reason was that while the King was inspecting some other troops earlier in the day his horse had reared and fallen on him doing him some injury though I believe not a serious one . . .

To K. A.   30 October 1915

. . . But when can you be going to send me the Trench photograph of yourself which was promised before I left? I have got a dinky little picture of Dilly and if

---

[1] Raymond's soldier servant.

that is found on my corpse instead of a picture of you I know you will give me a wigging in the next world . . .

Our C.O. has gone off on leave today for a week and my company Commander is taking his place pro tem. so I find myself in command of the Company which is funny enough if one comes to think of it.

Montgomery, the husband of the lady we met at lunch at Tits, and 2nd in command of the battn. was killed the day before the battn. left the trenches and a soldier whose letter I censored yesterday describing his death says "Major M. was a very good officer and a gentleman of independent means from London." I suppose that is what gives the men confidence when we go into action. Another soldier alluding to the fact of my joining the Battn. wrote "He seems a very decent officer as yet. If his military style is as good as his classics he will do well." . . .

To Lady Horner   30 October 1915

. . . I have been pleasantly supported by the conditions of life, both during the 2 days I spent at the base and also in billets here. They frighten one at home by saying that one's luggage will be thrown into the sea if it is over 35 lbs., whereas really one could bring everything one possesses without anyone objecting and use it too. We are in a French village about 10 miles behind the firing line and hear the guns booming all day, but otherwise know much less about the War than one does in England . . .

To K. A.   1 November 1915

I note what you say about Derby, and no doubt if it could be quietly arranged it would be a good thing, if only because it would mean a slight increase of income – tho' I suppose most of that would have to be spent in the constituency – but don't worry unduly about it, my pretty. You suggest that Derby is probably more luxurious than this; I don't know that there is much in it in the matter of material comfort, but I would far rather sit down to a lean chicken with a couple of gentlemen, than see old Fletcher waving his mutilated hand over the plumpest turkey ever bred on the Trent and am honestly less bored at the prospect of going into the trenches than I should be by a week of meetings and speeches on the Insurance Act and such like skimble-skamble stuff. No doubt when I have had more experience I may revise my values.

Yesterday I had a note from [Osbert] Sitwell asking me over to dinner with his Battn. which is quartered about 6 miles off but I did not fancy a ride on the pavé in dark and wet, so dined instead at Brigade H.Q. who are just opposite my billet with John Ponsonby who was very agreeable and amusing. I understood quite a large proportion of what he said [*i.e.* in spite of his having a severe speech impediment].

I have determined to devote 5 minutes a day to serious reading and began this morning on the Odes of Horace, pleasantly surprised as I always am to find how astonishingly good they are. It was wonderfully clever of you, my sweet, to find that minute Horace for me. I can see it will be a great resource and a constant reminder of my angel Fawn.

To K. A.   3 November 1915
                                                  Cras Animarum

I have just got a letter from you dated 31st Oct. which day you erroneously describe as All Souls. All Saints Day is Nov. 1, All Souls Nov. 2 and Nov. 3 is correctly designated above as *Cras Animarum* or (in English) the morrow of All Souls. For once however I will pass over the error, merely warning you that if it recurs this time next year I shall go back to Margot; or possibly even to Canada where men are economically independent.

I'm sorry you were disappointed of a letter from me that day – I haven't written quite 'every single' but don't think I have missed more than 2 days at the most since coming here. But I shall miss several unless that hog Selfridge sends me some envelopes . . .

This morning we did a little practical bombing. I threw some live bombs for the first time. It is rather exciting at first as the fragments fly back a good way, and also you never feel quite sure that some clumsy lout next to you won't drop his bomb on the ground in the excitement of the contest. "Presently I went for a walk" and got on to a small hill covered with turning birch trees from which one could see a great way over flat plains with poplars on the horizon and a large misty cathedral in the middle distance looking rather massive and mysterious under a stormy and sinister sky. Coming back I got soaked to the skin.

No, my pretty. don't send me any book by Conrad, however good, I couldn't bear it. It gives me a sick headache even to write the man's name. And as a matter of fact I never seem to read anything except an ode of Horace now and then. I still have a book by Wells which I brought out with me quite untasted. I play bridge a good deal, latterly with my customary good fortune. Yesterday I won 200 francs . . .

To K. A.   5 November 1915

. . . Yesterday was a beautiful sunny day. After the morning parade I sat at a table in an orchard in the sun and paid the company. In the afternoon I marched the men to a rather picturesque brewery 2 miles away and they all had hot baths in the vats. While I was waiting for them in a garden behind the brewery a sergeant of the Scots Guards came up and asked me to umpire in a drill competition. A corporal had bet a sergeant 5 francs that he – the corporal – had the better word of command. So I went into a field and heard them shout at a squad in turn; I awarded the apple to the corporal, because I thought that would be the popular thing to do: and so it was. This morning we have been for a march.

The French villages look rather sad and dirty in the Autumn, but just round here they are less ugly I think than the average and every now and again one comes upon a small rather mysterious looking duck-pond with one white duck paddling about under the golden birch trees in a dimly symbolical kind of way like a Maeterlinckian princess.

It is getting a little dull here but everyone is sorry at the prospect of a move. They seem to think that we shall be off on Sunday, but probably stop a night somewhere on our way to the trenches. I believe we are going to a part of the line which ought to be considerably quieter than that which we have occupied lately.

We had your marmalade at breakfast this morning. It was excellent and much appreciated by all. But I don't think it is much good sending anything but small parcels during our time in the trenches. Chocolate is always useful. Tomorrow I am going to get some champagne and give a birthday party to 8 officers. Hopley and Oliver and Mark Maitland, who has been imported from the 1st Battn. to command us in the absence of Corry on leave, are coming. After that Swan Song things will be rather bloody and uncomfortable for a month or so I expect . . .

To K. A.   6 November 1915

. . . My parcels are raining in these last few days – socks, nightshirts, jam, peptonised cocoa, meat lozenges, cigarettes, newspapers, strop case etc. The thing I want most and can't get is writing paper and *envelopes*. I shall never trust that bitch Selfridge again. These are literally my last sheets of paper and the last envelope I can squeeze out of my reluctant friends. "*Victory*" arrived yesterday. If I had know that it was actually on its way I wouldn't have been so bloody about it in my letter the other day. But the fact remains that I don't suppose I shall get my teeth in to it till the end of the War and probably not finish it till the next one begins. I've had a really beautiful day for my birthday, brilliant sun, a touch of frost in the air and birches with silver stems and golden leaves looking well enough against a pale blue sky. A perfect day for covert shooting.

We are having a large dinner party tonight with foie gras and preserved ginger and old brandy and champagne and everything handsome including caviare.

Our departure has been postponed from tomorrow to Monday when we start at dawn for an 18 mile march. I think we shall be billeted for a night or two close behind the line before moving into the trenches. Probably on the 14th we are going north to relieve the Indians: I am supposed not to say exactly where, and a churchwoman like you would probably be offended if I did.

Please thank Frances for a most welcome birthday letter. Is it true that Lady Londonderry has been arrested in France? and if so what for? . . .

To K. A.   8 November 1915

. . . We have just arrived in our new billets about 5 miles behind the line as far as I can judge. We have to be ready to move up at ½ hour's notice, but I don't think we are likely to get our notice for several days yet. We had a very tiring march and once lost our way. I rose at 5.15 a.m. as things had to be packed, and we were off by 7 – the whole Brigade with all its transport etc. The march was about 18 miles and we did not get here till after 2 p.m. I had rather a headache having lived too much of late on foie gras and champagne, but otherwise did not suffer much and was pleased to find my feet quite hard.

It doesn't sound a very severe test, but of course one carries a lot of weight, and the men still more. They fell out like flies by the roadside and by the time we arrived we looked more like the retreat from Moscow than the smartest regiment in the British Army.

This is a much bigger place than the last one we were in, but the people are much less hospitable. We had to bring much pressure and some cash to bear on our landlady to persuade her to give us the use of a dining room and kitchen, but now we have got them I think we shall be even better off than we were at Norreut, though I fear our stay will be shorter.

The Germans came over all this part in their retreat and the landlady is terribly voluble about it all and insists on showing us masses of coffee pots and forks etc. which were buried in the garden and broken by shells in spite of being under the earth.

Just before I left I got a large parcel of shirts and towels and also what I fear must be your best field-glasses. It was very sweet of you to send them and I must try to be careful and bring them safe back to you before the season for observing greenfinches sets in again . . .

To Lady Diana Manners   9 November 1915

. . . Your discussion of the Art of Love seems to me a step quite in the right direction. Take Iris [Tree]. It is her scholarship which enables her to indulge her appetite; and at the same time her appetite prevents her learning from being donnish; if she had beauty she would be as irresistible as she is insatiable. Lust without learning is blind, learning without lust is empty, as Hegel used to say I think . . .

To K. A.   11 November 1915

It is fine today but colder and orders have come out for elaborate preparations against frost bite. But the cold will be bearable if only the rain keeps off. I have so much kit now that I don't want you to send me out anything more in the way of clothes unless I specially ask for it. I have written to Cording explaining what I want in the way of waterproof trousers.

We continue our lap-dog experience here, eating far too much cake and taking far too little exercise. I have to take the men to bathe this afternoon which means a good deal of boring hanging about. Oliver and the C.O. have just gone to have a look at the trenches we are to occupy and we shall probably know tonight what we have to expect in the way of water.

· I have read the accounts of the Lord Mayor's feast. The P.M.'s speech seemed to me a good one. Our band has just arrived and is playing out in the square. It is extraordinary what a difference it seems to make to the men and to all of the officers except me. They stand in the cold for hours listening to it playing Gilbert the Filbert or any other nonsense, and talk about it afterwards too as if it were an important event . . .

To K. A.   12 November 1915

Another of your Havre letters has drifted in today: and I had one yesterday and another today dated Monday and Tuesday so I have done very well indeed. Also lots of parcels – 2 excellent tins of honey and the Old Gold tobacco. You have been very clever about getting what I want. I said in my last letter that I should never want anything else but as I may have to sleep on the floor from time to time I think it would be a comfort to have one of those circular pink rubber air cushions with a hole in the middle – you know the sort I mean – like a coral necklace, about a foot across or a little more. One's hip bone fits into the hole and doesn't get bruised by the floor. There is no hurry about it, but some day when you are passing a shop.

. . . How are you getting on for money? Let me know when you run short and I will try to provide some more. I think that I have still a few pounds in the bank as I have drawn no cheques since I came out here (except for the rates of Bed. Sq.) and manage to live pretty well on my bridge winnings and the parcels from home.

I took the men to bathe in a factory yesterday near here where they have great vats of hot water. It was very well arranged and they all got clean clothes afterwards. There were also real baths for the officers and I thoroughly enjoyed myself in one of them. Today I had my hair cropped by a bar-tender in the neighbouring town in the hope that I might fight on more equal terms against the vermin, the dangers of which are I believe very much exaggerated.

I still have one more day of comfort before facing the mud and water. But I believe we get back every 48 hours to a place where we can change our clothes and sleep under cover of a sort. If so it won't be so bad . . .

To K. A.   13 November 1915

. . . We march off tomorrow afternoon at 4. I don't suppose we shall be in much danger from bullets but my Captain who went to see our trenches today reports them disgustingly wet and muddy and rather ruinous, so I look forward to being extremely uncomfortable and also having a lot of digging to do and very little sleep. It's a mercy we are only in for 48 hours at a time and then get back to a little behind the line to a place where we can get dry clothes and a roof of sorts over our heads.

I was glad to get your packet of chocolates and handkerchief and Needham was also much pleased with his parcel. I am going to march in George's gum boots tomorrow, but from all I hear there is every likelihood of the mud coming over the top of them when we get into the trenches . . .

To K. A.   15 November 1915
                                                                (In the Trenches)

Just a line to tell you that I am up to the neck in a rich glutinous blue clay, otherwise well and happy. Every kind of gun shoots in a pointless sort of way from every quarter of the compass all day and all night but so far without causing either pain or panic.

It is pretty cold at night (and also by day) but very fine and though one gets literally no sleep for some strange reason one does not get very tired. No time for more now, but I will write again tomorrow night or the day after when we go 2 miles back for 48 hours rest.

To K. A.   16 November 1915

There is nothing much doing this morning except what they call an artillery duel, so I don't see why I shouldn't write to you, though I am too sleepy to be very fluent or amusing.

We marched into the trenches on Sunday evening by a rather circuitous route – about 7 miles I should think, and it took us over 4 hours as the last part was very slow going. About 6 p.m. we reached a ruined village on the road where we halted and put on our trench boots – long rubber things which go almost up to one's waist, but none too long. It was a fine frosty night with a moon and stars. There we picked up our guides and made our way by platoons across open country to our various positions. The point where we left the road was about 1½ miles from the trenches and the communication trenches by which we were supposed to go up were so full of water and mud that we had to go across the top of the open country instead – a wide flat expanse of dead grass elaborately intersected by the flooded communication trenches.

It was very slow work getting the men across these obstacles in their full kit and there were constant checks. Fortunately we were not shelled at all, but there was a certain amount of harmless and unskilful sniping. The Boches kept sending up rockets which seemed to illuminate the whole country and towards the end of our journey where we were only a few hundred yards from their lines it seemed impossible that they should not see us, but whether they did or not they never hit any of us.

The sniping is very puzzling at first because it seems to come from every direction at once and you hear the crack of rifles which seem to be no further off than the next gun is to one in a partridge drive. Yet nothing happens. There was only one place where the bullets seemed to be coming rather too near and I had to make the men lie down for 5 minutes. I had the rear platoon of the whole Brigade, but my guide was a skilful one, and we got into our trench before any of the others. It was a support trench about 200 yards behind our firing line, and as filthy and dilapidated as it could be – a very poor parapet, flooded dug-outs and a quagmire of mud and water at the bottom in many places 3 ft. deep. But for my long boots I should certainly have died of cold and dirt.

I got in about 8 p.m., but it was nearly 10 before the whole company was in. We set to work digging and draining at once and worked all night. I constantly got lost in the labyrinth both below ground and above. I had a tot of hot rum about 3 a.m. which made the whole difference. We worked away all yesterday and are at it again; tonight the trench will be a very tolerable one. I have a small but dry dug-out in which I got 3 hours sleep last night. It freezes hard in the night and early morning but luckily we have had no rain, and every now and then at irregular intervals Needham brings me a bowl of turtle soup which he seems to think a diet appropriate to the situation in which we find ourselves.

The support trenches are usually more shelled than the fire trenches because there is less risk of the gunners hitting their own men, but we have fared very well in this respect, as the Boches are directing most of their fire at roads in our rear. One shell lighted a short way behind us and spattered me with mud but as I was already thickly coated with it I bore no malice. Shelling, rifle and machine gun fire go on spasmodically all day and all night, but we have had only 2 men killed and about a dozen wounded in the whole battalion: these were shot by snipers while digging in front of the line at night.

This morning I had a man down with frost bite in my platoon and I am surprised there are not more, as there were not enough boots to go all round.

Tonight at 6.30 we are relieved by the Scots Guards and go back a mile or two to get clean and dry for 48 hours – back into the trenches again – the front line this time – on Thursday for another 2 days, then 2 days in the rest billets, and after that I think we get 4 days real rest in the comfortable quarters from which we came on Sunday. I am looking forward to scraping some of the mud and hair off my face and getting some continuous sleep; washing and shaving being out of the question here and sleep almost so.

I'm afraid this is a regular "letter from the front" saying all the boring things you have read 100 times in the Daily Anything but the truth is I am too sleepy to be ingenious or inventive . . .

To K. A.   17 November 1915

. . . John Ponsonby is going away tomorrow on leave and my C.O. takes command of the brigade and my company Commander of the battalion, so I am left in command of the Company, for which I am not sorry as I shall get a better dug-out and have more responsibility and less work.

I think we are going back again to the same trenches but they ought to be less muddy if the Scots Guards have done their duty during the 48 hours of their tenancy. On the other hand it has rained very hard today and the water may be deeper. I found Edward's waders waiting for me here and shall certainly take them in with me in case I can't get hold of another pair of jack-boots. Please thank him very much for them . . .

I hope your dream about my leave may come true. As long as we don't attack one's turn comes round fairly fast, but when there is a push in contemplation they always stop it for a bit; and I shouldn't be surprised if we had another small push before Xmas. The stupidity of the authorities in not making any adequate preparation for winter life in the trenches is very striking. There ought at least to be trench boots for every man, but in our division so far every other man has to go without and probably other divisions are worse off still. But I believe they are getting out a further supply. Then one would have thought they would have arranged to make watertight trenches by now after last year's experience but they seem to have learned nothing and there is just as much mud and water and discomfort as there was in 1914.

. . . I don't think it's any good your sending me Eddie [Marsh]'s new volume of Georgian poets. I never read anything but Horace out here and not much of him. But I suppose even Eddie would admit that Horace was better than [Rupert] Brooke . . .

To Lady Horner   19 November 1915

. . . I am writing this in the trenches where I am doing my second 48 hours. It is rather worse than the first, as there is more cold, more wet, more mud, more bullets, less rum and less novelty. This is no place for those who mind rats, as the little rascals are very numerous, well-nourished and daring. They gnaw the corpses and then gallop about over one's face when one lies down. Fortunately I was always a lover of animals.

So far I have had no trouble with insects or indeed with anything else except cold and dirt. From these no conceivable precaution can save one. Long waders and hot rum go as far as anything.

. . . But on the whole we have little to complain of in the way of bullets and shells. They go on coming over the whole time; but usually in just sufficient numbers to create a diversion rather than a panic. In fact I don't know where we should be without them. It will be a very different story of course if we are to have another of these damned attacks which everyone but the staff regards with undisguised loathing and horror; reasonably enough, I think, seeing that they are both extremely dangerous and utterly useless.

I thought Winston's speech very good and did not identify the parts of it which the P.M. thought would have been better left unsaid. We are all rather disappointed out here at the academic character of Kitchener's mission, as we heard it rumoured that he had been sent out to assassinate the King of Greece . . .

P.S. Since writing the above another letter from you has just been delivered to me in the trench enclosing another fountain pen – both Swans, so perhaps they will breed – not cygnets but signatures (as Gregory VII might have said). The temptation to re-open my letter in order to insert this witticism should perhaps have been resisted . . .

To Lady Diana Manners   19 November 1915

It makes me miserable to think of you being miserable about George Vernon . . . I was very fond of him; he was an attractive and pathetic creature and in various ways gave us a great deal of fun. How much he loved and feared you! and how little you either feared or loved him! Yet I do not think you have anything to reproach yourself with in the matter. After all you spent a large proportion of your adult life "getting him right", and if the job was like pouring Pommery into a sieve that was not your fault. The dangerous double phenomenon of your beauty, alternately delighted and dismayed him, and that alternation I believe was his principal pleasure in life.

I don't see why we should not allow ourselves to be a bit soppy about that Venetian party with its brief profusion and glitter, so lamentably eclipsed by the swift procession of Denny [Anson] and Billy [Grenfell] and George from the Lido to the Styx. One may almost be pardoned, (or do you think not) for quoting Omar.

> "And some there be the loveliest and the best
> "That rolling Time has from his Vintage pressed
> "Have drunk their cup a round or two before
> "And one by one crept silently to rest."

. . . I am, by the way, in what are called the trenches and have been for 3 or 4 days now. I won't labour the point, as they are exactly like what you read about them (if you do read it) in the ½d press. So far they are more uncomfortable and less dangerous than I had been led to expect. Waders are essential as the mud and water are well above the knee and the cold intense . . . An unpleasant feature is the vast number of rats which gnaw the dead bodies and then run about on one's face making obscene noises and gestures. Lately a certain number of cats have taken to nesting in the corpses but I think the rats will get them under in the end; though like all wars it will doubtless be a war of attrition.

The trenches are so filthy that there is a temptation, hard to resist, even by the most lily-livered, to walk about on the top of them instead of the bottom. One has to remind oneself that Mr. Don't-Care was eaten by lions. Rifle bullets, as long as they don't come in great numbers, are rather exciting than alarming; shells, I believe, can be terrifying, but so far only rather ill-aimed ones have come my way and no one pays much attention to them. The noise is rather irritating and pointless.

There is hardly a minute of the day or night when one or other of these idiotic engines is not banging away, and I am often reminded of my rare and unrefreshing visits to the Opera.

But good God, I am labouring the point like a navvy; hardly doing myself justice, really, because if I ever get back I think I can promise you not to be a war-bore.

I take about the same sort of interest in it as an ill-tempered tourist may take in an uncomfortable hotel.

To K. A.   20 November 1915

The sun is setting and in 2 or 3 hours we shall be relieved by our 2nd Battn. and shall get back into decent billets for 5 or 6 days rest. It will be a long slow march and I daresay we shan't be in till nearly midnight so I am scribbling you these few lines to catch tomorrow's post if possible.

I shall be glad of a rest. The cold and mud and the interminable nights when one tramps through the frozen slush visiting the sentries and either may not or cannot sleep are very wearisome – more to the spirit, oddly enough, than to the body. Physically I am perfectly well – not even a cold in the head – and not really very tired. But the monotony of the life is already rather appalling and even in this short time the noise of the guns has become as idiotic and tediously irritating as the noise of motor buses in London. I suppose I am too easily bored to be a soldier even in War time. Today there has been and still is a very severe bombardment and the air has been full of shells – not directed at us fortunately, but what they call 'an artillery duel' between batteries some little way behind the lines. We have had two or three cases of frost bite among the men and 2 or

3 of that voice-destroying disease which I had earlier in the year, but I think only 2 casualties today . . .

I had a letter from Frances brought to me in the trenches yesterday and also one from you enclosing the Income Tax demand. It made me laugh heartily as I extricated myself from a puddle of frozen mud to receive a request for £193.2.6 which is more than I have earned during the whole of my career in the army. Your other enclosure also amused me – I mean the Pankhurst manifesto stating that England was disgraced and that Miss Carrie Tubb was going to sing. Was it sent to me? If so I am disposed to write them an insulting answer – or how else did you get hold of it? It is interesting about Eddie going to Downing St.

What is Bongie going to do apart from marrying Visey which I see is fixed for the 30th?

To K. A.   22 November 1915

We got out of the trenches all right on Saturday night. It was bright moonlight and frost and I expected to have trouble, but we only lost 2 men, one shot in the head the other in the leg by a machine gun which they turned on to one of our platoons. It was very pleasant marching back – a clear beautiful night just the right temperature for a walk; and still pleasanter to get home to my kind landlady and a bottle of "the boy" [champagne] consumed with immense gusto just before midnight and followed by 10 hours in a soft bed.

Madame Brunel Gailly who owns this house which is much the best in the town has developed an elderly caprice for me which has not been displaced even by the confession that she forced from me the other day that I was 37 and had a wife and two children or my utter inability to sustain conversation with her in her own tongue. It is really most fortunate as the Commanding officer came here with 3 interpreters and an adjutant and tried to get the house as his H.Q. but the old lady obstinately resisted him – swore that she would have no one here but me. This is the first real success I have ever had with your sex. In another 10 years I shall be irresistible.

By an infernal piece of ill luck we are to be shifted out of here tomorrow to a place about 3 miles further back where we are almost sure to fare worse. I don't think we are for the trenches again till Saturday or Monday, no one seems to know which.

By an odd chance Winston was attached to the H.Q. of the Battn. (2nd Grenadiers) which relieved us last Saturday, and I might easily have seen him but just didn't. He is really a splendid fellow and comes out of the war better than anyone, I think.

There is no end to the tiresome things one has to do here. I have just come in from a ride of 20 miles to reconnoitre the country between here and Neuve Chapelle, and am quite sore and stiff from jogging along the frozen roads on a

3rd rate horse at an uncomfortable and unremitting trot together with the 3 other company commanders. We got to within 800 yds of the German lines and were then met by a hysterical Major in some territorial regiment who said that there was a machine gun trained on that particular corner of the road, and that unless we retired at once we should attract attention and his men (not we) would all be killed. Sure enough it did begin loosing off soon after we were out of the way, but I don't think the bullets can have come anywhere near the poor major. We have to do the same thing over some other roads tomorrow morning before moving to our new billets . . .

To K. A.   23 November 1915

I'm sorry for poor Cincie [Cynthia]. She has certainly been out of luck lately. Fancy Beb having a fit! there is really no end to his oddities. Is spinal neuritis a new disease? and has anyone else got it from being shelled? or from being drunk? I am in an ill temper tonight having been moved from my comfortable billet to a rather primitive farmhouse in the suburbs where my bed takes up the whole of the room and looks unappetising and flea-haunted – And now I find I have begun to write on the wrong side of the paper, which I always think vulgarises a letter more than anything else.

I had another long boring bump along the roads today on a tired horse which kept falling down if one didn't look after it all the time. And then, in the afternoon we marched out a few miles to these new billets.

Winston rode over and took tea with me. He seemed very well and in good spirits at having substituted the trenches for the Cabinet. He thinks that the war will last all through next year and that conscription is coming shortly.

I dined last night with Cavan [divisional commander] at Divisional H.Q. He was very nice, gave me a good dinner and an excellent bottle of champagne and played bridge afterwards quite well for 50 centimes a hundred.

The Prince of Wales was there and gave me a long and fragrant cigar – his only contribution to the evening's sport, but a sufficient one. Please thank Frances for letter and peppermints which arrived this evening, and also your papa for letter, without peppermints . . .

To Lady Diana Manners   25 November 1915

. . . Out here one's outlook on life, military life I mean, changes very rapidly – every now and then moments of excitement and almost of happiness even in the trenches, occasionally a moment almost of ecstasy when one marches in late at night after a week of dirt and bullets and finds a feather bed and a bottle of the Boy awaiting one; then horrible reactions of boredom and nausea as one's mind collapses under the pressure of prospect and retrospect and the monotony of a great desert of discomfort and danger with no visible horizon. But usually one is very equable, looking no further ahead than the next meal and feeling that really life is very much the same everywhere, war or no war . . .

To K. A.   25 November 1915

. . . There was an ugly rumour last week that we were going to pop the parapet, this time for the purpose of making a diversion while a big attack was proceeding further north; everybody was very gloomy and indignant about it – to such a point has cant become obsolete: but the whole idea has been dropped now much to the relief of subaltern officers.

I'm afraid this is even a more tiresome letter than usual but this life dries up the flow of general ideas and blurs the outlines of language. A message has just come in to say that a clergyman called Crawley is ill in the next house and very much wants to see me as I am an old friend of his. Did you ever hear a more unlikely story? But I suppose I had better go and see . . .

To K. A.   26 November 1915

We marched this morning from our old billets to a ruined French town about a mile behind the firing line. It snowed fiercely all the time we were on the march and was very cold and uncomfortable. We are better housed now than one has any right to expect so near to the front and in a place which has been (and occasionally still is) so heavily shelled as this. There is no glass in our windows and the walls and ceilings and furniture are all perforated with shrapnel, but we have a fire and beds which are unexpected joys in billets of this character . . .

I got an excellent luncheon of soup, omelette and beer at a local estaminet for 2 francs. The phlegm of the French contrasts very favourably with the hysteria of the English. People still live and do their business in these shattered houses and a few doors down this street I heard the children in an infants' school chanting their lessons just as they do in New Street at Mells.

. . . I have written to Visey to give her my good wishes on her marriage; though as I pointed out to her, it is something in the nature of a concession, as no single member of my family has sent me a letter or anything else during the 6 weeks or so of my life in France. I record this not as a critic but as an observer. There is no earthly reason why they should write. But there is no harm in having something up one's sleeve to throw back in their teeth when they perorate about my heartlessness . . .

To K. A.   27 November 1915

. . . The chocolate and cigarettes have arrived safely and pleased both Needham and me. We are getting into the cold snap here – probably the same as you complain of at Mells. Today was a beautiful winter day, brilliant sun and hard frost. The sky was very clear and full of aeroplanes. I counted 7 of ours in a sort of flock being terrifically shelled by the Huns. It is really a very pretty sight, the flash of the shrapnel and the little ball of white smoke which keeps its identity for a quarter of an hour or more before it is dissipated. But this again has been so often described that one is ashamed to mention it.

The battalion paraded this afternoon for an hour's drill in a field here but 2 shells burst about 100 yards off so they had to dismiss the parade. I was rather surprised, as it usually takes something more than that to make a guards battalion stop drilling. I'm afraid we shall suffer a good deal from cold in the trenches tomorrow but anyhow they are dry this time and if we can only be sure of getting back for our 2 days "out" to these excellent billets I shall endure the 2 days "in" with equanimity.

This is quite a pretentious house and the room where I am writing leads by glass doors into a sort of greenhouse or what P. Glenconner would call a "stone parlour" painted with frescoes representing the bay of Naples with gigantic hydrangeas, convolvulus, etc., in the foreground. Unluckily it is cracked through the middle by shell fire and looks as if it might collapse at any moment. There is one devilish thing about this billet – a dog in a kennel in the garden which hardly ever stops barking. It gets on my nerves much worse than a machine gun . . .

To Lady Diana Manners   28 November 1915

Your letter has forced its way through a very dirty night to my dug-out in an isolated fortress of sand-bags – A lotus in Lapland, a snow-flake stained with wine. The Baptist's head was not more welcome to Salome. I was near the end of my or anybody's bent, for damp and cold and boredom, when it came. But if there had been nothing else with it but the words "or even man" it would have carried me through another 24 hours, and nothing can do more than that. God bless you, Dilly, for your wit. It sometimes makes me think He loved the world after all.

When your letter came – (in the morning) – I was reading the Odes of Horace (the only book I have here or want) and was in the middle of one, in which he tells how Penelope and Circe were both soppy about Ulysses *"Laborantes in uno Penelopen vitreamque Circen"* and was thinking what an apt epithet for you was "vitreous" which means glassy – hard, brilliant and of an aquamarine tint, reflecting well too, which you do; not that this exhausts you, nothing does not even your mother. But somehow "vitreous" gives me the physical sensation of you which is what I want, (and of course what every one wants), but in truth I believe it is only because the adjective is eked out by the substantive – CIRCE – what a word! I know none to equal it in charm. Will you write me any word which you think better or as good? How I adore words don't you? better than all things and almost all people . . .

To K. A.   29 November 1915

. . . I am glad that you are going to meet Oliver [Lyttelton], I like him, but many of the junior officers think him too casual and conceited. He has some of the faults of youth, but also many of the virtues. His chief defect to my mind is one inherited from Alfred – viz. telling rather long and moderately good stories and laughing hysterically long before he comes to the point.

I am in command of a platoon in an isolated redoubt away from the rest of my company with orders to hold out to the last gasp in the event of an attack. Fortunately nothing is less probable as we have completely (so far as one can judge) broken the spirit of the Boche in this part of the line. We shell him every day for hours and he hardly ever replies. Last night it was freezing, but now there is a thaw with a raw wind and rain, but I am better off for dug-outs than ever before, having a bedroom (with mattress, looking glass and writing table) a sitting-room and a kitchen for Needham. The men all have dug-outs too, so that it is difficult to get them to do any work. The only disadvantage is the loneliness and having to walk a certain distance up an inadequate communication trench for my dinner in the front line, a wet puzzling journey in the dark with bullets singing over one's head; if it were not for the German rockets, I should get lost every time. Being the only officer, I have to stay up most of the night, but I doze a good deal, read a little Horace, write a few letters, or mesmerise myself by gazing at the lovely broad flame of my giant candle, aspiring like a spirit and shaped like an Achaean spear-head.

I hope to be relieved tomorrow night and get back to bed and soap again for 2 days, but there is an awful possibility that I may be left here for 6 days running, and that without a razor. You might by the way, send me the 2 remaining trench candles. These are a great comfort through long lonely nights. I'm afraid this life tends to make me even more egotistical than usual. It is a mistake, and a very common one, to suppose that the details of one's life are different from the details one is used to. Anyhow by this time War-life has become more of a routine and convention than peace-life ever was and it is the doings of all of you who live at home that have grown romantic and wild and highly-coloured . . .

To **K. A.**   1 December 1915

. . . I had my first experience of aimed shell-fire yesterday: previously anything which happened to burst near one had simply been a bad shot at something else, but yesterday morning the Boches made a dead set at my little fortress and the road immediately in front of it and fired shrapnel at us for an hour between 9.30-10.30 a.m. My redoubt was built of sandbags, not cut deep into the earth as a trench would be in dry country and only too often is in wet and if they had fired high explosives they would have made us look very silly; but with good narrow breastwork shrapnel is not frightening. The net result of about 100 shells was one of my men wounded not seriously. I had a guard of a corporal and 6 men in a ruined building on the far side of a road about 30 yards from my redoubt and they burst one shell right over the roof of the building throwing up a great cloud of dust and mortar and broken tiles. I made sure that the guard must have suffered severely but when I went over to see found that none of them had been touched. We shelled the enemy heavily yesterday and again today, I hope with more effect.

In the rest of the battn. we had only 2 casualties – both killed by snipers and both in my company. When we go back tomorrow I shall be with the rest of the company and not in my redoubt and shall be able to watch the shelling of the redoubt with amused interest through my glasses as my fellow officers did yesterday . . .

To **K. A.**   5 December 1915

A delightful long letter from you last night written from Berkeley St with all the gossip and scandal of the town. I'm glad that Visey and Bongie managed not to look too dilapidated at the altar. They are ill advised I should say, to honeymoon at the 2 coldest spots in Europe, Salisbury Plain and the Italian Riviera.

I envy old E. going to see Dottie *ondulée 'd*.[1] I should be very glad to see anyone *ondulée 'd* – let alone Dottie; or even to be *ondulé 'd* myself (note my grasp on grammar). I am tired of seeing nothing but very muddy men.

I got a poem, by the way, from Dottie this morning by [W. H.] Davies about a dying harlot, which she says is having a great vogue, as I can well believe. Personally I don't much care about it, and it belongs to the simple-obscure type which always exasperates me. And even in that genre it is neither so simple as Blake nor so obscure. You might tell me when next you write what it means and why, if at all, it is good. You often know these things when I don't. I've just finished a very disagreeable 2 days in the trenches. A great deal of rain and hardly any sleep: and then last night instead of being allowed my

[1] Having her hair waved.

usual 2 days rest in decent billets was put in command of 3 redoubts about ½ mile behind the line with a platoon in each of them.

I am the only officer so it is rather lonely, but less uncomfortable than I had feared. I sleep in a battered farm house – rather a nice stagey sort of kitchen with low oak beams and a hearth and chimney 10 ft. wide. In another part of the house are ½ dozen men with a machine gun and there is a room where Needham cooks me a pork chop at irregular intervals. I also have an orderly attached to me called Bunker, a tall thin man with no roof to his mouth whose business it is to take messages. I can never understand a word he says. But I daresay it is good practice for John Ponsonby. He also accompanies me with a rifle when I go out at night, as it is supposed to be unsafe in the region of the firing line to move a yard without an armed escort.

Today has been warmer and sunny with birds singing or at any rate twittering: almost like Spring. In these parts the evening instead of being full of linnets' wings is full of the humming of aeroplanes . . .

Last night was very black with a gale of wind and drifting clouds lit up spasmodically by German searchlights. I wished you were here to keep me company, my sweet, as I sat down at 10.30 p.m. to my pork chop. The décor was rather what I used to picture in old days when we used to make plans for roasting chestnuts together in lonely cottages on stormy nights. No wolves, but Boches do as well.

Tomorrow evening I return for 2 days more to the front line, then back to rest for 6 days in safety and comfort. I am so fat that I am unworthy to be called thy husband. It seems rather hard that you should be married to a portly man . . .

To K. A.   10 December 1915

. . . I did not expect that you would take much to Oliver, who I may say is becoming increasingly unpopular with the junior officers here who charge him with being both a bully and a toady. He is always very civil to me.

Poor Sweet, I am so sorry that Hyacinth[1] has already begun to oppress you. But I suppose if you want to eat your cake you must have it first. Give my love to Helen and Perdita. I was much amused at the nurse saying that Visey looked very sober. I am glad she is keeping her head even in this lyric period . . .

To K. A.   11 December 1915

. . . We live a quiet liverish life here in billets with much rain, and many petty annoyances, such as having to get up at an absurd hour tomorrow (Sunday)

---

[1] A joke name for the baby that she was expecting the following April.

morning to take the men to a bath-house about a mile off, which could be done every bit as well by a sergeant. One ought to be squeezing every moment of joy out of one's holiday from the trenches, but for some reason, I have relapsed this time into a fit of mopy stupor and utter abeyance of energies mental and physical.

I am beginning to feel gloomy about money too as when I have paid that damned insurance I shall be quite cleaned out till my January allowance comes in. I only hope the papers won't bully the ministers into giving up their salaries or the P.M. will also be irretrievably broke too and we shall all be in the gutter.

It seems very strange to anyone out here that you should think our life too gay and varied in comparison with your own. I feel as if I could be happy for ever with a good mattress and a few hollyhocks. Though on second thoughts I know I shouldn't be. I hope people have stopped by now talking about the elevating and revivifying effect of the War. The fact is that a thick pall of boredom and nausea has settled down on the whole world, soldiers and civilians, victor and vanquished.

The bubble of material luxury has burst and the bladder of spiritual exaltation is punctured in a thousand pieces, and "there is nothing left remarkable beneath the visiting moon". The prospect is a poor one both for parsons and for plutocrats. Still more for paupers and for parasites like ourselves. However I suppose one ought to be thankful to retain one's legs and arms and a decaying faculty or so; though God knows what there is to do with them. It is very stupid of me to write all this dreary stuff to you, my sweet Fawn, who are probably not feeling too bobbish yourself. But I *am* very stupid just now . . .

To Lady Manners   11 December 1915

. . . I have been out here about 8 weeks now and already begin to find it a little monotonous. It seems strange that it should be difficult to keep one's attention fixed on a war even when one is taking part in it—more difficult in fact than when one is at home. But so it is with me. I keep thinking of quite other things all the time – women or places in England, or even odes of Horace, just as one does during the 2nd act of a boring play; of course we have been going through rather a sedentary phase lately. No doubt if there was more movement one would be too frightened to be very "dreamy".

As things are, after a week or so one gets so used to being shelled at a certain hour every day and to meeting bullets at a particular corner of the road when leading men in or out of the trenches that it becomes a routine like everything else, more irritating by its monotony than alarming by its "frightfulness". So far we have been fortunate in the matter of casualties and have not had more than about 2 dozen in the battalion all the time I have been here. But the mud and wet and cold, the rats and mice, the dankness and darkness and interminable duration of the nights which one spends in patrolling the trench and visiting the sentries – all these things become more revolting as the weeks go on.

On the other hand the joy of getting back to a bed and a bottle of wine and a few days rest in billets is intense. In our part of the line – and I fancy elsewhere too – we have completely mastered the artillery of the Boches, who are apparently pretty short of shells. If they shell us we telephone at once to our own batteries and every gun fires 10 rounds a minute for 20 minutes which has a very taming effect. Nothing will persuade the men that the war is not practically over now and that they are merely marking time out here while the details of peace are being settled. I wish I could think so. I began this letter in my dug-out 2 days ago, and when I got back here to billets was delighted to find a stove waiting for me which Oliver told me he had brought out as a present from you. Thank you so much, dearest Con. It will be a great comfort on these cold nights. We have very few braziers in the trenches and an insufficient supply of inferior coke to burn in them.

Winston came over and had tea with me about 3 weeks ago. He was then attached to the H.Q. of our 2nd Battn. in order to study trench warfare. I believe he has left them now and gone elsewhere. His own regiment is doing nothing in particular somewhere near Boulogne. Apart from him I have seen no one outside the brigade. We are not allowed to go to Paris when we are in billets which we think rather hard, as the officers of the line all do. But I think we do better than they do in the way of leave to England and I am hoping to get my 10 days somewhere about the New Year.

This is a ghastly dull letter for you to plough through, my poor Con. But living in this muddy isolated rut one gets stupider and less inventive every day Write to me please when you have time and tell me the gossip of the town. I have a terrible nostalgia for the comfort and corruption of civilian life and even a paper contact with it has a wonderfully tonic effect on me . . .

To K. A.   12 December 1915

Absolutely no news today except that Winston rode over to see me. He is still with our 2nd Battn. and thoroughly enjoying himself and the war, very gloomy about Salonica, but at the same time very happy because he has always said that the troops we sent there ought to have gone to the Dardanelles instead.

I was asked to dine and play bridge with John Ponsonby and Cavan tonight but unluckily was entertaining my own C.O. here so could not go. I think it is a good thing to keep in with these nobs and get them used to one's face, and these two happen to be particularly nice . . .

To K. A.   13 December 1915

Last night we had the C.O. to dinner and gave him lots of champagne and let him win at bridge, so he went away quite pleased with us.

. . . The Salonica situation looks rather poor. Winston was very satirical about it and wondered why they didn't send an expedition to Barcelona instead as it has the same number of syllables. Is Ego at Salonica? or where? It looks any odds on their being, at best, interned. Personally I shouldn't much mind smoking my cigar in the Parthenon for the remainder of the war . . .

To K. A.   17 December 1915

. . . My last 2 days in the trenches have been perfectly bloody, wet and mud worse than ever and no decent place to rest in when off duty. I was alone too which I always dislike; and usually worse than alone because I had an officer of the Welsh Fusiliers and half a platoon of his men attached to me for purposes of instruction. He was a well-meaning little fellow, but a thorough-faced snitcher and I found his society irksome, as I daresay he did mine. His men were absurd and pathetic and made me more than ever glad that I chose a good regiment to fight with. They were little black spectacled dwarfs with no knowledge, no discipline, no experience, no digestion, and a surplus of nerves and vocabulary – the kind of men who I imagine give passionate little lectures on physic to junior classes in a minor Welsh University. They moaned and coughed and whined and vomited through the long night hours in a way that was truly distressing and paid so little attention to their duties that if they had been grenadiers I should have had to have had half of them shot. If they are a fair sample of K's army the repeated failures of our offensive are easily explained. The Queen's Westminsters were in a totally different class for efficiency. We came out last night for 48 hours in squalid farm-house billets not far from the line and go back again tomorrow to rather better trenches than before, then another 48 hours out and another 48 in, and then I believe 10 days rest in comparative comfort.

We had 4 or 5 casualties in our last spell and I had the nearest shave I have had so far. I was sitting in my dug-out having dinner when a machine gun was turned on and one bullet came through the wall (which consisted only of a sheet of corrugated iron) and entered a sand-bag on the far side of the room about 3 inches above my head covering my cap with dirt. They shelled us a little too with high explosives but did no damage.

Leave seems to be going on all right now and it looks as if I should get home about the 30th of this month. One arrives in London I believe about dinner time. I will try and let you know the exact day but one never has more than a few hours notice.

Where are you keeping my clothes? Berkeley, Bedford, Downing or Mells? I should like there to be some place in London where one could change and wash, as one usually arrives with nothing except what one carries on one's back. The post is going. Goodnight my sweet.

To K. A.   21 December 1915

. . . We had a better time in the trenches this last 2 days – nowhere much to sleep, but fine weather and a certain amount of liveliness. We had about a dozen casualties from rifle fire and at last the Boche succeeded in putting a shell right into the trench which damaged 3 men pretty badly. The company on my immediate right suffered much more and lost about 2 dozen men during the bombardment – largely their own fault as they went into dug-outs which are mere death-traps when high explosives are going over, instead of standing in the trench and taking their chance. But being only a line regiment I suppose they didn't know any better: one of the trenches held was called the Duck's Bill and ran straight out from our general line towards the Germans about 70 yards distant. The Germans have mines on both sides of it and we have counter-mines from which dirty looking engineers occasionally come blinking up into daylight plastered with bright blue clay. I spent a good deal of time trying to spot Germans working on the parapet opposite and then getting one of our portable machine guns moved along the trench and loosing off 50 rounds at them in about 5 seconds. We got two or three that way. It keeps the men happy and amused.

Then yesterday afternoon the Germans began firing rifle grenades into the Duck's Bill and wounded 2 of our men. A rifle grenade is a thing like one of those big blunt-nosed Italian fir cones on the end of a metal rod about 2 feet long. You put the rod into the barrel of a rifle and fire it with a blank cartridge. Ours will go about 300 yds. and the Germans' 500. It is a good form of sport because it is almost like shooting with a bow and arrow. You can see the missile all the time in the air. I fetched up 3 men who are experts in the game with a box of grenades and we gave them back volleys of these things – our plan now is always to give them back about 10 times as much of any particular form of beastliness which they begin to practise on us. We made very good shooting and kicked up great columns of black muck from their trench and parapet.

The grenade explodes like a bomb only much more violently when it touches the ground. The men get very excited when one of these duels is going on and swear and sweat horribly. It is almost the only fun they get in the trenches, poor dears.

One morning I was sent off at day break with 4 men to light some fires near a ruined building some hundred yards in rear of our lines with the object of making the enemy think that men were cooking their breakfast there and of diverting their shells from our real line. It was a warm misty morning and the ruin where we made our fires looked rather melancholy and impressive. It must once have been a very large and beautiful farm house and had a wide moat round 3 sides of it, a kind of Hobbema road with poplars behind it, and in front the wide level tussocky country in which we are fighting, a little like Romney marsh, but not so pretty. We call it the Moated Grange and in former days it was one of the German Head Quarters.

It took us about an hour to get our fires going as everything was very wet. I suppose you are thinking that there is going to be some point to this story, but I suddenly realise, that there is absolutely none and I have simply been writing like a Russian novelist. The Germans did drop a few languid shells into the building later in the day, but they had often done the same before and I don't suppose they even saw our wretched little fires. I suppose the moat and the mist and so on put me in a good temper at the time and my mind recurs to it.

The next 3 days from now will probably be about the most disagreeable I have ever had. Most of tonight (which is supposed to be one of my 2 nights' rest) I shall have to spend in taking 100 men to an engineers' store and superintending them carrying gas cylinders from there to the front lines in the rain. Then tomorrow we go into a filthy bit of trench with nowhere to eat or sleep and every prospect of being worried by the Huns if the Brigade next door to us use these bloody cylinders which I am carrying up to them this evening. Also we still have some of these wretched little Welsh Fusiliers attached to us, and in my company we have to stretch our limited resources in the way of beds and food to accommodate two of their harmless, rabbity little officers. They are terrified out of their lives by the discipline of the Brigade and a good deal startled at the gentlemanly way in which we contrive to live in trenches and billets. But the thing which has impressed them most so far has been my big candle. When it was lighted in the dug-out they fell down and worshipped it with strange Celtic cries.

I must stop this now and go out into the rain to look for these gas cylinders. It is really rather bloody to have the responsibility of a captain, the pay of a subaltern, and the work of a coolie – if not indeed of an elephant piling teak in a muddy slushy creek. Really they might find some more suitable work for the 1st regiment of Foot Guards than dunging. Au revoir, beloved.

To K. A.   22 December 1915

The chocolate cake arrived last night in excellent condition. Also the 2 presents from you and Helen which delighted me. The photograph is lovely and comes nearer to doing you justice than any you have had for a long time. Its little case is very business-like too. Helen's taste must be very similar to mine, if she really chose the handkerchief. I should have chosen just such another. Give her my love and gratitude. I will send her a line if I have time, but in a few hours we move into the trenches for our last 2 days.

I was amused to receive yesterday the small red diary which the aunts take it in turn to contribute to my Xmas fun, accompanied this time by a letter from Aunt Callie[1] stating that she is proceeding to Falmouth for the winter which I suppose is as big an adventure for her as the trenches for me.

Bluey tells me that Beb is producing a volume of poems shortly, and also that he was never really wounded but only ran his fork through his cheek in a frenzy of greed. I should think both rumours were untrue.

If all goes well we shall come out of the trenches on Christmas Eve and spend Christmas Day in these billets where we are already beginning to lay down a cellar and make every preparation for celebrating the birth of our Lord in a suitable manner. In the meantime we shall have an extremely wet and wearing 48 hours.

Nothing more to report at present so will stop and go and arrange about my packing.

To Lady Diana Manners   26 December 1915

. . . I cannot help talking a little trench shop to you now and then, just as you could not help talking hospital shop to all of us. Every now and then the purely scenic effects are so good, not really good, but operatic and sentimental, that I feel sure you would enjoy them if you were here. Shelling and counter-shelling – especially in the dark – quite comes up to Christmas number standards. The odd thing is that as a method of killing people, it somehow just fails to come off – aims at a million and misses a unit almost every time, but misses it, as far as one can judge, by inches only. Red and yellow flame and tall columns of dirt and smoke and sand-bags fly into the air all round you; clods of earth fall upon your neck, the nose-cap of the shell whizzes over your head with a noise of a thousand bad harmoniums played at once by a maniac, and the most respectable soldiers look too idiotically serious for words, while the most disreputable ones shout with laughter and pour out a stream of obscene jokes. You think at first that everybody in the trench must be dead except yourself and after the thing is over you find that 2 men are slightly wounded. Every now and then you pop your head above the parapet to see whether your shells are doing any damage to the Boches, and you see a line of terrific volcanoes bursting out at intervals of 5 yards all along the German line, but if you keep your head up for ½ a minute a 100 bullets whistle past it at once, showing that the Germans are suffering even less than you are.

Then the normal scene at night, when one patrols the trenches and there is nothing much doing, would make up amazingly well on the stage – the breast-work of sand-bags, so excellent in their drabness of colour, the rain coming down in torrents, the sentries singing, the Officer splashing round through 3

---

[1] Miss Caroline Horner, Katharine's aunt, who died in 1947 aged 99.

feet of water, and the men off duty plastered so thick with mud that you can hardly see their equipment, sleeping in attitudes of collapse and fatigue, which would penetrate the hardest heart, and defeat the cleverest pencil.

We had a Welsh regiment attached to us last time for instruction, tiny little tots, utterly unfit for anything more strenuous than a children's ball. They would pull a couple of sand-bags out of the parapet and nest in the crevice like swallows under the eaves. One asked oneself if Kitchener was serious.

Forgive me Dilly, for all this rigmarole, I have still big arrears of sleep to make up, and when one is tired the easiest thing seems to be to transfer vivid images from one's retina to the paper . . .

The things I want fly before me for ever down the paths of sleep.

To K. A. [after ten days' leave]   Hotel du Louvre,
                                                                                                        Boulogne.
                                                                                                        9 January 1916

You see I am, in spite of all difficulties, writing "every single". The channel was quite safe though rather rough and bumpy: wonderful storm clouds in the sky which never broke, and seagulls looking quite their best against sinister gleams of weak yellow sunlight. Quite according to the routine of idiocy which regulates military life, the trains are arranged to start from here half an hour before the boats arrive, so I had (not unwillingly) to spend the night here and am going up to Gagne by 12.30 train this morning. I hired quite a good bed in this rather smelly inn and dined at the Folkestone with Conrad and Gilbert. C. went off in a train at 2 a.m. and I have just breakfasted with G. who lives very comfortably in a house in the town. This place does not seem to me so dismal as it did to you.

Today is cold with a brilliant sun, and the river with its locks and bridges looked well enough in the morning mists. I'm afraid that I was rather testy yesterday morning; what with the short night and the late cabs I was not even civil to the servants, let alone as sweet to you as I should have been. You were a darling to me, Fawnia, all the time and even your too frequent fits of dewiness were more in the nature of a compliment than a reproach – or so I tried to construe them. From the first moment when you went out and brought me a handful of collar studs, you were sweeter than honey, and I suppose I was rather a brute to make you spend so much time in flashy company. But somehow a good glass of wine and the sight of Dottie's hard eye and dazzling skin, gives me the illusion of living fast and brilliantly which one rather needs under the circumstances . . .

To K. A.   3rd Grenadier Guards,
                                                          B.E.F.
                                                  10 January 1916

. . . I reported to Corry (my C.O.) and found him packing up. This morning he left for England and we see him no more. The 2nd in command is also away so Napoleon is commanding the battn. and I the Company, which now contains 2 ensigns, both called Parker – a joke which would have amused Shakespeare but leaves me cold.

This morning an odd thing happened, and this evening a distressing one – to me though I daresay not to you. First of all, while I was getting up about 9 a.m. which we regard as good going in billets, and was in fact washing in that rather naked style that you find so funny, I was conscious of that unintelligible but unmistakable brouhaha (as the French say) of John Ponsonby. Needham did his best, but the gallant fellow was not to be denied and burst into my room in a paroxysm of inarticulate enthusiasm. It appears that G.H.Q. has decided to Court Martial Iain Colquhoun[1] and another Captain in the 1st Scots Guards for allowing their men to fraternise with the Germans on Xmas Day. There is a great to-do about it all, both on personal and regimental grounds and they want me to act as "Prisoner's Friend" – i.e. counsel for the defence when the trial takes place. It seems a rottenish sort of case, but I said I would do my best – Colquhoun is on leave at present, I believe consoling or consolidating the shattered relics of poor Dinah. But the other officer is under arrest in a redoubt near here, where I went up to see him at luncheon and talk over the thing. He was pretty mopy, but I fancy they can be got off with a lightish punishment, if not absolutely. I don't know when the trial will be. On the way back from lunch I was nearly destroyed by a shell and when I got back to billets the Germans began shelling the town with heavy howitzers. This is a new move. There was an awful noise, but I don't think they did any serious harm.

Then I was rung up from Divisional H.Q. and our new Major General (Fielding, not Lambton) sent a motor for me, and I went to see him about the case. He was very nice and friendly, and ended the interview (this is the distressing thing) by producing a letter from G.H.Q. expressing the view of Haig that I could be "usefully employed on intelligence work either at G.H.Q. or on the Staff of an Army or Corps". He wanted me to go off tomorrow to G.H.Q. and I had to beg with tears in my eyes to be allowed my last 2 days in the dear old trenches, ostensibly on the ground that the battn. was short of officers, but really in order to think of some way out of this otherwise precipitate ending to a tolerably honourable career. The difficulty is that Fielding seemed disposed to regard the information as being in the nature of a command – like being asked to dinner by the King – terribly like. I must try and have a talk with Ponsonby about it. He is the only available man whose judgment I can trust out here, and see whether some compromise can be

[1] Sir Iain Colquhoun of Luss, married to Dinah Tannant.

arranged. I was afraid you were up to some devilry, Fawnia, when you exacted that "good promise" from me, but confess I was surprised that the damnable necessity for making a decision should come down on me so quickly as this. It is very difficult I can see, to refuse the bloody thing, and yet I shall be wretched and contemptible if I take it. Honestly, it is not very kind of you, Fawnia, to put me in such a position. And in 2 days I shall have to tell them something definite.

We go out for 6 weeks I believe when this time in the trenches is over, and after that we join the 14th Corps in the new 4th Army and go to perfectly delicious trenches in a rolling chalk country to the south of Amiens, a new experience which I should be loth to miss. I might arrange to give the staff a trial for those 6 weeks, and go on with it if I found I could be of any real use, if not returning to the regiment. But it is hard to make terms with a potentate. I don't know what will happen, but I do hate having to influence events in any way. In all probability I shall come down on the side of the poodles, that apparently being the line of least resistance, and like enough, die of a surfeit of lampreys instead of a high explosive. And then you and I and Helen and Perdita will all look silly together.

To K. A.   12 January 1916

. . . Corry's letter was about the Colquhoun case – owing to idleness at Downing St in not sending it round at once to L. B. Street it missed the motor at Boulogne, and came on by train next morning in the ordinary way. But it didn't matter in the least, as Colquhoun has not even yet returned from leave, and nothing serious can happen until he does, as they might have known. They took some more evidence yesterday, which turned out to be favourable to the other officer concerned, and I should not be surprised if they stop the Court Martial in his case, though I imagine they mean to proceed with it in the other. There is a good deal of excitement about it here, and I am regarded as such an important life now that yesterday morning the Brigadier issued a special order that I was not to accompany my battalion into the trenches for this last turn of 48 hours, but to remain here in billets. I am accordingly living in comfort (though not in gaiety) at the H.Q. of the 1st Scots Guards, who kindly offered me bed and board. I felt rather like a lost dog when the battalion marched off in the dark leaving me alone with an acetylene lamp in a large cold dreary house. Tomorrow I shall join them when they come out, and go for a night or two with them into proper billets before setting off to G.H.Q. to learn what they purpose to do with me. I had a few words with John Ponsonby about my future. He advised me to try the Staff job at any rate for a time, and seemed to think there would be no difficulty about my getting back to the battalion if I wanted to later on. I daresay that after a few weeks of the other life, my spirit will be so broken that I shall have no decent feelings left, but still suspect that when the fighting begins again I shall suffer from an uneasy nostalgia com-pounded of fascination and fear, which will involve me in another awkward decision.

How bloody everything is. However, I have got well into *Victory* now and agree that it is a remarkable book and moves faster than the ordinary Conrad. Perhaps it is as well to make up one's mind to spend the rest of the war reading moderate novels.

This is a boring letter, but I am suffering from terribly low spirits just now.

To K. A.   13 January 1916

. . . I need a prop just now for my tottering self-respect. It seemed to me that my only point (if any) was to be a potential corpse. And now I am merely a barrister without a fee, and about to become a poodle without a muffin. However, as you say, now's the time. I certainly should have been very much bored by 6 weeks of steady drill – a kind of rural and uncomfortable Chelsea. Specially as they say that tomorrow the redoubtable Jeffreys is coming to take temporary command of us. He has the reputation of being the strictest disciplinarian and most utter and undiluted soldier in the Brigade of Guards and *a fortiori* in the British or any other Army. Not the man for me at all.

The Court Martial is fixed for next Monday, the 17th. I don't yet know where. Ian Colquhoun came back yesterday – rather a sweet man of his type – arrogant, independent and brave. He is quite indifferent about his case and hardly interested enough to talk about it.

I got sadly bored during my 2 days with the Scots Guards – a dreary mess – Lord Esme Gordon Lennox commands them; he was kind and hospitable to me, but piano to a fault, quite without vitality or interest: the others were a very Scotch doctor, a very Scotch adjutant, and a still more Scotch minister. I am back again with Madame Brunel Gailly, who remains strangely faithful and enthusiastic. I don't know when they will pack me off to G.H.Q. I hope not till after the Court Martial . . .

To K. A.   15 January 1916

I am writing this because you say you like a letter however empty. I never felt more barren, jumpy and ill-conditioned than I am now. Our new commanding officer is a perfect soldier, and that always makes things very uncomfortable for a perfect civilian like myself. He is wonderfully efficient, and not in the least disagreeable, but patently limited. He is only here temporarily as he really commands another battn. and has been sent here on a special mission to repair the errors of the last reign. The result is that one doesn't get a moment to oneself. All subalterns parade at 8 a.m. and do the most elementary form of drill under a sergeant major. I cannot believe that this helps us to win the war, and I would far rather be shelled for an hour than drilled for an hour.

Tomorrow morning (Sunday) I have to rise at 6 to take the men to bathe, and on Monday there is this idiotic Court Martial, which has now begun to get rather on my nerves, because John Ponsonby is so excited about it and one of my 2 clients so terribly depressed. Ian Colquhoun, on the other hand, is perfectly haughty and indifferent, and impresses me more and more as being a man of great individuality and charm, so far as one can have those things without a brain.

The rigours of the new regime have at any rate mitigated the wrench of leaving the battalion – In fact I don't think I could bear this highly Prussianised life for many days more – I have come to the conclusion that I rather like war (though I prefer peace), but I utterly detest "soldiering". As soon as the Court Martial is over I am to be whisked off to G.H.Q. – i.e. probably on Tuesday next. It appears that after all we are not to be allowed to rest just yet. There has been a hitch about the division which was to take our place, and we are to do one more turn in the trenches at least. But I suppose we shall be doing nothing much after that for a bit.

Everything seems very black – I don't see daylight anywhere. I must go to bed now or I shall die of fatigue tomorrow. You can see from the limp letter how fatigued my mind and spirits are. I feel almost as if I were starting for a night at Derby.

To K. A.   18 January 1916

I got 3 of the sweetest letters from you yesterday all by one post. It is a comfort to find you sympathetic about my wretched predicament, but rather wish you had forbidden the P.M. to move in the matter without consulting me. However, things may turn out to be less black than they look at present, and I suppose I shall be able to get back here when I am sick of the other place; though my brothers in arms are frankly cynical on the subject, and refuse to believe in the possibility of my return.

Today we have yet another commanding officer, this time a permanent one, Brooke. I know him slightly, and should think he would be a great success.

Yesterday I had a pretty bloody and exhausting struggle with the Court Martial. I don't think I can blame myself in the matter, as the facts were sadly against us all the time. The sentence has not been announced yet, but I should think it would be a light one, something in the nature of a reprimand. I think there was no doubt that he committed a technical offence, but in reality he showed a good deal of decision and common sense, and his military character is so first rate that they ought to take a lenient view of the case. I became much attached to Colquhoun in the course of the case. His deportment was quite faultless, both before and during the proceedings. There is a finished arrogance and sullen grace about him which is very attractive, and there is no doubt that he is a man of exceptional dash and courage . . .

To K. A.   19 January 1916

. . . I like your idea of tracking the Severn to its source, but as you say, it is perhaps not the best possible moment for a walking tour. Why not try a day on the Wylye river instead?

. . . I saw a lot of John Ponsonby in connection with the Court Martial. He was a witness for the defence. A very jolly fellow, quite my favourite soldier among those in high places.

Well my sweet, I suppose it will be a long time before I am able to write a letter of any interest again, I am so thoroughly in the trough of the wave. Your injunction to take care of myself falls on my ears with an ironic cadence . . .

To Lady Diana Manners   19 January 1916

. . . I spent yesterday in legal work – 10.30 a.m. to 9 p.m. in a big dark stuffy room with 20 minutes interval for lunch defending 2 officers of the Scots Guards charged with breach of good order and military discipline in connection with the Christmas truce proceedings. One of them was acquitted, the other – Iain Colquhoun – practically your brother-in-law now – was convicted. I don't know that they will punish him much – probably only an official rebuke of some sort. I am sorry he did not get off, as I have seen a good deal of him this last week and am a trifle soppy about him – a perfect man of his type – insolent, languid, fearless and (in khaki at any rate) of a virile elegance which is most engaging. I give him absolutely top marks for deportment, especially in the dock where few look their best. Yet in peace and plain clothes I have often seen him, as I daresay you have too, without knowing he was there.

This is a pretty juiceless kind of letter you will say, but the fact is, Dilly, I am pretty wretched and have been for some days, having been summoned to G.H.Q. whither I may proceed at any moment to do a little something – God knows what – among the bottle-washers and boot-boys of the staff. The P.M., in disregard of a perfectly explicit order from me to take no steps in that direction without my express permission, has tipped the wink to Haig, and here I am in the scrip. However, I fully intend to get out of it again when a suitable occasion offers, unless a month at St Omer leaves me too degenerate and flabby to take the necessary trouble, but I hope things won't be as bad as that. I always dislike leaving people I have got used to, and putting out fresh roots in a different and (I should guess) a poorer soil. Naturally no one will ever believe that the job has been arranged without my knowledge and against my will, and everyone will think that I spent my 10 days' leave in making a plot to avoid the

Spring offensive. So in self-defence I shall have to try and get back to the regiment when the fighting season sets in. After all, death is the only solution of the problem of life which has not so far been definitely proved to be the wrong one, and to be killed in action would gracefully set at rest many urgent and recurring anxieties. It has seemed to me of late that my only point was being a potential corpse. Without the glamour of the winding sheet I have no *locus standi* in the world, and should become a menace and a burden to you certainly, and I daresay to many others – King Albatross, in fact, instead of a boy to be borne with and even a little petted before going back to school.

Don't think I am becoming heavy or heroic, Dilly. Nothing of the sort – I am as flippant and as dastardly as ever. But I am simply balancing my accounts in a purely commercial spirit . . .

To K. A.   20 January 1916

No letter from you today, and I, as usual now, have less than no news. I am very tired, having been on parade from 8-11 a.m., 2-3 p.m. and out from 6-7.30 p.m. training 10 men for patrol work, i.e. walking about ploughed fields in the dark and trying to remember how many willow trees you see. It always makes me very shy owing to the lack of true semblance to anything in real warfare – like pretending to be a polar bear at a children's party. But the men are very sweet about it, and cheerfully tolerate the absurdities. Still I call it a stiffish day for a battalion which is supposed to be resting from its toils in the trenches.

I had an excellent letter from Dottie today giving a brilliant and tawdry account of her visit to Hickling. It sounds a very romantic spot I must say – more suitable to Fawnia than Dilly – with mists and mallards and sucking and jingling noises like those described by Conrad in that boring story we used to hear read aloud so often at one time . . .

To K. A.   3rd. Grenadier Guards,
                                                                                   B.E.F.
                                                                       21 January 1916

Your letters put me to shame, mine are more barren and juiceless than sea thistles, and much less pointed. But I had 2 beauties from you this evening full of sweetness and news. I'm sorry that our financial situation is not very rosy, but apart from old debts I should have thought that our obligations were not very heavy for the moment, though what with your 7/6 cook and one thing and another, I suppose you do get through a good deal. Let me know at once when your funds run low and I will replenish them, because I can always borrow money from the bank much more easily than you, and I don't want you to begin selling and pawning things one minute before it is necessary, and if we have any luck with Aunt Lily, as you rather lead me to hope, it may never be necessary . . .

To K. A.   3rd. Grenadier Guards,
B.E.F.
23 January 1916

I've just got your letter written in the train. I'm sorry you had that horrible dream about the last supper. I'm afraid you must have got into the habit of regarding yourself as Cinderella. This must be discontinued, as the official orders always say in the Army.

I have just got back from a visit to G.H.Q. They sent a motor for me this morning, and I had quite a pretty drive in frosty sunlight over very skiddy cobbles, and was more frightened than I have been so far in France. I lunched with the head of the intelligence department, General Charteris, who was extremely civil and friendly about the whole thing. I suggested two months as a time limit, but he said it would take me a little time to get into it and he thought 3 months the shortest period that would be useful, so I eventually signed the contract on that basis, and they will take me back here when I have served my time. He called it "Secret Service" to make it sound attractive, but the work seems to consist mainly in collecting and editing the reports of our spies in various parts of France and Belgium. The most pleasing feature of the scheme is that the Department has an office at Folkestone and I shall be sent there for 2 or 3 weeks at the beginning to see how it works on that side. I am to go over again to G.H.Q. on Tuesday and I suppose soon after that to England. I will let you know when they tell me more definitely, and you might come down and live at Folkestone for a bit. It will brace you after a long course of Mells . . .

Again I am nipped by the Post Corporal. So goodnight my sweet, I feel that I ought to be more enthusiastic about all this than I am.

To Lady Diana Manners   24 January 1916

. . . As to the Haig affair, I think I told you some of my difficulties when last I wrote. Today, as a matter of fact, I motored over to G.H.Q. and interviewed the head of the Intelligence Department, a very civil Brigadier, who is going to employ me in what he alluringly calls the "Secret Service". I'm afraid it doesn't mean a sham beard and blue goggles as I hoped at first but a pleasing feature is that it appears to involve a residence of some weeks in Folkestone – when, I don't exactly know, but probably quite soon. I told the General that I wanted to return to my regiment and haggled with him a bit over the time limit. I tried for 2 months and in the end he agreed to three. He was very pleasant and elastic about it, as his original idea had apparently been to keep me in America for the rest of the War. I thought that would be going just too far. Don't you? . . .

To K. A.

Intelligence,
General Headquarters,
B.E.F.
25 January 1916

I motored over here this morning to take up my new duties, but no one seems to be very clear what they are. I sit in a large cold room with 3 or 4 other men smoking, gossiping and occasionally reading a book about the German army, or looking at a map of the Belgian railways. At irregular intervals I go out to meals with Lord Onslow, a pleasant friendly fellow whom I remember dimly at Oxford just before my time.

I have got quite a comfortable looking billet where Needham has laid out my things. It seems very queer to be living in this twilight world, half soldier half civilian, after the tropical glare of militarism to which I have become inured in my own regiment. At present I feel very like a new boy at school, unfamiliar with the etiquette, unwanted by either masters or pupils, and utterly supernumerary to the whole scheme of things. However, I daresay I shall get acclimatised by degrees. I have certainly learned during the last year or so to fit into queerer crannies than this.

My prospects of going to Folkestone are, I fear, less bright than they were and if I do go, it will probably be only for a short time . . . I have a terrible sinking feeling just at present, and don't know how I shall ever get through my 3 months of office work. But, as you know, I should be grousing wherever I was . . .

To K. A.

Intelligence,
General Headquarters,
B.E.F.
26 January 1916

I don't know whether the letter I wrote you last night was posted in time so you may get it together with this. Life seems very queer here still in comparison with what I am accustomed to. Needham finds it perfect, and says that you have only to ask for anything you want and you get it: which is far from being the custom of the country as we have known it hitherto. The only military feature about the life is the enormous amount of waiting about which it seems to involve – very long hours but nothing to do in them. We are supposed to be on duty at 9.30 a.m. and remain so in theory till 2 a.m. the following morning, most of the time there is literally nothing to do, but one can't write letters or read a book because someone is making a noise on a typewriter, or an orderly is knocking at the door, or you are signing a receipt for a cipher message which someone else deciphers, or a friend comes in for a cigarette and 10 minutes gossip. Presently you go out for a walk – never more than half an hour and usually in the rain – you buy a book or cash a cheque or get your hair cut. Every now and then telegrams arrive, usually at inconvenient moments as e.g. dinner time or bed-time. These contain reports from our spies as to the movements of German troops on the railways and a report has to be prepared at night, showing the effect of the day's news and the movements and marked with arrows of various colours on a railway map. A good deal of care and labour is needed to get the details right, and every now and then I imagine some ingenuity may be required in drawing inferences as to what these movements mean. Onslow is very friendly and helpful and shows me the ropes. There is a mess for the junior members of the department where he and I lunched yesterday – rather a dim affair – and you can get a moderate rubber of bridge afterwards if you fancy it. Then there is a much smarter mess where the King's Messengers and a few others have their meals, to which he introduced me last night. About 10 o'clock I came back and hung about the office again till after midnight, bedding down in my excellent billet about 1 a.m.

Maurice [Baring] came in to see me this morning. He is still at the H.Q. of the Flying Corps where I am going to dine with him the night after tomorrow. Tomorrow I dine with Gilbert [Russell] at the Railway mess, and tonight with an excellent fellow called Guy Rasch, a Grenadier who was Brigade Major to John Ponsonby, and is on a Staff College course here. So one has plenty of society. It is all very queer – quite the oddest part of the war to my mind. It is rather pathetic how some of the people here nourish the illusion that they are in danger, and will tell you that the life is pleasant enough except when the bombs begin to fall – a thing that has only happened once I believe during the whole 18 months, and that was a picnic compared to the ordinary Zeppelin raid on London. I hear that Philip [Sassoon] writes to his friends offering them battalions and brigades with the most Oriental profusion . . .

The hamper you spoke of arrived safely before I left La Gagne – the curried chicken and guava jelly excellent, tinned partridge not so good – I have had it before and it is always a failure. But as long as I am here it is quite unnecessary to send anything, except every now and then a pot of honey for breakfast, which I have in my room. At all other meals one lives on the fat of the land. You might order *The Times* to be sent here instead of to the old address, will you? I've heard nothing more yet about the Folkestone project, and begin to think it was only a carrot dangled in front of my nose for encouragement. I can't honestly say I'm very happy, my sweet Fawn, but as you are, that is some consolation.

To K. A.

Intelligence,
General Headquarters,
B.E.F.
27 January 1916

. . . The people here have done their best for me, but it is obviously impossible to provide occupation either mental or physical for a man as ignorant as I am of modern languages, and all technical matters. I don't even know how to feed a carrier pigeon. However, I remember finding even the dear old trenches rather trying for the first 2 days, and I daresay I shall shake down later on with the kind of sulky stupor which so often cushions one from the pricks of an unpropitious universe. For the moment I haven't a kick left, either in body or mind.

To K. A.

Intelligence,
G.H.Q.
B.E.F.
28 January 1916

. . . I as usual have nothing to report; except by the way, this, that I am to go to Folkestone next Wednesday 2nd Feb. and remain there till 6th then to London 6th till 12th. I don't know how much or in what way I shall be employed during the visit but I suppose I shall have a certain amount of leisure, and when in London shall be allowed to live at home – if I can find a home. This may all be changed of course, as things are apt to be which contain any element of pleasure. But these were the instructions I got this morning. It will make me happy to see my angel Fawn again.

To K. A.

Intelligence,
G.H.Q.
B.E.F.
31 January 1916

. . . I have been so bleached and blighted by the vacuum of official routine, that I have not had the spirit to write of late. It is settled that I am to go to Folkestone on Wednesday, and the present idea is that I shall stay there till Sunday and then go to London till the 12th when I return here. They tell me that the Metropole is the best place to stay in Folkestone, so I have ordered a couple of bedrooms there and hope to find you awaiting me on Wednesday – if indeed I arrive then. The channel crossing is very chancy just now owing to mines and the boats are constantly held up.

It will be a good change for you and also for me, and may help to make both of us less mopy. The enclosed slip was handed to me as I was lunching with Summy and Onslow today and on returning here I found Lloyd George and Bonar Law being initiated into all our mysteries. Both looked a little worn and moth-eaten, but were agreeable according to their respective lights. They will stand a good chance of being blotted out, either in this country or their own by Zeps, of which 7 are reported to be on the wing at Dunkerque. F. E.[1] is reported to be somewhere in the neighbourhood under close arrest for travelling without the necessary passes . . .

To K. A.

Intelligence,
G.H.Q.
B.E.F.
14 February 1916

. . . The moss is already beginning to grow on my mind and body and soon the barnacles will encrust me. My pulse barely beats and my pencil moves over the paper like a cab horse mounting a steep hill. I have not even the energy to go for a walk. I sit and smoke and stare in front of me. Whereas you I suppose are enjoying the most voluptuous and vivacious intercourse with your little Dilly, to say nothing of the "interesting people" you will meet in such numbers at the tables of Peggy [Lady Crewe] and Frances. However, no doubt you have your troubles too . . .

To K. A.

Intelligence,
G.H.Q.
B.E.F.
16 February 1916

. . . I was glad not to be in the trenches last night as it rained in torrents, or on the sea today as it blew like hell. But that is about all I have to be thankful for. We have had a rush of work lately – big German movements, both to the East and to the West: and on the 14th we lost 600 yds of trench south of Ypres. But I spend a great deal of my time fumbling with masses of stationery, punching holes in tissue paper, indexing obsolete documents, and misunderstanding the vast apparatus of Heygate machinery with which all offices appear to be congested. Yesterday, I suppose to bring home to us how thoroughly in the thick of things we really are – every one was served out with a gas helmet, which made me smile for a moment. Today they were all withdrawn again, which reminded me much more vividly of real war. I rather like the *Cadet de Contras*, though the English part of it is not *vraisemblable* – "*Une certaine pudeur empêche M. le duc de penser devant le monde, comme les elephants de faire*

---

[1] F. E. Smith was at this time Attorney-General.

l'amour" is witty and might apply to, say, His Grace of Portland. Personally, however, I am getting less and less able or inclined to think whether in public or in private.

It is a lonely life this, much lonelier than the regimental – or even the maternal . . .

To Lady Diana Manners   22 February 1916

Fond of old E. as I am, gaga with geniality as I am, I can't help feeling that all this valedictory ritual has been the least thing overdone. Where is he going, after all? Egypt – a country where the climate is notoriously favourable to invalids – and has he any lung trouble? No. A country moreover where there is about as much chance of bloodshed as there is at St Omer. True, he may be shot at with a bow and arrow by a seditious Copt on the horizon, or pelted with camel's dung by a drunken donkey boy, or teased by the unnatural but not unwelcome importunities of a camarilla of coffee-coloured connoisseurs. But nothing is here for tears. And how is he going? . . . in the best cabin of the biggest liner afloat, with a not unreasonable expectation on arrival at Port Said of "luring to his bed some ivory-horned tragelaphus". Beagling without tears, I call it – Then why all this dew on the hearth-rug, Dilly? and bouquets at Waterloo? . . .

To K. A.   Intelligence,
                                                                        G.H.Q.
                                                                        B.E.F.
                                                              23 February 1916

. . . It has been snowing here the last 2 days with fine frosty nights. It must be ghastly in the trenches, and an officer in the Welsh Guards who has tried life *in tents*, if you please, at Calais, tells me that that is infinitely worse than the trenches, and from what one knows of the seaside, I can well believe it. In spite of the dullness of things here I am driven to congratulate myself on missing this bit of the war. The snow is rather beautiful in the streets and squares when the stars come out and reminds one of one's sweet innocent childhood, Santa Claus, St Agnes' Eve, Virgil's description of life in Lapland (see the pocket book – one of the Georgics), and what not – not, mercifully of Switzerland, which though *in* snow, is never to my mind *of* it. It must be a very long time since we had snow in England: almost the last I can remember was that Xmas we spent at Hartham – tobogganing and so on – nearly 10 years ago I suppose.

The bombs I told you of the other night seem to have killed 2 civilians in the town and wounded 3. Yesterday morning our guns shot down an aeroplane over the station here. Unluckily it was one of our own – naval. The pilot was not hurt – so they put him under arrest . . .

To K. A.

Intelligence,
G.H.Q.
B.E.F.
24 February 1916

. . . What are the sensational newspapers which frighten you, and what are the corrections which reassure you? I see lots of things in the press which fill me with anger and contempt because of their perverse vulgar and malicious stupidity and ignorance, but nothing which alarms me.

The French have lost some more ground today near Verdun and are in rather a stew about it all and constantly egging us on to make a counter-demonstration somewhere. I rather hope that we shan't, as I don't think there is really much wrong . . .

I'm glad Helen and Per are looking "well and lovely" (clever no doubt, too). Give them my love and tell them to keep it up at all costs. I hope you also are looking as well and lovely as when I saw you last. Clever you certainly are to send me such excellent letters made out of the slender materials of Mells life . . .

To K. A.

Intelligence,
G.H.Q.
B.E.F.
28 February 1916

I am having a very idle day here – no messages coming in – I have read through 2 numbers of the *Spectator* this afternoon and 2 of the *Vie Parisienne* and am no nearer the secret of happiness than before. The last *Spectator* by the way, contained a poem about a Flemish Church which I take to be by Beb. He must be coining money during his rest cure. I saw in *The Times* the other day 2 judgments in important Privy Council cases in which I took part by deputy – Some day I suppose I shall receive half the fees – perhaps £100 or so, which will be welcome enough.

I've got through the cold snap without taking to bottles, though I confess I was reduced to sleeping in the woolley waistcoat you gave me. It is wet and horrible now but with a certain promise of spring.

They seem to have blown up one of our biggest P & O's on Sunday within a few miles of Dover – whether by mine or torpedo is uncertain. But the French were happier last night about Verdun. Troops are coming back from Egypt in great numbers – six divisions I believe, including (they say) some Australians. But I hope that Edward will not be forced to exchange the Nile for the Aisne.

Fancy your having daffodils at Mells and dancing classes – a perfect Prima Vera life it sounds . . .

Oh dear, the days here seem as long as the nights used to seem in the trenches – more comfortable but if possible more dull. How I loathe the war. I can't think of anything to do now except write an epic poem bringing in the names of all the railway stations in Belgium . . .

To K. A.
Intelligence,
G.H.Q.
B.E.F.
4 March 1916

. . . Here it continues to be wet and continuously and progressively tedious. The sameness and emptiness of the routine almost makes one scream. This afternoon I tried to vary the monotony by going to a place where there are hot baths to be had in the town, but they looked so unappetising and there were so many candidates that after waiting half an hour I went away in disgust. This morning my landlady sent me a note (on paper heavily decorated with coronets) bidding me to luncheon tomorrow at *noon* to meet her husband whose regiment is resting somewhere in the neighbourhood. She is a woman of plain but refined appearance, about 30 I should think, with nice manners, her name is De Guillebon. I fear that it means 3 hours at least of atrocious boredom, and probably some sweet champagne as well . . .

God forgive me for sending such a ghastly letter. I feel that the post box will vomit it up again in disgust. But my head feels like a 2nd body. My poor Fawn. I adore and commiserate you.

To K. A.
Intelligence,
G.H.Q.
B.E.F.
5 March 1916

How briskly we maintain our antiphony of ululation! our moans go to and fro across the channel like shuttlecocks across a net, each applauding the other's master strokes of woe.

Gilbert's office is in a nunnery. All the cells have mottoes inscribed on the wall, and I found when I visited him the other day that his cell bore the words LE PLAISIR DE MOURIR SANS PEINE VAUT BIEN LA PEINE DE VIVRE SANS PLAISIR. But I'm not sure that even this consolation is open to soldiers.

The one bright spot in my present situation is that I have got through my luncheon with my landlady. It lasted over 2 hours and there were masses of cousins and aunts and several children . . . ·

To **K. A.**   Intelligence,
                                                                    G.H.Q.
                                                                    B.E.F.
                                                              7 March 1916

. . . The snow has begun again here and came down pretty hard with clear intervals during the last 2 days – yesterday young [Humphrey] De Trafford got me a motor and we went off to a hill called Scherpenberg near Ypres, where I had been told that one got quite close to the trenches and could see the British and German lines stretching for miles across the plains and the air full of bursting shells. As a matter of fact it was most disappointing, and though the day was clear I could hardly make out a sign of a trench and the shelling (such as there was) was of the most moderate description. Certainly one got a very good view over the Flemish plain with Ypres showing up well about 5 miles away on the left. I suspect that the Boches have improved it and that it looks better as a ruin than ever it did in its prime. We got very cold on the hill and had a bad lunch at Bailleul . . .

Did you read Northcliffe's article on Verdun? The first part of it giving names of the Corps and regiments engaged was very accurate and must have been taken from official sources, but the latter part made one smile a bit – e.g. "the nearer you get to a battle the louder is the noise" – "in this part of France there is more bird life than in some others" – "here we saw vast quantities of shells for every type of gun from the heavy howitzer to the graceful *mitrailleuse*" – (the latter, as no doubt you know, fires the same bullet as a rifle) . . .

To **K. A.**   Intelligence,
                                                                    G.H.Q.
                                                                    B.E.F.
                                                              8 March 1916

. . . I was delighted to get your more serene letter. I'm glad you are so well and I would rather the child were strong and beautiful than clever. It will be pleasant enough to have a semi-opaque background for the forked lightnings of Perdita's wit and someone one can meet on terms of intellectual equality after the strain of puffing in Helen's wake.

Tell me about your Mother's "cracking row" with Anne. I always like to hear about rows. Also more about the amateur theatricals, I hear that Dottie was 'natural' but inaudible – a queer reversal of her normal form. Also that a parody of her at the Empire under the name of "Lady Di Customs" has been taken off owing to the Duke's protests . . .

To K. A.

Intelligence,
G.H.Q.
B.E.F
10 March 1916

. . . If the war goes on much longer everyone will be petrified into a permanent lethargy and we shall all have to pinch ourselves once a week to be sure that we are still alive. The dismal oppression of being cut off from everything worth doing or having works with cumulative effect from day to day. I wish there were some attic in St Omer where I could go out shooting like the old man in *The Wild Duck*. The need for illusion or even distraction becomes hourly more pressing. This infinite desert of tedium and idleness has no horizon.

You were asking the other day for books: someone told me that an American writer Leacock was very funny – *Half Hours with the Idle Rich* – I think one of his books was called. And someone else recommended Anatole France's *Barbe Blue*: but I daresay you have read that.

I wrote to Perdita this morning recommending her to pursue literature and follow up her successful effort about the widow and the snow man . . .

To Perdita Asquith [aged 5]   G.H.Q. 10 March 1916

My pretty Per,

Your mother sent me the other day a very nice little story about a widow in the snow which you had written. I thought it most interesting. If you ever feel inclined to write another you might send it to me, as I don't get many good stories to read out here. There are plenty of widows here but it is the rarest possible thing to see any of them making a snow man: not for want of snow either, because we have plenty of that. I went on to the top of a hill the other day to see a battle but it was a very poor sort of battle and I came away much disappointed. I hear that you have lost some of your front teeth. Please grow some new ones as quickly as possible, because I want you to be exquisitely beautiful again – as lovely as the best kind of fairy – when I next come home to see you. But I'm afraid that won't be for some time yet. Give my love to Helen.

Your loving Father.

To K. A.

Intelligence,
G.H.Q.
B.E.F.
13 March 1916

Our old friend Spring at last: really balmy weather here the last 2 days. I got letters from my daughters the other day about birds and flowers – very sweet both of them – also one from you saying that some of "them" were coming to Mells for Sat.-Mon. Tell me how it all went off and how Dilly and Patsy [Patrick Shaw-Stewart] comported themselves among the crocuses . . .

There was another bombing accident last week at Calais – in my battalion this time: an officer slightly wounded, 3 or 4 men killed, and 20 others injured according to the vague accounts which have reached me. It is very puzzling: I suppose they must be trying a new kind of bomb: otherwise I can't understand it. Haig reviewed the Brigade the other day and seems to have told them that owing to the Verdun affair, our offensive would be postponed to a later date than had been contemplated.

Apart from this I have no news either of business or pleasure. My life goes drivelling on in the same dreary round, with even less prospect than usual of variety or relief since all leave has been stopped indefinitely – some say till the end of the war, others the end of the summer, which is little better . . .

To K. A.

Intelligence,
G.H.Q.
B.E.F.
14 March 1916

. . . It is ½ past 6 now but still quite light, and warm enough to sit at the open window. This weather makes one yearn a good deal for one thing and another: specially perhaps for pleasant lawns and shade and lovely women in muslin dresses. But it will be some time before I dip my oar in that stream I fear . . . If I ever take part in another war, I hope that it will be in my own country instead of in someone else's. In spite of what people say, I believe it would be much more agreeable than this – beastly as the East Coast undoubtedly is . . .

To K. A.

Intelligence,
G.H.Q.
B.E.F.
15 March 1916

. . . I have been reading some letters from Indian troops this afternoon: one man says: "I never think about the chance of being killed, nor do I feel any particular satisfaction at the idea of going on living." This is a mood one recognises. Today has been again vernal and balmy and again wasted. The best I could do with it was to go for 2 walks in the public garden – one with Richard Hart-Davis whose battn. is billeted near here, and is in process of being broken up and sent home to leaven the newer formations; and the other with Philip Sassoon, who was very civil and talkative. He and Haig were down at Chantilly holding Joffre's hand most of last week. The French seem to have been in a pitiful state of nerves when the offensive began, and thought that it was all up with them whether Verdun fell or not, owing to the losses in men which they would suffer either way. They are certainly getting pretty short of men, but the Huns are shorter, and have now got the whole of their 1916 class (i.e. boys of 20) at the front, whereas the French have not yet brought theirs from the depots. The most reasonable estimates of losses at Verdun up to date give the French at 50,000 and the Germans at 100,000. Probably this is somewhere near the mark . . .

To K. A.   Officers Club,
                                                                   Boulogne-sur-Mer.
                                                                   18 March 1916

Thank you for a good long letter last night – neither ill-written nor "ill-composed". I send you this while waiting a few minutes to catch a train to Lyons whither I am proceeding on a confidential mission. It will take me a couple of days and is rather a windfall. Anything to get away from St Omer and introduce a little variety into one's life: though the 'mission' itself is not intrinsically very sensational . . .

To K. A.   Le Grand Hotel,
                                                                   Lyon.
                                                                   20 March 1916

This visit to Lyons is really the most agreeable thing I have done since the war began. I got here at 4 yesterday morning after rather a stuffy night journey, with just time for a small dinner at the station buffet at Paris. The place is very full owing to a fair which is going on, and I had to drive round the town sometime before finding a bed, but in the end got a very good room at this Hotel, with a bath which I have made the most of. It is one of the most charming towns that I have ever been in, a great manufacturing place of ½ million inhabitants – silk-making, shell-making, dyeing – every kind of industry – but not a whiff of smoke or a sign of a slum; broad streets, wide squares, handsome houses, excellent food and quite admirable wine. The town is built rather like Bath round an amphitheatre with one open side looking out towards the Alps, the rest steeply banked up towards the Cevennes, with slanting streets and steps almost like a magnified Clovelly laid out by a succession of civic archangels instead of by a tyrannical old woman.

I had tea yesterday in the highest part of the town, from which you see a fine panorama of orderly streets and the two great rivers the Rhone and Saone with their quays and bridges flowing together at the southern end of the town and beyond the town a wide green plain stretching away to Mont Blanc, which shows very plainly perhaps a 100 miles off, its precipices glistening with snow. But the atmosphere of the place is so wonderful, full of life and colour and effervescence under a hot and brilliant sun – A more utter change from the north of France it is impossible to conceive, or from England either for that matter. It is the gayest town I have been in since Venice. There are a lot of French Colonial troops about – in appearance at any rate, much superior to ours – Senegalese with Beardsley faces, Zouaves with baggy braided trousers and moors with turbans of spotless linen, far handsomer than Othello. Best of all, no khaki, so that I am quite an excitement to the populace and the most charming looking women – the only ones in France – throw me every now and then a voluptuous leer.

This change of paper is because the vice-consul (British) came in to my hotel and made me walk up the hill to lunch with his chief at a pleasant villa on the top, and then I walked back and am finishing my letters in the consulate. The consul and his wife are both very pleasant friendly people and the vice-consul is a most agreeable youth who was at Winchester and Oxford – long after my time. He showed me the sights yesterday, and in the evening took me to a play called *Je ne trompe pas mon mari* – quite well acted but not less boring than plays usually are in spite of the curtain rising upon a man and woman (illicitly) in bed together. The vice-consul took a fancy to the woman and wanted to go round with me afterwards and talk with her: but I very nobly refused: (a) I am very chaste (b) because the woman was very fat (c) because I hate talking to a woman in a language which they know better than I do. No. *Je ne trompe pas ma femme*.

I start back again after dinner tonight, and shall breakfast with my chief in Paris, report the results of my mission and then I fear, back to St Omer. A very pleasant little holiday. I hope I shall find lots of letters from you when I get back.

To K. A.

Intelligence,
G.H.Q.
B.E.F.
23 March 1916

I had a rather wearisome return journey from Lyons, pausing in Paris just long enough for bath and breakfast, and getting to Boulogne (in a train which took 8 hours from Paris!) for a bad dinner in rain and fog, and so here by motor, where I was comforted to find several letters from you awaiting me. A few bills too, of which I will make what I can. The £168 acknowledged by the Bank is apparently some Inland Revenue fees and not so good as it looks, as I have to give half of it to the man who does the work for me. However, every little helps.

What a strange child Helen must be to versify the siege of Londonderry. I don't think I had ever heard of it till the last Home Rule Bill came along, though I knew all about the siege of Troy at her age.

I am sending this to London, where I gather you must be by now. I wonder if you are still "like someone under spells"? if not too spell-bound you might send me 2 more tins of honey and 2 blue silk vests which you will find among my things at Berkeley St (if indeed that *is* where they are). The two which I have carried so far through the campaign are beginning to look like the flags of the Peninsular War which you see hung up in Cathedrals.

If you see Dottie, beg her to write to me, I have not had a letter from her for a month and fear that she must be engrossed in Patsy to the exclusion of all else. This will never do. You tell me not to take my leave until the baby is born. But when will that be? As a matter of fact I may not get leave at all and in any case should have to take it when the authorities see fit. I thought of making an application towards the middle of April and trying to put it in between my departure from here and my reunion with Napoleon. Is that too early?

Let me know when you go to Newmarket. I'm glad your poor papa is better. Mine seems to be still laid aside.

To K. A.

Intelligence,
G.H.Q.
B.E.F.
24 March 1916

. . . I'm sorry that the Government is thought to be rocky,[1] but it has happened so often that one can't attach much importance to it. If the only criticisms to be made of them are those one reads in the papers, I can't see that they have to fear. All this stuff about broken pledges, and the married men, is the worst bosh we have had during the War. And who the devil is going to take their place if they do go?

Even the spring has not been able to endure St Omer for more than a day or two, and now it is snowing again, so that life is deprived of the last shred of interest or amenity. It is settled now that we all move on 30th March to Montreuil – It is said to be more picturesque and salubrious than this place, but it is much smaller and less comfortable, and my mess will probably be broken up and we shall all be more bored and miserable even than we are here.

I am sorry that Libby is bursting out in literary recollections – and still worse – drama. Will it be called *The Way of the Worm* after Congreve, or *Colon and Semi-colon* after Shaw? Lord what a world we live in! My poor Fawnia.

---

[1] Heavy criticism of the government led to the resignation of his father as Prime Minister, soon after Raymond's death.

To K. A.   Intelligence,
                                                                   G.H.Q.
                                                                    B.E.F.
                                                           25 March 1916

. . . Nothing of any kind happens here except in the sky, where heavy snow and
bright sun alternate rapidly and disagreeably. I go for a little turn after
luncheon every day of about 45 minutes and usually with Gilbert. Otherwise
sit in an office moaning and writing out unimportant things with a bad nib. If
you see any nibs which will write you might send me a box. I can get none here
with which it is possible to make shapely or even legible characters. And few
things so much destroy one's self-respect as writing badly.

. . . The extent to which reason takes a back seat during war is truly amazing. Nothing seems to be of any account except shouting and shoving anything
and anywhither. The trouble is that however and whenever the War ends,
there can never be a great assize in which all these rampant fools can receive
appropriate sentences for their follies. When I think of the silly people who are
going about thinking and saying that they were right all the time after all, it
fills me with nausea. If they were, then the Huns were much worse right . . .

To K. A.   Intelligence,
                                                                   G.H.Q.
                                                                    B.E.F.
                                                           28 March 1916

. . . Here we are in the throes of moving. The luggage goes tomorrow and
ourselves on Thursday morning to Montreuil (or as the servants insist on calling it Montreal). I had a talk with my chief today about future plans. He was
most civil and accommodating and ready to oblige in every way, either by keeping me here or sending me to another staff or to my regiment or anywhere else
I wanted to go. I don't think I can put off my return to the Grenadiers beyond
the beginning of May as that was my understanding with my C.O. But I think
I could arrange to leave here about 25th or 26th April for 10 days in England
and then rejoin my battalion on returning to this country. So do your best to
get Hyacinth and Honeysuckle[1] on to the register by the 24th at latest.

I haven't seen anything of the P.M. or Bongie and as Haig is away, I don't
suppose they will come here at all, unless on the way back from Rome . . .

I see Margot got £1000 out of the *Globe* [in a libel action]. I had hoped it
would be more, but no doubt she won't make the mistake of squandering it on
charities . . .

---

[1] Joke names for the child she was expecting in April.

To K. A.

Intelligence,
G.H.Q.
B.E.F.
30 March 1916

Writing has been impossible in the nightmare of confusion which has reigned during the last 2 days – no ink, no paper, no light, no chairs and tables, no post – Probably it is not much use writing now. I don't know when the letter will go or how – One might as well put it into a bottle and throw it into the sea. They began dismantling St Omer yesterday morning, but are still far from having made Montreuil habitable. We drove here this morning in a motor – about 40 miles through rather pretty hilly country, followed by a vast stream of lorries and motor buses with servants, baggage and furniture. Montreuil is what is called a beauty spot, much visited I believe by tourists and artists – In fact there is, I am told, a Montreuil school. It is certainly a picturesque old town cocked up at the top of a hill and guarded by ramparts 30 or 40 feet high of Elizabethan brick-work, with yellow wall-flowers in the cracks. Neat clean white houses with irregular roofs of battered tiles and dormer-windows: and below it the valley of a pretty stream (rather spoilt by a railway) osier beds in the foreground, low rolling hills further back, and the sea within 7 or 8 miles.

I had quite a good lunch with my friend Trotter and a stray general who seemed rather lost and grateful to find someone to order his wine for him, in the principal inn: cooking and wine very fair, and a pretty forecourt with vines trellised across it, which will be pleasant enough in summer. The inhabitants are very hostile to us, partly because they hate all the English, and partly because they think we shall attract Zepps – as to which they are probably right. The place is made by nature for a target, conspicuous for miles round and easily accessible – whether by land or by sea. So you see I shall really be safer in the trenches.

As to the leave question, I expect I should be able to put it off till perhaps the 1st May, when I suppose people will be coming back from their holidays, but it is usually bad policy not to take leave when you can get it, as you never know when it may be stopped, and the sooner you take it the nearer you are to your next turn.

The Derby news leaves me quite cold. I really don't care whether I get in or not, as you know. My only views on the subject are: (a) that it would be better to postpone the contest at any rate till I have left G.H.Q. which is not a very dashing address for a War appeal to the electors, whereas the Ypres salient leaves nothing to be desired in this respect: and (b) that the thing must on no account be allowed to happen while I am in England. Nothing would induce me to spend my leave in making political speeches . . .

To K. A.   Intelligence,
                                             G.H.Q.
                                             B.E.F.
                                             1 April 1916

It has been a beautiful sunny day and I walked about a bit and explored the old ramparts, dungeons, drawbridges and other flotsam and jetsam of antiquity which still exist here.

The only news is that my General has found a bug in his bed and was carried away this morning kicking and screaming to a hospital, suffering from bronchial influenza and severe fright. I don't blame him . . .

To K. A.   Intelligence,
                                             G.H.Q.
                                             B.E.F.
                                             3 April 1916

. . . My poor General has pneumonia (not double) as well and is laid up in the Duchess of Westminster's hospital at Le Touquet, where I drove over to see him this morning. The hospital is in a sort of large hotel or Casino – not the one we stayed at, but more in the town – and looks very clean and airy and pleasant. I did not go on to the links or see that amazing annexe where we once spent such an unparalleled easter-tide. How sceptical I should have been if I had been told then (even by one risen from the dead) that my next visit to Le Touquet would take place under the present circumstances. (Forgive the reflexion if you find it a trifle banal). I suppose the late Lord Roberts could have told me if I had cared to ask him.

I see that the P.M. has been having a crack with the Pope. I hope he contrived to fight down his provincial prejudice against the Papacy and keep a civil tongue in his head.

I am sorry that old E is bored by Egypt, but as you say it only proves that one is bound to be bored by this War wherever one is – I honestly think that he would find it worse in France – specially with the Cavalry, who seem to spend their time wandering round the most retired portions of the Army area acting revues! . . .

To K. A.   Intelligence,
                                             G.H.Q.
                                             B.E.F.
                                             7 April 1916

. . . Personally I feel that I could stand anything if the bloody war came to a reasonably speedy end, and should be quite happy living on nothing a year with

3 daughters, but no doubt, as you say, one would begin grumbling again almost before the bells had stopped ringing. But talking about mental outlooks, and the kind of things which stir people's emotions or impress their minds, the whole attitude of England at the present moment – if reflected accurately in the Harmsworth press, the only mirror in which I see it – is to me astonishing and shocking beyond measure. The complete jettison of self-respect, the utter surrender to panic cowardice and the grosser forms of self-interest and self-advertisement, the boastful and self-satisfied manner in which it is now the fashion to evade obligations and disclaim liabilities which formerly it was the custom to grin and bear – all these things nearly incline me to devote my post-war energies to a crusade against the foulness and vulgarity of the modern world. To suggest e.g. that this man Hughes should represent the British Empire at an economic conference is almost as sensible as suggesting that Charlie Chaplin should do so. My only hope for England is that the majority of its inhabitants would at any rate prefer Chaplin to Hughes. Ignorance of economics is a tiresome thing enough (when it is tinged with emotion) but ignorance of the whole basis of any possible morality – Xian or Pagan – is almost worse. And that is what the remnant of old women and old Ulstermen who are all that is now left of my poor country, have seemingly come to.

What an absurd letter. Forgive me, Fawnia, for running on. The post just going and I am a little hectic. All this has been written in under 50 seconds, so you must excuse it . . .

To K. A.

Intelligence,
G.H.Q.
B.E.F.
10 April 1916

. . . I wrote the other day to my Birmingham book shop to tell them if they hadn't succeeded in getting Swinburne's *Shakespeare* for you, to send 3 other books instead which I saw in their catalogue, so don't be alarmed if you get some very absurd volumes – I can't even remember what they were now, but only that they were what I should have chosen – out of a very poor lot – for myself. You will probably find them terrible.

I am enclosing in this letter – heaven knows why – a specimen of the paper money of St Omer (what the private calls a 'souvenir') which may be interesting some day (one asks oneself when?) and a picture of a battle which I cut out of one of the German papers which we got here. I am afraid these things do not compare favourably with the presents you have given me – my wrist watch which still goes excellently, the leather photograph case, and my woolly waistcoat, a great blessing in this frightfully cold office – to mention only a few of your benefactions.

Please thank Perdita for the story which she sent me. I will write to her myself soon. It is terrible to think of your being in a house with so many pictures of horses. Do you think it is quite wise or even safe? It would be a blow to us all if you were to give birth to a foal instead of to a son; and there would be even more trouble about finding a name . . .

To Perdita Asquith (aged nearly 6)
G.H.Q.
11.4.16.

My sweet Perdita,
I was delighted to get your letter with the violets and the story. I enjoyed the story very much and was sorry when it came to an end – rather suddenly as I thought . . .

I live in a very pretty little town on the top of a hill with a river running on one side of it to the sea which is only 8 miles away. All round the town are enormous walls of brick and stone 40 or 50 feet high and on the top of them is a broad path on which you can walk and look down onto the fields below. The French built these walls, I believe, to defend them from the English long ago. Ask your mother who the Emperor Napoleon was. He lived here a hundred years ago when he was planning to take his army over in ships and attack England with it. Today I saw a German prisoner. He was a flying man who lost his way and brought his aeroplane down not very far from here thinking that he was among his own friends.

To K. A.
Intelligence,
G.H.Q.
B.E.F.
12 April 1916

. . . Here on the whole I think that time passes more swiftly than in the trenches, owing to the greater sameness of the days and weeks. The Boche continues to pour new troops into Belgium – including Austrian guns – I suppose for Verdun which I still think may fall in the end. It seems (from prisoners' statements) that there is considerable rivalry and feeling between the armies of the East and West. A Bavarian Divn. arrived at Verdun some weeks ago from the Balkans singing this elfin rhyme.

> *"Im Osten Steht das wahre Heer*
> *"Im Westen nur die Fenerwehr."*[1]

but after one day's fighting those of them who were not killed either went mad

[1] "In the East stands the true army
"In the West only the false."

or ran away or both. I'm told that our troops from Gallipoli also arrived here with the idea that they were the only men who knew anything about real war. But the famous 29th Divn. were bombed out of the line the first night they entered it, and their illusions are rapidly fading.

To K. A.
Intelligence,
G.H.Q.
B.E.F.
14 April 1916

. . . Yes, you are quite right: I do eat at an "Hotel or inn", and there is no need to send me any food – I over-eat as it is. Plovers' eggs are always welcome, but they are beyond your purse, my pretty. I am told they are very expensive this year. You might tell Bluey to send me some, but don't do so yourself . . .

To K. A.
Intelligence,
G.H.Q.
B.E.F.
15 April 1916

Only time for 2 paragraphs before the post. A capital long letter from you today with the word 'Thursday' written at the top of it in someone else's hand.

Yes, Gough is a very good General and a very young one too – only 47, and a relation of Hugo's. It would be an excellent thing to be in his army. I am glad Edgar [d'Abernon] thinks the Govt. is all right – I have got to the stage now in which I would rather beat Harmsworth than beat the Germans. He seems to me just as aggressively stupid and stupidly aggressive as they are, and much less brave and efficient.

To Lady Diana Manners
15 April 1916

The eggs were bluer than the lids of Juno's eyes or Cytherea's breath – And I am willing to believe you when you tell me that they were also more expensive . . .

I like your story of the American General who ate the shells – it shows that the Yanks are fine fellows after all (like Sir R. Grenville who always ate his wine glass at dessert). But after eating so many words I daresay it seemed quite a soft job. (I read the patriot press so much that I can't help every now and then saying this kind of bold witty thing). An egg in the cup is worth two in the ovary; but all the same I would rather have had your letter than every egg laid since the first plover took flight from the ark . . .

To K. A.

Intelligence,
G.H.Q.
B.E.F.
17 April 1916

I am extremely sorry about Phalaris.[1] So far as I know there is no grass of that name, but was at one time a tolerably well known man who bore it. He lived in Sicily and had a brazen bull in which he enclosed those who displeased him and then slowly cooked them. At the beginning of the 18th century an unfortunate Irish gentleman called Boyle (afterwards I believe the Earl of Cork & Orrery) was induced to edit and boom some forged Greek documents which professed to be letters written by Phalaris, whereupon Bentley, our greatest English scholar, and an ancestor of Tuppy Headlam, wrote a very brilliant and biting book on the subject (entitled *The Epistles of Phalaris*) proving conclusively that the letters were not written by Phalaris but by someone else living in quite another place and time, and that poor Boyle and everyone who had any thing to do with him were perjured and fraudulent dunces. You had better verify these statements by reference to the Bedford Square library in which you will find a classical dictionary and also *The Epistles of Phalaris*, which you will see immediately opposite the centre of your thyroid gland if you stand with your back to the window immediately to the right of my writing chair. Or perhaps a shorter way would be to consult Smyth, who is sure to have all the facts fresh in his mind, which I confess that I have not . . .

To K. A.

Intelligence,
G.H.Q.
B.E.F.
18 April 1916

It was delightful to get such a contented letter from you on your return to the old roof tree.[2] I'm sorry though that the battered old blue hangings have gone from your famous canopy. I wonder if we shall find any of our things again. I have a feeling that all the keys will be lost. Have you e.g. succeeded in opening the drawers and cupboards in our respective writing tables? I have a faint memory of putting a lot of keys away in boxes in the central cupboard of that funny bookcase we bought at Frome, which now stands in the dirt trap. I hope Baxter will wring some more money for you out of the tenants. But my cheque for £50 did arrive, didn't it? . . .

There is as little news here as ever. Almost everyone has influenza or pneumonia, but I keep myself as well as one can expect to be when one is bored. I do this by sleeping for about 8 hours every night and drinking a great

[1] A horse of the Lambtons.
[2] Katharine moved back into Bedford Square before the birth of her son.

deal of liqueur brandy. I am reading Leacock's *Half Hours with the Idle Rich* which Gilbert sent me. It is really very clever. I am also pushing along with *Eothen*, a pleasant surprise. It is extremely readable . . .

To K. A.   Intelligence,
                                                                                        G.H.Q.
                                                                                         B.E.F.
                                                                                 19 April 1916

Today I had a letter from Ettie [Desborough] asking me to contribute an appreciation of Billy and Julian [Grenfell] for a book she is making about them. It was a charming letter but it is a terrible request. I suppose I must try to put something together, but I have such a bad memory for the individual incidents or characteristic sayings which alone can make memorial prose tolerable.

What you tell me about the political situation is alarming. According to today's papers it still hangs in the balance. I should be sorry if Lloyd George came in for the last 6 months of the War, and got all the credit of winning it, which he assuredly does not deserve. Whether or not I should be more sorry if he made another bungle of it and Thomas called out the railway men and the war was prolonged for another 2 years, I hardly know. The compulsionists may be right, but if there is a God he will certainly never forgive them for the bosh they have talked.

I am so glad that being back at Bed. Sq. has revived your spirits. No doubt it is very much nicer to live in one's own house, but our resources simply would not have stood it if we had tried to do it all the time . . .

To K. A.   Intelligence,
                                                                                        G.H.Q.
                                                                                         B.E.F.
                                                                                 23 April 1916

My Angel
    You really are a wonder. It seemed hardly possible that you would get the sex right as well as the date. The whole thing is a triumph of organisation which the Government would do well to imitate. What with the Resurrection, Shakespeare's death and now Trimalchio's[1] birth, I hardly know whether I am standing on my head or my heels today. Shall we send him into the Cabinet or into the Grenadiers? Have you arranged a marriage for him yet? or will he have to attest? If so I shall raise the cry of "weaned men first". Above all, does he give away any of your guilty secrets or might he so far be mistaken for my own?

[1] Another nickname for the son that had just been born, which survived in the form of Trim.

My sweet, I do hope it was less long and tiresome for you than the other two and that you are already beginning to feel well again. But the last I suppose is too much to hope. Still a boy must be much less of a shock than a girl and will beckon you on up the hill of convalescence . . . Darling angel, I adore you.

To K. A.

Intelligence,
G.H.Q.
B.E.F.
25 April 1916

. . . I have no news to give you from here except that at last and for once we have a really hot sunny day. But what one reads in the papers is sensational enough. I hope the Zeps kept clear of London and will not disturb your convalescence. I am delighted that they have caught that swollen-headed, maggot-ridden idealist Casement, and heartily hope they will hang him. We owe it not only to ourselves but to Belgium for the fuss he made about the Congo.

To K. A.

Intelligence,
G.H.Q.
B.E.F.
26 April 1916

. . . It is said that Lord French of Ypres has taken 2 divisions over to re-conquer Ireland, and that young Hicks-Beach has been killed defending Dublin Post Office. It sounds almost incredible and amazes me more than anything that has happened in the War . . .

To K. A.

Intelligence,
G.H.Q.
B.E.F.
28 April 1916

Very many thanks for your letter and the *Daily News* attack on Lloyd George. I somehow missed it here and was anxious to read it. I have a letter from Bluey today who says that L. G. is hated violently now by both sides and that the P.M. has turned his last corner now. I rather doubt both theories and don't understand the withdrawal of this precious bill which was to save everybody's face.

I'm delighted to hear that the baby has your eyebrows; as you say, one is grateful enough for their having anyone's. I hope it may also inherit your eyes (not to mention "little classical") and my own kind heart and hatred of impurity . . .

To Lady Diana Manners   28 April 1916

Katharine has kept on telling me for weeks now that you have been very sweet
to her but very low in your spirits. I do hope that you are not sick of love for
one of these terribly young men? Or is it only that you have not been getting
your whack at the bottle? . . . And yet there is a bitter pleasure in your being
subject to chance and change like the rest of us . . . Much as one likes you, one
would like you less if you were not (occasionally) depressed. Do you think
yourself that you would love anyone who was so free from human vicissitude as
to be always on the top of the wave? Perhaps you do think so. But if you do it is
only because you regard people as if they were things. The Matterhorn would
certainly lose its somewhat dreary point if once a week it looked like a molehill,
and Venice similarly if it had moods of Manchester. But I do love to think of
your proud front sometimes – hardly ever – levelled with the dust and equal
made with the poor scythe and crooked spade . . .

To K. A.   Intelligence,
                                                                G.H.Q.
                                                                B.E.F.
                                                            29 April 1916

I have a beautiful long letter from you with a few complaints which I take to be
a healthy sign. I always understood that the first clutch of infant lips on the
breast was the most thrilling and exquisite moment in a woman's life. Don't
tell me that I have been misinformed. Really I think you must be mistaken in
supposing the sensation to be unpleasant.

It seems hard that they won't let you see people if you are really so well.
Margot's letter, I agree, is an outrage, and one which conforms to her well-
known type.[1] She can no other. But I do feel rather curious to know what she
was praying about.

I am glad to hear that the child has a curly mouth as well as curly eyebrows,
but a little surprised that it has not yet given proof of the exceptional cleverness
which your children have always been used to display during the first few days
of their lives at any rate . . .

To K. A.   Intelligence,
                                                                G.H.Q.
                                                                B.E.F.
                                                            3 May 1916

. . . There is utterly nothing to report from here – Winston turned up this afternoon and I took him for a walk on the ramparts. He was rather sentimental

---

[1] Not long before the war, Raymond had commented that Margot 'says and does things that you
never forget, and remembers things that you never say or do.'

about the spring and rather dismal about the War; says it would be madness to have an offensive this year and that we must wait until the Russians have 7 million men and look for victory in the autumn of 1917. His battalion is being disbanded and merged in another, so he is coming home on Saturday to oust Carson from the leadership of a patriotic opposition or co-operate with him in it if the worst comes to the worst . . .

To K. A.   3rd Grenadier Guards,
                                                       B.E.F.
                                                  20 May 1916

. . . Alfred Yorke I found in excellent form but somewhat shaken in nerve by his experiences in their part of the line; also a new subaltern called Jackson who seems very nice and anxious to do other people's work as well as his own which is an excellent quality in a young officer and none too common even in the youngest.

In this part of the line we are surrounded and overlooked by the Germans on almost every side and they have a great number of guns in good positions which they loose off pretty continuously. We were fairly heavily shelled on Thursday and had some casualties, but nothing really to matter. The weather being so fine puts a picnic complexion on the whole affair and obscures the less agreeable aspects.

All officers have to be up all night but the nights are so short that this is not a very severe tax and at 3.30 a.m. we have a cup of coffee and turn in, if there is anywhere to turn in; if not, sleep in the open, as I did last night with great comfort and enjoyment. One advantage of the weakness of our position is that it is impossible to work or even move during the day, so one simply lies about dozing in the sun till about 8.30 p.m. We have given up luncheon and have bacon and eggs at 11 a.m., tea at 4 and dinner – a substantial meal – at 7. We are in for 5 days on end this time – the longest I have ever done at a stretch but the conditions are so favourable that I don't think it takes it out of one so much as 2 days in the winter trenches . . .

To K. A.   3rd Grenadier Guards,
                                                       B.E.F.
                                                  22 May 1916

. . . After 10 days here we are going 10 miles or so further back to live in billets for 3 weeks. I am rather depressed at the prospect. The perfect way to do this war would be G.H.Q. for these waste spaces and regimental life for the spells of trench work.

To K. A.

3rd Grenadier Guards,
B.E.F.
23 May 1916

. . . As for me I am already more bored with this tiresome camp than ever I was with G.H.Q. We were allowed an easy time today but for the next week we live a terribly strenuous and wearisome life – a certain amount of drill and a great many "fatigues" – i.e. digging trenches, laying cables, fetching and carrying, hewing wood and drawing water for other people. Personally I prefer anything to drill. But it does seem rather queer that with masses of men in France who have never come within sight of a trench, they should yet find it necessary to take a battalion which has just finished 2 months in the worst and most dangerous part of the line and is supposed to be coming out for a rest and use it to do odd jobs every day (including Sunday) from 6 a.m. onwards, as if it consisted entirely of conscientious objectors.

I knew I should begin grousing as soon as I got away from G.H.Q. but I suppose I should have groused more if I had stayed there. There is no avoiding the boredom of this War, turn which way you may. There is more novelty and excitement about the trenches themselves than any other part of the show, but I should still be discontented if I were made to stay in them for a month on end instead of coming out and doing these bloody fatigues and things . . .

One fearful addition to the honours of War since I have been away is the steel helmet which we all have to wear now, when in the shell area. They are monstrously tiresome and heavy and I suppose if idiots like Pemberton Billing had not asked questions in Parliament about them we should have been allowed to go on with our comfortable caps. We make the bloody things better than anyone else does of course by sewing the blue and red brigade ribbon with a gold grenade on it, on to the khaki cover, but even so they are insufferable . . .

To Lady Diana Manners

25 May 1916

. . . We came out to this utterly bloody camp where we now are on Sunday night, marching between fields of deep cool green corn in the early morning. It was wonderfully like what coming home from a ball through Covent Garden ought to be, but, as we know, isn't – leaving behind one the flash and clatter of machine guns and pressing one's brow against the dewy peace of the vegetable world. After a week of "all the metals and more" there is a certain sweetness in transition . . .

Katharine writes that you have been an angel to her which I like to hear, and also that you are utterly stage-struck which I like less. Tell me when you next write, about the stage and why you like it. It makes me think that you might like Ypres, and God only knows if you wouldn't give even the Matterhorn a *coup d'oeil*.

A brutal orderly has come for the post while I still had much more to say. Write as much as you can without putting a burden on yourself.

To K. A.   25 May 1916

. . . I spent yesterday from 8.30 a.m.-4.30 p.m. in a wood near here with Ham. We took 100 men to put up wooden huts there and spent quite a pleasant and restful day lying on our backs on the moss drinking whisky, listening to the song of the nightingales and reading aloud to one another a book by Ouida called *Chandos* which we both thought very funny. It was a fine warm day and the only trouble was that we were harassed incessantly by midges and mosquitoes . . .

P.S. Did you read in the last number of the *Spectator* a flaming tribute to the P.M. and his gallant sons?

To K. A.   3rd Grenadier Guards,
                                                                                    B.E.F.
                                                                               26 May 1916

A sweet brace of letters from you yesterday and today. I'm so glad that you are getting over your tiredness and hope that you will be well enough to enjoy Esher.

Trim is making an early beginning with his country house visits. Is the Dean of St Paul's the gloomy one? I hope so. It is rather Brahms [i.e. recherché] to have a son christened Trimalchio by the gloomy Dean . . .

To K. A.   3rd Grenadier Guards,
                                                                                    B.E.F.
                                                                               28 May 1916

I notice a distinct change in the morale of this battalion since I was last with them – the officers I mean. They are more tired of the war, more frightened of shells and talk more constantly about the prospects of peace. I think it is almost entirely boredom which produces this effect, because it is absurd to pretend, as some people do, that there is anything in the nature of continuous nervous strain in this war. Shelling certainly has a cumulative effect, but even in the Salient there is hardly more than 1 day a month when it is bad enough to cause real distress.

We have a parson attached to us now – a Cambridge don – who wanted to hold a service today in our battalion mess room, but the walls have been so thickly papered with French pictures of naked women that he had to confess the site inappropriate for any holy purpose . . .

To K. A.

3rd Grenadier Guards,
B.E.F.
30 May 1916

Last night we had an open air concert in the dusk, a long succession of super-sentimental songs, about people being married for 40 years and still playing the same old tune on the piano and so on. I wondered what we should be like in 40 years; and came to the conclusion that you would still be very sweet indeed, though poor Trim would be just developing the "middle-aged spread". What a terrible place the world is. Even in war time one can't help having more apprehensions about living to be old than about being cut off in the flower of one's youth – if indeed one can still call it that.

Old E's return is most interesting. I wonder what he can have done already to make Frances plaintive, and what more he will do . . .

To K. A.

3rd Grenadier Guards,
B.E.F.
2 June 1916

. . . On Thursday I rose at 5 a.m. and the battalion marched off at 7.30. We went about 20 miles over hot hard dusty roads under a brilliant sun and one got nothing to eat or drink between 6 in the morning and 3 in the afternoon. Considering how little exercise I have had these last 3 months I was surprisingly little tired and hardly at all footsore. A long march is really more boring than tiring, provided one is going light. Our late C.O. used to make the officers carry packs but this one mercifully doesn't. It makes a vast difference.

We got to a pleasant enough town where we were by way of staying for 3 weeks – quite pretty country and excellent billets, but the authorities had omitted to notice that the whole district was under crops and consequently there was no possibility of training there. So we were at once moved on and this morning I again rose at 5 and the whole Brigade with John Ponsonby at its head marched off another 10 miles to a large Franco-Flemish village where we now are and where there is about 1000 yds of uncultivated ground on which we are to dig trenches and practise popping the parapet.

Again a hot lovely day but a terribly slow and tedious march. But there is something rather majestic about the movement of a Brigade with all its 4 battalions and their transport and the drums playing. My Company led the whole Brigade (which occupies about 1½ miles of road) and we marched past the G.O.C. 2nd Army in the square of a small town en route with great distinction and éclat. John Ponsonby rode up and talked to me for a little on the march, very friendly and congratulatory about my return to the battalion. Ham [Yorke] and I have got a billet together – not a bad one, except that my bed is a foot too short. We had to walk about the place for hours and call at nearly every house before we could find anyone who would let us have a room for a company mess. The French – what is left of them – are really too beastly. The population consists entirely of invalid old women who are incredibly timid, inhospitable, prejudiced, audacious and obstinate.

After marching for 2 days one gets rather irritable when the solitary inhabitants of large empty houses refuse to let one have a chair to sit down on or a bath to eat one's caviare off. There are many of these rheumatic old bitches I would gladly throw to the Boches. I believe we shall be here till the 18th, then back to our camp for a week or so and then the trenches again . . .

To Sybil Hart-Davis   3rd Batt. Grenadier Guards
                                                                                    3.6.16

After 5 very enjoyable days in the salient (which smells strongly at this season of dead Scotchmen) I marched through the deep green corn fields of Belgium in the cool of the summer morning to a wayside camp, as one might walk home through Covent Garden from the din and clatter of a ball, and was much pleased to find your letter awaiting me.

Now that the Huns have conquered Italy and Greece and sunk all our ships and killed all our Canadians and all but taken Verdun I suppose it will be the turn of the British Army next. Well, well, there is much to be said for being quietly under the sod. And yet I feel that I have a kick or two – not more – in me yet. And then Dalmeny has got the Military Cross, so no one can say the war is over. We have been marching like hell for the last two days along hot and dusty roads and have now got so far away from the enemy that we are allowed not to wear gas helmets or shrapnel helmets or anti-lachrymatory goggles or revolvers or field glasses or periscopes or breastplates or field dressings or any of the other knickknacks that make us so terrible in battle.

But at any moment we may be whipped back into the soup. Still, it is so long now since I have been allowed to stay in bed after 5 a.m. that a battle would do me a fair treat.

To K. A.   3rd Grenadier Guards,
                                                                                    B.E.F.
                                                                            4 June 1916

. . . Today for the first time we have been allowed to get up later than 5 a.m. and I have had nothing to do but listen to the twaddle of our parson in a field full of buttercups which hung down their heads.

Yesterday we spent digging trenches, from which to practise the attack. The government have bought 500 acres of the richest land in France for the purpose and we tramped down or dug up God knows how many tons of the best foodstuffs in the execution of our fatuous project. Luckily the weather has been beautiful and the country watered with the golden light of Dutch pictures.

To K. A.   3rd Grenadier Guards,
                                                                                  B.E.F.
                                                                           9 June 1916

. . . An intolerable thing has happened in the Expeditionary Force – much more deeply felt by the troops than Kitchener's death – leave has been reduced to 6 days or some say to 5; it is not quite clear which. It doesn't make so much difference to the line regiments, who, poor devils, never got more than 7 but it is perfectly bloody for us who have grown used to 10. There is some hope that the change may be only temporary, but I should think it would last all through the summer, and bitch my next expedition to Blighty.

We are supposed to be doing Brigade training here but life is really very much less strenuous than it was in the 'rest camp'. We have dug an elaborate system of trenches copied from aeroplane photographs of a particular part of the German line and every day we practise attacking them. There is a great deal of sitting about, and on a sunny day it is really very restful and not unpleasant.

This morning we spent an hour or two watching a demonstration with trench mortars and Stoker Guns. It was quite interesting from the rear and looked as if it would be very disagreeable from the front . . .

The night before I dined with John Ponsonby who told me that, without asking me, he had sent my name in on a list he was told to make out of officers eligible to be G.S.O. 3 (if you know what that means) – practically intelligence officer to a Division, Corps or Army. He has always been very friendly to me and anxious to do me a good turn, but I hope nothing will come of it for the present. I wouldn't mind having a shot at it for a while in the winter . . .

To K. A.   3rd Grenadier Guards,
                                                                                  B.E.F.
                                                                         11 June 1916

Certainly it was a formidable bundle you sent me from the Income Tax people. It is quite impossible out here to discuss what one's income is or what one's tax should be, so they will have to kick their heels for a bit. Luckily I have been paid a little for Revenue cases and enclose you £50 to keep the W. from the D.

I am glad that Trim's baptism went off nicely and that he scooped in some presents; also that Helen has the right instincts about Archbishops . . . How like Visey and Margot to make such a fuss about Lord K.[1] As if it mattered

[1] The news of Lord Kitchener's death arrived while Trim was being baptised at St Paul's Cathedral. Margot burst in with it and talked loudly all through the ceremony.

these old men being killed . . .

There is such a noise in the room that I can't write you a proper letter. An order has just come out that there is to be no cheering in the trenches when peace is declared. No one can say that our Generals don't look ahead.

To K. A.   3rd Grenadier Guards,
B.E.F.
13 June 1916

. . . I share your feelings about the badness of being drowned as compared with being shot, but can't help still suspecting that Kitchener will stroll into the House of Lords combing the seaweed out of his hair as strong and silent as ever.

To K. A.   3rd Grenadier Guards,
B.E.F.
17 June 1916

. . . I made the mistake of playing a game of football the afternoon we came in – a thing I haven't done for 15 years. It made me pretty tired and stiff and brought home to me the ghastly ravages of age. However I managed to get carried on a motor bus up to within about 3 miles of the line, so I didn't suffer much.

It was rather interesting though also very tiring and irritating getting into the new trenches and relieving strange troops who have no idea of discipline and I suppose were not at their best after some weeks of really heavy fighting. They reeled past us drinking rum and leaving everything else behind them, including numbers of loaded rifles and every kind of equipment. In fact we have fed and clothed 2 companies with their leavings and sent back to the base a vast amount of stuff which we couldn't use.

Luckily the weather has been very fine and so far it has not been unpleasant in any way. I am not in the front line at present, but shall probably move into it tomorrow. We have a line of dug-outs behind a lake. It is about as big as Rydal Water and is fringed with poplars. Last night under the full moon it was really quite beautiful.

A terrific reciprocal bombardment began at about 10 and lasted 3 or 4 hours. It turned out that we were in a very safe place, the shells being directed at trenches in front or in rear of us; so several of us went up and stood by the shore of the lake and watched it. It was really a magnificent sight. The lake without a ripple with a full yellow moon above the poplars and all round the horizon a ring of flame, the flashes of the guns and the bursting of the shells, bangs and screams and crumps and coughs and whistles in every key and from every direction. But like everything that happens, it went on too long and before it was over I was heartily sick of the noise. Specially as in the middle of it all a gas attack began and we all had to put on our gas helmets and stumble about spitting and slobbering and swearing and looking like the Wolf in *Little Red Riding Hood*. Some people said they could smell the gas, but I never did and after a time we took off our helmets and went to bed, and then in the morning the bloody noise began again and gave me quite a headache. However the Boches never attacked, and I don't believe they ever will now. I should think they are hustling back to Russia as fast as the trains can carry them. My brigade had about 50 casualties from shell fire including one officer (whom I knew but did not particularly like) killed and 2 wounded – really a very small bag considering the intensity and duration of the bombardment. Today has been sunny and fairly quiet and I have slept a good deal and won 7 rubbers of bridge.

To K. A.   3rd Grenadier Guards,
                                                                      B.E.F.
                                                            22 June 1916

. . . We came out of the trenches last night and marched into camp about 3 this morning. Now we are out, I suppose there is no harm in saying what I daresay you have already guessed that we were pushed in to relieve the Canadians opposite Hooge. The Canadians had almost all been killed in the recent fighting there (which was unlucky for them) and hardly any of them had been buried (which was unlucky for us). The confusion and mess were indescribable and the stinks hardly to be borne. No one quite knew where the line was and the men were spotted about in little holes in the ground or in the cellars of ruined cottages and the crypts of crumbling churches.

The first two days I was in a pretty comfortable place from which I wrote to you about the bombardment, but afterwards things were less agreeable. It was impossible to show ourselves for a moment without being shelled and there were no adequate arrangements for hiding. Sloper Mackenzie, Eddy Ward and another officer were shut up for 48 hours in a dug-out meant for 2 at the best of times and when half flooded as it was with blood and water and filth of every kind quite unfit for habitation. We did our best to clean out some of the muck but the process was so disturbing that poor Sloper was physically sick in the middle of it. I couldn't endure sleeping there so got hold of an old stretcher and lay on it in a shell-hole outside, which I think saved my life, though it might easily have ended it.

One would have given anything for a bottle of verbena or a yard of ruban de Bruges. Luckily after the first big bombardment the shelling was very desultory. I never saw anything like the foulness and desolation of this bit of the Salient. There were 2 woods near to us on which we roamed about picking up gruesome relics in the dusk – Maple Copse and Sanctuary Wood – not a leaf or a blade of grass in either of them, nothing but twisted and blackened stumps and a mesh of shell holes, dimpling into one another, full of mud and blood, and dead men and over-fed rats which blundered into one in the twilight like fat moths.

To my mind it was a far more impressive sight than the ruins of Ypres, because it was sheer abomination undiluted by a single touch of beauty, grandeur or sentiment. However after 2 days Sloper and I were moved to rather better quarters where we stayed till last night . . .

Goodbye, my blessed angel. This morning I took my boots off and washed for the first time these 8 days. It was delicious.

To Lady Diana Manners   23 June 1916

. . . But, 2 nights out of a dreary 7 did make me think of you perhaps harder than usual – one for beauty and one for ugliness. The first was on the shore of a biggish lake with poplars and a honey-coloured moon, and one of the most crashing bombardments of the War going on all round, shells bursting in front and behind to right and to left, but not just where I was, so that I felt as safe as if it had been the Charge of the Light Brigade and could enjoy the spectacle as such, and fancy almost that the lake was "Sutton Waters" and wished that you were there to enjoy it too as you would have done intensely – at any rate for a little. After an hour or two the noise gets on one's nerves like music. There was a gas attack too in the middle which was boring, and for 40 minutes we had to stumble about slobbering into rubber snouts like animals in a pantomime.

Another night I was in a much worse place than this – the most accursed unholy and abominable place I have ever seen, the ugliest filthiest most putrid and most desolate – a wood where all the trees had been cut off by the shells the week before, and nothing remained but black stumps of really the most obscene heights and thickness, craters swimming in blood and dirt, rotting and smelling bodies and rats like shadows, fattened for the market moving cunningly and liquorishly among them, limbs and bowels nestling in the hedges, and over all the most supernaturally shocking scent of death and corruption that ever breathed o'er Eden. The place simply stank of sin and all Floris could not have made it sweet . . . The only dug-out turned out to be a 'dirt trap' if not a death trap, awash with sewage, stale eyeballs, and other debris, so I spent 2 days on a stretcher in a shell hole in the gutter certainly, but looking all the while at the stars with which you have so richly studded my memory.

There is a great deal after all to be said for the existence of evil; it might almost be held to prove the existence of God. Who else could have thought of it?

We go into the line again in a few days – still the salient, but a different part of it. And in a fortnight or so I suppose we shall have won the war.

To K. A.   3rd Grenadier Guards,
                                                          B.E.F.
                                                    27 June 1916

We are moving tomorrow and I may not be able to get off a letter, so I send you
a line today just to tell you that we are all merry and bright, because that is
really all the news there is except that the rain has begun again and I'm afraid
the trenches will be rather sloshy and uncomfortable.

We captured a sparrow-hawk when we were up at Zillebelle; its leg and wing
had been broken, probably by shrapnel. It lives with my company now and
feeds on mice and is very tame and handsome.

This letter reads rather like one of Perdita's stories, but every day now we
get threatening messages from G.H.Q. telling us that if we ever say anything
interesting again we shall be court-martialled and all correspondence with
England will be cut off till the end of the war. All bloody nonsense, but there it
is . . .

To K. A.   3rd Grenadier Guards,
                                                          B.E.F.
                                                    28 June 1916

Thank you for a sweet letter today. I'm afraid I must have written of the
horrors of Maple Copse and Sanctuary Wood rather too much. But that is a
temptation one can't resist in these dull days.

It was sweet of old Richard [Haldane] to give you a cheque for brandy and
cigars. It is really not worth while sending good cigars out here, and for the
moment we get plenty of very decent brandy. If I want any later on, I will let
you know. In the meantime Patum Peperium (Gentleman's Relish) tinned
chicken (plain or curried) and honey are all acceptable in the trenches. But I
really would prefer you to spend the cheque on your own pleasures. I have no
time for more as we are just pushing off . . .

To K. A.   3rd Grenadier Guards,
                                                          B.E.F.
                                                    2 July 1916

I was delighted to get two letters from you yesterday in the trenches. I'm glad
you are going up to London again. It will be more amusing for you. I too am
getting rather tired of country life and a yearning for cities begins to revive in
me. Sixteen days in the same clothes is decidedly too much. However I
managed to shave this morning which always gives one back a tinge of self
respect.

. . . After dinner I went out into No Man's Land to see what our wire was like taking one man with me and some beggar threw a bomb at us – no one seemed to know where it came from. Some thought it was our own as the line is very muddled up there, but I think it was a Boche myself as they had been bombing one of my advanced posts a little earlier.

Anyhow it was a damned good shot and burst within a yard or two of us. Luckily we had just bobbed down behind a lump in the ground to avoid the glare of a German rocket. A few small bits hit me on the shoulder but without going through my coat or hurting me at all. The man got 3 or 4 biggish bits in his arm and leg and was a good deal frightened, but he managed to walk back to the trench where we bound him up and sent him off to the dressing station.

Then to put the lid on everything when I got back to my dug-out and lay down at 4.30 a.m. there were 3 loud-voiced over-nourished mosquitoes trumpeting all round me. I killed one and woke up this morning unbitten by the others, so perhaps my luck is in again now . . .

To K. A.   3rd Grenadier Guards,
                                                         B.E.F.
                                                 5 July 1916

I wrote to Helen yesterday but I think it is a day or two since I wrote to you. In the front line where it is at all lively one is so tired by night work that one has little appetite in the day for anything but sleep and food and drink.

Last night we came out for 4 days in the support line. That only means a retirement of about 100 yards or so, but one gets a more roomy dug-out and a great deal more rest. You probably know as much and more than I do about our offensive in the South. So far it certainly seems to be going better than our offensives usually do, though the northern wing of it seems to be tiresomely held up. In this part of the world we have our little flutters, but nothing on a big scale. Our 3rd brigade made a shallow advance on a short front the other night and so far as we know have held their new line against the counter attack.

Then on Sunday night the Irish Guards made a trench raid which I'm afraid wasn't a very great success as the enemy were waiting for them, killed a good lot on the way over and then cleared out of their trenches so that we got very few prisoners. In the territory just opposite to my platoon three Boches were very enterprising and we had bombing fights every night. The night before last, I think we frightened them a bit. I posted 3 men with bombs in a shell hole about 40 yards in front of my parapet while some others were putting up new barbed wire.

My bombers spotted the Germans coming down an old ditch between one and two in the morning and there was quite a good little fight in which the enemy made off in a rain of bombs. My men were certain they had knocked out 2 or 3 Huns, so I went out with them towards the German line to try and pick up dead and wounded. The grass was so long that it was like looking for a golf ball and we found nothing but an unexploded German grenade. But it was quite exciting crawling about among the grass and shell holes, though one got rather wet and muddy . . .

To K. A.   3rd Grenadier Guards,
                                                                              B.E.F.
                                                                     7 July 1916

I sent you back your p.c. yesterday with a few scratches on it. Never waste a penny stamp on one again, it is unnecessary and reckless. There is still no news.

Raids (which are terribly overdone and destroy far more of our men than the enemy) go on most nights with the usual artillery nonsense all along the front, but we have had a pretty quiet time since leaving the front line. At this moment the Belgian guns (of all unexpected and unsuitable instruments) are blasting off on our left. I am bored to death with all this senseless noise.

A few other 'comforts' have occurred to me which you might send from time to time out of the "Haldane fund".

(1) Tinned grapes
(2) Anchovy paste (in moderation)
(3) Kippers and smoked haddocks if they can be packed.

The Stornaway kippers are the best if obtainable. One rather feels the lack of fish here.

I have been in this line so long now that I am almost acclimatised to it and feel that it doesn't much matter whether we are here for a fortnight or 6 months . . .

To Lady Diana Manners   10 July 1916

Your letter was terribly sad and moving. How I wish that I could comfort you but I can't. Ego [Elcho] is irreplaceable – you will never find another man who can even pretend (as he used to) not to want to kiss you. And he had other strange and fascinating qualities which we shall not see the like of again. A blind God butts about the world with a pair of delicately malignant antennae to detect whatever is fit to live and an iron hoof to stamp it into the dust when found. It seems amazing that the bony fingers of fate and spite should push into what seemed the safest field of all the War and nip the finest flower in it. One's instinct that the world (as we know it) is governed by chance is almost shaken by the accumulating evidence that it is the best which is always picked out for destruction. But one ought not to jump to conclusions. Out here I believe one feels these disasters less than one would at home. If one thinks at all (which rarely happens) one feels that we are all living so entirely on the edge of doom, so liable at any moment to fall in with the main procession, that the order of going seems less important, the only text that comes into my mind at these times is "Let determined things to destiny take unbewailed their way" – I think from *Antony and Cleopatra*, isn't it?

Poor sweet Letty, I can well imagine her misery, and your darling labours to soften it and "get her right", she is lucky indeed to have such a comforter. As your way is, you put your finger on the core of all such miseries as hers – the conviction that love is over for life. And this I suppose you dare not even begin to displace or discredit in her mind. How right you are to go on claiming and expecting new love and new life, until physical decay throws us all back upon memories and ghosts and fables and films of the past. It seems hard to believe that time and chance which happens to all men can happen to you.

"For thy eternal beauty shall not fade
"Nor lose possession of that fair"

– and yet I suppose it will happen; but it has given me the worst twinge I have had in the War to think of the children not turning round to look at you any more.

Oh dear, this is a maudlin graveyard kind of letter, not at all what I meant to write. But after living in the same clothes for a fortnight one has no self-respect left, either physical or intellectual.

. . . Your letters are flowers in this noisy desert.

To K. A.
3rd Grenadier Guards,
B.E.F.
10 July 1916

. . . I agree with you about the utter senselessness of war, but I do not think about it even so often as one day in seven; one of its chief effects being to make one more callous shortsighted and unimaginative than one is by nature. It extends the circle of one's acquaintance, but beyond that I cannot see that it has a single redeeming feature. The suggestion that it elevates the character is hideous. Burglary, assassination, and picking oakum would do as much for anyone.

I'm glad that Frances pitched into Margot about the 'heartlessness' stunt. As a result I got quite a sensible letter from her (Margot) – the 2nd I have received from Downing Street since the War began. I answered it promptly and at considerable length, but I don't flatter myself that anyone but Margot's maid will read what I wrote. I also got last night a parcel of socks from Frances with your note inside and the frozen eau de cologne, which is very refreshing . . .

We are in the front line now and have 2 more days there, then 2 days in support, and then I think 8 days rest further back. One gets terribly tired of one's clothes after 16 days without a change. One dozes off in the day time with a pleasant humming in one's ears which makes one dream of woods and hay fields in England and when one wakes one finds that it is a covey of bluebottles quarrelling over a bit of bully beef that some blasé private has flung into the trenches.

Yesterday I saw a very handsome fly with a bottle green bodice and magenta skirt. This is the nearest I can get to a pretty woman . . .

To K. A.
3rd Grenadier Guards,
B.E.F.
12 July 1916

This is just a line to say that things are going on quite normally here. A little shelling this morning while I was shaving outside my dug-out, so that I had twice to stop and comb the mud out of my hair, but it soon calmed down. Great rewards are offered for catching a Hun alive and we do our best by patrolling every night between the trenches, but in vain; they don't come out . . .

I have heard from Bluey who says characteristically "your father has made a fatal mistake in putting L. G. at the War Office", and from Patrick who seems to be having an agreeable unadventurous kind of picnic with the French at Salonica . . .

To K. A.
3rd Grenadier Guards,
B.E.F.
15 July 1916

. . . I found a delicious cargo of luxuries awaiting me here – scent and morphia and marmalade and cold chicken and a really admirable ham for which Mrs. Gould[1] deserves quite full marks. The night before we went out we had a game of trench baccarat. Sloper and I got in 3 officers of the Scots Guards and we made ourselves rather drunk and gambled and argued about Germany and St Paul's and all the things drunken Scotchmen talk about – including Scotland – from dinner till dawn. I won quite a lot of money, but I don't suppose I shall ever get paid as there was a good deal of confusion and in the end the score blew away into a wet shell hole. But it was rather amusing while it lasted. I have sent £50 to your account at the bank by the way, which I hope will keep your head above water for the moment.

The news from the South continues to be good, and I hear from G.H.Q. that they believe the Germans have only 3 divisions in reserve in the West and 2 in the East. If this is so it looks as if we were pretty near the end.

[1] The cook at Mells, who survived till 1975.

275

You seem to be living a very fast life with McKenna and McEvoy. It is too bloody the way artists make guys of beautiful women and goddesses of plain ones. If he has really bitched Diana and Helen both, we must write him off as a painter . . .

To **K. A.**
3rd Grenadier Guards,
B.E.F.
16 July 1916

. . . Now we are out of the trenches, I suppose it is permissible to tell you that we were the left battalion of the British Army and had a brigade of French territorials on our left, separating us from the *Braves Belges*. I went along to see the French once or twice. They were pleasant enough, but rather nervous, taking themselves and the War very seriously, and whenever they were shelled they used to come into our trenches for company . . .

To **K. A.**
3rd Grenadier Guards,
B.E.F.
18 July 1916

. . . I was amazed at your clever little plan for a code. It has occurred ere now to many of the private soldiers and the censors know all about it. One man ingeniously wrote "I am in a place in Belgium; the name has five letters and begins with Y and ends with S; you will find it written inside the flap of the envelope." . . .

To **K. A.**
3rd Grenadier Guards,
B.E.F.
19 July 1916

Many thanks for the pencils which arrived with your letter this morning and seem much less fragile and futile than any I have had before.

I'm glad to hear that Trim repays your attentions, and especially that he smiles. It is the only hope for a baby and a pretty good card to play all through life . . .

The Huns have been rather aggressive of late round here.

Last night they put 500 big shells into Poperinghe 2 miles behind our camp and knocked out Crosse & Blackwell's shop where we get many of our suppers, but it is all in working order again now. Yesterday they flattened out the trenches we occupied during our last 16 days, but they say the casualties were not very serious. This morning they dropped bombs from aeroplanes fairly near the camp and this afternoon they put shrapnel into a lake near here where some of our officers were foolish enough to go for a swim – a risk from which my well-known indifference to aquatics preserves me.

I felt rather bored this morning with the routine of camp life so had the happy idea of being inoculated against para-typhoid which gets one off all duties for 48 hours. So far I feel no ill effects beyond a stiff arm . . .

To Lady Diana Manners   21 July 1916

Except for the banal booming and flashing of the guns one might be at one of those old-fashioned balls in Arthur Grenfell's garden at Roehampton – the same tiresome noise of electricity being generated in the too near foreground, the same scraggy oaks, the same scramble for sandwiches, the same crowd . . . the same band playing the same tunes, the same moon in the same sky.

The Brigadier (John Ponsonby) and the Prince of Wales (your 'future'?) dined with us tonight, and in order to get our last gulp of gaiety before resuming trench warfare tomorrow, we improvised a ball in camp with lights under the trees and open air supper and bagpipes, and all the hackneyed horrors which go with gaiety.

But much as I love these men (and specially Ponsonby) yet I love women so much more (and especially you) and music and dancing so much less and I have been to so many balls and so many trenches that it is a comfort to turn into the first open hut and write to you . . .

To K. A.   21 July

. . . I should like to have seen you all at the canteen trying to prevent Edward looking too garish. We live a sociable life here with a good deal of rather boring cricket, and lots of people to dinner. Last night we had John Ponsonby and tonight the Prince of Wales. The Huns have taken to having silly little air raids in these parts. Every morning at 7 and every evening at 5. There is one going on now. The bombs never come very near us, but bits of our own shells rain through the trees. We usually go in and have tea while this is going on . . . I was sorry to see in today's list the name of Foster Cunliffe, whom I was rather fond of at All Souls, I forget if you knew him – a most agreeable civilised man, very good, but laughing always louder than anybody at one's foulest jokes.

The papers astonish me nowadays – all this fuss about Registration and Home Rule and even Mesopotamia. In time of War you can only judge the quality of a government by the character of its critics, and this one gets nearly full marks by that standard – Carson, Hogg, Markham and Dalziel . . .

To K. A.
3rd Grenadier Guards,
B.E.F.
24 July 1916

. . . It is sweet of you to go on worrying about Derby. All those people seem to me "small and undistinguishable like far off mountains turned into clouds". As for conscientious objectors they are too far beyond the pale to be taken notice of. Besides they will, I hope, all be disfranchised and therefore politically as well as morally and socially negligible. Whatever you may think about War (and no one thinks worse of it than I do) it is fatuous to refuse to fight and yet claim to vote. If I ever go back to Derby I shall be disposed to jettison some of those hard-shelled partisans and rope in a wider and fresher public.

Perhaps it is as well that you are giving up your Canteen work. Staying up at nights makes one more tired in London than in the trenches, because in London there are always things you want to do in the day time, whereas in the trenches you get shot if you do anything to speak of between dawn and dusk – in the Salient anyhow.

Yesterday (Sunday) was very fine and warm. In the afternoon I went for a walk with another fellow to a place called Elverdinghe Chateau not far from here which is used for troops. There is a good big lake in the grounds and I was actually persuaded to bathe in it and found it quite enjoyable. Every now and then one ran into a large carp floating on the surface killed by shell shock. On the way home I practised my botany which I found rather rusty. There are plenty of flowers about here and rather nice trees. I got chicory and corn flowers and poppies and michaelmas daisies and St John's wort, and golden rod and corn cockles, and many kinds of vetches and clovers and some caryophyllaceae which I did not know or could not remember . . .

To K. A.
3rd Grenadier Guards,
B.E.F.
25 July 1916

. . . Do you know that today is the anniversary of our wedding? Nine years it is, as nearly as I can reckon. They seem very short and wonderfully pleasant as one looks back on them. You are sweeter and more lovely even than you were then, my Fawn, and I adore you a million times more and I am not sorry, not a bit. Give my love to Trim.

To K. A.

3rd Grenadier Guards,
B.E.F.
30 July 1916

You wrote me a very sweet letter to celebrate our golden wedding or whatever it is, and as luck would have it I had already written to you in the desired sense without prompting. I think that I have changed in the last 9 years a good deal more than you have, but not as far as you are concerned except for the better. As for you, you have preserved and even accentuated your original flavour and at the same time widened your scope, increased your range and amplified your field of fire. So you have no need to reproach yourself as you do with an excessive stability . . .

The war has become suddenly much more amusing since I last wrote – because for a day or two we have got away from the stereotyped and traditional stagnation and immobility of the Western front, and are really doing in a mild enough form the things one used to read about in military manuals.

Yesterday evening at 7.30 I marched off an advanced party to a station about 8 miles away where we loaded the battalion 1st line transport onto a train – a big business, as we have 70 horses and about 30 waggons and limbers, not to mention boxing rings, bicycles and all the apparatus of cricket and football. About 1.30 a.m. the battalion entrained, the men frightfully crowded in cattle trucks, the officers fairly comfortable 4 to a 2nd class compartment. It didn't look like getting any sleep, but somehow one did – that is the greatest change the War has wrought in me. I can sleep in a luggage rack or on a bicycle pedal.

About 6.30 a.m. we detrained and marched for an hour and a half along a rather pretty road, halting in a field where we were soon overtaken by the cookers and had an excellent breakfast and a rest of an hour or so. Then we marched on for 3 hours under a scorching sun up and down the undulations of chalk downs covered with corn and poppies with lovely woods in the hollows, till we got to a village where we are to spend tonight and most of tomorrow before marching on.

What with steel helmets and gas helmets and all the other paraphernalia which the variety of modern warfare necessitates (to which I see Conan Doyle with characteristic sagacity proposes to add a steel shield weighing 30 lbs.) the men fell out like flies under the terrific weight of their equipment and the fearful glare of the sun. I was marching light myself and did not feel the least tired or even bored at the end of it. Strange considering that for months and months one has hardly had any exercise beyond lifting a glass of old brandy from the table to the lip. One was a little sustained I suppose by an illusion of the romance of war which any kind of movement is enough to create after all these sedentary months. We were doing the same sort of thing as Wellington and Napoleon did – only incomparably better – I mean we do it incomparably better.

The terrific punctuality and excellent quality of the men's breakfasts and dinners – tea and bacon and raspberry jam in precisely the most shady corn field on the line of march, and an Irish stew, which no one would grumble at on a grouse moor, served without a hitch in the farmyard where we were billeted, the sun shining, the air motionless, the drums playing and the guns booming at a safe distance – really the whole thing was most enjoyable. But weather is the secret of everything.

To Lady Diana Manners   30 July 1916

. . . I assure you there has never been anything like the heat we encountered on those poppy-studded uplands. The men fell out like flies, and the pores opened as to the word "Sesame". But my grey hairs – so often the target of your heartless gibes – never turned. I can't tell you the joy of at last, after all these sedentary months, behaving as people do in military textbooks, or in the *Illustrated London News* of 40 years ago – and then at the end of it a clean billet in a farm, with liquor so good that it might be the best cider, and so ambiguous that it might be the worst champagne – stock doves crooning far more pleasantly than shells, white cats licking themselves silently on the summits of gables like fantails and the ecstacy of choosing your own *poussin* in the yard and knowing that it will appear perfectly roasted on the table at 8.15 . . .

To K. A.   3rd Grenadier Guards,
B.E.F.
3 August 1916

Two lines just to tell you that I am well and undamaged, though terribly tired. We have been moving about a great deal lately and digging all night and doing things in the day also.

The heat has been terrific. In the day time one sleeps when one can and drinks what one can. But I have only managed to get 6 hours sleep in the last 3 days and today I degraded myself so far as to drink both lemonade and ginger beer.

It is now 6.30 a.m. and I have just got back from the trenches ready for nothing but sleep. The post goes at 7, so goodnight and good morning.

To K. A.   3rd Grenadier Guards,
B.E.F.
4 August 1916

I haven't written much lately but really I have had no time to spare from drinking and sleeping. The weather has been terrific and the labour unremitting. On

1 Aug. we got up at 4 and left the pleasant village where Sloper and I had lived really comfortably for a couple of days on the best that the countryside could provide, and marched to a wood where we arrived about 9 and went to sleep. After luncheon we all bathed in a cold but fairly clean and green mill-stream, and then waited again in the wood for some motor lorries which were supposed to pick us up at 5. They didn't come till 9 and then we drove for hours through a dark country along incredibly dusty roads constantly losing our way.

About 3 a.m. we arrived on a rolling down country, rather like the uplands of Hants or Wilts and there bivouacked; which consists on lying on a rather wobbly bit of ground under a bath-towel stretched over a towel horse. Luckily it was too hot rather than too cold. We rose again at 7 and the officers rode 4 or 5 miles to a ruined sugar-factory where we left our horses and walked up to the line through miles of twisting communication trenches.

We got back for luncheon at 2, and at 7 we took our men up and began digging out a trench which had been blown in during the recent fighting. It was a tiresome job, very little room to work and every now and then the Germans sent over a trench mortar bomb – to my mind the most alarming things in this war. It is a thing about the size and shape of a very big rum jar, has a range of 400 yards or so and goes very high and very slow. At night you see it slowly elbowing through the stars with a trail of sparks behind it, and the probability is that the trench is too full for you to get as far away as you would wish. Then it falls and fizzes for a little in the ground and then the most ear-splitting explosion you can ever hope to hear.

This night I was up at the forward end of this trench, rather engrossed in directing the men's work, when suddenly I found myself surrounded by a mob of terrified figures from the battalion which was holding that part of the line (we were only working on it) who gibbered and crouched and held their hands over their eyes and generally conducted themselves as if the end of the world was at hand. It was very alarming; they had seen one of these damned rum jars coming and I hadn't. Sure enough in about 5 seconds the thing went off – luckily just the other side of our parapet. The sky was black with smoke and dirt, and the people butted into one in the fog screaming, but much more frightened than hurt.

The explosion was as painful as a sound can be. In the moment immediately preceding it I made up my mind I was dead, and in the moment immediately following I said to myself "I suppose this is shell shock at last, now I shall get home. But it wasn't. The cracking of one's ear drums is painful and the extraordinary tension in the air and pressure on one's head and a smell which I can only describe as the smell of infinite force. And then one found after all that one was not much the worse. I felt a piece of the thing hit me on the leg, but alas it only made a small blood blister. I picked another fragment out of the shoulder of my jacket – it had cut through the khaki but not through my shirt, and there was quite a big dent in my steel helmet. A most disappointing result. I don't know why I tell you all this. These new sensations are interesting to oneself at the time, but very boring I fear in narrative.

We got back for breakfast about 6 a.m. and I went to bed at 7 in my bivouac. One feels greatly tired after these nights of digging and a march of 6 miles or so each way. And as soon as one gets to bed the heat and noise begin, so that really one gets very little sleep. Then yesterday we went up again and did much the same thing. But this afternoon I felt slightly more bobbish and strong enough to write you a diary of our proceedings.

If it weren't for the heat and weariness and lack of shade and sleep parts of it have been quite pleasant. Our rest and bathe e.g. en route, and a lovely chateau near the bathing place with the ruins of an abbey and cloisters in the grounds, which some of us went to see. And the first part of our wait for the motor lorries wasn't so bad. We lay out in a cool field and the drums played and the men sang choruses and about 20 French children sprang up out of the ground and began dancing with extraordinary skill and brio to the popular tunes. But one got terribly tired of it before the lorries arrived. I wish I had more stamina. But really there are patches in this War which are a higher test even than talking to Lady Queensberry at dinner. We shall probably be doing this spade work for another 4 or 5 days and then I hope we shall have a little rest.

I am not favourably impressed by what I have seen of the 'K' [itchener] armies in this part of the line. I daresay they go ahead all right in an attack, but they are horribly nervous under the ordinary conditions of trench warfare . . .

The Australian attack at Fauquissart (our old line in the winter) was a great disaster. Entirely owing to the folly of generals who, I fear, have not suffered for it, and the official communiqué was allowed to pass it off as a moderately successful trench raid instead of an utter failure by 2 divisions . . .

To K. A.   3rd Grenadier Guards,
                                                              B.E.F.
                                                      8 August 1916

After the first night's rest for 10 days or so I feel more capable of writing a letter than of late, though there is very little to report. We went on night after night marching 5 or 6 miles up to some rather bad trenches which we had to improve. We used to start about 7.30 p.m. after an early dinner and march over flat open country under the setting sun for about 4 miles to a point where we entered the hindmost of the vast maze of communication trenches which heads up to and around the front line. Usually as we approached this point we were spotted by a German balloon or aeroplane which dropped lights to signal to the guns which began loosing off in a desultory kind of way about 5 minutes afterwards, usually just after we had reached cover when it was pleasant enough to hear the shells whistling overhead on to the road behind us.

Then we wandered for ages through the widening trenches constantly losing our temper and our way till we got to a dump where we picked up tools and sandbags etc., and then advanced to the scene of operations. We would get there usually about 10.30 p.m., sometimes an hour or so later and work for 4 hours under rather adverse circumstances, bodies of engineers constantly forcing their way past us carrying long boards, pit props, dug-out frames, and swearing horribly. The trenches we dug in ran out to what had been our front line but it is now (since the crumping it has had during the last month) only a series of isolated posts held or not held as the case may be by nervous and incompetent groups of the new Army.

The first night I found I had nothing at all between me and the Germans except a few dead men whom I found while reconnoitering, so I had to send out a covering party of my own as well as digging. I had to borrow some bombs from the battalion which ought to be there and they got into serious trouble for not covering us and for the remaining nights they took measures to do so. Luckily we were not molested by the enemy except for a few trench mortar shells and rifle grenades. But it was disagreeable, tiring and rather nervous work, as we couldn't possibly have held the line we were in if we had been attacked, and should have had some difficulty in falling back upon any other.

Then about 2.30 a.m. we would deposit our tools and march back, arriving in camp about 5. We breakfasted on an oil sheet on a high curve of the downs, eating our bacon under the rising sun, dog tired but listening at ease to the noise of the harmless guns, which never ceases in these parts. Then one would creep into one's bivouac and do one's best to sleep till luncheon, not always with success owing to heat, flies and noise. (The lotion you sent me by the way is excellent against mosquitoes). Then luncheon, then another attempt at sleep, then dinner about 6.30 and the same old round again.

Yesterday we marched about 5 miles to a camp in a wood further back. I got a good night's rest on a stretcher in a tent and this morning we have done nothing but a little bayonet fighting. I would willingly stay here for a bit where it is cool and peaceful, we were promised a fortnight's rest but orders have just come in that we are to move again tomorrow. The division is going into the line, but this battalion will only be in support to begin with. We are supposed to be in a Reserve Army, but it appears to be rather less reserved than one might have hoped from the name. However no one really knows what is going to happen. We have repulsed (yesterday) 5 counter-attacks on Pozieres and all the Staffs are very sanguine and say that we are going to 'break through' whatever that means.

In the circumstances there seems to be no chance at all of leave re-opening for some time yet. I have had no letters for 3 days and there is an ugly rumour that the post is stopped for a week in order that the ships may bring shells instead of letters.

To K. A.   3rd Grenadier Guards,
                                                              B.E.F.
                                                         9 August 1916

. . . Last night I dined with the Brigadier – an excellent party and very gay. I sat between Frank Mildmay whom you may remember in far off days when we used to mix with the Cowpers and such like (he is now a Lt. Col. in some obscure capacity on a Corps staff) and Valentine Castlerosse who jilted Libby and insulted Edward but is all the same a very pleasant companion and has some of the best and biggest cigars in Europe. He gave me several of these and also a nice tame horse to ride back on at midnight.

I wish one could form any idea as to whether our offensive is being a success or not. People here think that it is, but I hear from Bluey that Winston pronounces it to be a murderous failure.

The King came to see us this morning, looking as glum and dyspeptic as ever . . .

To K. A.   3rd Grenadier Guards,
                                                              B.E.F.
                                                        11 August 1916

The last 2 nights we have slept in tents on the top of a highish hill about 2 miles behind the line – rather a pleasant spot on a fine evening, meals served on packing cases out of doors and so little to do that yesterday I was able to have breakfast in bed or rather in the bloodstained stretcher in which I usually lie on these occasions. This morning we have moved back about a mile to another camp, lower down and not so nice. But it is a much more comfortable way of being "in support" than we are accustomed to. In the Salient being in support was very little better than being in the front line . . .

To K. A.   3rd Grenadier Guards,
                                                              B.E.F.
                                                        14 August 1916

Your gifts are as various as, and far more valuable than those of Caspar, Melchior and Balthazar. The socks look very soft and alluring. The treacle tart was in excellent condition and won loud applause at our subterranean dinner table last night. My own view has always been that there should be more treacle in proportion to the pastry. Is there any technical objection to this? You ask about Mrs Gould's cakes, but I can't recollect having had any from her, certainly not for a very long time. Cicely has sent me several of those brown ones, which are quite good, but I think rather less so than they used to be in

Pre-War days. I suspect some economy of material. The kind of cake I like is one which has a good many raisins in it and rather wet almond paste both on the top and surprisingly in the middle.

Yesterday we came into the new line – the best trenches I have ever seen cut narrow and deep into the chalk, and dug-outs which would keep one safe from anything but the very heaviest poundings. The one I am writing in must be quite 20 feet below the surface and has several openings. But of course they have the defects of their qualities; very stuffy and clammy and as dark as hell. This one is a long kind of tunnel. Our Company Headquarters is in the middle of it. Battn. H.Q. at one end and a sort of Orderly Room and telephone place at the other with a couple of kitchens in recesses and bunks let into the walls here and there. You hear distant voices and see candles gleaming far away. It is very weird and reminded me rather of a side show at the White City where you wander about in passages with distorting mirrors on the walls or find yourself on moving footpaths or haunted swings or gazing into the eyes of a tattooed woman. It is also rather like a coal mine, a mortuary, a station on the Two-penny Tube or the murderer's room in the Tussaud Chambers of Horrors . . .

To K. A.   3rd Grenadier Guards,
                                                                                      B.E.F.
                                                                        18 August 1916

. . . We had just settled the men in and sat down to luncheon in a very nice green mess tent when the damnable sound of an approaching howitzer shell smote our ears. We looked at one another with sickly smiles each holding an oily sardine suspended half way between the cup and the lip while the thing came slowly through the air. One's ear gets very delicate in these matters after a certain amount of practice and it was obvious to all that as far as direction was concerned the shell was coming straight for our tent; the only question was whether it would be short or over or just right. There were 4 tables in the tent, one for each company. Sloper and I were at the one nearest the enemy and at first I thought we were going to have the worst of it and then it became clear that there was just enough kick in the shell that would take it on at least as far as the other side of the tent say 30 feet away, and then came the bang. The tent swayed about and rattled with mud and stones and the 4 officers at the far table threw themselves flat on the floor. There was no harm done. It had gone another 30 feet or so beyond the tent.

Then other shells began bursting short of us where the main tents were and we dashed out to get the men away from the camp and separate them up into groups in the adjacent fields, taking the best cover we could get. There was not a great number of shells really but where there are a lot of men in a small open space, shelling seems (and is) more dangerous. However we got them all out with only 3 killed and then there was a very boring period while we waited about with our platoon and without our lunch in fairly heavy rain until it should be thought safe to return. It was 4 o'clock as a matter of fact before we were again sitting down to our sardines.

At 6.30 I was ordered to take out a dozen N.C.O.s to reconnoitre various ways out of the village up to the trenches. Just as we had finished our job and begun getting back the shelling began again with greater vigour than before. It was rather disagreeable having to march back in the sunset into the middle of the cannonade. The shells were falling all about the camp and the houses and the hollow in which the village lay was full of dust and fumes and rolling clouds of smoke. When we got to the camp we found that everyone had left it for shelter in the fields, so we went on and rejoined our platoons and after about ½ an hour the shelling stopped and the C.O. decided to move off to another bivouac in a safe position. We had just time for a hasty dinner off an excellent ham which Frances had sent and which arrived most felicitously and then we marched away about a mile to a site where we had bivouacked about 10 days ago unmolested. We managed to get to bed soon after midnight and spent a peaceful and comfortable night.

I have made rather a story out of all this as I always do. There was nothing much in it really, except the damnable inconvenience of the noise beginning twice exactly at meal times, and as usually happens when there is shelling we were all more frightened than hurt. We are staying here till Monday when we move further back for a couple of days, and then move further South again. After that our destinies are uncertain, but from what I hear I should doubt if we shall be in the line again for a fortnight or 10 days . . .

To K. A.   3rd Grenadier Guards,
                                                                              B.E.F.
                                                                  22 August 1916

I have 2 or 3 letters from you which I have not had time to answer. I was delighted with them all and also with the photographs. Trim looks as if he might turn out very presentable. I see a distinct likeness to your father, not at all a bad model. Perdita grows more and more like Voltaire, with her heavy lids and sagging lines of satire from nose to mouth – also not a bad model. Helen hardly does herself justice in profile. I always enjoy pictures of the Manor House and Church . . .

I wrote yesterday to the P.M. telling him frankly that [J. H.] Thomas knows much more about Derby than he does or even Gulland and asking him to get a move on in the matter. Whether or not this will promote good feeling I don't know. I also took the opportunity of pointing out that my last quarter's allowance is now nearly 2 months overdue, so I hope that I may soon be able to send you another cheque poor child.

If Margot talks any more bosh to you about the inhumanity of her step-children you can stop her mouth by telling her that during my 10 months exile here the P.M. has never written me a line of any description. I don't see why he should. He has plenty of other things to do; and so have I . . .

To Lady Diana Manners   22 August 1916

. . . I like your fears of deterioration – bad masters, but excellent servants – and (like all servants) never so officious as when you least need their services. If only I were with you how quickly and firmly I could put them in their place. Candidly, my darling Dian – and not merely because of your divine charity to me this last week or so – you seem to me to have been adding every day a string or two to your bow; and bows, unlike broth, in this respect can hardly be spoiled by too many. As for your body I know it to be perfect in every cell, and certain to remain so if not for all time, for all the time that counts. And for me, and I believe for all who have seen you as you are, with eyes not bunged by cant, or fat, or age, you have spiked the guns of change and chance, and anchored in all our hearts a steady image of inviolate loveliness, which no weather can ever stain nor wind disturb. And I believe too that the acutest of your sensibilities is enlarged, and every channel of feeling deepened but not cheapened. As to your mind, have no fears or doubts. You say that it is a labour to read. Of course it is – there is no surer sign of intellectual progress than the increasing difficulty with which one reads a book, and no more certain symptom of decay than the easy acclamation of masterpieces. Believe me, a half-disgusted adoration of the best is the last reward of finished scholarship.

I know, no one better, the feeling of effort of which you speak. But our minds are not asleep because they do not wink and chatter all the time. Better a Lapland night than the dance of St Vitus. Think for one moment of those who find it no effort to talk. Their minds are almshouses where outworn notions and wrinkled phrases and a host of dilapidated pensioners flaunt their threadbare fustian in the sun, and fight again their burlesque battles with purblind eyes and blunted swords over the shadow of a shade of nothing. We do not hunt the carted hares of 30 years ago. We do not ask ourselves and one another and every other poor devil we meet "How do you define Imagination?", or "What is the difference between talent and genius?", and score an easy triumph by anticipating the answer with some text-book formula, originally misconceived by George Wyndham in the early eighties at Glen, and almost certainly misquoted by Margot in the late nineties at the borrowed house of a Frankfort baronet, not because it was either true or witty or even understood, but because it was a sacred obligation to respect whatever struck the late Sir Charles Tennant as a cut above what he had heard in the night school at Paisley where they taught him double-entry – we don't do these things – but don't be discouraged my Diana, for all that. The game is not up. There are brains and brains. The one that can so easily produce your letters is good enough for me, and far too good for most.

I worship the clearness of your vision, I think that you see further and quicker than almost anyone; but I do not agree that there is nothing to unravel. For my own part I feel that there is hardly anything that I understand; but then there is hardly anything that anyone *can* understand. It is not for you and me to make our fingers bleed by picking the oakum of metaphysics, but if anyone has the fancy to speculate in a well-bred manner between the chinks, I am his man or hers.

. . . I have given you no facts as yet, of which for a wonder there is a certain supply to hand. But I cannot end I suppose without telling you that the day before yesterday Basil Hallam[1] was killed before my eyes by falling 6000 ft. or so from an escaped balloon. He came to earth in a village ½ a mile from where I stood, falling a few yards from Mark Tennant, shockingly foreshortened, but recognisable by his cigarette case. His companion descended more gradually by parachute just the right side of the German lines, over which the empty balloon drifted. I saw Edgy Knollys today, who had come from burying him. A frightening death, even to look at. I do not know how sad this will make you, I hope not too sad. But I cannot say.

To K. A.   3rd Grenadier Guards,
                                                                          B.E.F.
                                                              24 August 1916

I have just got your letter dated Sunday August 19th (which should be 20th but I like any date better than none). I agree with you it is ghastly the "cabinet" being "filmed". But certainly Harmsworth has no right to say so. It is just the kind of thing he has always maintained will win the war. If they must do it they had much better get Iris [Tree] to take the part of the P.M. and Sybil [Hart-Davis] pose as A. J. B.

I can't tell you the joy of getting into a house at last after this life of trenches and dug-outs, huts and tents and bivouacs. Last night we had an absolutely bloody camp, the worst I have seen yet. All the officers slept together in a hut with a canvas roof, through which the rain poured in on a floor of hard mud littered with the leavings of poultry, and just as I was going to bed a mole ran out from under my pillow and then ran in again.

We had to get up at 4 a.m. in the dark and wet and marched off – the whole division together – at 7. The weather cleared and we had a fine and fairly cool march of 12 miles or so pretty nearly due South through a very comely bit of country with hills and woods and fields of undulating corn. About noon we finished up in a biggish rather pretty village with an oldish rather pretty church. Sloper and I found an excellent billet in a cottage with a charming little garden

---

[1] An actor and admirer of Diana's.

full of pansies and dahlias and delightfully clean rooms where we have just had lunch. We are out of the sound of the guns and the countryside is smiling and peaceful, and I have seen one rather pretty girl in the village street – such a relief after the sour featured hags one is used to in this country of the middle-aged. The wine is getting better too as we get further South. We push off again tomorrow – by train this time – and I fancy – though no one knows from day to day – that we are likely to be in reserve for a little while yet. You would think it impossible on our limited front to cover as much ground as we have done during the last month. We never stop moving and yet we never seem to arrive anywhere, which is perhaps as well . . .

I am now reading the prefaces to Shaw's plays which I find stimulating. He has the gift of never being quite right about anything. No one who wears jaeger and disbelieves in vaccination ever could be. But he always says a number of true things in a very telling way. How right, e.g. to wipe off the slate those stale and senseless controversies about the exact date of the gospels and the authen-ticity of the miracles. And how true that beliefs are a matter of taste and taste a matter of fashion. This gets rid at once of the old trouble about so many clever men being Xians and the newer one of so many clever men not being Xians. I should like Ford's plays if you can get hold of a small (and cheap) edition, and you might also send me (if you can get a French version of it) *Mafarka Le Futuriste* by Marinetti.

The chief clouds on my horizon at present are (1) the near approach of the harvest – long season – always formidable and in a chalk country like this almost too frightening to be faced and (2) the hardening probability that I shall be let in to defend a brother officer who is to be tried by Court Martial for Homosexual offence at the base. I have drafted what seems to me an extremely moving petition to resign his commission instead of standing his trial and my only hope is that this may melt the heart of authority . . .

To K. A.

3rd Grenadier Guards,
B.E.F.
26 August 1916

. . . I have your letter of Tuesday. It is bad news about Helen being musical, but I am glad she can ride. I think it would be a great mistake for you to become a nurse (unless of course you are driven to it by sheer boredom). After all charity begins at home and you will contribute much more to the com-monwealth by suckling Trim and teaching him how to attract women and Helen and Perdita how to attract men, than by muddling about with com-pound fractures and spiral bandages. Also what would happen to me if I ever did come home on leave? There is talk of it opening again on 1st October, but I daresay it is only nonsense . . .

To Lady Diana Manners   27 August

. . . All the morning I have spent conferring with a bn. officer who wants me to defend him at a Court Martial on a charge of "homosexualism", as these over-educated soldiers persist in misnaming these elementary departures from the strict letters of "Infantry Training 1914". His story seemed a very queer one even to me who esteem myself a man of wide sympathies. But I am hoping to persuade Sir E. Carson to take my place, as I think the situation demands a deeper reservoir of cant than anyone but an Ulster covenanter can extemporarily command . . .

To K. A.   3rd Grenadier Guards,
                                                                    B.E.F.
                                                          2 September 1916

It is days since I wrote you a proper letter but I simply haven't had a moment to myself. This damnable trial has filled every hour with unbearable fatigue. The case was quite hopeless from the beginning but most of the witnesses were fearful liars and in other respects tarred with much the same brush as the accused, so it was possible to have a certain amount of fun cross-examining them. One of the 2 principal ones was a queer fellow in the Irish Guards who had been, I think, a quack doctor in peace time and a soldier of fortune whenever there was any kind of a war going on, a tiresome officious puritanical creature full of the missionary and detective spirit and apparently with a bee in his bonnet about the corruption and decadence of the English upper classes and particularly of Etonians.

The other was a nephew of Robert Ross, lately a scholar at Eton, who aroused everyone's suspicions by knowing Latin and Greek and constantly reading Henry James' novels. He was not ill-looking but with an absurdly cushioned figure and a rather hysterical temperament more like a girl than a boy. He was the accomplice who turned King's Evidence.

The others were queer grey-faced untruthful boys who saluted like guardsmen when they entered and left the room, but shuffled and stammered most uneasily in the witness box. There were 5 charges, and the Court sat (at Divisional H.Q.) for 2 days. 6 hours the first day and 10 the 2nd. We jogged over there on horses in the early morning and back again after dark. I found the unusual strain of concentrating one's mind on a – by now – unfamiliar kind of effort, most tiring – especially the 2nd day when I had to speak for about an hour and a half in the twilight. I think I gave the unfortunate boy a run for his money, but we both knew that there was not a dog's chance. They announced last night after some deliberation that they had found him guilty of something, but we shall not know on how many of the charges until the findings are confirmed by Haig and after that the sentence will be announced. He is certain, I imagine, to be turned out of the Army. It was a queer experience and now it is over, I am not sorry that I went through it, though I was very sorry at the time.

Anyhow all the authorities have given me good marks for bearing the burden and I have been allowed 24 hours leave to go into the cathedral city of —— [i.e. Amiens] some 20 miles from here this afternoon where I shall at any rate get sheets and baths and a good bottle of wine. I have also been offered a place on the staff of the Guards Division. I told them I would like to take it when the weather begins to break up. At present it is still hot and the flies are most annoying and are spreading an epidemic of mild dysentery said to be conveyed from the captured German lines. A whole German Corps is supposed to be down with it. I have had a touch myself, but am all right again now.

You seem to be having a pretty busy time with your children and their nutrition and education. Trim ought to be a terrific fellow after all this suckling. Many thanks for the razor blades and watch strap etc. And please thank Frances for the marmalade and treacle tart – the latter specially excellent. Mells must be rather pleasant now among the hollyhocks and dahlias. It is wonderful to have reached September without getting involved in this battle. Another 2 months and the pushing season will be over . . .

To K. A.

3rd Grenadier Guards,
B.E.F.
4 September 1916

. . . I'm glad you approved my contribution to Ettie's book – an almost impossible thing to write even tolerably and probably, after she has doctored it, even less presentable than it originally was. She told me that she was going to cut out a bit in which I had said that Billy was insolent (as he most assuredly was) and as far as I recollect, the excision is bound to make nonsense of some of the least infelicitous paragraphs. She also told me that she was going to put in Dunrobin and some of Bron's houses as places where B and J and I had had fun together – which perhaps lends some colour to your charge of snobbery. As a matter of fact Ettie is a snob in the same simple harmless sense as Patrick [Shaw Stewart]. She meant to give her sons the best mise-en-scène from a worldly point of view which could be had and I suppose she wants people to know that she succeeded as she certainly did. She promised me the book but has not sent it – probably it is too big to travel.

I had a pleasant enough sojourn in A[miens]. Oliver and I and Sloper got the Prince to lend us his car. We went in on Saturday afternoon, got excellent rooms with soft beds and hot baths, and had several very well cooked meals and some drinkable champagne. The town was seething with other officers from the division and we rollicked about on Saturday night visiting the ladies of the town who provided a certain amount of amusement, but without (you will be glad to hear) any loss of chastity on my part or indeed on that of most of my companions.

Cn Sunday night we drove back again and today in rain and wind have resumed the ordinary drudgery and beastliness of life. It was pleasant to get back even for 24 hours to the decencies and indecencies of civilisation. The cathedral is very beautiful, but the first thing one instinctively looked at on seeing it was the sandbag barricade in front of the doors to see whether it was properly built according to the classical canons of trench architecture.

Tomorrow we have a Brigade Field Day. Yesterday there was a successful British attack on Ginchy and Guillemont and if they capture Lenze-Wood (I don't know yet whether they have done or not) comparatively open fighting may set in.

We have been put at 3 hours notice to move, but that happens so often that I don't think it means anything. The French as usual have got on much quicker and further than we have – on our right. Everything seems to point to the Huns really going back some distance, perhaps 15 or 20 miles, shortening their line and taking up a new position roughly on the line from Lille to Cambrai. If they can be effectively harassed during the process it may make a good deal of difference . . .

To Lady Diana Manners

5 September 1916

Your lyric moan about Basil gave me an excuse for thinking of you even more tenderly than is my wont. One after another your loves are stricken by the shafts of fate, as the children of Niobe by the arrows of Apollo because they were fairer than the children of God . . . As for me, I suppose that if ever I get another chance I shall remind you, as you suggest, of the 'proximity of the grave' –

> 'The grave's a fine and private place
> 'But few I think do there embrace.'

– always one of my favourite couplets. And yet I half hope that I shan't. A caress loses much (though not all) of its value when it is no more than the conclusion of a syllogism. You should kiss people because you want to, not because if you don't do it today there may be no time tomorrow. Though I agree, that if the impulse is there the arguments may irrefutably reinforce it. You have always to remember that after all there may be any amount of time tomorrow, unless like Cleopatra, you take damned good care that there shan't be.

I had two terribly strenuous days last week – 10 hours each before a Court Martial defending a brother officer upon 5 charges of "homosexualism" – unsuccessfully. It was terribly tiring but not entirely unenjoyable as it was easy to make fools of most of the witnesses (though not unfortunately as to the facts to which they testified) and I wound up by making a speech of considerable length in which I wavered between being a blunt soldier and a cynical barrister, plunging rather recklessly from one extreme of idiom to another. I can tell you it takes some nerve to say to a bevy of flint-faced brigadiers "When one contemplates the picture of ——— (chief witness for prosecution) padding down the duck-boards in the twilight with muffled feet and gimlet eyes to spy upon the privacy of a brother officer, one asks oneself whether even the missionary spirit has ever exhibited itself in a more repulsive and ridiculous guise." However, as a reward for my services I was given 24 hours' leave to Amiens and whipped off there with 2 or 3 others, in young Wales' excellent Daimler on Saturday afternoon. We ate and drank a great deal of the best, slept in downy beds, bathed in hot perfumed water, and had a certain amount of restrained fun with the very much once-occupied ladies of the town. I took a particular fancy to a perfect *femme du monde*, with a voice as hoarse as the late Lady Westmoreland's, and a skin distinctly less exhausted who entertained a dozen of us for an hour or more with talk and sweet champagne and all manner of lingeries . . .

To K. A.

3rd Grenadier Guards,
B.E.F.
7 September 1916

Our 5 minutes notice to move has been cancelled again, as one guessed it would be, and we are continuing our strenuous training. Yesterday we had a Brigade Field Day under John Ponsonby illustrating all the newest and most elaborate methods of capturing German trenches with the minimum of casualties. It involved getting up at 5 a.m. but in other respects was funny enough. The "creeping barrage" i.e. the curtain of shell fire which moves on about 50 yards in front of the advancing infantry, was represented by drummers. The spectacle of the whole four battalions moving in lines across the cornfields at a funeral pace headed by a line of rolling drums, produced the effect of some absurd religious ceremony conducted by a tribe of Maoris rather than a brigade of Guards in the attack. After it had gone on for an hour or two I was called up by the Brigadier and thought at first that I must have committed some ghastly military blunder (I was commanding the Company in Sloper's absence) but was relieved to find that it was only a telegram from the corps saying "Lieut. Asquith will meet his father at cross roads K.6d at 10.45 a.m." So I vaulted into the saddle and bumped off to Fricourt where I arrived exactly at the appointed time. I waited for an hour on a very muddy road congested with troops and lorries and surrounded by barking guns. Then 2 handsome motors from G.H.Q. arrived, the P.M. in one of them with 2 staff officers, and in the other Bongie, Hankey, and one or two of those moth-eaten nondescripts who hang about the corridors of Downing Street in the twilight region between the civil and domestic service.

We went up to see some of the captured German dug-outs and just as we were arriving at our first objective the Boches began putting over a few 4.2 shells from their field howitzer. The P.M. was not discomposed by this, but the G.H.Q. chauffeur to whom I had handed over my horse to hold, flung the reins into the air and himself flat on his belly in the mud. It was funny enough.

The shells fell about 200 yards behind us I should think. Luckily the dug-out we were approaching was one of the best and deepest I have ever seen – as safe as the bottom of the sea, wood-lined, 3 storeys and electric light, and perfect ventilation. We were shown round by several generals who kept us there for ½ an hour or so to let the shelling die down, and then the P.M. drove off to luncheon with the G.O.C. 4th Army and I rode back to my billets. In the morning I went to an improvised exhibition of the Somme films – really quite excellent. If you haven't seen them in London I advise you to take the earliest opportunity. They don't give you much idea of a bombardment, but casual scenes in and on the way to the trenches are well-chosen and amazingly like what happens.

This morning we did some battalion training. It is certainly much easier and pleasanter commanding a Company than a platoon. You tell your subordinates what to do and then canter about the country damning them for not doing it.

Tonight we do some operations in the dark and tomorrow another brigade field day. The books and food you speak of have not yet arrived, but I have received 3 cakes of 'Violette' soap which smells very good.

The weather has become lovely again – bright sun with a touch of autumnal crispness in the air . . .

To K. A.   3rd Grenadier Guards,
                                                                    B.E.F.
                                                       8 September 1916

. . . We move either tomorrow or the day after. Probably tomorrow. We are only allowed 50 lbs. of kit, which is a bore. It would be awful to arrive in Berlin looking a perfect scarecrow. The noise of the bombardment makes me feel quite sick. I am so sorry for the wretched Hun . . .

To K. A.   3rd Grenadier Guards,
                                                                    B.E.F.
                                                      12 September 1916

After a long interval I have 3 letters from you today – one sweeter than another. By the way, the letter you enclosed from the Professor contained a fine fat dewdrop for you. After saying how poor all the letters of condolence in Ettie's book are he goes on "There's one letter better than all the rest, quite beautiful and simple, by your wife. She takes the only prize." I have always thought you first-rate in prose as well as in verse, my sweetly clever Fawn. Your other enclosure – the light bill – I will discharge forthwith. Thank you very much for the Ford plays which also came today. Then I have got a nice parcel of food, Lux, tinned grapes, honey etc. Diana tells me she sent some – I don't know if this lot is hers or yours. Anyhow very good.

My client in the Court Martial was an unfortunate fellow . . . He was convicted on 4 out of the 5 charges and sentenced not only to be cashiered but to serve one year's imprisonment – most barbarous I call it. His buttons were cut off in the Orderly room yesterday and he was taken off to Rouen by the military police, poor devil. His father was killed earlier in the war and he is the 6th consecutive generation of his family to hold a commission in the Grenadiers.

Your suggestion about leave to Paris may turn out to be feasible later on, but not till this push is over. A few lucky ones managed to get there last week, Sloper among them – but it is stopped for the present. I believe it is not difficult for women to go, but rather uncomfortable as I think they have to go round by Havre. It would be great fun if we could bring it off. Don't worry, my pretty, about money and never mind if you don't succeed in letting Bed. Sq. I have several hundred pounds worth of Exchequer bonds which I can sell at any moment for their full value if we get really short.

I liked your ironical passage about the mosquitoes. As a matter of fact I have been exceptionally lucky this season with the harvest bugs and hardly suffered at all. The flies here are what they call 'a caution'. Nothing seems to have any effect on them. As to the staff, you must see my pretty, that this is hardly the moment for seeking shelter. I don't think I shall have the least difficulty in getting a job whenever I want one. Probably they will keep this place on the division open for me a reasonable time, and anyhow my General at G.H.Q. told me he would always find a billet for me if I wanted one.

It would be not altogether disagreeable to come back and do something at the War Office during the winter months. I am getting terribly tired of not being at home, and not seeing my sweetest Fawnia. But I must see out the fighting season. Tomorrow we shall move forward again, probably into the line. Angel, I send you all my love. Remember me to Trim.

[V]

Epilogue

In the great movement of 15 September the Guards Division advanced from Ginchy on Lesboeufs. As one commentator put it, 'their front of attack was too narrow, their objectives were too distant, and from the start their flanks were enfiladed. It was not until the second advance on the 25th that Lesboeufs was won.'

In his last letter to Diana Manners, written the day before the attack, Raymond hinted that his own chances of survival were small. In the event, seventeen out of the twenty-two officers in his battalion who took part in it were either killed or wounded. One of the few who escaped unscathed was the adjutant, Oliver Lyttelton, who together with Sir Iain Colquhoun, so recently defended by Raymond, collected an assortment of Grenadiers, Scots and Irish Guards and pressed on through the heavy and confused fighting to occupy an extremely advanced and exposed position. They were eventually forced to retire when the Germans counter-attacked in overwhelmingly superior numbers. In the words of the regimental history of the Grenadiers, 'Captain Lyttelton, finding himself surrounded, threw his empty revolver at the Germans; thinking it was a Mills bomb, they ducked, and gave him time to scramble out of the trench and escape.'

Almost at the outset of the advance, Raymond was hit by a bullet in the chest while leading the first half of No. 4 Company into the attack. An eye-witness recorded that in order to prevent his men from knowing the worst at once, Raymond lit a cigarette after he fell, before being given morphia by the Regimental Medical Officer. He was carried to the dressing station on a stretcher, but died, without further pain, before reaching it. He was buried not far away, and his soldier servant, Needham, who was present, added that 'there was a frightful bombardment in progress'. He added in a letter to Katharine that 'such coolness under shell fire as Mr. Asquith displayed would be difficult to equal'. The tributes that were paid to his courage and sang-froid were by no means confined to the privileged circle in which so much of his life had been spent. Another private soldier in his platoon wrote home to an old schoolmaster at Walworth Vicarage in south London: 'There is not one of us who would not have changed places with him if we had thought that he would have lived, for he was one of the finest men who ever wore the King's uniform, and he did not know what fear was.' And eighteen months later, Raymond's father received a letter from a complete stranger saying 'It chanced that, travelling through the Midlands the other day in a crowded railway carriage, an NCO of the Grenadiers chatting to another soldier mentioned the occasion when your son was killed, and added "He was the finest officer I ever served under". I thought you would like to know this as it was a spontaneous remark of an NCO who, I gathered, had been a regular before the outbreak of war.'

At the other end of the chain of command, Lord Cavan, the divisional commander with whom Raymond had dined a few weeks before, wrote to Katharine that 'Raymond died in the greatest of all the war achievements of the Brigade of Guards', while Brigadier Ponsonby, his brigade commander wrote: 'What I think struck most of us out here was the extreme modesty and the really entire unselfishness in the way he never thought of himself . . . [In the front trenches] I know he was one of the officers who really did work all night and most of the day . . . He was always in such good spirits and saw the funny side of everything even when things got rather hot . . . Most of his friends in his battalion and in the Brigade have now gone – either killed or wounded or sick but those of us who are left will always remember his charming personality and his very gallant conduct under fire.'

His will, made before he left for France the previous October, consisted of two sentences: 'I give the whole of my property to my wife Katharine, absolutely. If any of my friends would like books or other things of mine for remembrance, she will know what to give and to whom.' The letters of sympathy from her friends all naturally harped on the theme that 'no one gave up more, or gave it up better, than Raymond'. Many friends also wrote that the intensity of their own loss gave them an inkling of how far greater, and how unbearable, hers must be. Gilbert Murray added that when he had examined Raymond for the Ireland at Oxford it had been his personality even more than his scholarship that had impressed him so unforgettably. Aubrey Herbert, with striking simplicity, wrote 'It is always best to be brave, and now there is nothing else, but who has had to give what you have given?'; the reaction of Maurice Baring was that 'R. having gone will make it more difficult for everyone who knew him to bear the war – and yet, dearest Katharine, I feel his death to be the most triumphant of all his brilliant achievements . . . only there is no one who ever lived who will be so much missed.' A strange episode was recorded in another letter of sympathy, from the novelist Edith Olivier: 'Some years ago I was very distressed over a servant girl who was to be tried for the murder of her child. Sir John Simon introduced me to Mr. Asquith who we thought might defend her . . . he said he *believed* he had already been retained as Prosecutor. He said "If this is so of course I shall not communicate with you again, but I shall remember all this." He did prosecute, and made a very fine speech, bringing out all the facts, and in such a way that the girl was acquitted, and on leaving the Court he sent me a telegram to say how glad he was . . . I know that in sorrow (though nothing said by outsiders can really help) yet it is some ease to hear more and more of what, the lost one was, and how he was appreciated.'

> Nothing is here for tears, nothing to wail
> Or knock the breast; no weakness, no contempt,
> Dispraise or blame; nothing but well and fair,
> And what may quiet us in a death so noble.

APPENDIX A

Characters mentioned in the text

BAKER, HAROLD T. Born 1877, R.'s closest friend at Winchester and Balliol. Liberal MP 1910. Financial Secretary to War Office, 1912-15. P.C. 1915. Later Warden of Winchester College, but in spite of intellectual powers achieved surprisingly little in later life. Nicknamed Blue Tooth or Bluey after Harald Blue Tooth, an unappealing figure in one of the Norse sagas.

BARING, HON. MAURICE. 4th son of 1st Lord Revelstoke. Born 1874. Diplomatic Service 1898-1904; Special Correspondent in Manchurian War 1904, in Russia 1905-8, and in Constantinople 1909. Author of many novels, and of plays, poetry and books on Russia. Eccentric and much loved figure. Served on staff of Royal Flying Corps, 1915-18; described by Air Marshal Lord Trenchard as 'the best staff officer there has ever been'. Roman Catholic convert. Died 1945.

BATTERSEA, 1st and last Lord. As Cyril Flower, barrister and Liberal MP, Lord of the Treasury in Gladstone's last government. Early and close friend of H. H. Asquith; married the daughter of Sir Anthony de Rothschild, and was a connoisseur and collector of pictures as well as a keen horseman, winning the House of Commons Steeplechase in 1889.

BERESFORD, ADMIRAL LORD CHARLES. Holder of many senior naval appointments, and introducer of important reforms on the Turf.

BILLING, PEMBERTON. Born 1880. Fought in Boer War, and in Royal Naval Air Service 1914-16. Contested Mile End division 1916 in support of strong air policy. MP (Ind.) East Herts, 1916-21, constantly criticizing Government conduct of the war.

BIRRELL, RT. HON. AUGUSTINE. Born 1850. Holder of various cabinet posts, 1906-16. Formerly Professor of Law, University of London; author of numerous books.

BONHAM-CARTER, MAURICE ('Bongy'). KCB 1916. Born 1880, Balliol contemporary. Barrister 1909. Private Secretary to H. H. Asquith 1910-16; married in 1915 Violet Asquith. Stockbroker with Buckmaster & Moore after the war, and director of other companies.

BRODRICK, HON. ST. JOHN, later 9th Lord Midleton. Unionist Secretary of State for War, and for India, 1900-05. Married Lady Hilda Charteris. Their daughter Sybil married Sir Ronald Graham.

BROWNING, OSCAR. Born 1837. Fellow of King's College, Cambridge, 1859, and a master at Eton 1860-75. Author of various books, including Life of Charles XII of Sweden. Known as O.B. Gave rise to the following rhyme, possibly by Raymond:

> O.B., oh be obedient to nature's stern decrees,
> Or else instead of one O.B. you will be too obese.

BUCKLE, GEORGE E. Born 1854. Fellow of All Souls College. Editor of *The Times* 1884-1912; biographer of Disraeli.

BUXTON, SYDNEY, later 1st Earl. Held posts in governments between 1892 and 1914. Governor-General of South Africa 1914–20. His second wife, Mildred Hugh-Smith, appears on p. 124.

CASTLEROSSE, LORD, later well known *bon viveur* and gossip columnist on the *Daily Express*.

CECIL, LORD HUGH. High Tory MP and Churchman. Later Lord Quickswood and Provost of Eton.

DE GREY, LADY. Sister of the 14th Earl of Pembroke, and patroness of the arts, later instrumental in bringing Russian ballet to London. Mother of Lady Juliet Duff. Died 1917.

ELCHO LORD, (Hugo), succeeded in 1914 as 11th Earl of Wemyss. Married Mary, daughter of Hon. Percy Wyndham, MP, a confidante of Arthur Balfour. R. often stayed with the Elchos at Gosford and Stanway. Their daughter Cynthia married Beb Asquith, and their eldest son 'Ego' (b. 1884, killed in April 1916) was a particular friend of R. and K.

FARMER, JOHN. Organist and Director of Music at Balliol, author of Harrow School songs. Died 1901.

FARRER, REGINALD. Balliol contemporary of R.; later a noted botanist and plant collector.

FRY, C. B. England cricketer, boxer and all-round athlete.

GLADSTONE, HERBERT, LORD. Born 1854. 4th son of W. E. Gladstone. Liberal Chief Whip, 1899, later Home Secretary. Married Dolly Paget.

GOSCHEN, 1st Lord. Chancellor of the Exchequer 1887-92, and twice first Lord of the Admiralty. Immortalized by the line 'Goschen has no notion of the motions of the Oceans.'

GRENFELL, MRS W. H. ('Etty'). 1867-1952. Perhaps the most illustrious of all Edwardian hostesses, with political and intellectual, as well as purely social, interests. Daughter of Hon. Julian and Lady Adine Fane. Married 1887, W. H. Grenfell, formidable athlete and sportsman, who stroked an eight across the Channel and twice swam across Niagara; Conservative MP, created Lord Desborough 1908. Their two elder sons, Julian and Billy, were contemporaries of Edward Horner, and were killed in May and July 1915.

HALDANE, RICHARD, 1st and last Viscount. Born 1856. Prize-winning scholar at Edinburgh. Closest early friend and associate of H. H. Asquith at the Bar and in politics. Secretary of State for War 1906-12, largely responsible for what had been done to modernize and strengthen the Army before 1914. Godfather of Perdita Asquith. Lord Chancellor 1912-15, when Asquith reluctantly accepted his resignation under discreditable Unionist pressure on the grounds that Haldane had been partly brought up in Germany, and had studied at Göttingen University. Lord Chancellor again in Labour Government of 1924.

HAY, MAJOR THE HON. ARTHUR, CVO. Commandant of Lower Burma Police, 1887-93. Later Gentleman Usher to Queen Victoria, King Edward VII and King George V.

HEADLAM, G. W., 'Tuppy'. Balliol contemporary; later housemaster at Eton.

HERBERT, AUBERON, ('Bron'). Born 1876, succeeded as Lord Lucas on death of his uncle in 1905. Remained one of R.'s closest friends after Oxford, and was his best man at his wedding. Wounded as War Correspondent in South Africa, he became Under-Secretary for War, and for the Colonies, and by 1914 was President of the Board of Agriculture and a member of the Cabinet. Although aged thirty-nine, transferred from Hampshire Carabiniers into the Royal Flying Corps, and failed to return from a flight over the German lines on 3 November 1916. His father, 'Auberon the Anarchist' (p.36) began his career as Unionist MP for Nottingham in 1870, but developed republican and other increasingly eccentric views, especially on health, which he aired in a newspaper that he founded. Neither is to be confused with Aubrey Herbert, Bron's first cousin.

HERBERT, HON. AUBREY. Born 1880, elder son, by second marriage, of 4th Earl of Carnarvon (Secretary of State for the Colonies, and Lord Lieutenant of Ireland). Balliol contemporary of R., later Unionist MP for Yeovil. Travelled widely, especially in the Balkans, where he became leading British expert. Later offered throne of Albania. Wounded and twice captured in 1914 war, died 1923 after becoming nearly blind.

HERBERT, HON. MERVYN. Born 1882, younger brother of Aubrey. Also ed. Balliol. Played cricket for Somerset, served in Diplomatic Service, d. 1929.

HORNER, SIR JOHN, KCVO. Born 1844. Commissioner of Woods and Forests, 1908. Married Frances, daughter of William Graham (Edinburgh merchant and art collector, close friend of Ruskin and Burne-Jones, by whom Frances was several times painted). The Horners had acquired the Mells estate at the dissolution of Glastonbury Abbey in the 16th century.

HUGHES, RIGHT HON. WILLIAM MORRIS ('This man Hughes', p.255). Became Prime Minister of Australia in 1915, having emigrated from England in 1884.

JEFFREYS, GENERAL LORD, famous military martinet, later Colonel of the Grenadier Guards.

LAWSON, EDWARD, later 1st Lord Burnham. Owner of *The Daily Telegraph*.

LIPTON, SIR THOMAS. Creator of a large fortune in tea, and a generous public benefactor.

LYTTELTON, HON. ALFRED. Born 1857, 8th son of 4th Lord Lyttelton, and a nephew of W. E. Gladstone, but went into politics as a Unionist under the influence of A. J. Balfour. Played cricket and football for England, Secretary of State for the Colonies 1903-5. Married Laura, 3rd daughter of Sir Charles Tennant.

LYTTELTON, OLIVER. Son of the preceding. Adjutant of 3rd Battalion Grenadier Guards, 1915-17. Later a prominent business man, and cabinet minister in Conservative governments after 1951. Married Lady Moira Godolphin Osborne.

MACLEOD, OLIVE. Vice Principal of Newnham College, Cambridge.

MALLOCK, W. H. Author or *The New Republic* and other books.

MANNERS, LORD AND LADY ('Hoppy' and 'Con'). Very close friends of Frances Horner, lived at Avon in the New Forest. R. was particularly fond of Lady Manners, and often stayed with K. at Avon both before and after their marriage. Their son John Manners was killed on 2 September 1914. Their daughter Betty married R.'s brother Oc.

MANNERS, LADY DIANA. Born 1892, youngest daughter of 8th Duke of Rutland. Many of her admirers in first youth were killed in the war; she married in 1919 Duff Cooper, later Viscount Norwich, on the threshold of a successful political career which she helped to finance by appearing, to great acclaim, in Max Reinhardt's *The Miracle*.

MARSH, SIR E. ('Eddie'). Private Secretary to Winston Churchill, *littérateur*, generously encouraged many young artists and authors, including Rupert Brooke. Lent R. and K. his flat in Gray's Inn for the first months of their married life.

MEDD, CUTHBERT ('Cubby'). Close Balliol friend of R. and a poet. Died in 1902.

MILNER, ALFRED. 1st Viscount. Born 1854. Fellow of New College, Oxford, and a barrister. Under-Secretary for Finance in Egypt, 1887-92; High Commissioner for South Africa, 1897-1905; member of War Cabinet without portfolio 1916. Married Violet Maxse, widow of Lord Edward Cecil.

MONTAGU, RIGHT HON. EDWIN, b. 1879, son of 1st Lord Swaything, Lib. MP 1906-22, Under-Sec. of State for India 1910-14, Fin. Sec. to Treasury, 1914-16, Min. of Munitions 1916, Sec. of State for India 1917-22, d. 1924. m. 1915, Hon. Venetia Stanley, q.v.

MORRELL, PHILIP. Born 1870. Brewer; Liberal MP 1906-10. Married Lady Ottoline Cavendish-Bentinck. Close neighbours of R. and K. in Bedford Square.

PLOWDEN, PAMELA. Daughter of Sir Trevor Chichele-Plowden, and much admired by Winston Churchill before his marriage. She later married 1st Earl of Lytton.

RAYLEIGH, LORD, O.M. Distinguished scientist; Nobel Prize winner.

RUNCIMAN, 1ST VISCOUNT. Shipping magnate and Liberal politician. President of the Board of Trade, etc.

RUSSELL, CONRAD. See p. 43.

SELBORNE, 2ND EARL OF. First Lord of the Admiralty, 1900-05.

SMITH, LIONEL. Son of A. L. Smith (later Master of Balliol). Fellow of All Souls College, and later of Magdalen. International hockey player. Director of Education in Iraq. Turned down headmastership of Eton, later Rector of Edinburgh Academy.

STANLEY, HON. VENETIA ('Vinny'). Daughter of Lord and Lady Sheffield. Close friend of R. and K., and godmother of Perdita. Confidante of H. H. Asquith, whose daily letters to her after the outbreak of war have been published. Married in 1915 Right Hon. Edwin Montagu, and d. 1948.

STEPHEN, J. K. Cambridge scholar and poet, first cousin of Virginia Woolf. Died insane, aged 23, in 1892.

TYRRELL, SIR WILLIAM. In 1914, private secretary to Sir Edward Grey at the Foreign Office, later Ambassador in Paris.

VINCENT, SIR EDGAR, afterwards Lord d'Abernon. Governor of the Imperial Ottoman Bank 1889-97; Ambassador in Berlin 1918; leader of Allied Mission to Poland, 1920. Married Lady Helen Duncombe, godmother of Helen Asquith.

WALLOP, HON. FREDERIC. Youngest son of 5th Earl of Portsmouth. Trustee of National Portrait Gallery for thirty years.

WARD, ARNOLD. Son of Mrs Humphrey Ward, the novelist, and great-nephew of Matthew Arnold; later a barrister, and MP for Watford.

WARREN, SIR HERBERT. President of Magdalen College. His weakness for titles inspired the poem on page 105 and was finally gratified when the Prince of Wales entered the college in 1912.

WEDGWOOD BENN, WILLIAM, 1st Lord Stansgate. In 1914 a Junior Lord of the Treasury, Chairman of the National Relief Fund. Awarded the DSO in 1917 and DFC in 1918 for gallant service with RNAS and RFC, as well as the Croix de Guerre, Legion of Honour, and other foreign decorations.

APPENDIX B

Places from which the letters were written

Altachiara, Portofino	A property of Aubrey Herbert.
Amisfield, Haddington	Original home of the Charteris family, rented in 1899 by H. J. Tennant.
Avon Tyrrell	Home of Lord and Lady Manners in the New Forest.
Breamore, Salisbury	Home of Sir Edward Hulse, who married the daughter of Lord Burnham.
Clovelly Court, Bideford	Home of Mrs Hamlyn, sister of Lady Manners ('Con'), whose daughter Betty married Raymond's brother Oc in 1918, and later inherited Clovelly.
Cortachy Castle, Angus	Home of Lord and Lady Airlie.
Dalmeny Park, Edinburgh	Home of Lord Rosebery.
Dunrobin Castle	Seat of the Duke of Sutherland.
Easton Grey, Malmesbury	Home of Mrs Graham Smith, a sister of Margot Asquith.
The Glen, Innerleithen	The Tennants' home near Peebles.
Glen of Rothes	Rented by the Asquiths in 1905 and 1906.
Gosford, Longniddry	Scottish home of Lord Wemyss and the Charteris family.
Hall Barn, Beaconsfield	Home of Sir Edward Lawson, later Lord Burnham, proprietor of *The Daily Telegraph*.
Hartham, Corsham	Home of Sir John and Lady Poynder, later Lord and Lady Islington.
Holker Hall, Cark-in-Cartmel	Home of Lord and Lady Richard Cavendish.
Hyndford House, and The Lodge, North Berwick	Rented by the Asquiths in 1897-8.
Lympne Castle, Hythe	Rented by Mr and Mrs F. J. Tennant in 1909.
Marshall's Wick, St Albans	Rented by the Asquiths in 1901.

Mells Park, Frome	Home of the Horner family. After the death of Frances Horner's mother in 1901, the Horners resolved to let the Park and move to the Manor, an Elizabethan house a mile away.
Panshanger, Hertford	Left to Mrs Grenfell (afterwards Lady Desborough) by her aunt, Lady Cowper.
Penrhos, Holyhead	Home of Lord and Lady Sheffield.
Pixton Park, Dulverton	Home of Aubrey Herbert.
The Pleasaunce, Overstrand, Cromer	Home of Lord Battersea.
St Salvator's, St. Andrews	Rented by the Asquiths in 1898.
Slains Castle, Aberdeen	Rented by the Asquiths in 1903 and 1908.
Stanway, Gloucestershire	Home of the Charteris family.
Sutton Courtenay Manor House, Abingdon	Home of Mr and Mrs Harry Lindsay, close friends of R. and K.'s parents.
Taplow Court, Bucks	Home of the Grenfells.
Terling Place, Essex	Home of the Liberal scientist, Lord Rayleigh.
Tulchan Lodge, Strathspey	Famous grouse moor rented by the Sassoons.

Index

Figures in italics indicate pages on which letters to individuals appear. Bold figures indicate pages where descriptions of characters may be found.